# Approaches to Economic Geography

The last four decades have seen major changes in the global economy, with the collapse of communism and the spread of capitalism into parts of the world from which it had previously been excluded. Beginning with a grounding in Marxian political economy, this book explores a range of new ideas as to what economic geography can offer as it intersects with public policy and planning in the new globalised economy.

*Approaches to Economic Geography* draws together the formidable work of Ray Hudson into an authoritative collection, offering a unique approach to the understanding of the changing geographies of the global economy. With chapters covering subjects ranging from uneven development to social economy, this volume explores how a range of perspectives, including evolutionary and institutional approaches, can further elucidate how such economies and their geographies are reproduced. Subsequent chapters argue that greater attention must be given to the relationships between the economy and nature, and that more consideration needs to be given to the growing significance of illegal activities in the economy.

The book will be of interest to students studying economic geography as well as researchers and policy makers that recognise the importance of the relationships between economy and geography as we move towards a sustainable future economy and society.

**Ray Hudson** is a Fellow of the British Academy, the Academy for the Social Sciences, the Regional Studies Association and the Royal Geographical Society and is a Member of Academia Europaea. He is also a long-standing Professor of Geography at Durham University, UK.

## Regions and Cities



In today's globalised, knowledge-driven and networked world, regions and cities have assumed heightened significance as the interconnected nodes of economic, social and cultural production, and as sites of new modes of economic and territorial governance and policy experimentation. This book series brings together incisive and critically engaged international and inter-disciplinary research on this resurgence of regions and cities, and should be of interest to geographers, economists, sociologists, political scientists and cultural scholars, as well as to policy makers involved in regional and urban development.

For more information on the Regional Studies Association visit www.regionalstudies.org

82. **Knowledge, Networks and Policy**
Regional studies in postwar Britain and beyond
*James Hopkins*

81. **Dynamics of Economic Spaces in the Global Knowledge-based Economy**
Theory and East Asian cases
*Sam Ock Park*

80. **Urban Competitiveness**
Theory and practice
*Daniele Letri and Peter Kresl*

79. **Smart Specialisation**
Opportunities and challenges for regional innovation policy
*Dominique Foray*

78. **The Age of Intelligent Cities**
Smart environments and innovation-for-all strategies
*Nicos Komninos*

77. **Space and Place in Central and Eastern Europe**
Historical trends and perspectives
*Gyula Horváth*

76. **Territorial Cohesion in Rural Europe**
The relational turn in rural development
*Edited by Andrew Copus and Philomena de Lima*

75. **The Global Competitiveness of Regions**
*Robert Huggins, Hiro Izushi, Daniel Prokop and Piers Thompson*

74. **The Social Dynamics of Innovation Networks**
*Edited by Roel Rutten, Paul Benneworth, Dessy Irawati and Frans Boekema*

73. **The European Territory**
From historical roots to global challenges
*Jacques Robert*

72. **Urban Innovation Systems**
What makes them tick?
*Willem van Winden, Erik Braun, Alexander Otgaar and Jan-Jelle Witte*

71. **Shrinking Cities**
A global perspective
*Edited by Harry W. Richardson and Chang Woon Nam*

70. **Cities, State and Globalization**
City-regional governance
*Tassilo Herrschel*

69. **The Creative Class Goes Global**
*Edited by Charlotta Mellander, Richard Florida, Bjørn Asheim and Meric Gertler*

68. **Entrepreneurial Knowledge, Technology and the Transformation of Regions**
*Edited by Charlie Karlsson, Börje Johansson and Roger Stough*

67. **The Economic Geography of the IT Industry in the Asia Pacific Region**
*Edited by Philip Cooke, Glen Searle and Kevin O'Connor*

66. **Working Regions**
Reconnecting innovation and production in the knowledge economy
*Jennifer Clark*

65. **Europe's Changing Geography**
The impact of inter-regional networks
*Edited by Nicola Bellini and Ulrich Hilpert*

64. **The Value of Arts and Culture for Regional Development**
A Scandinavian perspective
*Edited by Lisbeth Lindeborg and Lars Lindkvist*

63. **The University and the City**
*John Goddard and Paul Vallance*

62. **Re-framing Regional Development**
Evolution, innovation and transition
*Edited by Philip Cooke*

61. **Networking Regionalised Innovative Labour Markets**
*Edited by Ulrich Hilpert and Helen Lawton Smith*

60. **Leadership and Change in Sustainable Regional Development**
Edited by *Markku Sotarauta, Ina Horlings and Joyce Liddle*

59. **Regional Development Agencies: The Next Generation?**
Networking, knowledge and regional policies
*Edited by Nicola Bellini, Mike Danson and Henrik Halkier*

58. **Community-based Entrepreneurship and Rural Development**
Creating favourable conditions for small businesses in Central Europe
*Matthias Fink, Stephan Loidl and Richard Lang*

57. **Creative Industries and Innovation in Europe**
Concepts, measures and comparative case studies
*Edited by Luciana Lazzeretti*

56. **Innovation Governance in an Open Economy**
Shaping regional nodes in a globalized world
*Edited by Annika Rickne, Staffan Laestadius and Henry Etzkowitz*

55. **Complex Adaptive Innovation Systems**
Relatedness and transversality in the evolving region
*Philip Cooke*

54. **Creating Knowledge Locations in Cities**
Innovation and integration challenges
*Willem van Winden, Luis de Carvalho, Erwin van Tujil, Jeroen van Haaren and Leo van den Berg*

53. **Regional Development in Northern Europe**
Peripherality, marginality and border issues
*Edited by Mike Danson and Peter De Souza*

52. **Promoting Silicon Valleys in Latin America**
*Luciano Ciravegna*

51. **Industrial Policy Beyond the Crisis**
Regional, national and international perspectives
*Edited by David Bailey, Helena Lenihan and Josep-Maria Arauzo-Carod*

50. **Just Growth**
Inclusion and prosperity in America's metropolitan regions
*Chris Benner and Manuel Pastor*

49. **Cultural Political Economy of Small Cities**
*Edited by Anne Lorentzen and Bas van Heur*

48. **The Recession and Beyond**
Local and regional responses to the downturn
*Edited by David Bailey and Caroline Chapain*

47. **Beyond Territory**
*Edited by Harald Bathelt, Maryann Feldman and Dieter F. Kogler*

46. **Leadership and Place**
*Edited by Chris Collinge, John Gibney and Chris Mabey*

45. **Migration in the 21st Century**
Rights, outcomes, and policy
*Kim Korinek and Thomas Maloney*

44. **The Futures of the City Region**
*Edited by Michael Neuman and Angela Hull*

43. **The Impacts of Automotive Plant Closures**
A tale of two cities
*Edited by Andrew Beer and Holli Evans*

42. **Manufacturing in the New Urban Economy**
*Willem van Winden, Leo van den Berg, Luis de Carvalho and Erwin van Tuijl*

**41. Globalizing Regional Development in East Asia**
Production networks, clusters, and entrepreneurship
*Edited by Henry Wai-chung Yeung*

**40. China and Europe**
The implications of the rise of China as a global economic power for Europe
*Edited by Klaus Kunzmann, Willy A. Schmid and Martina Koll-Schretzenmayr*

**39. Business Networks in Clusters and Industrial Districts**
The governance of the global value chain
*Edited by Fiorenza Belussi and Alessia Sammarra*

**38. Whither Regional Studies?**
*Edited by Andy Pike*

**37. Intelligent Cities and Globalisation of Innovation Networks**
*Nicos Komninos*

**36. Devolution, Regionalism and Regional Development**
The UK experience
*Edited by Jonathan Bradbury*

**35. Creative Regions**
Technology, culture and knowledge entrepreneurship
*Edited by Philip Cooke and Dafna Schwartz*

**34. European Cohesion Policy**
*Willem Molle*

**33. Geographies of the New Economy**
Critical reflections
*Edited by Peter W. Daniels, Andrew Leyshon, Michael J. Bradshaw and Jonathan Beaverstock*

**32. The Rise of the English Regions?**
*Edited by Irene Hardill, Paul Benneworth, Mark Baker and Leslie Budd*

**31. Regional Development in the Knowledge Economy**
*Edited by Philip Cooke and Andrea Piccaluga*

**30. Regional Competitiveness**
*Edited by Ron Martin, Michael Kitson and Peter Tyler*

**29. Clusters and Regional Development**
Critical reflections and explorations
*Edited by Bjørn Asheim, Philip Cooke and Ron Martin*

**28. Regions, Spatial Strategies and Sustainable Development**
*David Counsell and Graham Haughton*

**27. Sustainable Cities**
*Graham Haughton and Colin Hunter*

**26. Geographies of Labour Market Inequality**
*Edited by Ron Martin and Philip S. Morrison*

**25. Regional Innovation Strategies**
The challenge for less-favoured regions
*Edited by Kevin Morgan and Claire Nauwelaers*

**24. Out of the Ashes?**
The social impact of industrial contraction and regeneration on Britain's mining communities
*Chas Critcher, Bella Dicks, David Parry and David Waddington*

**23. Restructuring Industry and Territory**
The experience of Europe's regions
*Edited by Anna Giunta, Arnoud Lagendijk and Andy Pike*

22. **Foreign Direct Investment and the Global Economy**
Corporate and institutional dynamics of global-localisation
*Edited by Jeremy Alden and Nicholas F. Phelps*

21. **Community Economic Development**
*Edited by Graham Haughton*

20. **Regional Development Agencies in Europe**
*Edited by Charlotte Damborg, Mike Danson and Henrik Halkier*

19. **Social Exclusion in European Cities**
Processes, experiences and responses
*Edited by Judith Allen, Goran Cars and Ali Madanipour*

18. **Metropolitan Planning in Britain**
A comparative study
*Edited by Peter Roberts, Kevin Thomas and Gwyndaf Williams*

17. **Unemployment and Social Exclusion**
Landscapes of labour inequality and social exclusion
*Edited by Sally Hardy, Paul Lawless and Ron Martin*

16. **Multinationals and European Integration**
Trade, investment and regional development
*Edited by Nicholas A. Phelps*

15. **The Coherence of EU Regional Policy**
Contrasting perspectives on the structural funds
*Edited by John Bachtler and Ivan Turok*

14. **New Institutional Spaces**
TECs and the remaking of economic governance
*Martin Jones, Foreword by Jamie Peck*

13. **Regional Policy in Europe**
*S. S. Artobolevskiy*

12. **Innovation Networks and Learning Regions?**
*James Simmie*

11. **British Regionalism and Devolution**
The challenges of state reform and European integration
*Edited by Jonathan Bradbury and John Mawson*

10. **Regional Development Strategies**
A European perspective
*Edited by Jeremy Alden and Philip Boland*

9. **Union Retreat and the Regions**
The shrinking landscape of organised labour
*Ron Martin, Peter Sunley and Jane Wills*

8. **The Regional Dimension of Transformation in Central Europe**
*Grzegorz Gorzelak*

7. **The Determinants of Small Firm Growth**
An inter-regional study in the United Kingdom 1986–90
*Richard Barkham, Graham Gudgin, Mark Hart and Eric Hanvey*

6. **The Regional Imperative**
Regional planning and governance in Britain, Europe and the United States
*Urlan A. Wannop*

5. **An Enlarged Europe**
Regions in competition?
*Edited by Louis Albrechts, Sally Hardy, Mark Hart and Anastasios Katos*

4. **Spatial Policy in a Divided Nation**
*Edited by Richard T. Harrison and Mark Hart*

3. **Regional Development in the 1990s**
The British Isles in transition
*Edited by Ron Martin and Peter Townroe*

2. **Retreat from the Regions**
Corporate change and the closure of factories
*Stephen Fothergill and Nigel Guy*

1. **Beyond Green Belts**
Managing urban growth in the 21st century
*Edited by John Herington*

# Approaches to Economic Geography

## Towards a geographical political economy

**Ray Hudson**

LONDON AND NEW YORK

First published 2016 by Routledge

2 Park Square, Milton Park, Abingdon, Oxfordshire OX14 4RN
52 Vanderbilt Avenue, New York, NY 10017

*Routledge is an imprint of the Taylor & Francis Group, an informa business*

First issued in paperback 2019



*British Library Cataloguing in Publication Data*
A catalogue record for this book is available from the British Library

*Library of Congress Cataloging in Publication Data*
A catalog record for this book has been requested

ISBN: 978-1-138-80408-1 (hbk)
ISBN: 978-0-367-87071-3 (pbk)

Typeset in Times New Roman
by Out of House Publishing

# Contents

# Preface

Some 15 years ago I published a couple of books which pulled together work that I'd been doing in economic geography and regional development since the early 1970s. This volume needs to be located and seen in relation to them. One of these was essentially a collection of already published papers (Hudson, 2000a). The other had a rather different purpose and was intended to offer a more substantial and synthetic statement of an approach to economic geography that I'd been exploring and seeking to develop over the previous quarter century (Hudson, 2001a). The starting point for this was grounded in Marxian political economy and its key concepts. It then sought to engage with subsequent developments deriving directly from Marxian approaches – for example in regulation and state theories – and I also began to explore ways in which analyses of economic geographies could be elaborated by drawing on other approaches that began from different conceptual starting points. In part, these points of departure related to conceptions of economic and social processes – such as evolutionary and institutional economics – and in part to approaches in the material and biophysical sciences, that had a very different purpose and epistemological starting point. This was – and is – not without its challenges. The rationale for so doing was two-fold. First, recognition that the capitalist economy had developed in many ways (organisationally, technically, spatially) since Marx was carrying out his seminal analyses in the nineteenth century. Second, recognition that Marxian political economy powerfully focused on the rationale of capitalist production and on so *why* capitalist economies were organised as they were. It revealed why spatially uneven development was an unavoidable aspect of the process of capitalist development, but did so at a high level of abstraction in terms of a particular conception of value theory. Switching from analyses at the level of values to that of prices (if you like, following the path from volume 1 to volume 3 of *Capital*) broadened understanding of how capitalist economies operated and developed particular socio-spatial forms but it seemed to me that there was scope to explore the extent to which other approaches to political economy, some of which had developed more or less directly from Marxian approaches (for example, regulation theories and state theories), others that developed from different conceptual starting points (evolutionary and institutional economics for example) could be profitably explored as a way of developing more nuanced 'middle level' conceptual approaches that could elaborate on the *what* and *how* of capitalist economies. In addition, parts of the social sciences in the last quarter of the twentieth century were coming to acknowledge the centrality of spatiality to economic, political and social life and as a result there were increasing openings for economic geographers to engage with a range of social science disciplines and theoretical approaches (for example, with work on structuration and the relations between agency and structure). While some of this was explored in *Producing Places* it was only done so in a preliminary and tentative manner. In subsequent years I further explored approaches in parts of the social and biophysical sciences and also sought to broaden the conception of what counted as 'the economy' in a critical geographical political economy via a series of papers and book chapters. It is this that is reflected in this book, which, with the exception of one paper published in 1999, draws together material published after 2001, with the intention of developing a more nuanced and expansive approach to a geographical political economy but one that remains grounded in its roots in Marxian political economy. As such, the present volume is perhaps best regarded as a further instalment in an evolving project, bringing together a number of papers written over the last 15 or so years, still preliminary rather than definitive but hopefully one that moves things on from where they were.

There are a further couple of points of clarification that I want to make about the material presented here. All of the chapters had their origins as single-authored papers. I have resisted the temptation to re-write them – while this has the disadvantage that I might now want to express some things differently, it would defeat the point of seeking to show how my approach to these issues has evolved over the years. Thus the chapters have been reproduced here more or less as they were originally, with only very minor editing to tidy up the text in places and the addition of an occasional footnote where events have moved on since the material was first published. The one substantive change has been to merge the references into a single section, in part to avoid repetition and save space. The restriction to sole-authored material is in response to comments by one of the reviewers of the earlier collection who – I can't remember who it was, but the name isn't the point – had taken issue with the fact that a small number of the chapters therein had been written as co-authored pieces, drawing on externally funded collaborative research projects (and of course with the permission of the co-authors, and making it explicit that the material had been co-authored). Rather than run the risk of similar criticism, it seemed safer to restrict the material here to papers that had been sole authored. That said, some (perhaps in various ways, given the nature of research and scholarship, all) of them do draw upon projects that were jointly carried out and I'd like to acknowledge the contribution of various colleagues who worked on them (including Ash Amin, Huw Beynon, Mike

Crang and Nicky Gregson) and as will be clear, there are also quite a few references to papers co-authored with these and other colleagues who I've worked with over the years, such as Costis Hadjimichalis. It goes without saying that working with them constructively influenced the way that my own thought and approach developed but they are in no way responsible for what follows.

Ray Hudson
Durham University
January 2016

# Acknowledgements

With the exception of Chapters 1 and 12, the chapters in this book were originally published as journal articles and in one case a book chapter. Except for some minor editorial changes, the chapters are as originally published. I would like to thank the publishers of this material for permission to reproduce it here: Chapter 2, 'Conceptualising economies and their geographies spaces, flows and circuits', first published 2004 in *Progress in Human Geography*, 28, 447–72; Chapter 3, ' "The learning economy, the learning firm and the learning region": a sympathetic critique of the limits to learning', first published 1999 in *European Urban and Regional Studies*, 6, 59–72; Chapter 4, 'From knowledge based economy … to knowledge based economy? Reflections on changes in the economy and development policies in the North East of England', first published 2011 in *Regional Studies*, 45, 997–1012; Chapter 5, 'Re-thinking change in old industrial regions: reflecting on the experiences of North East England', first published 2005 in *Environment and Planning A*, 37, 581–96; Chapter 6, 'Global production systems and European integration', first published in Peck J and Yeung H W-C (Eds.) *Global Connections*, Sage, London, 216–30; Chapter 7, 'Life on the edge: navigating the competitive tensions between the "social" and the "economic" in the social economy and in its relations to the mainstream', first published 2009, *Journal of Economic Geography*, 1, 1–18; Chapter 8, 'Thinking through the relationships between legal and illegal activities and economies: spaces, flows and pathways', first published 2013, *Journal of Economic Geography*, 1, 1–21; Chapter 9, 'Cultural political economy meets global production networks: a productive meeting?', first published in 2009, *Journal of Economic Geography*, 8, 421–40; Chapter 10, 'Critical political economy and material transformation', first published 2012 in *New Political Economy*, 17, 273–98; Chapter 11, 'Resilient regions in an uncertain world: wishful thinking or practical reality?', first published 2010, *Cambridge Journal of Regions, Economy and Society*, 13, 11–25.

Thanks to Oxford University Press (http://cjre.oxfordjournals.org and http://joeg.oxfordjournals.org) for permission to reproduce Chapters 7, 8, 9 and 11; to Pion (www.pion.co.uk and www.envplan.com) for permission to reproduce Chapter 5; to Routledge (www.tandfonline.com) for permission to reproduce Chapters 4 and 10; and to Sage (www.sagepub.co.uk) for permission to reproduce Chapters 2, 3 and 6.

# 1 Setting the scene

## Steps towards a geographical political economy

### Introduction

There have been great changes in the ways in which economic geography has been thought about and practised over the last 60 or 70 years. There were several phases in this process of change, though this claim needs to be qualified as the literature to which I am referring is mainly, though not exclusively, that of the Anglo-American world. Increasingly these changes also reflected the interaction among economic geographers and other social science disciplines, as spatiality became of increasing concern to their practitioners. This also involved engagement with other disciplines in other cultures and languages (for example, there were important influences from French and Italian social scientists). With these qualifications in mind, we can identify five phases. First, there was the shift from the descriptive geographies that had been dominant until the 1950s and the rise of spatial analysis, location theory and spatial interaction models in the 1950s and especially the 1960s. Then towards the end of the 1960s there was the brief rise and fall of behavioural approaches based on a critique of the unrealistic assumptions about individual behaviour and knowledge on which locational theories were based. The critique of both location theory and the behavioural approaches that developed in reaction to it centred on their preoccupation with, and idealised conception of, markets and exchange relations and/or the shallow conception of social process that they encompassed. As a result, they had limited explanatory power and for this reason economic geographers began to search for more powerful explanatory frameworks in the latter part of the 1960s and to engage with processes and relations of production as well as exchange and consumption. Crucially, they also sought to explore more powerful conceptions of social structure, the dominant social relationships that define particular types of economy, and relate social process to spatial form and in particular to deepen understanding of why economic geographies in capitalism take the forms that they do. Around this time social scientists more generally were re-discovering the traditions of classical political economy and more specifically the work of Karl Marx and a Marxian approach to political economy, with its focus on the totality of the production process and processes of capital accumulation and combined and uneven development. The next development in economic geography became part of this movement, a much more significant one, marked by the ascendance of various strands of political economy, initially and predominantly Marxian. From the 1980s onwards this in turn spawned the emergence of a plethora of approaches critiquing political economy, particularly its Marxian variants. Some of these were seeking to elaborate a more nuanced political economy approach – for example, emphasising the need to appreciate the relationships between structure and agency, giving greater attention to knowledge, learning and motives in accounting for economic behaviours (in a way harking back to the behavioural critiques of the 1960s), or giving greater emphasis to evolutionary and institutional issues. At the same time, however, the advocates of both the New Geographical Economics and New Economic Geography focused on these issues while cutting connections to the systemic concerns of political economy (Hadjimichalis and Hudson, 2014). Others were challenging political economy perspectives in other ways and seeking to espouse alternatives to it – for example feminist approaches and what we might describe as the somewhat inchoate world of 'post-isms', which themselves became subject to challenge. That said, there were points of constructive engagement between political economy and feminism and some parts of the post-isms literature. For example Coe *et al.* (2007) note that during the late 1980s and early 1990s, the political economy approach manifested itself in the post-Fordism debate. This focused both on the ways in which capitalist economies are regulated through institutions and also on the transactional relationships between firms in industrial districts, in new industrial spaces and in new high volume production systems (Hudson, 1989a; 1994a). The net result of these successive changes is that contemporary economic geography – indeed human geography more generally – is characterised by a plurality of approaches co-existing side by side. Different approaches have not so much displaced and killed off others but rather interaction and dialogue among them has led to their selective modifications so that economic geography today is characterised by a rich mixture and diversity of approaches, a fragmented form of 'engaged pluralism' (Barnes and Sheppard, 2010). I will return to these issues in the final chapter.

In the course of these changes in theoretical approach and inter-disciplinary engagement there have often been associated shifts in methodologies and the substantive foci of interest of economic geography, with varying emphases on different aspects of the economy and its geographies. These have generally been positive developments. The former included the increased use of a range of qualitative as well as quantitative approaches, generating a range of different types of evidence, while the latter included shifts in emphasis from production back to consumption, from territories to flows, and, in some ways reminiscent of an earlier era, a return to a concern with the importance of the specificity of places but in the context of their location as nodes within global networks. Picking up on what had been a somewhat neglected dimension of Marxian political economy, there was also a growing awareness of the significance of the natural world for economic processes (and vice versa), a renewed emphasis on the materiality of the economy and economic processes as material transformations. This in turn had epistemological implications as critical economic geographers had to engage with more traditional forms of theory developed in the realms of the biological and physical worlds (and also dominant in parts of the social sciences, notably but not exclusively mainstream economics) as well as critical theories of the social world (Horkheimer, 1937). In addition, there was a somewhat belated recognition of the persistence of non-capitalist social relations and the significance of the informal and illegal as well as the legal economies within capitalism. In short, the end result has been a more diverse and heterogeneous view of the constitution of 'the economy'. This, as well as the changes in theoretical perspectives, has implications for the ways in which spatial development policies have been conceived, as will be clear from several of the chapters in what follows.

There are several excellent accounts that comprehensively set out the history of this shifting terrain and the current and recent scope of economic geography (for example, Clark *et al.*, 2000; Coe *et al.*, 2007; Leyshon *et al.*, 2011; Sheppard and Barnes, 2000) and it is not my intention to seek to emulate them. My aims and ambitions here are much more modest. In the Preface I have sought briefly to locate the present volume in terms of earlier work, in particular *Producing Places* (Hudson (2001a). What I am seeking to do here is sketch out the subsequent trajectory of my own thought and practice of economic geography, a partial and selective pathway on what could be described as a journey towards an as yet unknown endpoint, but one that I hope will be of interest as an example of how individuals are both influenced, and to a small degree possibly influence, these broader movements in the evolution of a discipline.

In summary, this journey has been one that has sought to contribute to a more nuanced and subtle theoretical approach to economic geography. More specifically, it has been – and remains – an attempt to deepen understanding of geographies of diverse capitalist economies by elaborating a concern with the spatiality of political economy, with deepening understanding of the spatiality of uneven development, elaborating but never abandoning key insights from Marxian political economy. As such, it can be regarded as a project to elaborate a geographical political economy. The next section very briefly outlines some of the foundational Marxian concepts. Building from these, it is an approach that can be briefly characterised as follows (see also Chapter 2). First, it seeks to recognise both systemic and structural constraints and the ways in which people individually and collectively are both shaped by and reproduce these constraints. Class relations are pivotal but can take a variety of forms and inter-relate with other social relations such as those of ethnicity, gender and place. Second, it recognises the variety of socio-spatial forms that capitalist development can take through the social construction of institutions such as markets and a variety of regulatory mechanisms. Third, it acknowledges that such development is a product of what came before it but without necessarily being able to identify a discrete starting point ('there is no point of departure': Massey, 2014, 254, drawing on Althusser), and follows open ended though not unconstrained pathways to unknown end points. Fourth, it recognises that capitalist economies embrace diverse sets of non-capitalist social relations that can and do, in specific ways in particular time/space contexts, have an important bearing on the capitalist mainstream. Fifth, and finally, it recognises the complex reciprocal relations between economy and environment, between biophysical and social (perhaps best thought of as bio-social) processes. Whether seeking to develop such an approach does so in ways that are helpful is of course for others to judge.

## Marxian political economy: what makes capitalist economies capitalist?[1]

### *Value analysis and modes of production*

In contrast to the approach of location theories, with their focus on deducing spatial pattern from an impoverished conception of social process, political economy approaches seek a more holistic understanding of the economy and its geographies focusing on generative social processes and the relationships of individuals to society, the economy and the state (Routledge, 2011, 177). Among the various approaches to political economy, Marxian political economy provides a powerful entry point into analyses that seek to understand capital, capitalist economies and their geographies. It seeks to uncover the critical social relationships that define and shape economies and their geographies and provides the conceptual basis for understanding the economy and its spatiality, crucially recognising that analyses at different levels of abstraction are critical in this task.

At the most abstract level, the Marxian concept of mode of production seeks to reveal the essential 'inner logic' of particular types of economic organisation, characterising these via specific combinations of social relations and forces of production (such as factories, machines and tools). It insists that while the latter are important the former are decisive (thereby dismissing from the outset any simplistic notion of technological determinism). In the capitalist mode of production *the* key defining social relationship is the class structural one between capital and wage labour. This is a contradictory, dialectical and necessary relationship: capital and labour are mutually defining, the existence of each pre-supposing the other. Capital needs to purchase labour-power[2] – that is, the capacity of people to work for it – and organise the labour process and work in particular ways, deploying particular combinations of variable (workers), fixed (for example, factories and machinery) and constant (for example, raw materials) capital. This is because living labour is the only source of new value – that is surplus-value – created in production and embodied in commodities. Conversely, labour needs to sell its labour-power (its capacity to work) for a wage in order to survive and reproduce itself. As such, it is alienated labour. The capitalist mode of production is thus structured around the wage relation and commodity production, with labour-power bought and sold in a competitive market *as if* (although as will become clear it isn't) it was simply another commodity.

What then do we mean by commodities, commodity production and values? A starting point in beginning to answer these questions is the Marxian conception of value analysis, grounded in its particular and precise definition of value as social labour. Commodities simultaneously possess attributes as use values and as exchange values. As materialised human labour, they have use values, qualities that people find useful, which reflect specific concrete aspects of labour. At the same time, labour within capitalist relations of production also takes the form of undifferentiated abstract labour. In the capitalist mode of production the exchange value of a commodity is defined as the quantity of socially necessary labour time – that is, the amount of undifferentiated abstract labour needed under average social and technical conditions of production – required for its production. These concepts of abstract labour and socially necessary labour time are central to understanding the driving rationale of capitalist production: production for exchange and profitable sale through markets. Production finds its rationale in and is socially validated *ex post* by market exchange and the successful sale of goods and services, linking processes of production, exchange and consumption within the economy. The *purpose* of production, however, is the realisation of exchange values via sale in markets. Conversely, failure to sell at a price that realises a profit (via realising the surplus-value embodied in the commodity) spells a potential crisis for an individual firm as a result of competition from other firms producing the same or similar competitive commodities and expanding their market share as a consequence. But if the problem of realisation becomes generalised over the economy, capitalist production more generally may slide into crisis and this raises questions about how such crises may be temporarily resolved.

The moment when capital returns to the monetary form, a result of successful sale unlocking the surplus-value embodied in commodities, is critical. From the point of view of capitalist enterprises, there is a strong imperative to minimise the time taken for surplus-value to be realised and capital to return to the fungible money form, at which point it can again be invested in search of further profit. As a result, the various infrastructures that facilitate and permit the circulation of capital and its flow from one form to another – ranging from the means of transport and communication to credit and financial mechanisms and structures – are crucial. These infrastructures both require capital investment, fixing it for a time in particular forms, and as a result help shape the landscapes of capitalist economies. Thus these forms of fixed capital become necessary in order to facilitate the circulation of capital.

What then happens to the surplus-value following successful sale of commodities, once surplus-value has been realised as corporate profit and again become potential investible capital? The answer to this question is linked to the way in which the more general development of the economy and the capital accumulation process is conceptualised in terms of circuits of capital of various types (Palloix, 1977). Capital is above all a process of circulation and it circulates in the form of money and of commodities of various sorts. In terms of the key circuit of productive industrial capital – key because it is where surplus-value is produced – (see Hudson, 2001a, 14–47 and chapter 9), part of the newly expanded capital may be deployed as variable capital (used to acquire additional labour-power), part to acquire additional constant capital (for example, additional raw materials), part to expand fixed capital (in the form of additional machinery, or extra factory space, for example) and possibly part as interest payments or rent for the acquisition of land or in relation to money borrowed to further augment the scale of production. Furthermore, some of the realised surplus-value may be invested in 'fictitious commodities', forms of money capital and monetary and financial instruments that are not in themselves productive of surplus-value but can be highly profitable because (for a time) they can make claims on surplus-value already created or yet to be created elsewhere (Harvey, 2014, 239–42). In summary, as a result of decisions as to the allocation of surplus-value created and realised in one production period, it becomes re-invested in succeeding periods. This in turn enables firms that make successful investment decisions to grow and may also result in the economy expanding overall. Given certain assumptions about the proportional relationship between different sectors of the economy and forms of capital, growth can be smooth and uninterrupted. Whether such conditions are – or indeed can, over a period of time be – met in practice has been and remains a matter of debate, not least because of the implication that continuing capital accumulation requires that the economy sustain a compound rate of growth (Harvey, 2014). The periodic emergence of economic crises of varying severity and scope, which has characterised the history of capitalist economies, would suggest that at best such conditions can be met for a time in particular places.

It is important to emphasise that the discussion so far relates to the abstract conceptual space of the capitalist mode of production and the rationale – the *why* – of capitalist production. *Where* new capital is re-invested – in terms of product, sector or geographical location for example – is a different order question that needs to be explored via different forms of analysis and empirically, not least as such decisions are made in the realm of prices rather than values. As a result, a different form and level of analysis is required to begin to answer such questions.

### *Social formations, varieties of capitalisms and modes of regulation*

According to Hodgson (1981, cited in Streek, 2014, 50)

> [e]very socio-economic system must rely on at least one structurally dissimilar subsystem to function. There must always be a co-existent

plurality of modes of production so that the social formation as a whole has the necessary structural variety to cope with change.

The concept of social formation thus relates to the articulation of modes of production, the ways in which different modes of production – capitalist, pre-capitalist, non-capitalist – relate to one another. In so doing, it makes an important point in that capitalist modes of production may depend for their development and reproduction on their relationship to other modes of production. Consequently, 'actually existing capitalisms' exist in a variety of forms – perhaps more helpfully thought of as socio-spatial rather than simply social formations. Furthermore, this variety involves understanding the ways in which particular forms of 'actually existing capitalisms' emerge and (co-)evolve and reflects the ways in which capitalist social relations come together with other class and non-class (ethnicity and gender, for example) social relationships, in particular time-space contexts.

This has critical conceptual implications for thinking about the economy. For example, while recognising structural limits it is important to emphasise that the economic geographies of capitalism are not structurally predetermined simply by the dictates of capital or indeed competitive struggles among fractions of capital or between capital and labour. Rather, they result from the interaction of different causal structures, leading to over-determination, and unknown trajectories within the structural limits that define an economy as capitalist. Or to take a more specific example, commodities do not simply spring from the laws of supply and demand but constitute an arena of cultural production, involving a plethora of specific social practices (Tsing, 2005). More generally, then, recognising this over-determination creates conceptual space for different institutional forms and varieties of capitalism (for example, see Lane and Wood, 2011; Wood and James, 2006), allowing that capitalist economic relations may be socially and culturally constituted in varying ways in different places and at different spatial scales (a point developed further below).

An important implication of acknowledging this variety is a recognition that there is no one 'best way' of organising capitalist economies or predetermined end-point in their development but rather complex and over-determined outcomes as causal structures (for example of class, ethnicity, gender and religion) interact to produce different forms of capitalist organisation. Furthermore, they may also involve different articulations of legal and illegal, formal and informal activities. These 'actually existing capitalisms' in turn interact, compete and co-operate within the structural limits that define an economy as capitalist. Structural conditions and limits are therefore socially produced by human actions, discursive and material, individual and collective, which thereby produce capitalism in its various varieties. Such actions have both intended and unintended consequences, however, and so variable relationships to both the sustainability of specific forms of capitalism as well as to structural reproduction. The ways in which the structural limits that define economies as capitalist are socially (re)produced are therefore complex and a pivotal issue.

As a result of its contradictory as well as complex character, however, capitalist development is always prone to economic crisis as it tends to undermine and destroy the conditions that first made accumulation possible. Crisis tendencies are immanent, always latent. Polanyi (1944) famously recognised this contradictory character in terms of the 'double movement', as capital's attempts historically to dis-embed the economy from its social contexts provoked a reaction that sought to challenge the imperatives of capital and the market. Given this inherent tension, capitalist states have come to have a particularly important role in seeking to manage crises, to contain or displace (in time and/or space) their effects via a range of economic, credit and monetary policies so as to maintain the conditions that make accumulation possible. Consequently, recognising the centrality of capitalist states to capitalist economies led to increased attention to their role in ensuring the reproduction of capitalist social relationships – and of their own reproduction as states (for example, see Brenner *et al.*, 2003).

Focusing particularly on Fordism as a particular form of capitalist organisation, the work of regulation theorists (for example, Aglietta, 1979; Lipietz, 1987) has been particularly important in deepening understanding of the ways in which complex capitalist societies are reproduced through particular modes of regulation, combinations of state activities interacting with other social forces in civil society as well as the economy to contain crisis tendencies within socially and politically acceptable limits. However, state action cannot eradicate the tendency towards economic crisis but may – and often does – displace it into other social and political spheres. For example it may lead to rationality crises because of the disjuncture between the intended and actual outcomes of state policy interventions, or, more seriously, legitimation crises that question the authority of the state to act in the first place as the impossible becomes necessary, the necessary impossible in policy terms (Offe, 1975; see also see Habermas, 1976). This further emphasises the complex contradictory crisis-prone character of capitalist economies.

### *Prices and values*

As Harvey (2014, 26) succinctly puts it,

> 'value' is a social relation established between the labouring activities of millions of people all around the world. As a social relation, it is immaterial and invisible ... Being immaterial and invisible, value requires some material representation. This material representation is money.

So while at one level of abstraction Marxian political economy conceives of the economy in terms of value categories, conceptualising value in terms of social labour, at a lower level of abstraction it also recognises that the routine performance of the day-to-day conduct and market transactions of a capitalist economy (declaring profits, paying wages, paying the rent, purchasing commodities) is conducted in prices. Recognising the roles of money and prices raises a series of complications which reflect the complexity of the variety of 'actually existing capitalisms' – for example, the creation of credit and the capacity to defer payments in time, or the multiplicity of national currencies and their mutual relationships. But there is also a more fundamental question of conceptual relationships: how do values and prices relate? Is the relationship of prices and values one of quantitative equivalence or qualitative difference?

In capitalist economies economic agents (more or less) freely enter into market relations mediated by monetary prices. Money thus serves as both a medium of exchange and a measure of value, though one that does not equate to values defined in terms of socially necessary labour time. In much of *Capital* Marx proceeds for expository purposes as if money prices are perfectly correlated with the amounts of socially necessary labour time embodied in commodities. Given this (heroic) assumption, monetary exchange is equivalent to value exchange. In fact, this *never is* nor *can it be* the case: as Harvey (1996, 152) puts it, money is always a slippery and unreliable representation of value. Discrepancies between supply and demand in markets result in commodities being exchanged at prices that diverge from their values. Individual price transactions would only converge around an average price that represented the generality of value in a perfectly competitive market – a mythical entity that cannot exist – so actual prices unavoidably diverge from values (Harvey, 2014, 31). As production conditions diverge from social and technical averages, the amounts of labour time embodied in commodities deviate from the socially necessary amount that defines their exchange value. Commodities thus contain varying amounts of labour time but are sold at the same market price while money prices unavoidably diverge from exchange values. Consequently, value is re-distributed between sectors and companies (and so places) via the processes of competition. This is pivotally important in relation to the systemic dynamism and uneven development of capitalist economies, to Schumpeterian processes of 'creative destruction' as firms seek competitive advantage via radical innovation. The creation of various forms of money and 'fictitious' capital, capital that is non-productive of surplus-value but making claims on realised surplus-value from within the productive circuit of capital, can further complicate the overall relationships between prices and value. If the aggregate divergence of prices from values is perceived to reach a tipping point, then a systemic crisis of accumulation may be triggered which over time serves to bring this relationship back within tolerable limits in relation to accumulation and the circulation of capital via a process of class restructuring, with sharply unequal social and spatial effects – as the events following the widespread crisis that erupted triggered by the bankruptcy of Lehman Brothers in 2008 exemplify.

There are, though, no definitive solutions as to how value and price analyses should be quantitatively related, no unique relationship between them. To seek such solutions to the 'transformation problem' empirically is misconceived as value and price are most appropriately regarded as concepts of different theoretical status. Both are necessary but the difference between them is significant, as analysis simply in terms of prices conceals key relationships that structure capitalist economies while value theory cannot deal with other issues that are important: for example, many aspects of use values cannot be captured in exchange value categories. The value of value theory is that it is indicative of the way in which capitalist social relationships unite a wide range of qualitatively different types of labour in the totality of the production process (Massey, 1995, 307). Value theory describes a specific set of social relationships in which exploitation is a process of extracting surplus labour in the form of surplus-value that can only be understood in the context of the wider social forms that are constitutive of capitalism as a system of commodity production. Value theory therefore helps elucidate critical social relationships specific to capitalism, focusing attention on class structural relationships and the social structures of the economy that they help to define.

## A provisional summary of the argument so far

*In summary*, then, political economy approaches seek to develop a systemic view of economies and, within the broad spectrum of such approaches, Marxian political economy has two particular advantages as a starting point in seeking to understand economic geographies. First, it provides a powerful conceptual basis for understanding the economy. Via its concept of mode of production, a fundamental concept developed at a high level of abstraction, it focuses very directly on the critical defining social relationship of capitalist economies and why they are organised as they are. Via its concept of value analysis Marxian political economy goes straight to the heart of the matter in emphasising that capitalist economies are driven by the production of profit, recognising the centrality of the contradictory class structural relationship between capital and labour in this process, while also recognising competition among the class of capital as companies compete for profits in a variety of ways. As Davis (2015, 63) has put it, '[a]s all careful readers of *Capital* know, class struggle or competition takes many forms'. As such, Marxian political economy conceptualises capitalist economies as dynamic, as competitive companies switch processes and products – and as we'll see, locations – thereby literally re-shaping economic landscapes in search of profits. As a result, there is competition among groups of labourers in different places for paid employment. Second, because of its point of departure in value analysis at a high level of abstraction, it enables the parameters and conceptual boundary conditions of capitalist economies to be precisely defined and specified. There is of course a price to pay for such a level of abstraction in that there are issues that it cannot – and should not be expected – to address via value analysis but this absence can be filled by drawing on other different, or less, abstract concepts such as social formation and price within the framework of Marxian political economy and also, as I shall argue below, by drawing on other strands of political economy that are more attuned to issues of how, what and where as opposed to why – as we shall see.

## Geography matters: uneven development, spatial differentiation and spatial divisions of labour

In his magisterial re-working of capital, building on insights derived from the work of Marx, Lenin, Trotsky and Mandel, David Harvey (1982) locates spatially uneven development as a key integral element in the organisation of capitalist economies. Harvey's work in that respect is foundational. Recognising that all economic activities have to take place somewhere – literally in place – he identifies 'spatial fixes' as central to his 'third cut' at crisis theory. Spatial fixes involve a process whereby capital seeks to resolve economic crises on its terms by relocating its activities. It devalorises capital in some places (which may but does not necessarily involve the material destruction of machinery, factories, buildings, etc.) in which production is no longer profitable (enough), a recognition that capitalist development has an inherent tendency to destroy the conditions that first attracted it to a place as a location in which to operate profitably, and investing it in others that are (for at least a time) more amenable to producing profits. Put another way, 'capital never solves its crisis tendencies; it merely moves them around' (Harvey, 2014, 11). Smith (1984), building on Harvey's work, further developed the notion of capital flowing into and out of places, and back again.

While thus identifying changing economic geographies and landscapes as an integral part of the development of capitalist economies, Harvey's and Smith's analyses did not – indeed arguably could not – engage with the issue of which places experienced the effects of relocation, devalorisation or fresh investment. As a result, there can also be a tendency, albeit an erroneous one, to see changes in geographies of economies as simply a result of capital's logic of accumulation. Smith' s 'see-saw' theory, suggesting that new capital flows into a place would always follow in response to the outflow of other capital, with no recognition that capital might simply abandon places and never return, is prone to this interpretation, for example. Others have rightly pointed out, without denying the major role of the decisions of capital, that the processes of re-shaping economic geographies are more subtle, complex and over-determined than this, with a wider range of social actors and capitalist states involved in them (for example, Lipietz, 1977; Massey, 1995). This led to a greater emphasis on the role of a range of people in their places as active agents, individually and collectively seeking to shape spatial divisions of labour, while recognising the asymmetries in power relations between capital and labour, big capital and small capital, national states and capitalist interests and so on. Spatial divisions of labour emerge, and change over time, as capitalist firms seek to locate parts of their operations in those places most appropriate to them in their pursuit of profit. Capitalist enterprises can respond to a crisis of profitability – or the threat of such a crisis – by relocating with their existing technology to a location in which this can be deployed profitably; or by relocating in order to be able introduce new technology linked to process and/or product and/or organisational innovation. Alternatively, companies may stay put and introduce new technology and ways of working in situ if labour market conditions are favourable and/or can be made so by threatening to relocate (Massey and Meegan, 1982). Nonetheless, there are other social forces that will seek to influence these decisions to take account of the particular interests (industrial or territorial, for example) that they represent. The net result of such decisions is that both the geographies of individual companies and the overall economic landscape fluctuate and alter – contra mainstream economics and neo-classical location theories there is no state of static equilibrium to which they return.

## Introducing greater sophistication in thinking about how capitalist economies operate: exploring other theoretical perspectives

What I wish to argue at this point is that there needs to be more emphasis upon who are the key actors and decision makers, how actions evolve and decisions are taken and what various individuals, groups and collectivities are seeking to achieve via their actions in the economy. Building on the insights and entry point provided by concepts such as social formation and mode of regulation, more explicit and fuller consideration needs to be given to the socio-political and cultural contexts in which and the practices through which economic life is performed and takes place. Equally there needs to be recognition of the major changes in the technologies and forms of capitalist economic organisation since the foundational texts of Marxian political economy were first written. For example, there is scope to give much fuller and also critical consideration to issues of meaning and the constitution of commodities (for example, via advertising and brand creation: although see Chapter 9; Pike, 2013) and to innovations in production processes and related changes in forms of knowledge and learning, going well beyond the critique of 1960s behavioural geography approaches to these issues. While considerable emphasis has been placed upon learning, and knowledge-based economies, however, it is important to remember that economies have always involved learning and been grounded in a knowledge base (Chapters 3 and 4). Indeed, it is difficult to imagine economic activities that did not involve and depend upon knowledge.

As well as this renewed interest in knowledge and the cognitive basis of economies, there is potentially considerable value in interrogating evolutionary and institutional approaches to political economy and economic geography. Rather than seeing these as alternatives to Marxian political economy, however, I seek to bring these together with it to provide a more powerful explanatory framework in which to understand the geography of economies, the shifting restless landscapes of capitalist economies and economic landscapes of uneven development. I will also give some consideration to an emergent environmental economic geography and, more briefly, to more recent relational approaches, and how insights from these may also be drawn upon and linked to Marxian concerns – which of course are themselves relational.

### *Institutional approaches*

These approaches focus on the role of institutions in economic life (Hodgson, 1988; Hollingsworth and Boyer, 1997). Institutions can be thought of as generally accepted rules and regulations that shape human behaviour, and which are maintained and reproduced either by individuals themselves, by collectivities of various sorts (individual firms, employers' organisations or trades unions, for example) or by some kind of external authority, such as the state enforcing or otherwise securing compliance with them. In short, they help elucidate *how* economies are performed and develop. It is helpful to distinguish between institutional environments (for instance, rules, customs and routines) and institutional arrangements (organisational forms such as markets, firms or trades unions). Institutions, understood as sets of durable systems of social rules and conventions that are constituted by habits and routines, help structure social interactions. They are rendered durable precisely as a result of the development of collective intentionality, habits and routines. It is important to emphasise that neither agency – individual or collective – nor institutional arrangements exercise ontological primacy, and that their relative weight is a matter for empirical investigation in specific instances. Indeed as MacKinnon *et al.* (2009, 135) put it, the focus should be on 'the interaction between social structure and human agency mediated by institutions'.

In addition to formal rules and regulations, informal conventions and various forms of habitual behaviours have become seen as more significant in some economic contexts (although in others they have always been so – for example in relation to the regulation of illegal activities: see below). This recent growth in interest is because economic processes in contemporary capitalist economies have become much more uncertain and complex. As a result those in work and seeking work in their labour markets often face a precarious existence and informal conventions can help provide some degree of assistance in mitigating uncertainty. Capitalist firms and their managers are also facing a much more challenging and uncertain operating environment. Consequently they also require some kind of 'stabilisers' in the form of organisational conventions and corporate cultures to make sense of and manage in the face of this uncertainty, and to maintain some degree of coherence in the corporate structure in the face of constant change (Thrift, 2000). Such conventions and cultures influence ways of thinking, material practices, social relations and power relations.

### *Evolutionary approaches*

As noted above Marxian political economy is sensitive to the importance of history in understanding present processes and future trajectories. Evolutionary approaches in the social sciences also emphasise the importance of historical development in *how* economies change. They focus upon principles and metaphors such as variation, selection and retention or replication, routines and co-evolution of firms, markets, regulatory systems and their related spatialities. There is a considerable variety of evolutionary approaches in different social science disciplines, some of which draw on biological analogies. Evolutionary economic geography in turn draws on a variety of these to differing degrees in seeking to explain the spatial evolution of firms, industries, networks, cities and regions from elementary processes of entry, growth, decline and exit of firms and their locational behaviour (Boschma and Frenken, 2011, 295). This competitive dynamic produces a variety of organisational forms among firms, some of which succeed, others of which fail, depending upon their adaptation to the environment of existing market conditions or their adaptability in moving into or creating new markets.

As a result, over time successful firms build up routines as the competitive basis of their success (Nelson and Winter, 1982), linked to path dependencies (Arthur, 1989; David, 1985) and lock-ins of various sorts (cognitive; functional; political: Grabher, 1993), and to processes of learning and technical change (Dosi *et al.*, 1988). Emphasising the cognitive grounding of economic activities and the importance of functional, organisational or spatial proximity, embodied knowledge in dynamic learning processes and the diffusion of successful routines has spatial effects. For example, it is seen as central to the emergence of clusters of related firms in particular places through a 'snowball process' (Klepper, 2010) via an evolutionary process of spinoff formation. Evolutionary economic geographers have therefore emphasised the importance of the evolution of territorial variation in developmental trajectories, and conversely of the place-dependent character of processes of regional evolution, while placing varying emphases on the causes of such path dependencies. In addition, and as part of this they have also drawn attention to issues of path contingency, recognising that the evolution of economic geographies involves contingency as well as path dependency in varying measures, and path destruction and the replacement of obsolete and decayed paths by new ones (Chapter 5). This emphasises that territorially de-limited economies are open and complex systems, with development trajectories significantly different from those of specific technologies as a result (Martin and Sunley, 2006).

There have also been suggestions that evolutionary approaches can be constructively combined with those of an emerging environmental economic geography. This is because they share common roots in institutional methodologies, emphasise cumulative causation and path-dependent behaviour, have strong interests in regional scales of analysis and are intimately tied to the causes and consequences of innovation. As a result, Patchell and Hayter (2013) argue that they can be brought together to provide a conceptual framework that focuses on co-evolutionary and multi-scalar processes that are situated within a 'reasoned history' interpretation of economic development. The recognition that environmental and socio-economic processes are co-evolutionary – that is, mutually causative – and multi-scalar is both important and challenging for understanding economic geographies.

### *Combining and merging environmental, evolutionary and institutional approaches?*

There are those who argue that the distinction between evolutionary and institutional approaches is overdrawn (Essletzbichler, 2009). Rather than pursue the development of distinct evolutionary or institutional approaches, an alternative perspective is to recognise that these approaches can be productively combined, since institutions and organisational routines can be seen to co-evolve (Boschma and Frenken, 2009). Others hold differing views. MacKinnon *et al.* (2009, 137) caution against the dangers in such approaches of reliance upon imported theoretical frameworks which tend to privilege firm learning, technological change and self-organisation over institutions and social relations. Gibbs (2006) suggested bringing together ecological modernisation and regulationist approaches as one route to an environmental economic geography, which would have a strong political economy and institutionalist inflection, while Patchell and Hayter (2013) provide a further variation on this theme in arguing that environmental and evolutionary economic geography approaches can be combined to good effect, especially in those instances where evolutionary approaches have paid attention to political economy and institutions.

I argue for an approach that both recognises and goes beyond this fusion of environmental, evolutionary and institutional approaches, allowing for the incorporation of evolutionary and institutional issues within a broad political economy perspective, informed and framed by Marxian analysis (Hudson, 2001a; also MacKinnon *et al.*, 2009; Martin, 2015; Sunley, 2009). While Marxian approaches are strong on why capitalist economies and their geographies are organised as they are, evolutionary and institutional approaches provide greater depth of insight into how they are organised and into the what and where of economic activities within capitalist relations of production. It is also important to remember that there are well-established examples of the incorporation of evolutionary as well as institutional concepts into political economy approaches to understanding capitalist economies and their geographies from the 1990s (for example, Grabher, 1993; Hudson, 1994b), well before concern about developing distinctive evolutionary economic or institutional economic geographies emerged.

### *Actor-network theory and other relational approaches*

There are those who claim that relational economic geography provides a further option for economic geographers and such approaches can provide valuable insights, which I agree they can, but overall I tend to agree with Bathelt (2006) that it is little more than a loose assembly of theories and ideas that share some common articles of faith but differ in important respects. This includes post-structural approaches such as actor-network theories and while these have severe explanatory limitations, they can also offer something to a more comprehensive approach to understanding the economy, providing these limitations are acknowledged and addressed, as I argue below.

In particular, drawing on actor-network theory we can add – or perhaps more accurately, help re-discover, along with the emergence of an environmental economic geography – a further dimension to a critical geographical political economy. Not least, the influence of actor-network theory is helpful in reminding us that the economy is not just grounded in social relationships among people but also in relations among people, non-human life forms and inanimate objects and materials and the transformation of these objects and materials into socially useful products (a point developed more fully below). However, that said, it does so in ways devoid of considerations of the social bases of power and asymmetries in power relations among social classes and groups, issues that are central to Marxian political economy and to the practices of actually existing capitalisms. The flat ontologies of network perspectives are ill-suited to an appreciation of the significance of hierarchical social structures and power relations while adopting a decentred view of power underplays the centralised decision-making capacity and power of major economic actors, such as multinational corporations. Recognising this, I agree with Sunley (2009, 11) that the pressing task is to blend and combine network approaches with other institutionalist and evolutionary perspectives, with the key proviso that this involves a critical appraisal of network approaches (Hadjimichalis and Hudson, 2006). I would also add that a further part of this pressing task is to integrate environmental perspectives. In this way, bringing together these various perspectives with Marxian political economy will enhance the capacity to address questions of how capitalist economies and geographies co-evolve and are co-produced and further enhance understanding of them.

## Varying spatialities: from industrial districts to global production networks

In discussing evolutionary approaches, I briefly mentioned the emergence of clusters of related activities as one spatial form of capitalist development, one particular expression of the way in which restless capitalist landscapes are, for a time, fixed in a particular spatial form. For example such industrial districts can be identified in nineteenth century England and in the late twentieth century in many parts of southern Europe – though in both cases many have since been transformed or disappeared entirely (Chapter 6). Such industrial districts can therefore be seen as one example of *temporarily* stabilising flows of capital, commodities and people in place.

There are, however, many other spatial forms of capitalist development, other ways in which these flows are for a time stabilised in particular spatial forms that economic geographers have identified and analysed. In strong contrast to these locationally concentrated forms of development, with a dense tissue of relationship between firms and other relevant actors in place, there are other forms of development characterised by distributed geographies, 'spaced out' economies. Such spatial divisions of labour can be constituted at varying spatial scales from intra-national to global (for example, see Lipietz, 1977; Massey, 1995). Others argue that in fact both clustered and distributed forms of organisation can be and are combined, with localised clusters in particular places forming nodes in global networks, linked to other clusters in place. For example, building on the initial insights of global commodity chain analyses (Gereffi and Korzeniewicz, 2004), there has been considerable attention given in the economic geography literature over the last two decades to global value chains and global production networks (for example, see Yeung and Coe, 2015). Both these approaches analyse production flows from suppliers through lead producers to end users or consumers, with flows between places across scales, space and time. However, while both are concerned in different ways with the territorial segmentation of value chains, they are also concerned with the extent of embeddedness in linked geographies that incorporate clusters and spatially dispersed functions. Although such approaches tend to play down the role of organised labour and national states in the spatial organisation of these chains and networks (Smith *et al.*, 2002), and tend to ignore the circulation of commodities as 'wastes' and their revalorisation (Gregson *et al.*, 2010), they nonetheless provide a useful point of entry into understanding an important form of capitalist spatial organisation.

## Broadening the conception of the economy

The previous section considered various theoretical and epistemological developments that could help elaborate understanding of geographies of economies. In this section the focus is ontological, on broadening the conception of what counts as part of the capitalist economy (although this in turn has epistemological implications). There are two sets of issues to address, building on earlier brief comments: first, a more diverse conception of the social relations of capitalist economies; second, a fuller consideration of the materiality of the economy and relations between nature and the economy.

### *The diversity of social relations within and beyond those of capitalist economies*

So far, discussion has focused on the formal mainstream capitalist economy, markets and the class relations of capital but there is more to the economies of capitalism than this. In broadening the substantive scope, there are three particular issues that I want to discuss here. First, there is the issue of unpaid household labour, an ethics of care and the reproduction of a labour force, issues emphasised in feminist approaches that insist that these are critical in the understanding of economic processes (McDowell, 2004). I previously noted that capitalist economies treat labour *as if* it were a commodity. In fact it isn't. It is a 'fictitious commodity' (Polanyi, 1944). People do not produce children or reproduce themselves as commodities for the convenience of capital but as socialised human beings. The key issue for capital is how to ensure that people will become a labour force, suppliers of the commodity labour-power in a labour market and agree, willingly or unwillingly, to sell their capacity to work for a fixed period of time to, or to produce an agreed number of outputs for, capital. Historically, this involved processes of proletarianisation and, contemporarily, continuing processes of accumulation by dispossession (discussed more fully below), both stripping people of the capacity to reproduce themselves without selling their labour-power.

It is crucial to appreciate that wage labour by some depends upon unwaged labour by others. As a result unpaid household domestic work, through which people are reproduced and sustained, became and remains critical to capitalist economies but does not enter the cost calculations of capitalist enterprises. Such costs are borne by some combination of unpaid domestic workers in the home (historically, largely women, who for reasons of biology continue to remain crucial to the process), other members of families, national states and various charitable organisations. Often these costs are displaced spatially and temporally, with labour reproduced in one time/place but with labour-power consumed in another, primarily as a result of flows of migrant labour at scales varying from the intra-national (for example, in recent years in China) to global.

Second, it is important to consider what Gibson-Graham *et al.* (2013) have graphically described as 'the iceberg economy', the economy beyond – or metaphorically submerged below – the mainstream. Building on the older recognition of the importance of the informal economy in particular times/spaces (that is, activities that are legal but performed by people not authorised to do so, often out of necessity as a survival strategy), this encompasses a range of other forms of economic organisation on the fringes and in the interstices of the capitalist mainstream. These include the social economy (activities not driven by the profit motive: Chapter 7) and the illegal economy (of arms, drugs, illegal migration, prostitution, scammed brands and so on) and how these varied activities are socially constructed and regulated in ways other than those of formal regulatory systems (Chapter 8). Recognising that illegal activities are now structurally inscribed in globalising formal economies (Hudson, 2015) necessitates consideration of relations between the legal, informal and illegal economies, and how they are interdependent and co-constituted in various ways. The reproduction of informal and illegal economies depends upon a range of institutions, mechanisms and values (such as trust; reciprocity; non-monetary value; non-mainstream monies and exchange; different concepts of value and processes of valuation; and on occasion the threat of violence, extreme force or death).

Third, building on earlier work around the articulation of modes of production, there also needs to be consideration of what lies beyond the capitalist economy – that is, the worlds of non-capitalist economies and their relation to those of mainstream capitalism. Such non-capitalist economies are predicated upon different concepts of value and processes of valuation and their relationships to those of capitalism. Processes of accumulation by dispossession remain important – and indeed in the recent neo-liberal phase have become more important – in subjugating non-capitalist economies to the imperatives of capital accumulation, a point elaborated below.

### *Relations between economy and nature*

Building on some remarks in previous sections in relation to actor-network theory, there is a pressing need to re-think and give much greater attention to the relationship between economy and nature, or more precisely between social and biophysical processes. One implication, which can pose tricky issues, is a need to engage with the biological and physical sciences, whose practitioners typically work within different epistemological frameworks to economic geographers, especially those of a more critical inclination. Zimmerman (1951) presciently observed that natural resources are not naturally resources but become so via social processes and societal appraisals. However, prior to the 1980s much of post-war economic geography 'did not so much overlook nature as be actively complicit in its abstraction and marginalisation' (Bridge, 2011, 219–20). Economic geography had very little to say on resource or environmental issues at a time when the linkages between economic growth, development and the environment were acquiring huge social and political significance.

Subsequently, however, economic geographers began to address this lacuna. Initially they did so by drawing on strands of Marxian political economy and political ecology (Chapters 9 and 10), recognising capitalist development as a social process grounded in asymmetrical social relations between people that allows capital to appropriate elements of nature. In turn this led others to engage with a range of other approaches to the social construction of nature. This has enabled a more detailed examination of the economy's grounding in biophysical processes and materials, its relationship to non-human life forms and natural materials, and the effects of economic activity on those processes, life forms and materials. Consequently, 'nature' and apparently 'natural' phenomena such as soil erosion, floods and famines have become increasingly understood as social products, 'socionatures' (Swyngedouw, 1999). Others have sought to disaggregate production to understand the effects of specific processes, such as the enclosure of global commons, the commodification of bodies and life, the marketisation of environmental goods and services, the normalisation of environmental rationalities and the proliferation of different forms of environmental governance. To relate back to earlier discussion, this entails recognition that natures are 'enacted' and performed through the actions of institutions and individuals so that 'nature' is increasingly produced within the social relations of capital, as so-called 'second nature'.

There are two more specific aspects of the relations between economy, nature and the environment that are of particular interest here. The first of these is the reason for the recent renewed emphasis on accumulation by dispossession and its effects on the natural environment and socio-economic inequality. Marx analysed primitive accumulation as a temporary precursor to the emergence of a fully fledged capitalism, as a process whereby private capitalist interests and/or imperialist states forcibly acquired wealth and natural resources from non-capitalist societies in what was later to be defined as the 'Third World' and later still the 'Global South' but one which would disappear once a more mature capitalism became established. History took a rather different path, however. More recently, accumulation by dispossession has come to be understood as an active and on-going accumulation strategy, given added emphasis and greater salience as a result of the rise to dominance of neo-liberalisation as capitalist values are forcibly imposed on non-capitalist societies (Hadjimichalis, 2014). Accumulation by dispossession refers to processes whereby the possession of communal resources (such as plant life, forests or various minerals such as metal ores, oil and gas) is transferred from local communities to global traders who concentrate their corporate wealth elsewhere. Furthermore, this process is advanced globally by one capitalist state exerting its influence over another, often through direct negotiation between governments (for example, trade agreements) or through multilateral arrangements (for example, the structural adjustment programmes imposed by the International Monetary Fund). This new form of political-economic domination has been dubbed the new imperialism (Harvey, 2003). It can also extend beyond the acquisition of raw materials and natural resources. For example, Lee *et al.* (2015) describe recent tourist development in the Seychelles as a process of accumulation by dispossession in the context of neo-liberalism.

The second set of issues relate to the economy understood as material transactions and the transformations of nature, as a consequence acknowledging that both other species and inanimate objects can exercise causal powers. Bennett (2010, viii) refers to the 'vitality' of non-human bodies and matter as 'the capacity of things – edibles, commodities, storms, metals – not only to block the will and designs of humans but also to act as quasi agents or forces with trajectories, propensities, or tendencies of their own'. Sometimes this capacity can have positive economic impacts. For example, cows have become enrolled as active participants in computer-controlled, robotised automated milking systems (Holloway, 2007). Another striking recent example of this is the ways in which over the last two or so decades various species of insect – bumble bees for example – have been enrolled as actors in the production of fruit and vegetables in the 'artificial' ecologies of greenhouse production in northern Europe (Harvey *et al.*, 2002). However, such instances of a positive enrolment of non-human species in production are perhaps an exception to a more general tendency. For more generally other species and inanimate objects exercise causal powers that are less efficacious for human intentions in the economy, doing so unintentionally simply because biophysical processes have their own logic and cannot necessarily be contained to give only economically intended and socially desired outcomes. For this reason if no other relations between people and these elements of the natural world are central to economic processes.

Contrary to social constructivist accounts, nature has an irreducible non-social agency and biophysical processes have an unruly aspect that needs to be taken into account because they may have a noticeably unco-operative and disruptive quality that refuses to be corralled by purely social interpretations and human intentions. The materials and processes that comprise the biophysical world are not infinitely malleable: nature possesses lively and generative capacities and sometimes behaves in ways that confound efforts to produce it in particular ways and/or defies properties that are attributed to it (Prudham, 2003). Echoing earlier emphases on the effects of the friction of distance on economic processes, this has graphically been described as 'the friction of nature' on the way the economy works (Braun, 2006).

Furthermore, the unintended and/or unwanted effects of these transformational processes can impact back on the natural world in a way that may threaten the sustainability of the economy itself (as through the effects of global warming as well as more localised pollutants for example). The threats to sustainability have in turn led to growing interest in issues such as economic and environmental adaptability, resilience and sustainability, and the possible (partial) closure of urban and regional economies in the search for enhanced sustainability (Chapter 11). This has often involved reaching beyond the social sciences to disciplines such as ecology in seeking deeper understanding of how capitalist economies adopt and survive crises.

## The end of the beginning …

The rest of the book follows from this introduction, with a series of chapters that reflect the way in which I have explored broadening the scope of a geographical political economy approach that remains grounded in Marxian political economy. I have indicated some points at which particular chapters relate to aspects of this broadened agenda in the preceding sections. However, I want to end this introductory chapter with a recognition of what it doesn't cover – put another way, with a recognition that the book is inevitably a reflection of my own positionality, history and geography, and particular interests. This is most definitely not to say that those things that I don't consider are less important than those I do (and indeed in other publications, both singly authored and co-authored, I have considered some of them, (for example Gregson *et al.*, 2012; Hudson, 2005), and there is a voluminous literature that does comprehensively cover these other aspects of the sub-discipline (for example see the excellent edited collections by Clark *et al.*, 2000; Leyshon *et al.*, 2011; and Sheppard and Barnes, 2000). Substantive issues that are not covered here, except for occasional passing comments (for example in Chapter 2), include final consumer consumption, the commodity form as an arena of cultural production, shaped by culturally specific preferences and tastes, wastes, sustainability (except for some discussion in Chapter 11 examining regional resilience and in the final chapter) and the pivotal role of finance, credit and money. In terms of conceptualisation and other approaches to understanding economic geographies, while recognising the importance of unpaid domestic labour there is little about important approaches such as those of feminist economic geographies or about the diverse cluster of perspectives gathered together under the rubrics of 'non-representational theory' and 'performativity'. That said, this latter exclusion perhaps should be qualified at least in part because I have always seen a feature of critical political economy from Marx onwards as being politically 'performative', seeking to change the world in particular ways, not merely represent it as it is and this is reflected in a couple of the following chapters.

## Notes

1 For a fuller discussion see Hudson, 2001a; also Hudson, 2006a. For seminal statements, see Harvey, 1982; 2014.
2 Note that for the purposes of analysis within the context of the capitalist mode of production this assumes (a) that there is a labour market and (b) that money has come into existence. The historical formation of both markets and money precede, or co-evolve with, the development of capitalist social relations.

# 2 Conceptualising economies and their geographies

## Spaces, flows and circuits

### Introduction

I begin with two introductory questions and sets of issues. First, how do we best conceptualise the production of social life in general, in terms of relations between structures/practices/agents and between people and things? Second, and more specifically, how do we most appropriately conceptualise 'the economy', its temporalities and spatialities, its circuits and spaces and the links between them in capitalism? By the 'economy' I refer to those processes and practices of production, distribution and consumption through which people seek to create wealth, prosperity and well-being; to those circuits of production, circulation, realisation, appropriation and distribution of value, recognising that value is *always* culturally constituted and defined and so what counts as 'the economy' is always cultural. The economy is, therefore, always culturally defined, constituted in places and distributed over space, linked by diverse flows of value, monies, things and people within circuits and networks that conjoin a diverse heterogeneity of people and things in recognition of the simultaneous discursive and material construction of economies. By 'capitalism' I refer to a particular mode of political-economic organisation defined by socially produced structural relations and parameters, which are always – and necessarily – realised in culturally and time/space specific forms. There continues to be debate as to the extent to which the contemporary phase of capitalism represents continuities with or a break from past trajectories of capitalist development. Although there is now more emphasis on continuity than on radical ruptures between – say – Fordism and post-Fordism, or other dichotomous binaries, there are still claims and counter-claims about the extent to which the economy is characterised by greater 'flexibility' or has become more 'cultural'.

The prime focus of this chapter is the second question, the conceptualisation of capitalist economies, but it is framed by the first. Capitalist economies are constituted via a complex mix of social relations, of understandings, representations and interpretations, and practices. Certainly the class relations of capital are decisive in defining such societies *as* capitalist but these are (re)produced in varying ways and in relation to both non-capitalist class relations and non-class social relationships of varying sorts (such as those of age, ethnicity, gender and territory). There is undoubtedly a great variety of forms of the social relationships of economies that are non-capitalist, and some reference will be made to them, but in order to allow some depth of analysis the focus will be on the economies of capitalisms and the social relations of capital that define and dominate them. I first outline some principles that should be adhered to, on the basis of six assumptions about the economy and how best to conceptualise it. I then consider cultural economy and political economy as complementary perspectives. This leads to further consideration of issues of circuits, spaces and related issues before drawing some brief conclusions.

## Six assumptions and guiding principles and some of their implications

In seeking to answer the two introductory questions, I begin from six assumptions that shape the approach I seek to develop. First, there is a need for concepts at a variety of levels of abstraction, in part related to the differing temporalities as well as spatialities of individual and collective practices. This theoretical variety is necessary in order to describe and account for the diverse practices involved in processes of production, distribution, exchange and consumption and in the flows of materials, knowledge, people and value (variously defined) through time and over space that constitute 'economies'.[1] All social life occurs in irreversible flows of time and has a necessary spatiality. Second, however, there is a need to conceptualise the 'economy' in such a way that these diverse practices are seen as necessarily inter-related and avoid fragmenting the economy into dis-located categories such as production and consumption, seeing these as at best unrelated and at worst hermetically sealed off from one another. For a considerable period of time much social scientific analysis of the economy – whatever its theoretical stripe – tended to separate the analysis of consumption from that of production[2] and explicitly or implicitly prioritised production over consumption. Consumption was simply seen as a necessary adjunct to production. Now it is important to emphasise that this is the case in capitalist economies in one very precise sense. For both production and consumption – or, more accurately, exchange and sale – form moments in the totality of the production process and the point of sale is critical as this realises the surplus-value embodied in commodities and returns it to the monetary form. However, it is equally clear that this is only a very partial perspective on consumption. While services of necessity are (co)produced and consumed in the same time/space, in the case of material commodities the moment of sale marks a shift in emphasis from their exchange to their use value characteristics, to what can be done with material commodities post-sale in a variety of spaces of private and public consumption in homes and civil society. This emphasises that the life of commodities after they have been sold has important instrumental, material and symbolic connotations and dimensions (ranging from the creation of waste, to the giving of gifts based on relations of family, friendship, love and reciprocity, to the creation of identities).

Third, knowledgeable and skilled subjects, motivated via a variety of rationalities, undertake *all* forms of economic behaviour and practices.[3] Although people are certainly not the all-knowing one-dimensional rational automatons of neo-classical theory, what they do, how they do it and where they do it, are the outcomes of purposeful behaviour, underpinned by knowledge and learning, although understanding these determinants can pose serious methodological challenges. People are not cultural dupes, not passive bearers of either structures or habits, norms and routines. Conversely flows of people in the course of their actions within the economy (and also in other arenas, such as those of family and community) can become a mechanism and medium for flows of information and knowledge. Such flows can occur both in the form of embodied knowledge (often tacit) and that of the transmission of information in a variety of codified forms (written, spoken) and via a variety of media (letter, telephone, fax, e-mail, for example).

Seen from this perspective, the economy is performed and (re)produced via meaningful and intentional human action but knowledge does not translate in any simple one-to-one relationship to behaviour. Knowledge is a necessary rather than sufficient condition. Action is much more than simply a product of information and knowledge. Moreover, people and organisations have differential abilities to acquire and use information and knowledge in pursuit of their various projects (although this is not to equate such behaviour with generalised self-reflexivity and the continuous monitoring of individuals' life projects: see for example, see Giddens, 1991; Lash and Friedman, 1992). What people come to know and do depends in part upon their positionality in terms of class, ethnicity, gender and other dimensions of social differentiation and identity and the powers and resources available to them by virtue of their position within a given social structure, its organisations and institutions.

Furthermore, intention does not translate in any simple one-to-one relationship to outcome. Purposeful behaviour may have unavoidable unintended as well as, or instead of, intended outcomes. This is so because people chronically act in circumstances in which they lack complete knowledge both of the context, of other people and objects, and of the relationships between the people and objects on which they act. There may be emergent properties because of the excess of practices, and the messy conjoining of people and things in heterogeneous networks and processes of ordering that produce emergence. Consequently, it is necessary to take seriously the unintended consequences of human action, at all levels from the individual to the formal organisations and institutions of the state (see Habermas, 1976; Offe, 1975). As Urry (2000b, 4, emphasis added) notes, complex change may be unrelated to agents actually seeking to produce change. They may simply recurrently perform the same actions but 'through iteration *over time* they may generate unexpected, unpredictable and chaotic outcomes. Often the opposite of what human agents may be seeking to realise'. Miller (2002, 166) draws attention to 'the degree to which the political economy around us is the result of the unintended consequences of intentional actions'. Nevertheless, given these qualifications about uncertainty, ignorance and unintended outcomes, a concept of an economy that is not underpinned by intentional, purposeful behaviour, knowledge and learning is simply, literally, inconceivable, although of course the ways in which, and forms in which, knowledge and learning influence economic practice can and do vary over space and time. As such, economic practices are performed by knowledgeable, socially constituted subjects, although the outcomes of their actions may differ from those intended.

The fourth assumption follows from the third: the economy is socially constructed, socially embedded, instituted in a Polanyian sense (with institutions ranging from the informality of habits to the formal institutions of government and the state: Hodgson, 1988). These various institutions exhibit a degree of stability over the medium-to-long term, set within the longue dureé of structural parameters and necessary relationships that define a particular mode of political-economic organisation (such as capitalism). As such, the economy can be thought of as a relatively stable *social* system of production, exchange and consumption. However, while emphasising institutional stability, it is equally important to recognise that this is always conditional and contingent, as there are processes that seek to disrupt and break out of established institutional forms as well as processes that seek to reproduce them.

Hollingsworth (2000, 614–15) elaborates upon the social character of the economy and suggests that a social system of production

> is the way that a society's institutions, its institutional arrangements and its institutional sectors are integrated into a social configuration. A society's modes of economic governance and co-ordination and its institutional sectors develop according to a particular logic … institutions and institutional arrangements within sectors are historically rooted.

Even so, while a useful elaboration, this emphasis on 'sectors' suggests only a partial grasp of the institutions and processes through which the social relations of capital are (re)produced. However, Hollingsworth (2000, 624) goes on to add that 'there is a great deal of path dependency to the way that institutions evolve'. Thus embeddedness/institutionalisation also implies that economic change and institutional development are path dependent, emphasising that economic practices are performed in and create real, irreversible time. Again, however, this is a conditional dependence, for there are forces that seek to break path dependency as well as those that reproduce it. Therefore it would be more accurate to describe trajectories as path contingent, with periodic cyclical crises along a given path and the potential for secular changes from one path to another.

The fifth assumption is that behaviour (individual and collective) is both institutionalised and enabled and constrained by structures, understood as

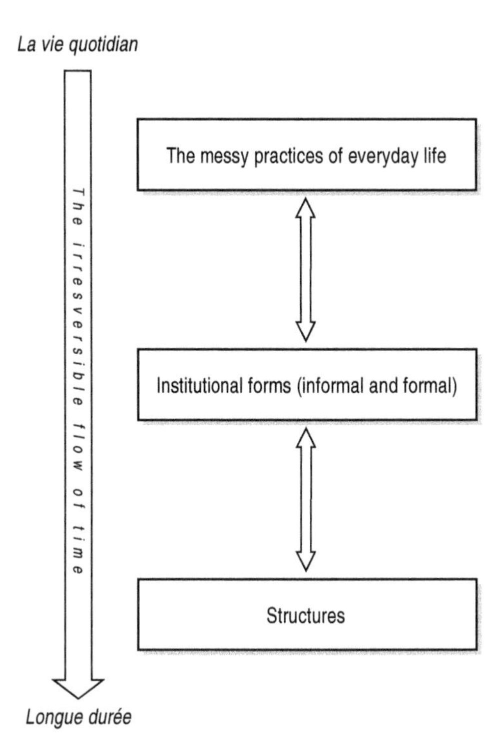


*Figure 2.1* Temporalities of practices, institutions and structures

stable yet temporary (albeit very long-term) settlements of social relationships in particular ways (see Figure 2.1). Structural relations specify the boundary conditions and parameters that define a particular mode of political economic organisation as *that* mode. For example, the class structural relation between capital and labour is one of the defining features of the capitalist mode of production – if this was not met, some other mode of production would exist. There are certainly varying instituted forms in which this relationship can be constituted – and indeed behaviour is always necessarily instituted – and this is central to the possibilities of creating many capitalisms and their historical geographies. Whatever the specific form, however, economic agents behave in instituted ways that are shaped by such structural relations and at the same time help reproduce them. There is a definite relationship between practices in the short-term and in the long(er)-term. This is not to say that such relationships may not be challenged – they often are. However, such challenges are typically folded into and absorbed in ways that may alter, but do not radically break and transform, the defining structural characteristics and boundary conditions defined by capitalist social relations. Nonetheless, there is theoretical space for structural change, a point of immense political significance.

The sixth assumption follows from the previous two. 'The economy' is constructed via social relations and practices that are not natural and typically are competitive. They are not naturally (re)produced but must be socially (re) produced via a range of regulatory and governance institutions that ensure the more or less smooth reproduction of economic life. These range from very informal governance institutions such as habits and routines in a variety of spheres, including those of civil society, community, family and work, to the legal frameworks and formal regulatory mechanisms of the state. In short, there is a need to ensure the reproduction of the social relations of capital*ism* and not just those of *capital*, while acknowledging that the latter are both defining and dominant in capitalist economies and societies. However, while dominant, they are neither singular nor uncontested and it is important to recognise this. Equally, there is a significant difference between the existence of rules and behavioural conformity with them. People may seek to break rather than obey rules and this raises key questions as to the circumstances in which they will do so (not least in terms of issues of predictability of behaviour; see below). A distinction may be drawn between the formally regulated economy, the informal economy and the illegal economy. The formal economy consists of legal activities governed and regulated within the parameters of legislation. The informal economy consists of legal activities but which are regulated by mechanisms and practices that fall outside the legal framework. Other activities are illegal but nonetheless form part of the economy (the economy of criminality, of the Mafia for example). However, the boundaries between formal, informal and illegal are not fixed but may be fluid and vary over time/space.

The variety of institutions leads to complex spatialities of governance and regulation. These combine the diverse spaces and spatial scales (national, supra-national and sub-national) of state organisations and institutions within civil society. Systems of governance and regulation are now more multi-scalar (Brenner *et al.*, 2003; Jessop, 1997) but national states still have a critical role to play in them (Sassen, 2003; Weiss, 1997; Whitley, 1999). While generally concerned with regulating the conditions that make markets possible, state activity can – and does – extend to supplementing or replacing market mechanisms in resource allocation. National states may, in particular circumstances, become involved in the provision of collective conditions of consumption (via the (in)direct provision of educational, health and welfare services) and the direct production of key goods and materials needed to enable private accumulation but that in themselves are (insufficiently) profitable to attract private capital. 'The economy' is chronically re-produced in situations of contested understandings, interests and practices because of the construction of governance and regulatory mechanisms that keep such potential disputes within 'acceptable' and 'workable' limits. However, it is important to stress that such mechanisms themselves must be socially (re)produced, often via processes of conflict and struggle – and do not simply emerge automatically to meet the functional needs of capital. Thus the practices of government, governance and governmentality are of critical importance. Furthermore, within forms of capitalism that encompass formal political democracies these mechanisms must be generally regarded as acceptable and legitimate but in dictatorial capitalisms they may be more violently enforced as a result of state power. One way or another, however, modes of governance and regulation must be sufficiently held in place, or at least for a time.

The requirement for a degree of admittedly contingent institutional – and even more so – structural stability reflects the need for a degree of predictability in the outcomes of economic practices and transactions. The issue is not simply one of institutional stability for its own sake but rather that this is a necessary condition for a required degree of predictability in performing the economy. This requirement for predictability is complicated precisely because of the dynamic character of the capitalist economy, the constant becoming of the economy. The economy is not something that simply is but always something that is *necessarily* in the processes of becoming (as, for example, companies constantly strive to produce new things, in new ways). The capitalist economy is performative, a practical order that is constantly in action, based in the irreversible time of strategy (Thrift, 1999). On the other hand, economic actors – workers, banks, manufacturing companies and so on – do require a degree of predictability in order that the transactions and practices of the economy can be performed with some certainty as to outcome over varying time horizons. Companies need to be confident that their customers will pay their bills on time, workers that they will receive their wages regularly at the end of the week, and governments that tax revenues will arrive at the due date. As such, there is an unavoidable tension between destabilising processes that would undermine predictability, stabilising processes that seek to assure it, and the necessarily dynamic character of capitalist production that complicates processes of governance and regulation and the smooth reproduction of capitalist economies.

In summary, I assume an instituted and structurally situated economy produced by knowledgeable people behaving purposefully in pursuit of different, and often competitive, interests, which can be pursued with a tolerable degree of predictability of outcome, and which are contained within 'acceptable – or at least tolerable – limits via a range of governance and regulatory mechanisms. There is an unavoidable tension between processes of institutionalisation, that seek to create a degree of stability and predictability, and the emergent outcomes of practices that seek to disturb this, either deliberately or inadvertently. I therefore also acknowledge that there is no single totalising meta-narrative that can explain everything about economies and their geographies but that nonetheless meta-narratives remain valuable – indeed are necessary – in seeking such explanations (cf. Massey, 1995, 303–4).

More specifically, I want to argue there are, broadly speaking, two analytic strategies for understanding the economy and its geographies. The first approach can be defined as '(political) economic', taking categories such as value, firms and markets as given, with these assumed to exist prior to their being observed and described from 'on high', prior to an analysis of the economy in terms of such categories. However, it is recognised that different types of economics conceptualise and represent these in different ways. The second can be thought of as 'cultural (economic)' and focuses on the discursive and practical construction and 'making up' of these categories. It emphasises the ways in which the 'economy' is discursively as well as materially constructed, practised and performed, exploring the ways in which economic life is built up, made up and assembled, from a range of disparate but always intensely cultural elements.

## A couple of caveats

There are two qualifications that I want to enter at this point, however. First, while recognising the different inflections of (cultural) economy and (political) economy and the recent growth of interest in the former, I reject suggestions that somehow the 'economy' has (ontologically) become more 'cultural'. As Hall (1991, 20) cogently argues, 'we suffer increasingly from a process of historical amnesia in which we think just because we are thinking about an idea it has only just started'. I think it important to avoid such amnesia – hence the need for eternal vigilance to guard against the constant danger of confusing new movements within thought (the (allegedly) new understanding that culture and economy cannot be theorised separately) from new empirical developments. The history of classical political economy (as evidenced, for example in the writings of Smith and Marx) prior to the marginalist revolution and the rise of neo-classical economics and its claims to universal economic laws was one that recognised the cultural constitution of 'the economy' (see Amin and Thrift, 2004). For 'culture is everywhere and little has changed in this respect ... economically relevant activity has always been cultural' (Law, 2002, 21). 'Is it the case', Slater (2002, 78) asks rhetorically, 'that culture is more central to the economic process than it was before? ... the answer, I think, is only in particular circumstances and instances but, in general, "no" '. Seeking to recover the ground conceded by the rise of neo-classicism in economics and acknowledge the long history of a cultural dimension within political economy is a very different matter to assuming that there has been a qualitative change involving the 'culturalisation' of the economy – the hard realities (if not quite iron laws) of commodity production and the production of surplus-value remain invariant.

Second, it is also important to insist from the outset that any simple equation of production/economic and consumption/cultural, and of the primacy of the latter over the former, or vice versa, must be firmly rejected. While there is clearly a case for paying more attention to issues of consumption, there has been a tendency for the pendulum to swing too far, replacing one-sided accounts that were overly productionist in their emphasis with equally one-sided consumptionist accounts (for example, see Gregson, 1995). This was especially so with 'first wave' consumption studies. For example, Bauman (1992, 49) asserts that

> in present day society consumer conduct (consumer freedom geared to the consumer market) moves steadily into the position of, simultaneously, the cognitive and moral focus of life, the integrative bond of society … in other words, it moves into the self-same position which in the past – during the 'modern' phase of capitalist society – was occupied by work.

Bauman alludes here to the elision of (allegedly) post-productionist consumer society with post-modern society. Echoing this, Lash and Urry (1994, 296, emphasis in original) claim that 'the consumption of goods and services becomes *the* structural basis of western societies. And via the global media this [pleasure seeking] principal comes to be extended world-wide'.

There are two kinds of lessons to be drawn from this, which are reflected in 'second wave' consumption studies. First, politically, it clearly exemplifies the dangers of confusing fashions in academic thought based on very class and socially specific experiences of a minority in the West with substantive changes in the living conditions and lifestyles of a much broader spectrum of the world's population. For the vast majority of people in the West at best only a fraction of consumption activities could be said to be 'pleasure seeking'. McRobbie (1997) criticises the political complacency of recent work on consumption that emphasises pleasure and desire precisely because it, at best, marginalises issues of poverty and social exclusions in its urge to reclaim the 'ordinary consumer' as a skilled and knowledgeable actor. For as Miller (2002, 182) remarks ordinary mundane consumption was (and indeed still is) neither hedonistic nor materialistic nor individualistic but was above all the form by which 'capitalism was negated and through which labour brought its products back into the creation of humanity'. For the vast majority of people living beyond the affluent West, hedonistic consumption and pleasure seeking behaviour – let alone the attainment of pleasure – is a distant pursuit of the affluent minority, occasionally glimpsed on TV screens in a world characterised by perpetual hunger and malnutrition for the impoverished majority.

Second, theoretically, it illustrates the dangers of divorcing a concern with consumption from issues of production, both specifically in the context of capitalist economies but also more generally.[4] Understanding capitalist economies and their geographies requires a more nuanced and subtle stance in theorising relations between the moments of consumption and production within the totality of the economic process.[5] Equally in terms of epistemology, there is, for example, a long history of rich ethnographic accounts of life in the workplace that seek to build an understanding of work and the social relations of the workplace in terms of the categories, understandings and practices of those engaged in the process (for instance, Beynon, 1973).[6] Conversely, there are powerful political economies of consumption (for example, Fine and Leopold, 1993; Miller, 1987). My argument is that such approaches are equally valid and should be seen as complementary. We need both to grasp the complexity of capitalist economies and their historical geographies, examining diverse practices of production, exchange and consumption from both political economy and cultural economy perspectives.

## Cultural economy approaches to understanding the economy

As suggested above, there has recently been a considerable resurgence of emphasis on 'cultural' approaches to understanding economies and their geographies, although these are far from uniform, broadly falling into ontological and epistemological concepts of a 'cultural economy'. For example, Ray and Sayer (1999, 14) argue that it is possible to distinguish between an economic logic concerned with means/ends calculation and a cultural logic concerned with ends per se. On the other hand, Lash and Urry (1994) argue that there has recently been a significant 'culturalisation' of economic life. They suggest that there are three expressions of this. First, there has been a growth in the numbers of innovative companies producing cultural hardware and software. Second, 'there is a growing aestheticization or "fashioning" of seemingly banal products whereby these are marketed to consumers in terms of particular clusters of meanings, often linked to lifestyles' (p. 7). Third, that there has been a growing 'turn to culture' in the worlds of business and organisations, precisely because maintaining or enhancing competitiveness requires companies changing the ways in which they conduct business and the ways in which people conduct themselves in organisations.

However, the significance and validity of these epochal claims of 'increased culturalisation' are far from assured. The evidence in support of 'the exemplary oppositions between a more "use"-value centred past and a more "sign"-value-centred present' is simply 'empirically insubstantial' (du Gay and Pryke, 2002, 7). Typically the evidence is fragmentary, at times simply anecdotal. However, the issue is not simply one of adequate empirical evidence, but also one of adequate theorisation and conceptualisation of the links between 'economic' and 'cultural'. For as Slater (2002, 59, emphasis added) points out, in practice, social actors cannot actually define a market or a competitor, '*except* through extensive forms of cultural knowledge'. He goes on to argue that producers cannot know what market they are in without extensive cultural calculation; and they cannot understand the cultural form of their product and its use outside of a context of market competition. Understanding culture and (local) cultural difference is vital in order successfully to produce and sell globally (Franklin *et al.*, 2000, 146). In like fashion, the economic practices of advertising, evocatively described as the 'magic system' (Williams, 1960), are intrinsically caught up with the cultural understanding of the role, functions and nature of advertisements (McFall, 2002, 161).

This foregrounds the way in which (to adopt a famous phrase from the cultural analysis of resources: Zimmerman, 1951): 'products and markets are not, they become'. This is perhaps most sharply emphasised by the iconic commodity of twentieth century capitalism – the automobile – in which the cultural and economic are inextricably fused via the segmentation of the market and the symbolic meanings associated with automobiles and automobility (Sheller and Urry, 2000). Furthermore, in order to be(come) a particular kind of economic institution, a market must also be a certain kind of culturally defined domain, because it depends on the social categorisation of things as (dis)similar (Slater, 2002, 68).[7] The dependence of markets upon such social categorisation has important implications for proponents of the increasing 'culturalisation of the economy' thesis and those who argue for the increasing, even complete, separation of the material and sign values of commodities.

Various forms of culturalism reduce the product to its sign value and semiotic processes. As a result, the object becomes entirely dematerialised as a symbolic entity or sign, infinitely malleable and hence never stabilised as a socio-historical object; its definition can be entirely accounted for in terms of the manipulations of codes by skilled cultural actors. As such, both the materiality of the object and the material economy and social structures through which it is elaborated as a meaningful entity are ignored. Consequently, there is also a tendency to reduce market structures and relations to semiotic ones. It is rather difficult to imagine how markets could exist over time, as they patently do, if products have actually undergone the kind of semiotic reduction that culturalists assume. As Slater (2002, 73, emphasis added) notes, '*markets are in fact routinely institutionalised, and are even stabilised, around enduring definitions of products*, whereas the semiotic reduction would assume that – as sign value – goods will be redefined at will'.

However, while the definition of a commodity, or of a thing, cannot be resolved by drifting off into the realm of floating signifiers, neither can its definition be simply and solidly anchored in given material properties. In contrast, the meanings of things, and things themselves, are stabilised or de-stabilised, negotiated or contested, within complex asymmetrical power relations and resource inequalities. This emphasises three things. First, it emphasises the processes and interplay between the realms of the material, the symbolic and the social through which the meanings of commodities are created, fixed and re-worked. Second, it draws attention to the instituted social field within which multiple actors seek to intervene to establish the meaning of things. Third, it highlights the political-economic structural relations within which both actors and social fields are located – although these can tend to get lost in the emphasis on meanings.

Moreover, Law (2002) argues that culture is located and performed in human and non-human material practices, which extend beyond human beings, subjects and their meanings, and implicate also technical, architectural, geographical and corporeal arrangements.[8] As such, social production systems comprise a heterogeneous mix of people and things and links among and between them – that is, the social has an irreducible materiality. He further suggests that this is – or ought to be – old news. 'Perhaps Marx told us this. Certainly Michel Foucault and a series of feminist and non-feminist partial successors have done so' (Law, 2002, 24).[9] The reference to Marx is important as it reminds us that one strand of the Marxian view of production centres on the labour process and transformation of elements of nature by people using artefacts and tools. In this regard, Law does no more – nor less – than re-state an old proposition from Marxian analysis that conceptualises the economy as therefore *always* a product of interactions between heterogeneous networks of people, nature (both animate subjects and inanimate objects) and things; of relationships between the social and the natural.

In summary, the conceptualisation of the economy remains contested terrain. Indeed that terrain is now more complex, and in some ways more slippery in its analysis of relationships than it used to be. Furthermore, they raise some important issues about the relationships between 'culture' and 'economy'. Miller (2002, 172–3) is particularly scathing in his comments about the 'culturalisation of the economy' thesis. He suggests that there seems to be 'a sleight of hand' through which a shift in academic emphasis is supposed to reflect a shift in the world that these academics are describing, that is, an assertion that the economy is more cultural than it was in earlier times.[10] He goes on to argue that it seems 'quite absurd' to suggest that we live within some new self-conscious, self-reflexive economy. There are undoubtedly powerful marketing discourses in the contemporary economy, but 'advertising and Hollywood were extraordinarily important' in the USA of half a century ago, and these made as much use as they could of the current psychological theories about how to create subjects (for example, see Williams, 1960). On the other hand, the economy was just as cultural 'at the time when most academics saw themselves as Marxists' (Miller, 2002, 173). It is undeniably true that a small, affluent minority live more self-reflexive (self-centred) lifestyles. It is also almost certainly something of an exaggeration to claim that there was a time when 'most' academics were Marxists. Neither point, however, negates the force of Miller's argument about the need to avoid conflating changes in the economy and changes in academic fashion.

However, I am not primarily concerned here with those arguments to the effect that the economy has become more 'cultural' in terms of both its processes and outputs. I do not deny that in certain limited respects this may be true although to claim that the economy overall has become 'more cultural' is much more problematic. However, as Law, Slater and others have demonstrated, positing a binary opposition between 'economy' and 'culture' is simply implausible and unhelpful. What is of interest here are those approaches that envisage the 'cultural' as a 'bottom up' method of analysis,[11] complementary to a more top-down political economy.

## Political-economic approaches to understanding the economy

There are also contested versions of 'the economic', based on differing forms and levels of abstraction (neo-classical and mainstream orthodoxies, heterodoxies of various sorts including Marxian political economy and evolutionary and 'old' and 'radical' institutional approaches[12]). From the outset I reject the technicist conceptions of the economy and its geographies exemplified by neo-classical and mainstream orthodox economics, which persistently seek methodologically to fix economic categories as self-evident or natural (and which are central to the (allegedly) new 'geographical economics': for example see Krugman, 2000; Glaeser, 2000).[13] Indeed, Slater (2002, 72) argues more generally that within economic analysis

> needs and goods appear as a natural and self-evident environment. In more critical theory, the use of the use value/exchange value distinction within the commodity form has generally functioned as a proxy for the distinction for a 'natural metabolism' between man and nature, and the warped social form taken by need and things within capitalist market relations.

While I agree with Slater's comments regarding neo-classical and mainstream orthodoxies, his view of critical theory reveals at best a partial and warped understanding of Marxian political economy. For 'critical' heterodox positions embrace more than Marxism while the notion of some 'unwarped' natural form is difficult to reconcile with *any* notion of 'the economy' as socially constituted and embedded.

Recognising the heterogeneity of heterodox economics, I seek to argue that a political economy approach needs to combine the differing but complementary levels of abstraction of various heterodox positions – Marxian, institutional and evolutionary. This multiple approach is needed in order to begin to grasp the complexity of 'the economy' as constituted by labour processes, processes of material transformation and processes of value creation and flow in specific time/space contexts.[14] Marxian analyses allow a specification of the structural features common to all capitalist economies that define capitalist economies *as* capitalist. This is emphatically not to claim that such structures exist independently of human practice; quite the contrary. They are both a condition for and an expression and a result of such practices and are always contingently reproduced. Practices may give rise to emergent effects that challenge the reproduction of these structures, although there are powerful social forces and institutions that seek to assure their reproduction. In short, there is a permanent tension between processes that seek to destabilise these structural relations and those that seek to reproduce them that is generally – but by no means inevitably – resolved in favour of the latter. This may involve folding disruptive processes into new institutional forms of capitalism while leaving the defining class structural relations unchanged.

Indeed, in making the distinction between modes of production and social formations, Marxian political economy recognised that capitalism was – and is – constituted in variable ways, an insight that has been considerably developed within other strands of heterodox political economy, in particular within evolutionary and institutional economics and sociology. Institutional approaches emphasise the ways in which these economies are constituted and embedded in specific cultural and time/space contexts. Evolutionary approaches foreground the path dependent character of development. At its most abstract level, the 'economy' in capitalism is certainly dominated, indeed defined, by the social relations of capital – and hence we need powerful analytic tools to theorise these. At this level, Marxian political economy and its value-theoretic account of the social relations and structures of capital provide powerful conceptual tools to understand accumulation by, through and as commodity production and surplus-value production. However, this is a highly abstract approach and so there is a need to develop less (or at least differently) abstract concepts to understand how capitalist production and the (re)production of capital come about. This requires other theoretical constructs to capture the ways in which capitalism is instituted in specific time/space contexts, discursively and materially formed and concretised in and through specific informal and formal institutions. As such, it necessarily includes theorising the state, regulation and governance within capitalism and also links between the formal and informal sectors of capitalist economies.[15] Put another way, it requires understanding how practices, institutions and structures inter-relate in the reproduction of capital (understood as a social relationship).

This in turn, however, requires acknowledging that the commodity form within capitalism is a slippery one, temporally and spatially (see Appadurai, 1986), and that the social structural relations of capital intersect with those of other social structures (such as ethnicity or gender) in varying ways. While there may be co-evolution of structures, this is a variable and contingent process. Massey (1995, 303–4) recognises that there are broad social structural relations – of class, gender and ethnicity, for example – which have determinate though non-deterministic effects. Recognition of such broad structures

> is not the same as the commitment to, or the adoption of, a metanarrative view of history. None of the structures ... need to be assumed to have any inexorability in their unfolding ... outcomes are always uncertain, history and geography have to be made.

These effects are determinate rather than deterministic precisely because of the multiplicity of structures, the conjunctural specificities of which combination of structures intersect and interact in a given time/space (which may also activate specific 'local' contingencies),[16] and the emergent properties of practices.

Commodification is a process that brings about, albeit unevenly, the extension and penetration of capitalist mechanisms and forms into aspects of the world and life world from which they were previously absent. However, these processes result in uncertainty about the fate of commodities once they have been sold. The purchase of commodities depends (inter alia) upon the meanings that consumers attach to them. Consumption is one source of meaning and identity, both for those purchasing the commodity and those consuming it (not necessarily the buyer – for example, the recipient of a gift). There are claims that we are what we eat, what we wear and so on and, beyond those, that the body itself has become an accumulation strategy (Harvey, 1998), with bodies worked on in terms of physical fitness, health clubs and plastic surgery to re-shape various parts of human anatomies in socially sanctioned ways. Goods acquire meaning and value, becoming 'culturally drenched' and so taking on 'identity values', expressed in rituals around possession and the giving of gifts, for example (Featherstone, 1991). However, such identity values are themselves subject to change and re-negotiation. Not least this is because commodities are manufactured with their own pre-planned trajectories, with built-in obsolescence within a product life cycle. As commodities reach the end of their socially useful lives to their original purchasers, they may be 'sold on', both formally and informally in a variety of settings (including street markets and car boot sales: Gregson and Crewe, 1997a; 1997b). In this process, the meanings attached to commodities by their original purchasers are typically re-worked (as, often, are the things themselves) so that there are recursive circuits of things and meanings rather than simply a linear path or a single circuit of meaning.

However, commodity production and consumption are also processes of material transformations. The resultant 'environmental footprint' of these activities emphasises the critical grounding of 'economies' in nature. Not only do elements of 'first nature' become commodified but a 'second nature' is also increasingly produced from within the social relations of capital. There is a significant difference between the appropriation of an 'external' first nature into capitalist social relations and producing a second nature within those relations. With recent developments in biotechnologies even life itself has become capitalised and produced as part of second nature (Franklin *et al.*, 2000).

Notwithstanding the increasing production of nature as second nature, within capitalist economies there remain 'economic activities' that are not under the direct sway of capitalist relations of production, both within and outside the spaces of capitalism (Figure 2.2). This raises questions as to how the capitalist and non-capitalist economies relate to one another and about strategies of 'accumulation by dispossession' – that is, (forcibly) taking things/people not produced as commodities and commodifying them (Harvey, 2002).[17] Not least, *the* key requirement of any form of capitalist production – the availability of labour-power – requires that people produced in a non-commodity form become commodified as labour-power, willing to sell their capacity to work on the labour market in exchange for a wage. This requires on the one hand understanding of the processes whereby people are reproduced as sentient, thinking human beings, conscious agents with their own agendas, pathways and plans – that is, *not* as commodities – and the circumstances in which and the processes through which they become commodified as labour-power.[18]

The key point in terms of conceptualising 'the economy', however, is that recognising the existence of non-capitalist social relations within capitalist economies and non-capitalist economies alongside capitalist ones requires considering different concepts and theories of value and other economic categories to those appropriate to the mainstream, formal capitalist economy. It requires consideration of different processes of valuation, in which value is not defined as socially necessary labour time but in terms of some other metric, perhaps in a more multi-dimensional way that reflects a broader range of cultural and social concerns.[19] This raises the issue of how best to understand processes of production and consumption in these 'alternative' economies and their circuits, flows and spaces, both in themselves and in their (lack of) relationships to the mainstream.[20] This raises questions of political character of political economy and leads into a normative question of future alternatives, of 'sustainable economies' and their spaces.

## Cultural economy and political economy: complementary not alternative approaches

While some see cultural economy as an alternative to political economy approaches, the inflection here is to see them as complementary perspectives: understanding the geographies of economies necessarily needs to embrace both. This is to do no more than seek to recover a position that was central to classical political economy but that was generally (there were exceptions) denied for many decades following the ascendancy of neo-classical orthodoxy (and that continues to be denied within the discipline of mainstream economics). Nonetheless, such recovery is vital to a more nuanced understanding of economies and their geographies. Thus the objects of analysis can be both taken 'as given' and can be problematised in terms of their discursive and material constitution. For example, consider the central concept of 'market'. A market 'is physically a place, a set of socio-technologies, and a set of practices. ... Socially it is also a set of rules' (Law, 2002, 24). In contrast, du Gay and Pryke (2002, 2) suggest that 'the turn to culture' reversed the perception that markets exists prior to and hence independently of descriptions of them. A cultural approach indicates the ways in which objects are constituted through the discourses used to describe them and to act upon them. As such, economic discourses format and frame markets and economic and organisational relations, ' "making them up" rather than simply observing and describing them from a God's-eye vantage point'. This has critical analytical implications since it suggests that 'economic discourse is a form of representational and technological (that is, cultural) practice that constitutes the spaces within which economic action is formatted and framed'. Put slightly differently, the discursive space of the economic decisively shapes the practical spaces of the economy; and vice versa. Discursive and practical spaces are co-determining, co-evolutionary.

In summary, economic categories (for instance firms or markets) need to be analysed in complementary ways that acknowledge the processes through which commodities are produced and the meanings of commodities created, fixed and re-worked and the political-economic structural relations in which people are unavoidably located. Therefore what is required is a culturally sensitive political economy that begins from the assumption that the economy is – necessarily – always cultural and a politically sensitive cultural economy that is alert to the power geometries and dynamics of political economy. These are seen as complementary approaches, viewing the economy from different analytic windows rather than an 'either/or' ontological and epistemological choice. Indeed these approaches in some respects interpellate one another rather than being discrete and self-contained. As such, the space currently occupied by culture-economy divisions and reductions could be at least partially reconstructed by treating concepts such as competition, markets, products and firms as *both* lived realities *and* as formal categories (cf. Slater, 2002, 76). Indeed, it could reasonably be argued that Marxian political economy has always contained strands of both approaches (for example, see Anderson, 1984).

## Re-considering the issues

Given the above, I now want further to explore in a preliminary way two sets of inter-related issues. First, the conceptualisation of relations between agents, practices, representations and structures and their varying temporalities (Figure 2.2).[21] Law (2002, 21–3) defines practices as 'materially heterogeneous relations' that 'carry out and enact complex interferences between orders or discourses'. As such, economic practices in their various and multiple specificities interfere in different and specific performances with other, alternative strategies and styles. Moreover this interference and multiplicity produces an 'irreducible excess' which is necessary to the survival of discourses and performances grounded in them. Second, the conceptualisation of relations between spaces, flows and circuits, addressing the question of how to explain which parts of circuits are 'fixed' in which spaces for a given period of time. Three points can be made briefly in relation to this second question. First, spaces must be understood relationally, as socially constructed. Second, economic process[22] must be conceptualised in terms of a complex circuitry with a multiplicity of linkages and feedback loops rather than just 'simple' circuits or, even worse, linear flows (though for convenience the terminology of 'circuits' is used below: see also Jackson, 2002, for a similar argument).[23] Third, the economy must be conceptualised as a complex system, a fortiori given recognition that it involves material transformations and co-evolution between natural and social systems.

There are two important implications of 'complexity' in this context. First, that economic practices may have unintended as well as, or instead of, intended consequences, because people chronically act in circumstances of partial knowledge. Second, 'complexity' implies emergent properties that

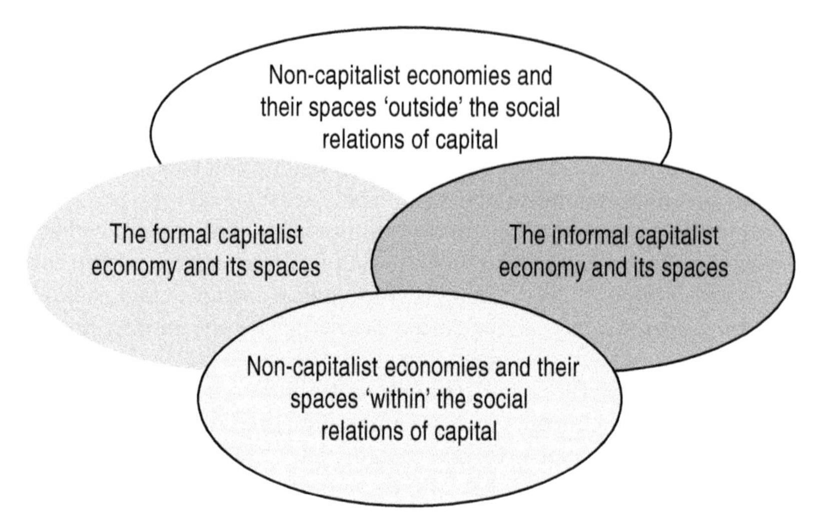


*Figure 2.2* Conceptualising the complex relations of economies and their spaces in capitalism

*may* lead to a change between developmental trajectories (for example, radical innovations of various sorts) rather than simply path dependent development along an existing trajectory. There is a danger that concepts of path dependency (especially if grounded in biological analogy) can lead to an under-estimation of the role of agency and reduce actors to 'cultural dupes' (Jessop, 2001). People thus cease to be knowledgeable actors and come to be regarded as the passive bearers of habits, norms and routines (much as structuralist readings of Marx reduced them to passive bearers of structures). As a result, the concept of path contingency, rather than that of path dependency, better expresses the possibilities of moving between as well as along developmental paths (Hardy, 2002). This is because actions and practices and systemic interactions may create emergent properties that alter, incrementally or radically, the direction of developmental trajectories. Consequently, evolutionary paths may be far from straightforward. As such, recognition of complexity and emergent properties can aid understanding of a shift from a simple evolutionary perspective of change along a given trajectory to evolution understood as a change from one trajectory to another.[24]

There has been a lively – at times, heated – debate as to the conceptualisation of contemporary economy and society in terms of circuits, flows or spaces, and of the relations between them. There are those that argue that 'fixities' no longer matter, or at least matter less, in a world of flows and (hyper)mobilities (Castells, 1996; Urry, 2000a). There is undeniably evidence of greater mobility, albeit unevenly, across a wide range of activities and spatial scales.[25] But for social life to be possible, for the economy to be performable, fluid socio-spatial relations and flows still require a degree of permanence, of fixity of form and identity – whether in terms of the boundaries of the firm, of national states or of local places. The 'same' event or phenomenon can be viewed through the analytic lenses of 'space' or 'flow', depending upon the purpose of analysis.

However, there is also a dialectic of spaces, flows and circuits. The key issue is the *necessary* inter-relations of mobilities and fixities, spaces and flows. Circuits and flows require spaces in which their various 'stages/phases' can be performed and practised, while stretching social relations to create spaces of different sorts, fixing capital in specific time/space forms and ensembles (Hudson, 2001a, chapter 8). Spaces are both discursive and material. Discursive spaces enable meanings to be both contested and established, permissible forms of action to be defined and sanctioned, and inadmissible behaviour to be disciplined. Material spaces are constituted as built environmental forms, a product of materialised human labour. Recognising that spaces are discursively as well as materially constructed implies that this process does not simply describe the economy. It is also in part constitutive of it, defining the economy as an object of analysis, constructing the spaces of meaning and the meaning of the spaces in which the economy is enacted and performed. These spaces of meaning then become guides to social and individual action. The same point can be made about concepts of circuits and flows, which are also constitutive rather than simply descriptive. As such, spaces, flows and circuits are socially constructed, temporarily stabilised in time/space by the social glue of norms and rules, and both enable and constrain different forms of behaviour.

Spaces, flows and circuits are thus both the medium and products of practices (over varying time scales), based on human understandings and knowledges. Moreover, flows, circuits and practices are also instituted (that is, situated in specific time/space contexts). As such, they are socially constructed and shaped (but not mechanistically determined) by prevailing rules, norms, expectations and habits and by dominant power relations. As Law (2002, 24) remarks of factories, markets, offices and other spaces of the economy, each is 'a set of socio-technologies and a set of practices. But socially it is also a set of rules'. Such spaces of the economy are thus simultaneously materially constructed, a fixation of value in built form, both a product of and an arena for practices, defined and regulated by socially sanctioned rules which both prescribe and proscribe particular forms of behaviour. In this sense there are structural limitations on action and understanding but, reciprocally, these limitations are a product of human action, beliefs and values. It is in this sense that structures are both constraining and enabling. Structural constraints are most powerful when they are hegemonic, taking effect not as a result of active domination but because they have become taken-for-granted, unquestioned determinants of everyday behaviour (Gramsci, 1971). Everyday routine then – even if unintentionally and unconsciously – reproduces these structural relations. Not least this is because of the existence of 'enabling myths' (Dugger, 2000) that are deeply embedded in the beliefs and meanings in which such routine is grounded and which have the effect of 'naturalising' the social and reproducing the structural. However, this does acknowledge that structures do not exist independently of human action and understanding and are always immanent, contingently reproduced. As such, they are in principle changeable. This is a key theoretical point and – potentially – one of immense political importance.

Bourdieu catches this sense of hegemony via his concept of habitus. Habitus emphasises the doxic (taken-for-granted, unthinking) elements of action, social classification and practical consciousness. Bourdieu (1977, 72) argues that the structure of a particular constitutive environment produces 'habitus, systems of durable, transposable dispositions, as structured structures, that is, as principles of the generation of practices and representations which can be objectively regulated and "regular" without in any way being the product of obedience to rules'. They are 'objectively adapted to their goals without pre-supposing a consensus aiming at ends or an express mastery of the operation necessary to attain them, and being all this collectively orchestrated without being the product of the orchestrating actor of the conductor'. Bourdieu later makes a critical point in insisting that habitus varies by and is differentiated between social groups. He argues (1981, 309) that the habitus is 'an analytic construct, a system of "regulated improvisation", or generative rules that represents the (cognitive, affective and evaluative) internalisation by actors of past experience on the basis of shared typifications of social categories, experienced phenomenally as "people like us". Crucially, however, 'because of common histories, members of each "class fraction" share similar habitus, creating regularities of thought, aspirations, dispositions, patterns of action that are linked to the position that persons occupy in the social structure they continually reproduce'. While Bourdieu refers specifically to 'class fractions', commonality of experience and identity could as well be based on 'people like us' defined via a variety of other social attributes, such as ethnicity, gender or place of residence. Furthermore, historical processes of class formation will reflect the intersection of structures of class relations with those of other social structures (cf. Massey, 1995, 301–5).

## Taking stock

We need to take what people do and their reasons for doing it, their actions and performances, seriously if we are to understand how structures are (un)intentionally (re)produced and constitute 'guides to action', informing social agents of appropriate ways of 'going on'. For example capitalists and workers behave in particular ways because they understand the world in terms of a specific class structural representation of capital: labour class relations. Nationalists and regionalists behave in particular ways because of their understanding of the world as principally organised around shared territorial interests and identities. Moreover, such behaviour may well be paradoxical precisely because social actors behave in circumstances beyond their control. For example, radical trades' unionists go to work, by various means and in varied workplaces, even though they understand the capitalist labour process as exploitative, since on a quotidian basis they and their families need to eat, to have a place to live and so on.

The 'economy' is thus instituted, based on shared understandings, discursively established, regarding 'proper' behaviour and conduct by the owners and managers of capital and the vast variety of workers in factories, offices, shops, consumers and so on. But these shared understandings and resultant practices/performances are structured by understandings of what capitalist production *necessarily* requires (a sufficient mass and rate of profit) and of how this can be produced – that is, they are shaped by structural constraints and the materiality of the economy and, simultaneously, help reproduce these constraints and that materiality. Thus, capitalist business is based in a material culture[26] that ranges from the vast number of intermediaries required to produce trade, through the wide range of means of recording and summarising business, to the different arrangements of buildings (spaces of work) that discipline workers' bodies. 'These devices and arrangements are not an aid to capitalism; they are a fundamental part of what capitalism is' (Thrift, 1999, 59). Of course, not least this is the case because a large part of these 'aids' is produced as commodities.[27]

The recognition of different arrangements of buildings as spaces of production that discipline workers' bodies touches on an important aspect of the spaces of economies and the ways in which these are both a medium for and product of human behaviour. More generally, economic spaces, circuits and flows (both discursive and material, of production, exchange, consumption) both help produce and are (re)produced by performance. They both constrain and enable different forms of economic practice. In this way consumers and producers of these spaces both produce and consume their own (formally economic) citizenship. Those who cannot produce or consume in this way cease to be legitimate citizens (for example, consigned to the ranks of the unemployed and welfare recipients or cleared from the streets and malls to let legitimate economic citizens buy and consume without hindrance, or excluded from the proliferation of gated communities within which the wealthy reside and consume: Minton, 2002). Spaces and practices are 'binding agents' in terms of how economies are performed and subject positions created and inflected (Thrift, 2000); the same point can be made about circuits and flows. Alternatively, and simultaneously, they are agents of social exclusion for those denied access to them.

However, these relationships between agency, practice and structure are even more complicated because (as the Foucauldian comment about disciplining workers' bodies hints) there are typically contested and competing understandings of what is and what is not possible in terms of action and change. For example, Beynon (1973) refers to a struggle within workplaces between managers and workers, a contest to define and dominate a 'frontier of control' running through every workplace as workers seek to increase their autonomy over the labour process and managers seek to discipline them to work in specific ways. Equally, as well as struggles between capitalists, managers and workers, there are typically competing practices between capitalists for markets and profits and among groups of workers seeking to promote their interests in competition with other groups of workers (Herod, 2001; Hudson, 2001a). Both capitalists and workers must also be disciplined to accept the 'rules of the game' of the commodity producing market economy in conducting these struggles, though these rules vary through time/space. As a result, there is a complicated and multi-dimensional struggle for domination between competing views of the world and material interests. Consequently, the reproduction of structural constraints is a product of contested processes, unless, of course, one particular view becomes generally if not universally accepted as hegemonic.

## Conclusions

My focus in this chapter has been on capitalist economies and the spaces, circuits and flows through which they are constituted, especially in capitalism's late modern phase. There are claims that this represents a radical break with earlier phases, and that in particular it is marked by an enhanced 'culturalisation' of the economy. This is an argument that I broadly reject, not least as it conflates changes in intellectual fashion and perspective with alleged changes in the economy. Practices of production, exchange and consumption, linked to flows of capital, commodities, information and people, are central to the constitution of the spaces of capitalist economies and are neither more nor less cultural than they previously have been (although they may be differently cultural). As such, spaces of consumption, exchange and production are linked via a complex circuitry of flows and at the same time constitute the material and discursive spaces through which these flows can and must occur. Circuits, flows and spaces exist in relations of mutual determination, socially produced in historically geographically variable ways. As Dicken and Yeung (1999, 125) put it, 'we need to recognise the organisation and geographical diversity of internationalising, regionalising and globalising processes and forms, ... together with the multiple scales at which they are enacted'. A corollary of recognising this diversity is a need for a variety of theoretical and methodological approaches in order to comprehend the economy: for example, political economic and cultural economic approaches.

People have different motives and rationalities, depending upon their positions in the economy: for example, as capitalists, managers of capital, workers or consumers. For example, corporate managers may seek to create meanings for products via advertising; potential consumers may accept these views or they may challenge and contest them. Decisions as to what/where to buy will be influenced by this, along with material considerations such as income constraints – that is, there is a material as well as a discursive dimension to such economic activity. The social relations and practices of 'the economy' are not necessarily harmonious and are not naturally (re)produced but must be socially (re)produced. A range of governance and regulatory mechanisms help keep potential disputes within 'acceptable' and 'workable' limits as different social agents seek to make the geographies of capitalist economies in particular ways to further their interests.

Recognition of the co-existence of spaces of production, exchange and consumption also points to the ways in which the same individual may fulfil different roles and niches within capitalist economies at different time/spaces. They may also participate simultaneously in the social relations of the economy in different ways in the same time/space – for example as consumer, producer and indirect owner of capital via their participation in company pension schemes. Because of this multiplicity of positions in the social relations of the economy, people develop multiple understandings of capitalist economies and their implications, depending upon their own variable positionality, not just in terms of class relations within capitalism but also in terms of ethnicity, gender, age and so on. This has manifold implications for the creation of (multiple) identities within the circuits and spaces of economies. Once again, the cultural and economic fold into one another, with profound implications for political action.

## Notes

1 Gough (2003) takes me to task for not rigorously deducing such concepts from the value categories of capital (see Hudson, 2001a). But to seek to do so would be to seek a single totalising meta-narrative account that can explain anything and everything (see also below).
2 Economic geography was handicapped for some time by the legacies of 1960s spatial sciences approaches to location theory that sought to develop specific partial equilibrium theorisations of the space economies of exchange, sale and production – consumption as such was simply ignored.
3 Giddens (1990) emphasises the significance of knowledge and learning in the contemporary economy. However, the key issue is the new ways that knowledge is important economically, not that knowledge has suddenly become economically important.
4 One of the strengths of the commodity chain approach is that it seeks to connect consumption and production practices: see Smith *et al.*, 2002.
5 If this smacks of meta-narrative, it is only one, not the only one, of relevance here.
6 However, Beynon's work is cast more in the mould of political economy and economic sociology than cultural analysis.
7 There are parallels here to the definition of an economic sector.
8 The economy conceptualised as a heterogeneous networked association of people and things is a more general characteristic of Actant-Network Theorists such as Law and Latour (1987).
9 Thus capitalist production is always more than just the production of commodities by means of commodities (as neo-Ricardians such as Sraffa, 1960, argue). Furthermore classical political economy embraced relations between economy and environment as well as recognising the cultural constitution of 'the economy', as noted above.

10 Law (2002) makes the same point about relationships between change in the world that social scientists analyse and changes in style and fashion of analysis that they deploy.
11 Methodologically, this involves ethnographic and participant-observation approaches as well as interview-based approaches. However, in several respects such approaches are not new. Hermeneutic/interpretative and ethnographic approaches have a long history, both generally in the social sciences and specifically in seeking to understand economic forms and practices (albeit not in the framework of cultural economy: for example, see Beynon, 1973).
12 The distinction between 'radical', 'old' and 'new' institutional analysis is important. 'New' institutionalism is closely allied to mainstream orthodoxies (Williamson, 1975). 'Old' institutionalism emphasises the institutional and social embeddedness of 'the economy' (as expressed in the work of Common, Polanyi or Veblen: see Hodgson, 1993). Radical institutionalism emphasises issues such asymmetrical power relations in shaping economic life (Dugger, 1989; 2000).
13 Thrift (1999, 59) notes the irrelevance of most formal economic – that is mainstream orthodox – theory to business practices. Indeed, these seem more in tune – albeit only implicitly – with heterodox theories which emphasise the need to extract surplus-value from workers, to ensure the creation of monopoly rents via product and organisational innovation, and so on. Equally many trades' union practices have been shaped historically more by Marxian political economy than by mainstream orthodoxies. While much public sector economic policy is guided by mainstream theoretical orthodoxies, this may well account for the chronic disjunction between policy intentions and outcomes, although there is an increasing influence of various heterodox strands of thought on local and regional economic development policy.
14 In turn, methodologically, it requires a variety of forms of evidence (quantitative and qualitative) relating to concepts such as firms, markets, or labour productivity.
15 For comparable arguments, see McFall (2002).
16 Miller (2002[5], 166) likewise emphasises the degree to which the political economy around us is the result of 'structural conjunctions', as different structures interact in specific time/space conjunctures.
17 Historically, within radical political economy this was reflected in literatures on the articulation of modes of production (for example see Amin, 1977).
18 There are circumstances in which slavery and indentured labour become mechanisms to assure the supply of labour-power outside the normal sphere of market transactions.
19 There is a connection here between concepts of space (defined in terms of capital's one-dimensional interest in locations as a source of profit) and place (reflecting people's multi-dimensional attachments to a location via relations of family, friendship and community): see Hudson, 2001a, chapter 8.
20 There are, for example, three ways of conceptualising the relationship between the mainstream formal economy and the social economy or 'Third Sector' (Amin *et al.*, 2002). First, the social economy can be seen as a route back into the formal economy. Second, it can be seen as complementary to the mainstream, filling the interstices in which the mainstream has no interest. Third, it can be seen as the potential seeds of a radical alternative conception to – or even of – the mainstream.
21 This may well be anathema to non-representational theorists. However, I want to explore the notion of practice as what people do in the economy as a way of better grasping relationships between agency and structure by emphasising doing rather than just thinking, the material and affective as well as the cognitive.
22 Such as commodity chains (Gereffi and Korzeniewicz, 1994) or production seen as a linear series of materials transformations (Jackson, 1995).

23 My argument involves a move from linear commodity chains to more complex circuits and networks as a way of subverting dualistic thinking and unsettling the kind of linear logic that sees consumption at one end of a chain that begins with consumption (Jackson, 2002, 5).
24 It is an open question as to whether emergent properties lead to changes within the parameters of capitalist social relations or to a shift onto alternative non-capitalist paths. This also raises key political questions about 'steering' changes along or between developmental trajectories (Hudson, 2001a, chapter 9).
25 Damette introduced the concept of hyper-mobility of capital in the 1970s (see Damette, 1980). Thus the notion that the capitalist economy has suddenly 'speeded up' in the last decade or so requires some careful re-consideration.
26 Material culture denotes the study of the relations between persons and things, the manner in which people convert things to their own ends. As both means and ends will vary with time/space, material cultures are inherently geographical.
27 There are strong echoes here of Sraffa's (1960) neo-Ricardian account of capitalist production as the production of commodities by means of commodities.

# 3 'The learning economy, the learning firm and the learning region'

## A sympathetic critique of the limits to learning

### Introduction

The context of, and focus of concern in, this chapter is the recent growing interest in – one might almost say obsession with – 'learning' and 'knowledge' as a – maybe *the* (only) – route to corporate and regional economic success. This is one facet of the growing, and generally productive, engagement between economic geographers and regional analysts on the one hand and evolutionary and institutional economists on the other (Maskell *et al.*, 1998; Storper, 1997). This focus on knowledge, and the processes through which it is transmitted, is often presented as a dramatic new breakthrough, of epochal significance, promising radical theoretical reappraisal and opening up exciting new possibilities for the conception, implementation and practice of policy (Braczyk *et al.*, 1998). It would of course be futile to deny the significance of knowledge, innovation and learning to economic performance. Production as a process that simultaneously involves materials transformation, human labour and value creation, necessarily depends upon the knowledge and skills of individual workers and on the collective knowledge of a range of social and technical conditions and processes that make production possible. This also directs attention to the institutional bases of knowledge production and dissemination, recognising that these are social processes and 'instituted processes' of a Polanyian type. Competitiveness and economic success is thus seen to be grounded in a variety of types of knowledge and knowing.

The argument in the chapter, however, is that recognising the importance of innovation and knowledge creation to economic success is hardly novel and that the contemporary focus on learning is in many ways simply a new twist on an old theme that 'knowledge is power'. This is an important insight. It is also a partial one – not least because of the relationship between the possession of power and the capacity to shape the production and/or appropriation of knowledge. Not all economies are capitalist but the historical geography of capitalism cannot be sensibly understood without giving due recognition to the revolutionary impacts of innovation on the what, how and where of production. It would be a foolish enterprise to seek to deny the importance of learning and knowledge creation, and the institutional settings and forms in and through which these processes occur, to innovation and to the dynamic of uneven development in capitalist economies. Indeed, one cannot over-emphasise that the creation of knowledge has been integral to the competitive dynamic of capitalist economies since they were first constituted as capitalist. As Marx emphasised well over a century ago and Schumpeter later re-stated, much of the revolutionary dynamic of capitalism has *always* rested in its capacity to create new commodities and new ways of producing them via a sequence of radical transformations of the forces of production and of the organisation of the labour process (Aglietta, 1979). So what, one might reasonably ask, is new? What, one might inquire, is all the fuss about?

The first point that can be made in response to these questions is that the current 're-discovery' of the importance of knowledge and the processes through which it is produced brings with it a baggage of strong claims about new and enriching and empowering forms of work (Florida, 1995). The alienated and de-skilled mass worker is apparently now no more than a subject of history. The emphasis on knowledge is also associated with claims about the possibilities for increasingly egalitarian, more equal and progressive forms of economic and social development. It likewise brings related claims as to new possibilities for urban and regional regeneration strategies, and suggestions of new developmental trajectories for problematic cities and regions (Morgan, 1995; Simmie, 1997). There is no doubt that in particular cases, times and places, such claims have a certain validity but they also require careful and critical scrutiny. Such a scrutiny must acknowledge the necessary structural limits to a capitalist economy and the disciplines (if not quite iron laws) that these set on what is both necessary and possible (as opposed to what may be desirable but impossible – to adopt a memorable phrase from Offe, 1975).

The structure of the remainder of the chapter is as follows. First, the claims made by the proponents of 'learning' approaches are briefly summarised, and some links are drawn between the pre-eminent emphasis that they place upon knowledge and learning and other literatures that analyse on-going changes in the organisation of production and work in contemporary capitalism and which have differing emphases. The aim is to situate and contextualise claims about the significance of 'learning'. Second, these claims are placed within the context of continuities and changes within capitalism, and the ways in which these have been understood, as a further step in this process of contextualisation and situation. Finally, some conclusions are briefly drawn around the limits to learning and questions of learning by whom, for what purpose, in the context of the politics and policies of social, economic and territorial development.

## The learning economy: learning firms and learning regions

There has been a growing recognition of the importance of knowledge in the contemporary organisation of production in what many commentators see as an era of globalisation (Giddens, 1990; Strange, 1988).This takes a variety of forms but the central point is that the production, distribution and exchange of knowledge is claimed to have attained an unprecedented significance in the operations of the economy. Much of the discussion about the significance of knowledge takes place under the rubric, and around the theme, of 'learning'. There are, however, several strands to the learning literature, which emphasise different aspects of, and ways of, learning: learning-by-doing (Arrow, 1962); learning-by-using (Rosenberg, 1982); learning-by-interacting (Lundvall, 1992); and learning-by-searching (Boulding, 1985; Johnson, 1992). Perhaps the most influential of these within recent debates has been Lundvall's emphasis on learning-by-interacting, informed by a concern to understand how (predominantly small) companies in open economies can remain competitive in an environment of rapid technological change and uncertainty. It essentially focuses upon companies learning about and adapting to 'best practice' via interaction with other firms and institutions as the route to competitiveness.

Lundvall (1995) has recently remarked that the term 'learning economy' signifies a society in which the capability to learn is critical to economic success. For Lundvall contemporary capitalism has reached the stage at which knowledge is the most strategic resource and learning the most important process. There is a recognition that this process is to a considerable degree path dependent, although significant breakthroughs often involve shifting onto new, rather than further along existing, paths. The learning process could thus involve the capability to move from already successful to potentially even more successful new 'state-of-the-art' development trajectories, or to learn how to sustain currently successful trajectories of development, or how to shift onto more from less successful paths. Learning both pre-supposes and produces knowledge (although the learning literature tends to gloss over the different forms and processes of knowledge production: Odgaard and Hudson, 1998) but knowledge is not an undifferentiated entity and it exists in a variety of forms. There is, in particular, a critical qualitative difference between information, which is codifiable (and so commodifiable and tradable) knowledge that can be transmitted mechanically or electronically to others (for example, as bits along the fibre optic cables of a computer network), and in principle can become ubiquitously available, and tacit knowledge in the form of know-how, skills and competencies that cannot be so codified and ubiquified. Foray (1993, 87) defines tacit knowledge as 'knowledge which is inseparable from the collective work practices from which it comes'. He goes on to emphasise that 'some tacit knowledge is always required in order to use new codified knowledge'. Foray thus emphasises the asymmetric relationship between these qualitatively different types of knowledge. Acknowledging that knowledge is 'tacit' problematises its communication and transmission to others who lack access to the unwritten codes of meaning in which such knowledge is embedded and upon which its meaning depends.[1] Such tacit knowledge may indeed be unique to particular individuals rather than collective in character – in which case the problems of communication are, a fortiori, problematic – but it *is* often collective rather than simply individual, locally produced and often place-specific. Know-how thus cannot be divorced from its individual, social and territorial contexts and in that sense is only partially commodifiable. It therefore can only be purchased, if at all, via the labour market as embodied knowledge and not in the form of patents, turn-key plant or other forms of 'hard' technology.

Recognition of the uncodifiable aspects of learning and knowledge creation[2] is important since it signifies that these processes are qualitatively different from the simple transfer of codifiable knowledge as information. As a consequence, learning involves more than simply transactions of information within markets or hierarchies. Lundvall (1992) has emphasised the national context of innovation systems and learning and the significance of shared language and culture as well as formal legislative frameworks in shaping trajectories of innovation and learning. This emphasis on the national as a key site of regulatory processes resonates with broader critiques of claims as to the decreasing significance of the national in the face of processes of globalisation. The notion of 'globalisation' has become increasingly contested and questioned, with a growing number of analysts stressing the continuing salience of the national in terms of the organisation and regulation of the economy (Boyer and Drache, 1995; Gertler, 1997; Weiss, 1997).

While recognising that the national territory can and continues to be a crucial milieu in some circumstances, it is also becoming increasingly clear that there is no a priori reason to privilege this particular spatial scale, irrespective of time and place. Nevertheless, the renewed emphasis on the salience of the national has implications not just for the proponents of globalisation but also for those who wish to privilege the regional over the national in terms of the production of knowledge and learning (Storper, 1995; 1997). Regional and locality-based learning and knowledge production systems can be of equal or greater significance (Maskell, 1998; Maskell and Malmberg, 1995), not least in the context of arguments that innovation systems are constituted sectorally – and at least potentially globally – rather than nationally (Metcalfe, 1996). The sectoral constitution of innovation systems globally across rather than within national boundaries emphasises the significance of the place-specifically local within the global and of the links between corporate learning and territorially embedded knowledge (a point re-visited below). Such tacit knowledge and learning capacity is seen as *the* key competitive corporate and territorial asset. While the debates as to the relative importance of sectoral versus territorial bases of learning, and of the relative importance of different territorial scales in processes of learning and innovation, do not challenge the importance of knowledge per se to the contemporary economy, there are, however, other reasons for treating such claims which foreground the role of knowledge and learning with a degree of circumspection.

A corollary of the renewed emphasis on the generalised significance of knowledge in production is a recognition of the need to move away from the old 'linear' R&D model as dominating the production of knowledge, associated in particular with a Taylorist conception of the technical division of labour. This approach was informed by a perceived need for the separation of mental and manual labour as the key to achieving scale economies and labour productivity growth within mass production systems. Such separate R&D departments and the associated routinisation of R&D activities formed one element in an historically specific form of organisation of the labour process within large firms. Such an organisational model has now been recognised as an historically specific one, which in some circumstances remains appropriate and powerful but in others can incorporate crucial weaknesses, especially in an era of rapid shifts in product markets, for there are no necessary feedback loops from the users of and customers for innovations to those within the firm charged with responsibility for producing them. Consequently, new products may not be attuned to consumer tastes and fail in the market place while, conversely, opportunities for new products may be missed. Furthermore, the growing significance of the symbolic meanings attached to consumption, a fortiori in circumstances in which the commodity is an event or spectacle rather than a material object, places an even greater premium on knowledge of consumer tastes and on the ability to shape them via advertising.

Knowledge creation and innovation is accordingly seen as something that must become all pervasive throughout the firm, at all levels and in all departments and sections. The ideal is to emulate the (originally Japanese) process of 'kaizen', continuous improvement through interactive learning and problem solving (Sadler, 1997), a happy state which it is claimed is brought about as a consequence of the existence of an actively committed and engaged workforce within particular types of corporate organisation, dedicated to enhancing corporate performance. The emphasis is upon creating dense horizontal flows of knowledge and information within and vertical flows of knowledge and information between the various functional divisions of the company, while opening the ears of those involved within the company to voices from outside its boundaries. The aim is to build a 'seamless innovation process', bringing together everyone in the firm involved in product development, from those who had the initial idea to those who finally took it to the market place. Creation of multi-disciplinary and cross-departmental 'concept teams' with responsibility for product development is seen as a way of sharply reducing the socially necessary labour time taken to bring new products onto the market. Increasingly these are organised as 'globally distributed teams' which 'meet' via video-conferencing and other forms of electronic technology. This reliance on such distanciated social relationships of intellectual production, rather than face-to-face meetings, reflects increasing pressures on managerial time and resources but can also create problems as these teams seek to work to very tight deadlines (Miller *et al.*, 1996). While these globally distributed teams are not quite 'virtual organisations' or 'virtual corporations' (Pine, 1993), they do represent a significant change in the organisation of processes of knowledge creation and innovation within companies.

Complexity theory strongly suggests the need to adapt a view of social systems as evolving in a non-linear fashion (Amin and Hausner, 1997). One implication of this in the context of innovations is that revolutionary innovations (both organisational, product and process) may be produced in unexpected ways. The emphasis now is therefore upon recognising that innovation is an interactive process that involves the synthesis of different types of knowledge rather than privileging the formal scientific knowledge of the R&D laboratory over other forms of knowledge. As a consequence, there is considerable emphasis on acknowledging the legitimacy and 'voice' of different types of knowledge (not least as radical innovations may well challenge the dominant 'logic' within an industry), of re-uniting the mental and the manual which were torn asunder by Taylorism, on re-inventing polyvalent multi-skilled workers, and so enhancing corporate competitiveness by producing higher quality products more flexibly.

Such tendencies are observable in both small flexibly specialised firms and units and in new forms of high volume production that seek to combine economies of scale and scope, ultimately in mass customised production with a batch size of one (Hudson, 1994a; 1997a; 1997b). Intensifying competition and shorter product life cycles (which may be part of an aggressive, offensive competitive strategy rather than simply a response to changes in consumer tastes) are necessitating a closer integration of R&D with the other functional sections within companies, with far-reaching implications for the internal organisation and operation of those companies. This growing emphasis on the significance of learning and knowledge creation, and new forms of production organisation, links in with propositions about the emergence of new forms of more rewarding, satisfying and engaging work than was available to the vast numbers of workers who manned the mass production lines of factories and offices, alienated in de-skilled and dehumanising jobs. It is, however, worth recalling that even at the high point of Fordism only a minority of labour processes were organised on Taylorist principles and that a considerable amount of manual work was performed by knowledgeable craft workers (Pollert, 1988). Innovation and learning have nonetheless become seen as creative processes that must be suffused throughout the entire workforce, capturing the knowledge of all workers to increase productivity and product quality and at the same time enhancing the quality of work. In essence, this amounts to the re-invention of polyvalent skilled craft workers, a return to a pre-Taylorist era prior to the invention of scientific management. Florida (1995) writes approvingly of the emergence of a new form of production organisation in a knowledge-based economy, in factories that are claimed to be becoming more like laboratories, with knowledge workers, advanced high technology equipment and clean room conditions free of dirt and grime. This does indeed powerfully suggest that the old distinctions between manual and mental workers are being cast aside, that every worker is now becoming an innovative knowledge worker.

Know-how historically was, and in large measure still is, typically a kind of knowledge developed within, and then kept within the confines of, a firm. Furthermore, the boundaries of the firm still remain significant for knowledge that is central to the core competences and strategic goals of a company. Nevertheless the increasing complexity of the knowledge base upon which the totality of the production process depends is increasing the social division of labour in knowledge production and resulting in growing numbers of collaborative long-term relationships between firms (Kitson and Michie, 1998). A variety of processes, ranging from the growth of out-sourcing and contracting out to the increasing prevalence of joint ventures and strategic alliances between even the largest global corporations, is indicative of a rather different model of shared corporate learning. As a result, know-who is becoming of growing importance in the production of know-how (Lundvall and Johnson, 1994). This growing emphasis on knowledge and learning therefore also links in with claims as to new forms of relations between companies, based on co-operation, trust, and the sharing of knowledge for mutual benefit. These forms of interactive inter-firm relations for knowledge creation are particularly associated with the supply chains of major Japanese manufacturers[3] (which is not to imply that they are in some sense culturally defined and confined to Japan and Japanese companies). Considerable emphasis is placed upon new forms of network relations, both 'horizontal' relationships between small and medium-sized enterprises and 'quasi-vertical' relationships between big firms and their suppliers and/or customers, which stress the sharing of R&D, of knowledge and the products of learning to the benefit of all partner companies in the network. For example, institutional innovations such as placing resident engineers in customers' factories allow efficient channels for inter-corporate learning within networks of inter-firm relationships.

Some of these networks are based upon spatial propinquity, others are not. A useful distinction can be drawn between spatial propinquity and organisational proximities (Bellet *et al.*, 1993). The former may (but does not necessarily) facilitate the latter by increasing the probabilities of encounter between agents within a system but is not necessary for interaction between individuals or groups. Organisational proximity does not necessarily require spatial adjacency or proximity but does presuppose the existence of shared knowledge and representations of the environment and world within which the firm exists, although the various units and sections of the firm may be in spatially discrete and distant locations. Such a form of proximity also enables the synthesis of varied forms of information and knowledge via co-operative and collective learning processes between firms within the institutions of an industry. Organisational proximity is therefore a necessary condition for creating innovations and resources through processes of collective learning and is simultaneously a product of these processes. However, the networks through which learning is enabled and expressed are not necessarily territorially defined and demarcated and in some respects the growing sophistication of IT and communications technologies has weakened this link further. The emergence of 'globally distributed teams' in innovation and product development is indicative of this weakened link (Miller *et al.*, 1996). Conversely, the technological facilitation of information flows has simultaneously enhanced the significance of place-specific tacit knowledge within key nodes of command and control in a global economy (Amin and Thrift, 1994).

Some networks are without doubt deeply spatially embedded and recognition of this provides a bridge into more general notions of the significance of territorially based knowledge to economic competitiveness and success. The concept of the learning firm as an institution for the production of knowledge is thereby transposed into the notion of the learning region (Morgan, 1995; for related concepts see Camagni, 1991). This perspective emphasises that regional economic success is heavily based upon territorially defined assets derived from 'unique', often tacit, knowledge and cognitive assets, and stresses the importance of spatial proximity in collective learning processes. Considerable emphasis is placed upon the pivotal role of regional institutional structures which allow regions (and firms within them) to adjust to, indeed anticipate and shape, changing market demands. Innovation and knowledge creation are seen as interactive processes which are shaped by a varied repertoire of institutional routines and social conventions. This involves not simply inter-corporate collaborative links but also links between companies, the (local) state and institutions in civil society, emphasising the permeability of the boundaries between economy, state and civil society in the creation of regional competitive advantage.

This notion of a cohesive society, with permeable boundaries between economy, civil society and state, is powerfully captured in the concept of the 'negotiated economy', originally developed in relation to analyses of the specificities of the Danish case (Amin and Thomas, 1996) but of a more general provenance. Within the negotiated economy, the state fulfils a distinctive role as arbitrator and facilitator of relations between autonomous organisations, as well as continuing with its more traditional roles of providing specialised services and defining the legislative framework of rules and regulations. This is a model of state activity which emphasises enablement and which falls between the concepts of the 'liberal' and 'interventionist' states (Offe, 1975). The concept of the negotiated economy can thus be linked with that of 'the learning state' and a mode of regulation positioned between market and hierarchy through which an enabling state seeks to create the conditions for a dialogic approach to conflict resolution and policy formation in general and innovation, knowledge creation and learning in particular. This approach rests on discursive, moral and political imperatives rather than formal contracts and legal sanctions in achieving consensus and taking decisions. It thus places the emphasis on shared values, meanings and understandings, specifically territorially embedded and tacit knowledge and the institutional structures through which it is produced. These emphases are caught in notions such as those of 'institutional thickness' (Amin and Thrift, 1994), 'social capital' defined as those features of social organisation, such as networks, norms and trust, that facilitate co-ordination and co-operation for mutual benefit (Putnam, 1993) or, perhaps most powerfully, as 'regions as a nexus of untraded interdependencies' (Storper, 1995, 210). As Storper puts it, 'the region is a key, *necessary* element in the "supply architecture" for learning and innovation' (emphasis added) while the emphasis on 'untraded interdependencies' or 'relational assets' focuses attention upon the necessary territoriality of critical elements of non-market relations and tacit knowledge. This signals a decisive shift in focus from firm to territory as the key economic actor in the knowledge-based competitive struggle, to a collective and territorialised definition of competitive advantage which emphasises the cultural and social underpinning of economic success. Insofar as this represents a growing recognition of the limits of narrow neo-classical and technicist views of the economy based on analogies with the behaviour of physical systems (Barnes, 1996), then this in itself is a very important step forward – the re-discovery and re-emphasis of the economy as a social process. Equally, it is important to be aware of the limits to such an approach and emphasis.

Rather than privilege territorial over corporate knowledge production and learning (or vice versa), the critical point is to explore the *relationships between* these two institutional bases of learning. Camagni (1991, 127) emphasises that firms seek to combine codified information and tacit knowledge into 'firm-specific knowledge'. More specifically, insofar as globalised forms of corporate organisation are emerging, they are predicated upon the integration of fragmented products of local learning to further corporate interests. This may well involve dis-embedding them from the contexts in which they were initially produced, and perhaps therefore finding ways of converting tacit knowledge into codifiable information. Alternatively, in situations in which knowledge is so organisationally and technically specific to a firm and so deeply embedded that it cannot be alienated from its origins, it may simply involve big firms acquiring smaller ones as a way of gaining access to such knowledge (a familiar story within the historical geography of mergers and acquisitions: see Athreye, 1998). Global corporations are, it is suggested, developing organisational forms focused upon ensuring the repatriation of the varied results of different localised learning experiences and their integration within a collective body of knowledge to serve strategic corporate interests (Amin and Cohendet, 1997). The implication is that the processes of seeking to secure access to locally produced knowledges are also processes of inter-corporate competition. The issue is therefore one of the relationships between knowledge production and acquisition and competition and co-operation between various territorial and corporate interests.

## Old wine in new bottles: or another trip around the mulberry bush?

The learning firm is, however, hardly a novel concept in the sense that knowledge has always been crucial to capitalist development. There are, however, limitations in the way in which learning approaches deal with the production of knowledge. Their emphasis is upon learning as a way of catching up with 'best practice' in a selection environment, and adapting to significant innovations in organisation, process or product. The issue of how radically new knowledge is produced, and re-defines 'best practice' as radical innovations are created, is left largely unexplored (Odgaard and Hudson, 1998). Moreover, the emphasis on the transmission of knowledge per se in a 'learning economy' may well lead to an under-estimation of the significance of other forms of learning that are more ubiquitous and central to capitalist competitiveness. Capitalist corporate success in production has always depended on ensuring one or both of two things, either finding ways of making existing commodities more profitably and/or finding or inventing new commodities to produce sufficiently profitably. Companies have evolved a variety of strategies to reduce the costs of production of existing commodities, involving a variety of 'spatial fixes' (Harvey, 1982) to enable the costs of producing with existing technologies to be reduced and for them to remain competitive. Such strategies typically involve a search for and learning about locations offering lower unit costs of labour or other material inputs to the production process. Storper and Walker (1989) contrast this approach based on 'weak competition' with a Schumpeterian one based on 'strong competition', a strategy based on the creation of new commodities and products and/or new ways of producing existing commodities rather than on seeking ways of making existing commodities competitively by searching out sources of lower cost inputs within the parameters of existing process technologies. Strategies of strong competition are thus also based upon innovation, learning and the creation of knowledge but of a very different sort to those which underpin strategies of weak competition.

These differing 'weak' and 'strong' competitive strategies and their grounding in different types of knowledge and learning are reflected in the extensive literature on spatial variations in conditions of supply and markets for various inputs to production processes and in the equally extensive literature on process and product innovations, respectively. Both types of innovation are based upon knowledge generated at the corporate level, though typically knowledge of new processes and products soon diffuses through a particular branch of production (albeit with its trajectory of diffusion legally regulated by patent – assuming of course that such regulations are enforceable). This tendency towards the erosion of a temporarily conferred competitive advantage by the diffusion of knowledge as information and of technological innovation underlies the continuous 'hunt for technological (and other) rents' (as Mandel, 1975, graphically and memorably expressed it). This diffusion of knowledge in turn provides the impetus for capital's continuous search to revolutionise the how, what and where of production. One has only to look at the economic history of the 'successful' regions of the nineteenth century in which industrial capitalism was first born and then consolidated to recognise the *key* role of product and process innovation from the very beginnings of the process.[4]

There are also strong grounds for critically evaluating the claims that this renewed emphasis on knowledge is associated with empowering workers in satisfyingly enriched – as a result of reducing, if not eliminating, the alienation of workers from their work – and multi-skilled jobs (Blyton and Turnbull, 1992). It is worth recalling in this context that the rationale of Taylorism was to break the power of the multi-skilled craft worker to challenge the imperatives of capital and disrupt the smooth flow of the production process. Taylorist scientific management therefore sought to disembody knowledge and know-how and to break up the production process into a myriad of separate and de-skilled tasks whose pace was controlled by the speed of the line rather than the inclination of the individual worker. The emergence of separate R&D departments and a linear model of learning and innovation within the firm that separated manual from mental labour and privileged the latter over the former, and privileged codifiable formal scientific knowledge over the practical and often tacit knowledge of the skilled manual worker, was equally an integral part of this process. Taylorism was invented precisely as a way of wresting control of the labour process from skilled craft workers and insofar as the economy remains a capitalist one, there remain pressing reasons why capital should want to retain such control in many types of contemporary production; indeed, there are now frequent references to the growing Taylorisation of office work and a range of 'white collar' occupations (Beynon, 1995) at the same time as others enthuse about the re-invention of the multi-skilled manufacturing worker.

It is difficult to imagine, therefore, that capital would willingly wish to return control of the production process to workers that it potentially could not control. The search for alternatives to mass production reflects capital's need to break the capacity of the mass worker collectively and spontaneously to challenge its quest for profits – although unintentionally, this may in turn create potentially new opportunities and points of leverage for organised labour since the contradictory character of the class relations between capital and labour can be re-fashioned but they cannot be abolished in an economy that remains capitalist. While the probabilities of strikes and other forms of disruption to the production process are certainly much lower now than in the decades of 'full employment' in the 1950s and 1960s in the territories of the major advanced capitalist states[5] (for reasons which are discussed below), it is clear that any form of disruption to production organised on lean, just-in-time principles can quickly spread along the entire supply chain, bringing production to a precipitate halt (Hudson, 1997a). Given this disciplining context of more or less permanent high unemployment, this recent and ongoing re-working of work can more plausibly be seen as representing a new way of ensuring managerial control and intensifying the labour process, of reproducing in enhanced form the asymmetries of power between capital and labour. Managerial strategies and regimes of labour regulation remain focused on seeking to ensure the continuity of production and the compliance of workers.

Rather than empowerment in new forms of satisfying work built around notions of re-skilling and team working, the new forms of work are based upon multi-tasking and new ways of intensifying the labour process. Workers are enmeshed within disempowering regimes of subordination, characterised by control, exploitation and surveillance, accepting arrangements through which they discipline themselves and their fellow workers, while bound together through the rhetoric of team working (Garrahan and Stewart, 1992). As a result, these may be actually worse jobs than those on offer on the old mass production lines, increasing stress (Okamura and Kawahito, 1990) and changing the mode of regulation of the labour process. No longer is it 'us' versus 'them'; 'them' are now part of 'us'. Considerable ambiguities and uncertainties follow from this change of identities, not least in relation to forms of organisation and representation of workers' interests.

A further point needs to be made concerning the number of such jobs and the criteria on which people are selected to fill them. For even when the claims that these are better quality jobs are shown to be true, there is still a savage sting in the tail for labour. The capacity of firms to create these new regimes of work depends upon their ability to exercise great selectivity in who they choose to employ and the terms and conditions on which they employ people, often in no-union or one-union factories, especially in countries or regions in which neo-liberal regulatory regimes have become dominant. Employees are selected more on the basis of their attitudes, psychological profile, age and physical condition, and personal and family circumstances than on their technical skills. For example, in many service sector occupations, personal appearance and social skills have become key recruitment and retention criteria (McDowell, 1997). Many manufacturing companies typically seek to recruit physically fit young males, with family and other financial commitments, who will be loyal to the company and accept new ways of working on the factory floor. Only a tiny fraction of those who apply and of those who feasibly could fill these jobs is employed, typically after an extensive selection process. Firms can only exercise this degree of selectivity against a background of high unemployment and for this reason are also very careful in their choice of locations in which to introduce these new forms of work and employment (Hudson, 1997b).[6]

There is also some scepticism as to the validity of the notion of new forms of network relations between companies as involving equal partners. It is certainly the case that there has been a considerable increase in out-sourcing and sub-contracting by many major companies. In this sense one can reasonably refer to a shift from vertical integration within companies to quasi-vertical disintegration, involving a re-definition of the boundary of the firm and a re-definition of the criteria on which to make the 'make or buy' decision. But to argue that these new relations are between equal partners is to ignore the sharp asymmetries in power between companies, and the extent to which such networks involve not co-operation based on trust but often not too subtle coercion if companies wish to keep their customers or suppliers. There is no doubt that the systems of relations between automobile or computer companies and their suppliers or between major retailing chains and their suppliers definitely are not relations between equals (Hudson, 1994a; 1997a). Indeed, there is no a priori reason why one should expect relationships between firms in a capitalist economy to be between equals; in fact, one should expect quite the reverse. In assessing the claims as to networks of equal partners, it is also important to remember that one of the features of the last couple of decades of the twentieth century has been wave after wave of mergers and acquisitions as the centralisation of capital has reached renewed heights after a couple of decades in which merger and acquisition activity was very subdued – and it is these massive transnational corporations, the 'movers and shakers' who dominate the global economy, that are frequently at the centre of decisive network relationships.

The concept of the learning region and the proposition that regional economic success reflects specifically regional assets and institutions for the production and dissemination of knowledge is also hardly a new one. Even the most cursory glance at the historical geography of capitalist development indicates that this has long been the case. In the United Kingdom in the latter part of the nineteenth century, for example, 'coal combines' lay at the heart of carboniferous capitalism in the industrial boom regions of the nineteenth century (Harvey, 1917). These combines comprised interlocking intra-regional networks of highly innovative firms, extending across sectors, integrated by physical input-output linkages and various forms of formal economic and financial linkages (such as inter-locking directorates and mutual share ownership). More importantly, they were underpinned by non-economic relationships between key individuals and families and by networks of supportive institutions that evolved around, in and through the formal economic relationships between companies. These spanned the boundaries of local civil society and the state, as a dense network of interlocking institutions, attuned to the needs of the dominant regional firms and sectors, emerged there. For many such regions the problems subsequently became those of 'institutional lock-in', an inability to make the change from one development trajectory to another precisely because the institutional bases of the region reflected the past dominance of now declining firms and sectors (Grabher, 1993; Hudson, 1994b). This is a salutary reminder that institutional thickness per se is no guarantee of successful regional economic adaptation and innovation as it can constrain rather than facilitate processes of collective learning and change.

Furthermore, the fetishisation of knowledge and learning, and their institutional bases, may lead to a neglect of *other* institutional factors that underlie regional competitiveness. There could be no clearer illustration of the point that in order to understand the historical (including the contemporary in this) geography of capitalist production, it is necessary to grasp the ways in which such successful regional economies in the nineteenth century were grounded in social relationships that extended far beyond the workplace into home, community and the institutions of local civil society, and in due course, the state (Beynon and Austrin, 1994; Carney and Hudson, 1978). Moreover, central to the embedding of industrial capitalism in these regions was the construction of discourses and ideologies that represented this as the 'natural' course of regional and socio-economic development. These representations constituted an attempt to present one view of a particular trajectory of capitalist development as 'natural' and 'unavoidable', to instil this as a hegemonic and uncontested view, subliminally learned and accepted by the populations of these regions.

This attempt to establish such a view as hegemonic was important because it was clear in the nineteenth century that economically successful regions, which were certainly learning regions containing learning firms, were also deeply socially divided ones. They were characterised by enormous disparities in incomes and wealth, juxtaposing extremes of conspicuous consumption with widespread abject and absolute poverty. The contemporary claims that the learning region offers a new and socially inclusive model of development are ones that need to be scrutinised carefully since they tend conveniently to ignore the point that the social relations of capitalism are at least as deeply marked by social inequality now as they were then. There are critical issues related to *who* controls the processes of knowledge production and learning. 'Learning firms' within a region may be successful economically and the institutional structures of a 'learning region' may both be produced by and facilitate the reproduction of 'learning firms'. This, however, does not necessarily equate to an egalitarian model of regional socio-economic development. Such firms remain unavoidably built around antagonistic class relations and may well also presume inequalities in other social relationships such as those of age, ethnicity and gender as an integral part of their strategies for competitiveness and success in the market place (cf. Massey, 1995, chapter 8).

## Conclusions and reflections on the limits to learning: learning by whom, for what purpose?

There is no doubt that firms have a great variety of possible approaches to production. Equally, there is a variety of forms of capitalist development model, nationally and regionally, and this indicates that there is a fair amount of 'room for manoeuvre' (to borrow Seers *et al.*'s 1979 phraseology) in seeking to define regional development strategies (Albert, 1993; Lash and Urry, 1987). While acknowledging the room for manoeuvre that exists as a result, the key point to emphasise is the continued existence of the social structural constraints which set limits to what is possible within a capitalist economy. These cannot simply be conveniently forgotten or assumed away. One implication of this is that capitalist development of necessity remains driven by competition and the search for profit. Another implication is that such development must therefore remain uneven – both between classes, between and within other social groups, and within and between regions, a fortiori if it is recognised that regions themselves are constituted as socially heterogeneous and as spatially discontinuous, whatever the claims about social homogeneity and spatial contiguity (Hudson, 1990). Certainly in some circumstances, development models may be based on less rather than more divisive guide rails – but capitalism requires the existence of reciprocally defining classes of capital and wage labour, although of course there may well be attempts to represent the situation in ways which deny this.

'Learning' and the production of knowledge are undoubtedly necessary elements in the processes of competitive commodity production and in some respects can themselves become commodified. The diffusion of information about new organisational, product and process innovations is a central element in the competitive dynamic of capitalism. The greatest competitive advantage is, however, conferred by precisely that knowledge that remains tacit and uncodifiable, not amenable to generalised transmission to others. It is thus the most valuable form of knowledge in conferring competitive advantage, precisely because it cannot have a price put upon it. Successful firms and regions thus guard it jealously. If, however, firms 'learn' via producing and protecting such knowledge, if 'regions' seek to learn in the same way, in the final analysis this is to enhance their competitiveness in a range of markets. As a consequence uneven development within and between regions and their constituent social groups is unavoidable. Knowledge and learning may be necessary for economic success but they are by no means sufficient to ensure it; nor, even more so, are they sufficient to ensure equality, cohesion and social justice.

For some firms, becoming 'successful learners' is the route to competitive success, and these firms have to locate their operations somewhere. Conversely, other firms lose as part of this struggle, and they have to devalorise capital, close plants and dismiss workers somewhere. There is no necessary territorial correspondence between these two faces of creative destruction – indeed, there are strong grounds for expecting the production of new commodities often to take place in new production spaces. For some regions, becoming 'learners' likewise offers a route to competitiveness, albeit one characterised by internal social division, if not strife. This may involve developing institutional structures to enable existing firms and sectors to evolve successfully, or new ones to become established in a region, or some combination of the two. It is important to acknowledge that for those regions that do successfully embark on the 'high road' to regional economic success, this very success raises new problems in terms of a requirement continuously to learn and anticipate, if not create, market trends. Moreover, if some regions 'learn' and 'win', many more will fail to do so and 'lose'.

The command and control functions of an increasingly spaced out global economy will doubtless continue to locate within the few global cities, economic 'winners' but marked by deep social divisions (Sassen, 1991). These global cities are characterised by intensely dense institutional structures for producing and disseminating information globally but at their heart lie inter-personal contact networks decisively bound together by the ties of critical tacit knowledge (Amin and Thrift, 1994). They are also deeply divided places, with socio-spatial differentiation deeply etched into their urban landscapes as a necessary feature of the ways in which their economies are constituted (Allen *et al.*, 1998). Moreover, beyond the boundaries of the global cities, a post-mass production, post-Fordist world of specialised regional economies, all on their own successful learning trajectories, and all winning, is not a feasible option within the social relations of capitalism. Equally, a post-mass production, post-Fordist world of product specialised high volume production regional complexes, all producing just in time and in one place in their own unique niche in the global market place, is not a feasible option. There may be some cases in which some regions 'win' by following one or other of these strategies – but there will be many more that 'lose', either failing in the attempt or doomed to failure by the success of others.

There is no doubt that an explicit recognition of the role of the production and dissemination of knowledge in a capitalist economy can help further understanding of uneven development. Cognitive assets can certainly be crucial is defining competitive advantage. Equally, the case for a regional political economy that remembers the lessons of a Marxian political economy and recognises capitalism as a structurally and necessarily, an inherently and unavoidably uneven process of growth and decline remains as valid as it ever did. Acknowledging that capitalism is shaped within particular structural boundaries which pivot around class relationships is not to imply that social life can be, is to be, or should be, reduced to such relationships, nor to deny that gender, location, ethnicity, and much more besides are constituted as separate cleavage planes of social division and at the same time as foci of individual and collective identities. It is, however, to suggest that class relations cannot be ignored – not least in the production and diffusion of knowledge itself.

There is no doubt that innovation and learning can be important concepts in understanding why some firms and regions are economically successful and others are not. Equally, it is evident that the 'learning' paradigm may both legitimate the success of some firms and regions, the failure of others, and seem to hold out the enticing prospect of a more prosperous future to still many others. Nevertheless, it would be as well to recognise the limits that 'learning' entails, both as an explanatory concept and as a guide to territorial development policies. Not least, learning the political economy of learning implies a need to unlearn – or at least ignore – other concepts of political economy, with different developmental implications. 'Learning' is by no means a guarantee of economic success. Still less is it a universal panacea to the problems of socio-spatial inequality and in some respects is used as a cloak behind which some of the harsher realities of capitalism can be hidden. Addressing the problems of uneven development and inequality undoubtedly poses very hard policy and political choices for those who seek to devise progressive development trajectories in such a world, torn between attachments to place, class, gender, ethnic groups and no doubt a lot more besides.

## Notes

1 There may be a danger of 'tacit knowledge' thereby being invoked as an unknowable residual explanatory variable, in a way analogous to neo-classical growth theorists' treatment of technical change. This is not to deny the existence or significance in some circumstances of tacit knowledge. It is to suggest that there are methodological problems in revealing its existence and effects.
2 It is important to note, however, that the processes of *producing* new knowledge, knowledge that comes into existence for the first time, are not dealt with directly in learning approaches, as a corollary of their grounding in associationist, stimulus-response conceptions of learning and their concern with outcome rather than process (Odgaard and Hudson, 1998). This represents a major problem with the learning approach *in its own terms*.
3 This chapter was originally written in the second half of the 1990s. Such organisational forms subsequently became much more common.
4 *En passant* it is worth noting that this creates problems to characterising the nineteenth century as a regime of extensive accumulation: cf. Brenner and Glick, 1991.
5 This was originally written in the second half of the 1990s; if anything, it remains even more valid in the context of post-2007 depression in much of the capitalist economy.
6 This also raises broader questions as to the maintenance of social order and the perceived legitimacy of capitalist relations of production and the state policies that sustain them, especially when such locationally concentrated pools of surplus labour have become a permanent and structural feature of labour markets.

# 4 From knowledge-based economy to … knowledge-based economy?

## Reflections on changes in the economy and development policies in the north east of England

### Introduction

There is widespread agreement that all economic activity – as purposeful human behaviour – necessarily depends upon knowledgeable behaviour and intentional human action; without a knowledge base, such activity would clearly be impossible. Thus an economy that is not based upon knowledge is, literally, inconceivable. The creation of knowledge has been integral to the development of capitalist economies since they were first constituted as capitalist, as Marx and Schumpeter (among other political economists) emphasised. Much of the revolutionary potential of capitalism has always rested in its capacity to create new commodities and new ways of commodity production via successive radical transformations of the forces of production and the labour process. Marxian political economy, conjoined with more recent approaches such as those of the French regulationists (for example, see Jessop and Sum, 2006) continues to provide a powerful perspective through which to understand the contemporary economy, especially in those versions of cultural political economy that seek more explicitly to incorporate consideration of issues of meaning and semiosis with more traditional concerns of commodity production and value. Such perspectives of Marxian political economy inform the interpretative approach adopted in this chapter.

Much has also been written in recent years about knowledge creation and transfer and related issues from more recent and different theoretical perspectives, such as those of knowledge creation, learning and national and regional innovation systems that place considerable weight upon knowledge and learning per se as sources of competitive advantage and economic success (Lundvall, 1992; Nonaka and Takeuchi, 1995). There are three main ways in which knowledge is now seen as more important in the economy. First, there is greater emphasis on knowledge per se as a commodified output, in part linked to the greater significance of symbolic products. Second, there is greater emphasis on increasing the knowledge intensity of existing commodities, both material and immaterial, shifting up the value chain towards more knowledge intensive activities. And, third, partly linked to this, are the increasingly blurred boundaries between material commodities and services produced via the interaction of people and things.

Initially, influenced heavily by the experiences of parts of the USA, such as California and New England, and the advocates of the 'triple helix' approach (Etzkowitz and Leydesdorff, 2000) these placed most emphasis on flows of codified knowledge within formal organisational and institutional structures and upon links between 'high tech' industries and entrepreneurial universities in the translation of scientific knowledge into innovative products and processes (Lundvall and Maskell, 2000). However, later and more nuanced approaches placed more emphasis upon tacit knowledge and the interactions and relationships between codified and tacit knowledges (for example, see Amin and Cohendet, 2003; Asheim and Coenen, 2005; Jensen *et al.*, 2007).

This growing emphasis upon knowledge has been influential in shaping new conceptions of urban and regional development policy and strong claims have been made as to the potential of such developments for urban and regional regeneration, linking the knowledge-based competitive advantage of firms with that of territories defined at various spatial scales (Braczyk *et al.*, 1998; Simmie, 1997). This draws attention to the significance of the place-specificity of processes of knowledge production and translation and the importance of tacit knowledge in enabling codified knowledge to be effectively deployed in the economy in place. The successful economies of fin-de-siécle capitalism are seen to be those of territories (cities, regions, national states) that, by good luck or judgement, have become constructed around activities grounded in valuable knowledges that can be literally capitalised and become a source of profit. The future success of these territories is seen to depend on the continuing production of new knowledge, translating this into innovative products and processes and maintaining first-mover advantages. This emphasis within policy discourse reflects perceived changes in the ways that knowledge is now seen as important in the economy. The task of public policy is then to try to ensure that the knowledge-based process of moving forward, ever onward and upward, is facilitated in successful places and that the lessons of their success are translated to unsuccessful places, insofar as this is possible within the parameters of capitalist social relations.

Claims about the emergence of new knowledge-based economies can therefore also be seen as recognition that the knowledge bases of formerly successful economic activities (as registered in mainstream indicators of capitalist development) and the regional economies that these helped constitute have been rendered redundant by sectoral, technological and spatial shifts in the capitalist economy. Consequently, commodities that could once be profitably produced in a given place can no longer be so. This recognises that the economy is knowledge-based but that capital valorises some forms of knowledge while devalorising others. Therefore, so the policy story goes, it follows that reconstruction of the economies of places that have become unsuccessful requires shifting to new activities with different knowledge bases that can be successfully capitalised and valorised and learning from the experiences of economic 'hot spots'. It is this that is signalled by normative claims about the perceived need to move trajectories and encourage and facilitate the emergence of a new knowledge-based economy via specific forms of public policy that privilege particular sorts of knowledge and institutions in the creation and dissemination of that knowledge. In this, of course, there are two major assumptions. First, that the bases of success of the 'successful places' have been correctly analysed and diagnosed in terms of the primacy of such knowledge as the main source of competitive advantage. Second, that the direction of the causal links between theory and practice has been correctly specified. However, this is a matter of debate – some see theory as shaping practice, others see theory as reflecting practice while others see links between the two as reciprocal and complex, not easily amenable to sweeping generalisation, leaving the issue of the effects of policy unresolved (Chapter 3, this volume; Lovering, 1999; Morgan, 1995).

Seen in this context, the issues to be addressed in this chapter can be re-stated in terms of a number of questions. First, and centrally, how have changing conceptions of the role of knowledge been reflected in successive strategies for regional development in north east England, and in particular in the recent turn to an explicitly knowledge-based economy? In turn, this requires some consideration of broader questions. What is the role of knowledge relative to other factors and processes as a source of competitive advantage? What is new and specific about the role of knowledge at the leading edges of contemporary capitalist development? What sort of knowledge, development strategy and policies are required for what sort of economy? Indeed what may well be at issue is what we mean by the economy, what counts as 'the economy' and how we conceptualise it. This may involve consideration not simply of the differing knowledge bases of varied types of economic activity but more fundamental questions relating to different concepts of value and processes of valuation within a more heterogeneous and plural conception of what is to be counted as 'the economy'. But this is to anticipate …

In this chapter, therefore, and against the background of more general claims made about the emergence of a new knowledge-based economy (Allen, 2002; Hudson, 2001a; 2005; Jessop, 2000; Leinbach and Brunn 2001), I want to explore the changing role of knowledge in the economy through the lens of the successive transformations of a particular regional economy – that of north east England – and the successive conceptions of development policy that have been pursued there and, if only implicitly for much of the time, shifting conceptions within policy of the required knowledge base for that economy to prosper. The remainder of this chapter falls into five sections. First, I consider in more detail some of the claims as to what is seen to be new in terms of knowledge and the new ways in which knowledge is now seen as economically significant. The next section considers the emergence and development of the north east region's economy from the nineteenth century as a centre of radical innovation and knowledge creation that underpinned its economic success. Third, in response to the secular decline of that economy from the late 1950s, I examine the emergence of an alternative branch plant economy, with its very different requirements in terms of knowledge, and various alternatives that were explored to that largely unsuccessful development policy, such as the pursuit of endogenous growth through small firms. Then, in recognition of the limitations of all these various policy options, a new suite of policies that self-consciously sought to promote the emergence of a new and more managed knowledge-based economy in the region began to appear from the 1990s. These are considered in the penultimate part of the chapter. Finally I reflect upon this developmental and policy history and seek to draw some lessons from it.

## So what's new about knowledge in the 'new' economy and the way we think about it now?

Given that there is a general acknowledgement as to the importance of knowledge in the economy, why then the recent widespread fascination, even obsession, with knowledge-based economies, both in academic discourse and development policies? What is seen now as novel about the role of knowledge in the 'new' economy? What's all the fuss about?

In recent years the social science and business literatures have become replete with claims as to the growing importance of knowledge and information flows in an (allegedly) weightless, de-materialised 'new' economy of informational capitalism (Castells, 1996), in particular in terms of the extent to which knowledge can be digitised, commodified and capitalised to underpin a new knowledge-based economy. There are strong claims to the effect that this new economy operates in a complex, non-propinquitous, multi-dimensional cyberspace, with novel spatial dynamics grounded in the possibilities that cyberspace offers for simultaneous co-location of myriad entities and relationships (Jessop, 2000, 4; see also Leinbach and Brunn, 2001). Moreover, there is no doubt that there has also been some growth in the importance of some sorts of knowledge and information in the economy in relation to material commodity production, to the production of high level services, and to the production of a range of 'symbolic' commodities.

The selectively increased importance of flows of knowledge and information in some sectors of capitalist economies has highlighted the importance of processes of knowledge creation and flows of information within firms via a range of types of learning (such as single and double loop) and ways of learning (by doing, by imitating, by watching, in working and so on). These become linked in inter-related and recursive ways so that learning and innovation involve complex circuits of knowledge and information rather than the linear flows of the hierarchical R&D model. The growing distanciation of many economic relations within an increasingly spaced-out economy as the locations of activities both within and between firms become further separated by physical distance is made possible by increasing digitalisation and other improvements in information and communication and transport technologies. Flows of information both increase in volume and in distance travelled, as do flows of people as sites of embedded and tacit knowledges, in the process re-working the meaning of work in the globalising economy (Jones, 2008). More generally, there is evidence of the creation of new global circuits of intellectual capital (Thrift, 2005).

Recognising these recent changes, it is nonetheless equally important to acknowledge that the economy has always depended on knowledgeable workers, flows of knowledge and information and mixes of codified and tacit knowledge so that claims as to the increased importance of flows of knowledge and information for economic performance must be carefully qualified. What is at issue is the changing significance of knowledge, the varying 'mixes' and types of knowledge, and the routes through which they flow into the production of *any* commodity. For example, Allen (2002, 39–40, emphasis in original) emphasises 'the symbolic basis of *all* forms of economic knowledge'. Furthermore, 'different economic activities play across a variety of symbolic registers – abstract, expressive, affective and aesthetic – and *combine* them in ways that render sectors distinctive'. Symbolic knowledge is not, therefore, confined to the production of cultural commodities, and it may have become relatively more important across a range of other commodities. Conversely, producing symbolic outputs, as with services, typically requires substantial material underpinning and infrastructure, not least in creating specific settings to enable co-presence of producers and consumers. For example, information technology services require particular sorts of buildings, computers, network connections, electricity – which requires power stations, which in turn require coal, oil, nuclear fuel, or some form of non-fossil fuel generating technology. The issue here is the complex connections between different bits of commodity production that allow the production of new 'symbolic commodities' rather than the emergence of de-materialised commodities in a digitalised, weightless economy. The material basis and weight remain critical, albeit distanciated from the particular sites from which flows of information and knowledge emanate.

Jessop (2000, 2) suggests that 'what is novel in the current period [of capitalist development] is the growing application of knowledge in developing the forces of production and the increased importance of knowledge as a fictitious commodity in shaping the social relations of production'. For example, one indication of this is the expanding volumes of patents awarded to companies involved in biotechnology and bio-engineering, which are positioned at the forefront of the new 'knowledge economy' in which 'information and ideas have become critically important economic assets' (Bowring, 2003, 118). At least three processes are involved in transforming knowledge into a fictitious commodity, although it is important to acknowledge that these are not new to a capitalist economy but that they have increased in intensity and extent. These involve both qualitative transformations and flows of knowledge between people, companies and other organisations involved in the economy. First, there is the formal transformation of knowledge from a collective resource ('intellectual commons') into intellectual property as a basis for revenue generation (for example, as a licence or patent). Second, the formal subsumption of knowledge production under exploitative class relations through the separation of intellectual and manual labour and the transformation of the former into alienated wage labour, producing knowledge as an exchange value rather than as a use value. Third, the real subsumption of intellectual labour and its products under capitalist control through their commodification and integration into a networked, digitised production-consumption process controlled by capital, of information produced by a firm not for its own use (as a use value) but to sell to another to deploy in its production process (as an exchange value).

Thus the distinctive features of recent developments in circuits of knowledge and intellectual capital are seen to relate to their global reach and speed of flow within them, changes enabled by technological innovations in information and communication technologies and the deployment of different combinations of knowledge in commodity production as the role of knowledge in the economy has changed qualitatively. Paradoxically, however, the greater fluidity in the movement of codified knowledge has enhanced the significance of tacit knowledge and the key material sites in which it is produced and circulated. It is these changes in the movement of information rather than knowledge and learning per se becoming distinguishing features of the capitalist economy that are crucial. There are, however, limits to such processes. Cyberspace is not a 'neutral third space' between capital and labour, market and state, public and private. Rather, it is a new terrain on which conflict between these forces, institutions and domains can be fought out. Consequently, irrespective of the extent to which capital migrates into cyberspace, like all capital 'it still depends on territorialisation' – that is, on materialisation in specific spaces, cities and regions. Indeed, 'even e-commerce needs such an infrastructure, even if it involves a "celestial jukebox" sending digitised music on demand' (Jessop, 2000, 4). This in turn suggests that those cities and regions in which such activities have become materialised have become pivotal and will become of still greater significance in shaping the development trajectories of capitalist economies and in reproducing the map of uneven development. This suggests that the extent to which peripheral places can gain as a result of the new developmental trends may be severely circumscribed. In turn, this calls into question claims that such policies constitute the panacea for the problems of such places.

## The knowledge-based economy, version I: the creation of a 'workshop of the world'

It is often remarked that north east England was once one of the 'workshops of the world', a region transformed in the nineteenth century into one of the birthplaces of industrial capitalism, a major site of production for key commodities and raw materials of the era of carboniferous capitalism.

This remarkable transformation of the region via the creation of a new form of economy was above all based upon invention, the creation of new knowledge, typically initially in the form of tacit knowledge as a result of the practical activities of engineers and working men, and its deployment in production via a range of radical product and process innovations in chemicals, coal mining, the production and use of metals in making ships, armaments, power stations and equipment and other complex commodities linked to the production of the means of production (McCord, 1979; North, 1975).

Thus this emergence of new forms of economic activity based around radical product and/or process innovations and their deployment in commodity production was nothing less than the creation of a new knowledge-based economy. Newly produced scientific knowledge was combined with existing knowledges, both codified and tacit, to form the epistemic basis of a new regional economy via translating new knowledge into radical innovations. The interplay of codified and tacit knowledges, of new and existing knowledges, and their resultant emergent effects, decisively shaped the competitive advantage of firms in the region. As such, the region became a pivotal location in the development of industrial capitalism, centred on major capitalist enterprises. These were typically linked into 'coal combines' via a variety of economic and non-economic relations and ties and deployed strategies of strong Schumpeterian competition, based on first-mover advantage and oligopolistic market domination, if not quite monopolistic control of markets (Hudson, 1989b).

Moreover, this emergent knowledge-based economy was based on a combination of endogenous capital and locally produced knowledges with imports and inflows of both human labour (from Ireland and other regions of the UK), knowledge and raw materials (for example, by the 1870s, iron ores from Spain: Beynon *et al.*, 1994) and resulted in substantial outflows and exports of commodities and capital to the markets of both formal and informal Empires. For example, around the turn of the twentieth century, around 80 per cent of all capitalist ship production emanated from the region. In these senses, it was from the outset a global region, deeply involved in the production of globalised relationships and global flows of capital. However – and this is a key point – all stages of the production process in these varied industries, from R&D and the production of knowledge and its translation into new processes and products to material commodity production, were located in the region which became, for capital at least, the centre of a virtuous spiral of accumulation and growth.[1] Moreover, high level scientific and technical knowledges to support such R&D activities were underpinned by the development of Durham University's activities in Newcastle, as Armstrong College focused on activities such as engineering, with a direct feedback to the economy via the transfer of codified knowledge about production processes and products (prefiguring proposals and developments around a century later: see below).

The depression of the 1920s and 1930s had severe impacts upon this 'old' industrial economy ('old' in the sense that it no longer enjoyed its former first-mover advantage as innovations had diffused internationally). Nonetheless, it managed to survive well into the 1960s, with a continuing although more selective and sporadic history of knowledge creation, R&D, and radical product and process innovation (much of it associated with the chemical production activities of ICI on Teesside). The inter-war depression was characterised by severe job losses but, in general (there were exceptions: colliery closures in west Durham and the closure of Palmer's Jarrow shipyard by National Shipbuilders Securities: see Wilkenson, 1939), it did not lead to large-scale capacity closure. While fixed capital was mothballed and to a degree devalorised, in general it was not physically and materially destroyed. Consequently, when demand recovered the region's industrial economy could respond and revive in terms of output and employment, though less so in terms of fresh fixed capital investment. In a way that typifies the contradictions of capitalist development, the regional economy was pulled from economic crisis by the combined effects of the war economy and post-war reconstruction. As a result, the sclerosis that had set into much of the economy did not become visible in terms of indicators such as output, employment and unemployment until the late 1950s, initially in coal mining and shipbuilding, but then in a progressively wider range of 'traditional' industries.

However, the design and R&D teams of the major shipbuilding and engineering companies (for example, Swan Hunter and Reyrolle Parsons) and especially chemicals (ICI at Wilton alone employed more than 200 PhD research chemists) in the region remained intact throughout this period; some even expanded. Indeed, the concentration of highly qualified research chemists at ICI can be seen as emblematic of the way in which knowledge creation had become intentionally designed to underpin commodity production and the process of capital accumulation. Moreover, to the extent that knowledge became patented and licensed to others, knowledge itself became capitalised, a commodity to be traded, bought and sold in markets. Nonetheless, in general this 'old' industrial economy had lost its radical innovative edge and the competitive advantages once conferred by its distinctive knowledge bases.

There were a number of reasons for this, related to private- and public-sector decision-making processes. First, there were changes in corporate strategy: as commodities became mature, companies either went out of business due to intensified global competition or switched product and/or process and/or location and moved their R&D and related activities out of the north east (a process that was still continuing into the 1990s: Pike, 2005). This locational switch was an integral part of changes in the international division of labour, and the rise of new production centres in other parts of the world. Second, nationalisation led to the centralisation of R&D in coal, energy and steel in locations outside the region. Privatisation of formerly nationalised industries had the same effect: the move by newly privatised British Gas of its R&D activities from Killingworth to the south east of England in the 1990s was the last in a series of such relocations. One critical consequence of these moves was that the potential for translating high level knowledges and skills into new activities in the region and a resultant transformation of the regional economy onto a new knowledge base was lost.

Interestingly, however, in one or two rare cases such a transformation of existing firms onto a new knowledge base did occur, registered in development discourse in the region (which is discussed more fully below) by recognition of the emergence of new clusters from the late 1990s. For example, on Tyneside this led to the emergence of a sub-sea technology cluster, evolving from offshore activities that in turn had developed from previous shipbuilding activity. A second example emerged in the Tees Valley, with a cluster of high level globally competitive engineering service firms evolving from firms that previously had been builders of bridges, railways and related products but that now sell their knowledge and expertise in design and project management in a global market. These transformations are a product of the link between two sets of processes. The first relates to the creation of 'redundant' or 'slack' resources (human, technical and infrastructural) left behind by the decline of traditional industries. The second focuses on the processes of corporate and sectoral re-organisation, the identification of new market opportunities, the selection of promising avenues of development, the organisation or creation of a new architecture of knowledge production and utilisation and the discovery of new methods of production organisation to enable the emergence of a new technological and/or market trajectory to absorb this slack and put it to productive use.

While recognising the potential significance of these examples of successful adaptation for development strategies in the region, the fundamental point is that these remain just that – rare examples of a counter-tendency.[2] The dominant effect of eroding the competitive edge provided by the knowledge bases that underpinned the growth of the region's 'traditional' industries is that of decline – in capacity, output and jobs. This was disclosed and registered as a profound regional de-industrialisation, with all the socio-economic and political difficulties that it brought, Recognition of this led to attempts to create a different sort of regional economy, with a different knowledge base.

## The knowledge-based economy, version II: the branch plant economy and beyond

As the 'old' knowledge-based economy began to exhibit signs of decline as early as the 1930s, there were moves to develop new forms of state policy that would help construct an alternative form of economy based around inward investment in 'new' – to the region – industries. This policy shift was initiated by established capitalist concerns which sought to construct a state regional industrial policy to protect their own interests and to counter the threat of social unrest as a result of rising unemployment and poverty. After a period of relative quiescence due to the effects of the war economy and post-war reconstruction in stimulating demand for products made in the north east, this policy of industrial diversification was prosecuted with renewed vigour from the late 1950s once it became clear that the decline of the region's 'old' industrial economy was secular rather than cyclical.

While a strengthened central government regional policy had been in place from the late 1940s, it had been implemented very selectively and with little enthusiasm or vigour in the north east. Specifically, only branch plants and back office activities that would not compete on the labour market with established industries (coal mining, steel, shipbuilding and so on) were permitted to locate in the region because their outputs were seen as vital to post-war economic recovery and national economic performance in the 1950s (Hudson, 1989b). Blocking the entry of potential competitors for male labour was crucial in ensuring that their labour forces remained intact and production was not endangered by labour shortages. As a result, such new branch plants as were permitted were concentrated in sectors such as clothing and consumer electronics, in which firms were primarily seeking to recruit female labour, while the expansion of public services such as education and health was also based upon enhanced female activity rates.

However, once the 'old' industrial economy was seen to be in secular decline, political-economic priorities changed. Not only was there a perceived need for alternative sources of male employment in the north east but unbalanced regional growth became recognised as a major impediment to achieving faster non-inflationary national economic growth. The solution to these problems was seen to lie in a more vigorous implementation of a further strengthened central government regional policy, attracting new investment and jobs to the north east (and like regions), creating new sources of male employment there and reducing inter-regional differences in economic performance and growth rates.

The emphasis in building a new form of regional economy around branch plants to a degree also reflected the emerging academic literature on corporate reorganisation and the new ways in which companies were using spatial difference as part of their competitive strategies as new geographies of production and spatial divisions of labour were emerging. Regional policy sought to use this and attract particular routine branch plant functions to the north east. This new branch plant economy required different sorts of knowledge and skills, with little or no demand for people with high level decision making, design and R&D skills. Instead it required people with more basic knowledge and limited qualifications but willing to accept the disciplines of Taylorised production in branch plants and back offices. This was still a knowledge-based economy but one based upon the import of codified knowledges as to how to organise routine production activities and requiring a limited range of skills and expertise within the region. Not only was there a much lower level of demand for people with mental and non-manual skills but such manual jobs as were provided were typically unskilled or semi-skilled and required different types of social and technical skills and competences to those of the 'old' industrial economy. As a result, there were often problems in getting men who had worked in coal mines, steel works, shipyards and engineering works – above all those engaged in skilled work, with occupationally specific skills, often based upon tacit knowledge acquired 'on the job' – to work on factory assembly lines in the new (to the region) consumer goods component production and assembly plants, in the paper processing assembly lines of back offices, or in the new public service activities of education and health, with their emphasis upon caring and cleaning work. This was a key reason why this second version of a knowledge-based economy in the region was associated with increased female employment and with feminisation and a shift in the gender composition of the labour force.

This shift in the industrial and occupational structure of the regional economy and its enabling and requisite knowledge bases was also facilitated by a variety of state-sponsored and/or organised training schemes to ensure the availability of workers with appropriate knowledge and skills. While the skill levels required of the 'new' activities were generally modest, they were nonetheless skills (technical, personal, social and communication skills) that were not readily available in the region's labour market. Thus part of the offer to potential inward investors was that training would be provided to ensure that suitably qualified labour was available in sufficient quantity. This included specific training schemes for assembly line workers in the new automobile and electronics companies and later for the substantial numbers recruited by a variety of call centres. However, the rigorous recruitment criteria of the new companies, in a labour market in which supply far exceeded effective demand, meant that participation in these training schemes was no guarantee of employment – for example, at one point in the early 1990s Nissan had over 33,000 applications in response to advertising the availability of 600 new jobs (Hudson, 1995).[3]

The new manufacturing branch plants, increasingly a result of inward investment by multinational corporations, were by-and-large demonstrably 'global outposts', subject to capacity cutbacks or closure because of decisions taken in distant locations, with often devastating effects in terms of job loss in the north east (Hudson, 1995). Some closed very quickly, others never even opened (such as the Siemens integrated circuit factory on north Tyneside), and on average the lifespan of branch plants shortened as more and more locations competed for them. Despite claims about changes in the character of inward investment and the emergence of embedded branch plants, with deeper commitments to the region and wider mandates (for example, to include limited incremental R&D activity), in practice such plants are rare and hard to find. While Nissan has been located in the region for many years and elements of its supply chain have co-located in the north east, its factory at Washington New Town lost its mandates for R&D and some aspects of purchasing following merger with Renault. Nissan is therefore both a rare example of a plant that has remained for decades, which sets the standard in terms of labour productivity and product quality for other plants in Europe and North America and by the standards of the north east provides well-paid and stable manufacturing employment, but also one which has become less, rather than more, embedded with the passage of time.

While public sector back office activities of government departments have proved relatively stable, the later re-location of private sector back offices has exhibited greater volatility. Equally, while there has been an influx of call centres and particular types of business process activity across a wide range of sectors, these too are susceptible to closure and re-location in an intensely competitive global market as locations in Canada, China, the eastern *Länder* of Germany, India and Russia seek to attract such labour-intensive (for now at least) activities. Although these are mostly 'white collar' non-manual jobs, they too require only basic knowledge, skills and competencies, with often a greater premium on communication, personal and social rather than technical skills.

By the late 1970s it was becoming clear that the dominant policy approach of attracting inward investment was failing to provide an adequate answer to problems of unemployment and lack of work in the region. The response to this was to shift the emphasis in policy to encouraging endogenous growth and the creation of self-employment in an (allegedly) emergent enterprise economy (Hudson R, 1998). This spanned a range of manufacturing and service activities, including tourism – the unifying factor seemed to be firm size rather than any more coherent shared characteristics. However, such a policy shift also valorised a new set of social and technical skills and competencies – summarised in terms of 'entrepreneurship' and 'enterprise' – but these proved to be in short supply in the region. Put another way, the policy switch to small and medium-sized enterprises was predicated on untenable assumptions as to the availability of particular sorts of knowledges and skills in the region – and was silent about the need to devise an appropriate supply-side policy response. When this conception of policy failed in practice to produce economic regeneration, the stage was set for a different policy-led version of the knowledge-based economy to emerge, centred on new forms of knowledge and sites of knowledge production, diffusion and transmission. In this, the emergent regional policy was influenced by growing emphasis in parts of the social sciences on the (alleged) emergence of a 'new' knowledge-based economy and on the primacy of particular socio-spatial formations of this economy. It was also influenced, decisively, by the dominance of neo-liberal perspectives on the economy that transcended party political divides and emphasised the role of competition, markets and self-reliance in shaping the fate of people and places.

## The knowledge-based economy, version III: regional devolution, new science-based industries and knowledge transfer from the region's universities

While the election of the New Labour government in 1997 in many ways was marked by continuities with the neo-liberal policies of its Conservative predecessors, in other ways it registered important changes. In the context of policies for the regions in general, and the north east in particular, these changes reflected the convergence of three different sorts of pressures, two 'economic' and the third 'political'. First, there was recognition of a persistent national productivity 'gap', especially between the UK and USA, reflecting lower levels of R&D and high level 'knowledge-based' activities. This was linked to policy makers' changing understandings of the determinants of economic growth that emphasised the quality of ideas, innovation and knowledge (Aghion and Howitt, 1998). This influenced national government policy and in turn filtered down to shape emerging conceptions of regional development policy. Second, there was recognition of continuing problems of regional uneven development as the north east persistently performed at the bottom of the regional economic performance league tables. This strongly suggested that previous economic development models (in all their varied forms) simply had not had, were not having and would not have their intended effects. Third, there were increased pressures for growing regional devolution in parts of central government and in some regions. These pressures were particularly prominent in the north east among certain business and political elites. The newly elected government saw the possibility of dealing with all three sets of issues simultaneously via new innovative devolved regional organisations in England, regional development agencies (the Celtic fringes had had their own stronger versions of such institutions for many years).

The regional development agencies (along with appointed regional assemblies) were launched in the context of national initiatives intended to help resolve the national productivity problem via encouraging knowledge transfer from universities to regional economies and promoting an entrepreneurial culture in higher education. This drew heavily on one particular conception of scientific knowledge and its translation into the economy (Etzkowitz and Leydesdorff, 2000; Lundvall and Maskell, 2000) and was a process that was to be heavily influenced in the north east by the subsequent involvement of international consultants Arthur D Little (ADL). Problems of poor regional economic performance were to be solved by, literally, capitalising and capitalising on knowledge produced in the region's universities, facilitating the production of more knowledge intensive and higher value added commodities, principally in manufacturing but to a degree in services, reflecting the increasing de-differentiation of manufactures and services. Enhanced economic performance would result from both capitalising upon on-going scientific research in universities and via specifically seeking to shape their research agendas and activities, especially in science and engineering. This potentially raised difficult issues regarding the autonomy of universities and the determinants of research, the production of scientific knowledge and the ownership of intellectual property arising from that research. Implicit in this approach to economic development policy was a territorially based model of knowledge production and dissemination, centred on a concept of regions as bounded and contiguous territories and regionally defined organisational structures and intra-regional flows. Universities in the region responded to these schemes (Duke *et al.*, 2006). Individually and collectively, often in collaboration with other regional partners, they explored ways to encourage knowledge transfer to companies and public sector organisations (such as the National Health Service) in the region and commercialise the results of their scientific research. At the risk of (over) simplification, these may be categorised as falling into one of five types: research centres; collaboration and consultancy; intellectual property transactions; promotion of spin-offs, incubators, science parks; training and labour mobility.

While these national initiatives evoked specific responses within the north east, they also created tensions, both nationally and specifically within the region. The Treasury and Department of Trade and Industry were primarily concerned with productivity and national economic performance, seeking to use these national initiatives to narrow the productivity gap between the UK and its main international competitors and ease the transition to a high productivity, new knowledge-based economy. They saw the prime role of regional development agencies as the elimination of regional productivity differentials and the barrier that these posed to non-inflationary national economic growth.[4] In contrast, the Office of the Deputy Prime Minister had a much stronger commitment to regional devolution per se, a cause long championed by the 'Old Labour' Deputy Prime Minister John Prescott, whose 1983 alternative regional strategy was based upon greater regional devolution, regional development agencies and elected regional authorities. As a result, there were visible tensions within national government over the role of the new regional development agencies between the Treasury and the Department of Trade and Industry and the Office of the Deputy Prime Minister.

Equally within the region there were divisions between those who wanted elected devolved organisations as part of a process of regional democratisation that would – inter alia – allow the formation and implementation of more effective regional development strategies and those who opposed them. These disputes reflected different conceptions of 'the region' as a social actor, differences as to the appropriate site of policy formation, and divergent views as to which social interests should be prioritised in regional development policies. The opposition was something of an unholy alliance, bringing together three distinct factions. First, those who opposed unelected bodies because they were anti-democratic. Second, those who opposed the proposed form of elected Assembly because it was simply too weak to be effective. Third, those who opposed an elected Assembly because they saw it as disrupting existing and well-established organisational arrangements that originated in the 1930s and subsequently evolved into a succession of organisations 'in and for' for the region. These organisations were manned (the term is deliberate) by groups drawn from a small political and economic elite and served their interests and those of their various constituencies (Hudson, 1989b; 2006b; 2006c).[5] The opposition prevailed as the offer of an elected Assembly was decisively rejected in a regional referendum in 2004.

However, the establishment of ONE North East, the north east regional development agency in 1999, was a significant extension of past policies. Its main task was to forge a regional economic strategy but within strictly defined parameters as to what constituted the economy ('the capitalist mainstream'), what constituted development (increases in productivity and GDP/caput) and as to the targets that had to be met and the tasks that needed to be achieved to ensure this. These constraints were not unique to ONE North East, applying to all the English regional development agencies. However, especially when combined with the influence of a few consultants who were involved in the production of these strategies and who were selling essentially the same generic model of development to all regions,[6] they led to the counter-intuitive result that their various economic development strategies bore a close generic resemblance to one another, despite the very different regional contexts that they were supposedly addressing. As such, the creation of the regional development agencies and the ways in which they were steered and monitored by central government can be seen as one expression of a new form of governmentality, of governing 'at a distance', apparently devolving authority and power to regions but in practice tightening the grip of the centre over the regions (Hudson, 2007b).

The emergent regional economic strategy in the north east had a clear and explicit focus on promoting a new sort of knowledge-based economy – a product in part of the perceived inadequacies of previous forms of regional policy, in part of a growing emphasis among international organisations such as the OECD and the EU with its Lisbon agenda upon a certain sort of knowledge-based economy as the route to future prosperity. The region's universities were assigned – or, perhaps more precisely, sought for themselves – a key role in this as important regional actors, centres of research excellence and producers and disseminators of knowledge. University laboratories were to become key nodes of 'high level' knowledge production, predominantly in the form of codified knowledge, and its transfer to private sector companies and public sector organisations in the region. While partly a response to pressures from the universities, this was also a realistic reflection of the absence of feasible alternatives to fill this role as key nodes of knowledge production and dissemination. By the late 1990s there was very little private sector R&D activity left in the region and there were no major government or public sector R&D facilities there. The regional economic strategy (ONE North East, 1999; see also 2003; 2007) specifically focused on universities as the prime mechanism for rebuilding the knowledge base, identifying 'Placing universities and colleges at the heart of the Region's economy' as one of six main priorities.

However, there was no serious consideration of the knowledge transfer process, of the necessary relations between codified and tacit knowledges in this process, and of how new codified knowledge would be used in combination with existing tacit knowledge. Rather it was simply assumed that the production of such knowledge in universities and its (non-problematic) translation into the regional economy as a source of new products, processes and profits would act as a necessary – at times it even seemed sufficient – condition to set in motion a virtuous spiral of growth in the region. As a result, putting the region's universities at the heart of the regional economic strategy in this way was not without risks. From ONE North East's point of view it left its economic development strategy – with its strong claim that it would generate 90,000 jobs in the new knowledge-based economy (whatever that in practice would mean) in ten years[7] – heavily dependent upon universities filling their assigned role. From the point of view of the universities, it created a weight of expectation as to their capabilities in knowledge transfer in circumstances in which they had little experience of, or track record of success in, such activity. Consequently, it was unclear as to whether this expectation was reasonable, not least because successive UK national Innovation Surveys reveal that only 2 percent of companies regard universities as a highly important source of information (Miles and Daniels, 2007, 9). Nonetheless, in the end, the knowledge-based economy – or, more precisely, the specific form of its elaboration in ONE North East's strategy – became accepted as a politically neutral leitmotif to which all those in the region who were 'partners' in the strategy could sign up (after all, who could be against knowledge?).

This still left unresolved the question of how to translate research from the universities to produce the desired regional knowledge-based economy. In seeking to answer this question, the production of the regional economic strategy became entangled with the debate on 'clusters' and the promotion of Porterian clusters as central to the process of knowledge transfer and successful regional economic development (although in fact ideas of cluster-based development were not new, having been floated in the north east in the 1960s: see Hudson, 1989b). Government White Papers in 2000 and 2001 emphasised the role of regional development agencies and of universities in underpinning economic vibrancy via support for clusters and innovation (DTI, 2000; DTI and DfEE, 2001), uncritically accepting claims that territorial clusters were the best – indeed the only – feasible economic development model and failing to explore alternatives based around different spatialities and forms of inter-firm relationships.

However, the question of which regional organisations could perform the role of broker and translator of knowledge from universities to economy still remained unanswered. While there were various national initiatives (such as University Innovation Centres) ONE North East set out to create its own set of new regionally specific intermediate organisations as an integral component in its emerging regional economic strategy. Initial 'guidance' from government required each English regional development agency to develop an innovation action plan, building upon existing innovation strategies developed through the government regional offices, often with funding from EU programmes. However, the resources available to support this were minimal (between £250k and £440k per regional development agency per annum) while regional; development agencies were highly constrained in their use of central government funds because funding streams were locked into central government programmes delivered in the regions. Furthermore the legacy of historically low levels of government R&D expenditure in the regions was seen as a key obstacle in moving towards a new knowledge-based economy As ONE North East (1999, 59) emphasised, '[t]here is a widespread belief throughout the Region that the Government must direct more Treasury funded research to Universities outside London, particularly to the North East. This is essential to underpin the Region's approach to promoting knowledge transfer'.

One suggested approach to knowledge transfer was via Advanced Centres of Excellence which like the, then new, International Centre for Life would combine research, exploitation, spinoffs, educational outreach, training and public understanding of science. Four additional Centres were proposed, but without specifying technology areas or delivery mechanisms or locations. To help clarify their potential role, in early 2001 ADL was commissioned to review the research base in the north east in relation to current and future needs of key industry clusters. The ADL Report (August 2001) combined lessons learned from a parallel study in the north west with refinement of previous work in the north east and provided a clear template for the region. The response to the report (ONE North East, 2001) was very rapid – indeed so rapid that it seems reasonable to assume that the response had already been decided ahead of receipt of the report. Submitted to the Department of Trade and Industry in September 2001 it incorporated most of ADL's recommendations. The core of the *Strategy for Success* was the formation of a Science and Industry Council (established in December), a regional exploitation agency – NStar – to provide access to finance, proof of concept investment and commercialisation advice and assistance and five 'Centres of Excellence', to be established as non-profit companies and located in different parts of the region. The five Centres would focus on life sciences (Centre of Excellence for Life Sciences – CELS), new and renewable energy technologies (New and Renewable Energy Centre – NaREC), nanotechnology (Centre of Excellence for Nanotechnology, Photonics and Microsystems – CENAMPS), digital technologies (Codeworks) and process industries (Centre for Process Industries), this last based on the legacy of ICI's former R&D activities on Teesside (see Chapman, 2005) – a mixture of technologies novel to the region and existing regional industrial and academic strengths.

The Centres were intended to form a bridge between business and scientific research in the region's universities – concentrated in Durham and the Newcastle Universities – facilitating the commercialisation and capitalisation of knowledge produced through research, while also recognising the need to forge extra-regional links. Each Centre evolved a distinct strategy, reflecting the characteristics of the technologies and sectors it supported and the legacies of existing Centres and activities. ONE North East provided pump-priming resources but each Centre was required to plan for self sufficiency from commercial and investment income within five years. Whether prioritising short-term concerns with financial self-sufficiency over longer-term concerns with qualitative regional economic transformation was sensible remains a moot point. Overall it was estimated that the regional development agency would invest £200 million over five years while aiming to leverage a similar level of investment from the EU and national programmes (ONE North East, 2003). In addition NStar sought to invest £33 million in innovative technologies through proof of concept funding. However, in total and in relation to the task of shifting the regional economy onto a qualitatively different developmental trajectory, this was very modest funding.

Following an appraisal of the *Strategy for Success* by the Regional Assembly in summer 2004, ONE North East identified three Centres as presenting the greatest potential for future economic growth. Accordingly, the programme was restructured around the three 'pillars' of Healthcare, Process Industries and Energy and Environment, associated respectively with CELS, CPI and NaREC. Each pillar was to be directed by a Leadership Council, responsible for setting a strategic vision and overseeing delivery of the project, and incorporate industrial clusters and other 'delivery partners' (including universities). ONE North East anticipated that each pillar could potentially contribute £2 billion towards closing the north east's perceived £9 billion productivity gap. The remaining two Centres (CENAMPS and Codeworks), along with NStar, the Northern Way Design Centre and a management skills programme provided via the Regional Skills Partnership, would have more of a generic underpinning and complementary role, supporting activity across the three pillars. Reflecting its aim that the pillars should become self-financing, ONE North East proposed that it should finance their public duty activities, with a separate trading arm, responsible for commercialisation and other income generation.

The emergence of the Northern Way growth strategy in 2004 involved ONE North East in discussions with two other regional development agencies (the North West and Yorkshire and Humberside) around a wider pan-regional strategy for investment in science in collaboration with eight research-intensive universities in the north, known as the N8. However, the scale of additional funding was again modest – a 'growth fund' of £100 million over the period 2005–8 spread across the three regional development agencies, with only £10 million targeted at knowledge transfer and science and innovation priorities (Northern Way, 2005). Clearly there is limited scope for new initiatives within these budgetary limits. In addition, Newcastle was one of three cities designated as science cities. The regional development agency, Newcastle City Council and Newcastle University acquired a development site, 'science central', near to the University and intended to be a new translational research campus. This, however, generated visible tensions between those who saw science city in this place-bound way, eliding it with 'science central', and those who envisaged science city as a distributed regional network, encompassing other key nodes of scientific knowledge production and research, both new (such as Netpark in County Durham) and more established (such as CPI on Teesside, which merged with CENAMPS in 2007).

How successful these various initiatives will be in facilitating the emergence of a new knowledge-based economy and closing the inter-regional output gap remains to be seen. There is some initial evidence of the 'pillars of excellence' developing as nodes in knowledge flows (Tully *et al.*, 2006) and innovative firms in the north east being more likely to exploit contacts with universities as compared to other English regions (Johnson and Reed, 2008, 24–5) but this is some way from the effective translation of results from scientific research into the cognitive basis of a 'new' regional knowledge-based economy. It remains to be seen how effectively science city and the 'pillars of excellence' will evolve as mechanisms for delivering the transition to a new regional knowledge-based economy. Influential analysts have cast doubt on the wisdom of relying on developing new industries on the basis of new knowledge and novel technologies, seeing it as high risk and arguing for a different strategy that sought to build more upon the legacies of previous versions of the knowledge-based economy (OECD, 2006).

## Conclusions and some questions

By the 1990s it was abundantly clear that the various policies pursued in the north east had failed to have their intended effects of producing a stronger, more diversified and resilient regional economy. The region continued to bump along at the bottom of league tables of regional economic performance, with persistent high levels of multiple deprivation and sharp intra-regional socio-spatial disparities in well-being. This encouraged – some might say politically necessitated – an urgent search for fresh policy approaches. Clearly the policy initiatives at both national and regional levels since the late 1990s, heavily influenced by new claims as to the significance of knowledge of particular sorts in shaping success in the contemporary economy, represent an ambitious attempt to remedy the situation and shift the region's economy onto a qualitatively different developmental trajectory, seeking to position the region more advantageously in relation to the (allegedly) emergent 'new' economy while echoing its nineteenth century 'golden age' but on the basis of a much more consciously managed process of knowledge production and translation. The aim is to facilitate the production of new commodities, with unique selling points and dominant market positions, and/or to enhance the knowledge intensity and move up the value chain in producing existing commodities via capitalising (on) knowledge produced in the region's universities and translated through new intermediary organisations.

The success or otherwise of these initiatives raises important questions. First, are they working – or will they work in future – in their own terms, to meet their defined goals? The answer to these questions remains as yet uncertain. Not least, this is because knowledge, no matter how original and novel, remains only one determinant of successful commodity production, corporate profitability and successful regional regeneration and too much weight may be being loaded onto knowledge per se as an agent of economic transformation.

While there have been some promising signs, it is by no means certain that this developmental strategy will succeed.[8] There will undoubtedly be knowledge transfer from the universities but it remains to be seen whether this will be on the scale required to transform the regional economy – not least because of lack of demand and the limited capacity of the region's economy to absorb such new knowledge and associated innovations. Moreover, there are unresolved tensions between the production of scientific knowledge as a research goal per se – which *may* then open opportunities for commercial exploitation, or then again may not – and the subsumption of such knowledge production to the pressing imperatives of capital. In short, it remains an open question as to whether the current round of policies in the north east will have their intended effects in facilitating the emergence of a knowledge-based economy, especially as they are based in a limited and partial – even naïve – view of the knowledge transfer process (see also OECD, 2006). For as Miles and Daniels (2007, 21) note, 'Increasingly it is not individual companies that compete but trans-border supply chains of integrated companies positioned in global markets. In the face of such massive unbundling, whither a national innovation strategy (let alone a regional strategy)?' This clearly calls into question the efficacy of territorially bounded innovation strategies.

Second, the region is seeking to pursue these policies in an increasingly competitive global environment, as cities, regions and national states all compete for investment. Many places that have gone through the same sequence of growth and decline as north east England are now seeking to develop knowledge-based economies, centred on the same restricted set of high technology activities and sectors. The pursuit of science-based – even science-led – investment in sectors such as biotechnologies and nanotechnologies is rife. However, these are also broad and diverse sectors of activity. One implication of this is that 'the way forward is to nurture "niche positions" ' (Miles and Daniels, 2007, 4). Consequently there is a need to identify precise niches and spheres of activity in which companies in north east England could, in principle at least, develop first-mover advantage and significant competitive advantage and then to develop equally precisely targeted strategies to support their further successful development. However, this degree of sophisticated targeting has not, as yet, developed; nor have its wider implications been thought through in a systematic way. For example, it could have important implications for the types of university research that would be supported – and for those that would not be, with potential longer-term dangers of narrowing the gene pool in terms of the diversity of research in universities.

Moreover, even if there was to be this degree of sophisticated targeting, it is important to remember that these policy-led attempts to both use the results of existing university research in regional innovation strategies and indeed shape such research in future so that it is directly linked to the needs of capital are constrained within the parameters defined by capitalist relations of production. Consequently, there are precise limits to such processes, circumscribed by the limits to capital itself (Harvey, 1982; Jessop, 2000) and by the limits to political strategies that seek to influence the form of capitalist development, which remains inherently and unavoidably uneven. Seeking to commodify existing knowledge and/or to produce future knowledge in commodity form cannot escape the contradictions inherent to processes of capitalist development and commodity production. Two are of particular relevance here: first, such development typically has unintended as well as – or instead of – intended results; second, such development is dynamically uneven and typically erodes the bases of its success over the longer-term. This is something that proponents of approaches that prioritise knowledge, information flows and learning per se are prone to ignore.

Third, however, if the strategy does succeed in facilitating the emergence of a new knowledge-based economy that, for a while, is both quantitatively and qualitatively significant in its transformative effects on the regional economy, there are two qualifications to be borne in mind. The first is that the historical-geography of the north east economy suggests that even when there was substantial indigenous R&D activity in the region, this was no guarantee of continued long-term economic success in/of the region. Profits made in the region were invested elsewhere, in other places and sectors (for example, railways in South America and banks in London). As the miners' checkweighman George Harvey put it in 1917, 'capital knows no county'; no doubt if he were to come back now, he would emphasise that capital knows no country, indeed no continent. The second qualification is that even a successful knowledge-based economy as envisaged within current policy discourse regionally and nationally would fail to engage large numbers of people in the region, for two reasons: first, it would generate insufficient jobs relative to the number of people seeking work; second, there would be great selectivity on the part of employers as to who would get those jobs. This strongly suggests the need for a more plural and heterogeneous conception of the economy, of development and of relevant knowledges in the context of a regional development strategy in the north east (and like regions). These are essentially theoretical tasks but the key issue is not so much re-theorisations per se (vital though that is) but rather which theoretical conceptions become dominant – even hegemonic – in policy discourse and practice and in politics. Most fundamentally, there needs to be acceptance of a broader conception of the knowledge-based economy to encompass a wider range of activities and valorise a greater range of knowledges. There is a pressing need to recognise that all forms of economic activity are knowledge-based and to embrace a more heterodox and plural concept of the economy, to acknowledge that there is – of necessity – still a place for the branch plant economy alongside an emergent more sophisticated 'knowledge based' economy. More than that, however, it is vital to acknowledge the presence of a social economy and an informal economy that will be crucial to any sustainable development strategy for the north east since the scale of employment creation in the formal economy, whether in its branch plant or more 'knowledge-based' variants, will simply be insufficient to absorb all those seeking work there. There is some evidence of growing recognition of such points in ONE North East's evolving approach to its regional development strategy although it remains uncertain as to how much weight will in practice be attached to such concerns.[9]

Finally, although the empirical focus in this paper has been upon the experiences of one region, this raises broader questions as to how different regions relate to and are positioned in the inherently uneven process of capitalist development and the changing knowledge bases and requirements of its leading edges. For however much the emphasis switches to the significance of flows of knowledge in cyberspace as underpinning economic success and a resulting migration of capital into cyberspace, like all capital 'it still depends on territorialisation' (Jessop, 2000, 4) – that is, on materialisation in specific cities and regions, which compete to be the sites of such materialisation and territorialisation. Thus many other regions with economic histories similar to that of north east England are pursuing similar policies to create new knowledge-based economies – all believing that this will enable them to shift onto the high road of economic success, emulate the processes of self-reinforcing endogenous growth present in the key nodes of the global economy, and break with their peripheral status. Put another way, the assumption is that all regions will be able to engage in 'win-win' scenarios. Some may indeed succeed in making this transition. However, as the history of north east England shows only too clearly, this is a far from easy task. Moreover, it is difficult to see how all can be winners in a capitalist economy that necessarily continues to be characterised by combined and uneven development. There are therefore clear limits to policies to create the new knowledge-based economy – as there were with previous generations of regional policies – in addressing issues of uneven development within the social relations of capital.

## Notes

1 Two qualifications are worth making regarding the growth process. First, there were often wild cyclical fluctuations around the upward trend. Second, the main beneficiaries of growth were local capitalists and their allies; working people and their families were commonly living in poverty, especially in cyclical downturns.
2 There was no inevitability about this, however. In other similar regions such transformations took place on a much larger scale. For example, in the Ruhr a significant new cluster of environmental technology companies emerged from the declining coal and steel sectors.
3 State training schemes were by no means new. Local technical colleges (and later polytechnics) provided courses for engineers and skilled manual workers required by the 'old' industries. Training courses were organised in response to the requirements of earlier rounds of branch plant investment – for instance in consumer electronics in the 1960s (Hudson, 1980). However, then, the probabilities of acquiring employment requiring these newly acquired skills were much higher.

4 Those with a sense of history – and irony – pointed out that this was precisely the argument used in the 1950s by Macmillan's Conservative government to justify introducing a revived and strengthened central government regional policy and soon afterwards specific initiatives for the north east of England: Hudson, 1989b.
5 They included the Northern Economic Planning Council set up in 1966, the Government Office for the North East, established in 1993 to bring together central government activities and operations and the delivery of central government policies in the region within a more coherent framework and the appointed Regional Assembly created in 1999.
6 There are strong echoes here of Thrift's (2005) emphasis on the significance of the global 'circuit of cultural capital' and of the pervasive influence of a small set of consultants and their associates.
7 Although the commitment to a knowledge-based economy remained in successive iterations of the strategy, this specific claim was not repeated.
8 This was written before the onset of the major recession that began in the wake of the financial crisis of 2007/8, which revealed the continuing fragility of the regional economy.
9 The answer to this question is and will remain unknown as ONE was abolished in March 2012 following the election of the Conservative-Liberal Democrat coalition government in 2010.

# 5 Re-thinking change in old industrial regions

## Reflecting on the experiences of north east England

### Introduction

In this chapter I want to reflect upon regional economic change and the ways in which this is conceptualised and understood, drawing heavily but not exclusively on some 30 years of research on economy, politics and society in the north east of England (Hudson, 2000a). The economy of this region been transformed from a booming core in the nineteenth century to a marginalised and near-bust periphery by the end of the twentieth century, while the region has been blighted by widespread poverty and inequality throughout this long period. The principal question that this chapter addresses, therefore, is this: how are the long periods of continuity, punctuated by occasional major shifts, in developmental trajectory and the region's place in the global economy, allied to the persistence in socio-spatial inequalities within the region,[1] to be understood?

In the nineteenth century, the north east was one of the birthplaces of industrial capitalism, a new industrial region materially and discursively constructed in a space that was formerly largely occupied by a pre-capitalist and non-industrial economy and society. It became a veritable 'workshop of the world', at the core of capitalist production, the British Empire and an emerging nineteenth century globalising economy, built around coal, iron and steel, engineering (notably shipbuilding, armaments and railways) and chemicals. Now it is an 'old' industrial region, with very little remaining of the growth industries of the nineteenth century. To use the adjectives 'old' and 'new' in relation to industrial regions is simply to acknowledge that the nature of capitalism ensures that all industries at some point become 'old', as, in a sense, do the regions in which they are – or were – embedded.

The extent and pace of decline in the last quarter of the twentieth century was nonetheless spectacular. As a result, and in strong contrast to the nineteenth century, the north east is now a profoundly de-industrialised region on the periphery of the European Union and on the margins of the global economy. It is very largely disconnected from the decisive circuits of capital and the major growth mechanisms of the contemporary capitalist economy. As a result, not only have the 'old' industries largely disappeared but there has been at best a partial and weak 're-industrialisation' via the endogenous growth of 'new' industries or the introduction of 'old' industries (such as automobile or consumer electronics production) that are 'new' to the north east.

In short, the north east has experienced a long wave of growth followed by decline (Mandel, 1978), although with cyclical fluctuations around this long-term trend. Throughout, however, the region has been characterised by deep intra-regional socio-spatial inequality (for example, in terms of incomes, wealth, health and living conditions). This was the case from the boom years of the nineteenth century to the profound economic decline that set in during the last quarter of the twentieth century. In the nineteenth century north east England was and now still is a region marked by intra-regional inequalities as nineteenth century liberalism was echoed by late twentieth century neo-liberalism in national politics and the dominant conception of the national political economy. Intra-regional socio-spatial inequality has remained a constant characteristic in its trajectory of growth and decline.

Seeking to explain the region's particular sequence of growth and decline, combined with persistent intra-regional inequality, requires drawing upon a variety of theoretical perspectives. A critical insight of Marxian political economy is that uneven development, including spatially uneven development, is structurally embedded within the capitalist mode of production and economies dominated by it. It stresses that uneven development is, as it were, genetically encoded into the capitalist mode of production. This emphasises the broader structural determination of regional uneven development and contextualises the possibilities for regional autonomy and pro-activity. However, while such a highly abstract approach can identify key causal mechanisms and the necessary structural relations that define the capitalist mode of production *as* capitalist, it cannot reveal *which* regions will grow and prosper, which will decline. Nor can it reveal which fractions of the classes of capital and labour, in which regions, will 'win' and 'lose' as an integral part of the dynamism of such processes.

A further related limitation of such a structural analysis is that it cannot uncover how the strategies and practices of capital, states and workers combine in complex ways to create regions that become critical nodes in the accumulation process and regions that become marginal to it. Equally, and critically, it cannot reveal the mechanisms through which regions change from being focal points in processes of growth to locations that are eviscerated by the flight of capital and abandonment by the (national) state as it ceases to regard them as locations for productive activity. Such regions are characterised by a 'surplus population', at best of direct interest to capital or state as a source of migrant labour that could move elsewhere in search of work and meet labour-power demands in other regions. Nonetheless, these are regions that require regulation and surveillance, and forms of state involvement to ensure the reproduction of a population there, not least for reasons of political legitimacy.

Answering such questions about the changing developmental trajectories of regions requires a different type of approach to that of Marxian political economy, drawing on theories grounded in other complementary strands of heterodox social science that seek to reveal the mechanisms, 'messy practices' and emergent effects through which capitalist economies are performed and (un)intentionally (re)produced. In particular, I want to draw on strands of evolutionary and institutional approaches and upon state theory and concepts of governance and governmentality to seek to deepen understanding of the production of 'old industrial regions'. I seek to use these as three inter-related and to a degree overlapping perspectives through which to examine and seek to interpret the socio-economic development of north east England. As such, there is a deliberate selectivity in choice of evidence.

I am not therefore seeking to give a comprehensive account of the region's development and historical geography. My aim is both more focused and limited: that is, to explore the extent to which continuity and change in the region's developmental trajectory can be understood in terms of evolutionary and institutional concepts and the varying engagement of the state with issues of socio-economic development and change. This has important practical as well as theoretical implications. Not least, how does the state seek to deal with such regional economic problems and legitimate its activities? What is the capacity of the state to manage the maintenance of or changes in developmental trajectories? Should state policies seek to maintain existing developmental trajectories or seek to move regional economies onto new and different ones?

## Path dependency or path contingency?

One way of seeking to understand the changing trajectories of regional growth and decline is to draw upon strands of evolutionary thinking, especially evolutionary approaches in economics that eschew biological analogy and emphasise that path dependence is socially constituted (Metcalfe, 1998). As such, path dependence is grounded in the reproduction of instituted forms of behaviour (which are discussed in the following section). Concepts of path dependency are undoubtedly useful in accounting for the long period of secular growth in the economy of north east England. This lasted from the early nineteenth century to the 1920s, albeit punctuated by sharp cyclical fluctuations characteristic of the capitalist business cycle in an economy dominated by a liberal mode of regulation that allowed markets great scope as resource allocation mechanisms. The booming regional economy was dominated by a small number of major conglomerates (or 'coal combines': see Hudson, 1989b, after Harvey, 1917), linked via a range of untraded as well as traded inter-dependencies (which are discussed more fully in the next section) that forged connections between them.

Rapid regional economic growth was therefore based upon close and mutually reinforcing links of intra-regional traded dependencies between the mining of coal and the production of iron and steel, and a wide range of engineering products manufactured from iron and steel (armaments, ships, railways and so on) and chemicals. Markets for these booming industries were often constituted as international, rather than simply national, markets from the outset. Such markets were constructed within the political frameworks of both the formal and informal British Empires, the latter constituted by areas of the world that were not under formal UK political rule but in which UK-based capital held a dominant position. For example, companies based in north east England had an iron grip on the market for constructing railways over much of South America. The combination of continuously growing markets and close inter-connections between the inputs to and outputs from production processes in the north east created a virtuous spiral of path dependent growth. This served the interests of the owners of capital and of the coal combines in the region well for around a century.

If, however, this was a successful and path dependent trajectory of growth, the conditions on which it relied were contingent and conjunctural, albeit relatively stable over a long period. As such, the concept of path contingency captures the character of the growth process, and in particular the transition from growth to decline, more adequately than that of path dependency (Chapter 2; Hardy, 2002). There are a number of issues of particular significance in this context. The first is the collapse of markets, both national and international, for commodities produced in the north east. The second is the transition from a liberal to an interventionist mode of regulation of the regional economy, shaped by dominant capitalist interests in the region. The third is the shift from a social democratic politics of nationalisation and state ownership of key industries in a state managed region from the mid-1940s to mid-1970s (Hudson, 1989b) to a subsequent neo-liberal politics of privatisation and pre- and post-privatisation rationalisation.

The secular collapse of international markets for many of the industrial commodities produced in north east England began in the depression of the 1920s and 1930s. As a result, whole swathes of industry in the region collapsed and in some cases this led to the permanent destruction of productive capacity. For example, in shipbuilding there was a state-sponsored strategy to cut capacity (Wilkenson, 1939) while in coal mining the cessation of pumping activities from the mines led to permanent closure due to flooding, especially in south west Durham (Dalton, 1953). By and large, however, it involved mass unemployment rather than the mass destruction of industrial capacity.

The scale and persistence of unemployment was sufficient to generate political concerns and at the same time the owners of capital in the region began to seek new ways of promoting and protecting their interests. One result of this was the invention for the first time, albeit haltingly and uncertainly, of a nascent national government regional policy from the late 1920s. This emergent policy concern registered that regional uneven development had ceased to be simply an undesirable characteristic of capitalist development and had become a political problem for the state. Prominent capitalists in the north east, coming together as the self-styled Northern Industrial Group, took an active role in seeking to construct this policy in ways that served their own interests, relying on their political power to do so, and became key figures in the new regional institutions established to develop and implement it (Hudson, 2006b). Re-armament in the 1930s and then the war-time economy (1939–45) restored effective demand for many industrial commodities produced in the region and the post-war settlement involved the nationalisation of industries that formed key sectors of the regional economy (coal mining, iron and steel and the railways). While the nationalisation of iron and steel was short-lived, it was subsequently re-nationalised in the 1960s while shipbuilding was nationalised in the 1970s.

These various nationalisations were informed by a variety of motives, depending on their specific timings (Hudson, 1986). Generally, however, nationalisation reflected the fact that industries seen in various ways as central to national or regional economic performance or national interests (notably in terms of defence) were no longer sufficiently profitable to attract the required investment in fixed assets and means of production by private capital. Public ownership via nationalisation in this way became a strategy to underpin the region's development trajectory around these industries, as the state replaced private capital as the proximate guarantor of the region's path dependent developmental strategy. It did so, however, in ways that created a trajectory locked-in to existing industries. For example, the newly created National Coal Board was confined to the mining of coal and legally prevented from diversifying into activities such as the manufacture of mining machinery and equipment – activities that remained a source of profit for other private sector companies (Grundy Warr, 1989). Thus this shift to the state as guarantor of the regional development trajectory, and of selected private sector interests, was politically negotiated on terms that were very favourable to the latter. For some it created captive markets while for others it was a means to liberate capital from obsolete and unprofitable fixed assets. In practice, nationalisation became a mechanism to restore capital to a money form that private sector companies could use to diversify their interests, spatially and sectorally.

Nonetheless, those industries that were nationalised continued to decline within the north east. There were two main sets of reasons for this. First, changes in the international division of labour as a consequence of the emergence of new centres of production for coal, steel and ships (as well as industries such as chemicals that remained in private ownership) in other parts of the world. Second, technological developments led to the creation of alternatives to coal as an energy resource and raw material for carbon-based chemicals production, and to plastics and other materials as alternatives to steel as an industrial material. Continuing decline in the regional economy led to further policy responses from the state. One response, informed by political concerns over socio-spatial equity and maintaining the legitimacy of state involvement in economy and society in the region, was that national governments strengthened their regional policies to try and attract new private sector investment. Initially, this was typically in the form of branch plants in manufacturing and their analogous workplaces in both private and public service sector activities. However, while there was diversification of industries and sectors, there was homogenisation in terms of stage of production and location in value chains, with a proliferation of low skill, low value added activities. These factories were 'global outposts' (Beynon and Austrin, 1979), located at the end of corporate chains of command and control that stretched across the globe. As the limits to these policies became visible over a number of decades, the emphasis switched more to the formation and growth of indigenous small and medium-sized enterprises – again without conspicuous success (Robinson and Storey, 1981; Storey, 1982).

From the mid-1970s the UK state faced growing fiscal pressures, with fears of a fiscal crisis of the state triggering capital flight from the national territory. In response, the scope and extent of state involvement in economy and society began to rein back as part of a transition from a social democratic to neo-liberal mode of state engagement with economy and society (Hudson and Williams, 1995). Two aspects of this are particularly relevant here. The first is the cutback in central government expenditure on regional policies. However, it was second, the privatisation and associated rationalisations of the formerly nationalised coal, electricity supply, steel and shipbuilding industries that was of greatest significance in revealing the contingent character of the developmental trajectory in the north east. The nationalised industries were increasingly unprofitable and as such were adding to public sector borrowing in order to ensure their continuing existence. In order to address this problem the state sought to dispose of these industries to private sector interests. Consequently, to try and render them more attractive (that is, potentially profitable) to private capital, the formerly close and politically mediated ties between the nationalised industries were broken as they were allowed to source and sell globally. For example, the electricity supply and steel industries had formed markets for coal, which disappeared as they were allowed to buy coal on the international market, with imports from Australia, Colombia and South Africa. This led to a series of colliery closures in the north east (Beynon *et al.*, 1991). In addition, and relatedly, these industries were subject to successive rounds of capacity closure and job loss in the north east (as well as elsewhere), with the specific intention of making them more attractive to potential private sector purchasers. Furthermore, following privatisation there were further rounds of rationalisation, as the new private sector owners of these companies sought to make them more profitable (Hudson R, 1998).

The net result was that by the early years of the twenty-first century, little remained in the north east of the coal, steel and shipbuilding industries: one steelworks on Teesside (currently under grave threat as a result of Corus' continuing crisis and a specialisation in producing semi-finished steel),[2] one shipyard on the Tyne and one deep mine (Ellington in Northumberland, the sole remnant of the Great Northern Coalfield and due to close in three or four years).[3] There was also a few opencast (strip) mines, which had expanded relatively and absolutely in scale as deep mining contracted, precisely because their costs of production per tonne of coal were less (Beynon *et al.*, 2000). However, these too are now declining in extent. In addition, the restructuring of ICI, from a company producing commodity bulk chemicals to one focused on speciality chemicals, and the subsequent fragmentation of the formerly integrated chemicals production structure on Teesside, and the elimination of swathes of heavy engineering, led to substantial capacity reductions. In total these industries employ around 20,000 people; even 50 years ago they employed about well over 400,000 in the north east – a reduction that provides a stark indication of the contingent character of the region's earlier developmental trajectory.

## The perils of instituted behaviour: institutional and cognitive lock-in

In recent years there has been a considerable re-emphasis upon the 'instituted' character of human behaviour. This is partly a result of the re-discovery of (neo) Polanyian approaches to economic analysis, partly a corollary of a more general concern in parts of economics and sociology with the socially embedded character of action (Granovetter, 1985). There is a long tradition of institutional approaches in economics, but the main source of inspiration here is the 'old' institutional economics of Commons and Veblen rather than the new institutional economics of Williamson, which is closely linked to neo-classical approaches (see Hodgson, 1988; 1993; Hudson, 2001a). 'Instituted' behaviour can be thought of as embracing a wide spectrum from the informality of habits, norms and routines (often unexamined and unthinkingly performed, symptomatic of a Gramscian hegemony of some ideas and ways of thinking over others) to the formality of behaviour within the state and its constituent apparatuses and organisations.

In the 1970s and 1980s political-economy approaches to analyses of regional uneven development placed great emphasis on the role of extra-regional relationships in shaping regional (under)development trajectories. The 'institutional turn' in analyses of regional development (Amin, 1998) led to a much greater emphasis upon intra-regional relationships between firms and between economic and non-economic processes. As well as the traded inter-dependencies of the supply chain, appropriate 'institutional thickness' (Amin and Thrift, 1994) and the untraded inter-dependencies of non-economic social and cultural ties (Storper, 1995; 1997) within an associational economy (Cooke and Morgan, 1998) were increasingly seen as pivotal to regional economic success in the late twentieth century. However, such untraded inter-dependencies had clearly been of crucial importance in the new capitalist boom regions of the nineteenth century such as north east England. Furthermore, the importance of untraded inter-dependencies there in the nineteenth century exemplifies the importance of distinguishing innovations in thought from actual developments in the economy that are being thought about (Hall, 1991).

The net result of the intersection and interaction of the linkages of traded and untraded inter-dependencies was to create and reproduce the conditions underpinning a particular growth trajectory for the regional economy. Many economically successful regions, including for a time north east England, can therefore be seen to possess an appropriate institutional thickness, one that underpinned and supported economic activities located within the region, and helped reproduce regionally specific competencies, tacit knowledge and trust, regarded as critical determinants of continuing economic well-being. Conversely, however, an inappropriate institutional thickness, often a relict form from an earlier era when it *was* supportive of regional economic success, can act as a barrier to moving a regional economy onto a new and more promising developmental trajectory (Hudson, 1994b), revealing 'the weakness of strong ties' (Grabher, 1993). Just as economic growth in north east England in the nineteenth century had been grounded in a supportive institutional formation, by the late twentieth century its legacies and relict form constituted a barrier to a transition to a new regional growth trajectory.

The effects of the legacies of habits and routines established as constituent moments in the formation of the north east region's 'traditional' economy are easily observed. Some of these were relatively permeable and transformable. For example, the strict gender division of labour established as a necessary part of the 'old' industrial economy broke down. As male employment fell in the coal mines, steelworks and shipyards, many of the 'new' jobs attracted to replace them were in industries that targeted female wage labour (for example, clothing and consumer electronics, as well as a range of service activities). In part, this had been presaged during the First and Second World Wars, when shortages of civilian male labour because of conscription led to large-scale incorporation of women into factory work forces for the duration of the two Wars. Post-war, however, married women returned to their place as unpaid domestic workers 'in the home' while unmarried women found work in a range of 'female' industries and occupations, not least the expanding public sector services of education and health, performing 'caring' work socially defined as appropriate for women. This is not to say that such transformations were smooth and uncontested; quite the contrary. There were protracted debates about the replacement of 'male' with 'female' jobs and many men found genuine difficulty in coming to terms with permanent unemployment and their role as domestic workers whilst their wives worked outside the home for a wage. Indeed, many women became both sole wage earner and carried on as the main unwaged domestic worker, a combination bringing its own socio-psychological pressures and tensions.

In other respects, however, established informal habits and routines proved much more resistant to change. For example, the 'old' industrial economy had involved the construction of working class settlements to house workers close to their workplaces. Archetypically, this involved the colliery, shipyard or steelworks at the end of the street, and a very short journey to work, typically on foot. Furthermore, sons would follow fathers into jobs in these workplaces, often based on recruitment practices structured around networks of personal relations of family and friends. As a result, the educational aspirations of many boys were low, as they simply expected to follow in their father's footsteps in this way. Such training as was needed would, typically for most workers, be provided 'on the job', via processes of learning-by-doing, learning-by-imitating and learning-by-watching. With the closure of virtually all the workplaces in these industries, however, such individual trajectories through the labour market are no longer possible.

The instituted legacies of the past remain, however, in three important ways in relation to people's commuting behaviour, activity spaces and aspirations and expectations about employment and work. All three represent examples of cognitive 'lock-in' in terms of the ways in which people think of the labour market and their possibilities in it. First, there is a marked reluctance to commute, with even modest journeys-to-work of a few kilometres regarded as unreasonable. In many ways, the region remains a series of small, discrete and spatially bounded labour markets, rather than forming an integrated labour market in which people are linked to employment opportunities across the region. The distance from Newcastle to Middlesbrough, the towns at the heart of the region's northern and southern conurbations, is only 50 kilometres, but per capita car ownership rates are low and public transport provision is often poor and expensive, which militates against intra-regional labour mobility. It is, however, important to qualify this by pointing out that there is a continuing imbalance between the demand for and supply of labour in the region, with many more people seeking waged work than there are available jobs in the region. One response to this has been a growth in long-distance weekly commuting and international labour migration, albeit limited in extent (Beynon *et al.*, 1994).

Second, there is a continuing legacy of recruitment into the 'traditional' industries via sons following their fathers in terms of low expectations and limited ambition in relation to education and skills acquisition among many young people, especially but by no means wholly young men. This cognitive lock-in lives on despite the disappearance of the coal mines, shipyards and steelworks.

Third, there is an enduring culture of wage labour, a culture of dependency on wage labour and employment by others. People by and large expect to be employed in either private or public sector workplaces rather than to become self-employed, let alone employ others. This is not to say that there is an absence of entrepreneurial attitudes and ambitions, but it is to recognise that these are not funnelled into the more conventional channels of the formation and development of small and medium-sized enterprises. Such behaviour, especially when seen to be associated with a reliance upon welfare state transfer payments,[4] is often regarded as one reason for the persistent failure of state policies that aim to encourage the formation of indigenous small and medium-sized enterprises as the route to a new developmental trajectory in the north east. Many redundant workers have considered establishing their own businesses but have taken the economically very rational decision not to do so. They are acutely aware that the possibilities of successfully developing a new small enterprise are very slim in regional and sub-regional economies that are profoundly depressed by the effects of permanent, large-scale unemployment and lack of waged work in a thriving formal sector economy. Many of those losing their jobs regard investing their redundancy payments in their home as a safer and more rational investment of their money (albeit a home that they will have great difficulty selling should they subsequently decide to move in search of work). In some cases, former industrial workers display considerable entrepreneurial ability and ingenuity in developing business in the informal sector or in or on the fringes of the illegal 'black economy'.

Cognitive and institutional lock-in also exists in the more formal realms of governance, regulation and the state. The origins of regional policy in and for north east England can be traced back to the 1920s and 1930s. During this period a cross-class regionalist alliance, dominated by major capitalist interests, successfully lobbied central government and used their political influence and power to push for the creation of new forms of regional policy. This centred on the attraction of new industries and inward investment to diversify the regional economy and labour market, and helped create new opportunities for capital based in the region while seeking to protect existing capitalist interests and the jobs that they provided. This policy was intensified following the ending of the Second World War, both via strengthened forms of regional policy to attract new branch plant investment and via the nationalisation of sectors that were central to the regional economy (coal mining, iron and steel production, rail transport). This was allied to policy innovations such as the creation of New Towns as an integral part of settlement policies. Public sector infrastructure investment was concentrated in key settlements ('growth points' and 'zones'), with the intention that these became more attractive to private sector investment, seeking to bring together new employment and people in selected locations (Hudson, 1982). With varying emphases, these policies remained in place for some three decades, and in certain important respects their legacy in terms of cognitive and policy lock-in within the state continues to the present.

The implementation of these policies required the assignment of new, related powers and responsibilities to existing state organisations (for example, the planning responsibilities given to local government). It also required the construction of new formal institutional arrangements in the region. Many of these took the form of appointed quasi-state organisations (such as the New Town Development Corporations and the Regional Economic Planning Council, established in the 1960s), with little electoral accountability in the region because their members were appointed by central government. These bodies tended to be manned (the choice of verb is deliberate) by the same combination of representatives of capital and organised labour as had lobbied for and run the new institutions of the inter-war and war-time periods. As a result, they became locked into a conception of the 'regional problem' that centred on notions of industrial obsolescence, 'old' industries and derelict and polluted built and natural environments that required 'modernisation' as a pre-condition to attracting fresh rounds of manufacturing branch plant investment, increasingly from outside the UK (Hudson, 1989b).

As the limits to this response became increasingly clear in the 1970s, the policy prescription switched from state to private ownership, from large to small firms, from manufacturing to service sector activities, from inward investment to indigenous growth. This was no more than a reflection of dominant perceptions of the causes of growth in more economically successful regions. As such, the transition to a more market-oriented approach was embraced and actively promoted with some enthusiasm by some public sector policy makers in the region, often encouraged by consultants that they hired to give advice on developmental strategies for the region (for example, see Northern Regional Strategy Team, 1977). Others were much more sceptical, more wedded to a stronger directive role for the state, so that there were tensions within the public policy community. These tensions were often exacerbated by the effects of the new policy priorities. For example, the influx of call centres was evidence of new service sector growth but in activities that reproduced a 'branch plant' syndrome of unskilled, low wage work in establishments controlled by firms located outside the north east and vulnerable to competition from lower wage locations in south east Asia and Russia.

In short, official conceptions of public policy, of the causes of the 'regional problem' and of appropriate policy responses to it, remained locked into a restricted conceptual space. This left no alternative to the contradictions of particular forms of state engagement with economy and society and the decline of some sorts of private sector activities, other than the encouragement of different sorts of private sector activities, as the limits of existing policies became increasingly visible. The market as resource allocation mechanism became increasingly seen, normatively, as *the* right and proper solution to the 'regional problem'. If it failed to produce prosperity in the north east, this reflected failings in and of the region, to be addressed by people in the region, allied to appropriate supply-side policies. These varied shifts increasingly formed integral components of a more general shift away from the long post-war social democratic consensus towards a new neo-liberal governmentality.

## New modes of regulation, new governmentalities: seeking to break out of lock-in

In the preceding sections I have argued that we can conceptualise the trajectory of socio-economic change in north east England in terms of path contingency and dependency, encompassing various forms of lock-in and instituted behaviour. I have suggested that the state had a central role in these processes of continuity and change in this quintessentially state-managed region. The state was centrally involved both in creating and reinforcing lock-in to ensure path dependent development between the late 1920s and mid-1970s and subsequently seeking to erode such lock-in to facilitate new developmental trajectories. This has involved seeking to address the problems posed to such a transition, especially in terms of the attitudes and behaviour of people in the region as part of neo-liberal supply-side approaches. In this section, I further explore such issues via concepts of regulation, governance and governmentality.

Regulationist approaches emphasise the social and political grounding of the economy and the non-random coupling between a particular regime of accumulation and the social mode of regulation that makes it possible (Boyer, 1990; MacLeod, 1997). The latter encompasses both the formal regulatory mechanisms of the state apparatus and a range of non-state regulatory mechanisms located in the spaces of civil society – that is, processes of both government and governance. While stressing the centrality of the coupling between accumulation and the political and social conditions that make it possible, however, regulationist approaches have little to say about the actual practices of government, or about how particular modes of thought and policy styles become (and cease to be) dominant, even hegemonic. Thus regulationist approaches tend to assume the existence of forms of lock-in and the persistence of instituted practices but have little to say about their (re)production. They have even less to say about how one set of practices is replaced by another and radically different set as a shift from one coupling to another is enacted.

There have been attempts to address such issues, however. For example, Jessop (1990) seeks to build upon regulationist perspectives by drawing together neo-Gramscian ideas as to how hegemonic practices are channelled through complex ensembles of institutions dispersed throughout civil society with Foucault's 'capillary' notion of power in theorising the mechanisms of state power and knowledge. This views power as fluid and relational, exercised from innumerable points within civil society, the economy and the state, in productive networks of power that extend beyond the state. Nonetheless, Foucault privileged the role of the state (the 'macro-physics of power') as 'the point of strategic codification of the multitude of power relations ("the micro-physics of power") and the apparatus in which hegemony, meta-power, class domination and "sur pouvoir" are organised' (Jessop, 1990, 239). As such, the state is centrally located in relation to processes of regulation but the specific ways in which state power is developed and deployed vary. Consequently, in theorising the state, it is necessary to allow a significant degree of autonomy to state apparatuses and allow for variation in the administrative manner, style and logic by which the state regulates economy and society as it undertakes the practical tasks of 'real regulation' (Clark, 1992). Practices of implementation can decisively shape regional development trajectories.

The Foucauldian concept of 'governmentality' emphasises the practices of government and governance (Dean, 1999) and further illuminates these issues. Governmentality

> is intrinsically linked to the activities of expertise, whose role is not one of weaving an all-pervasive web of 'social control', but of enacting assorted attempts at the calculated administration of diverse aspects of conduct through the countless, often competing, local tactics of education, persuasion, inducement, management, incitement, motivation and encouragement.
>
> (MacKinnon, 2000, 296)

However, concentrations of expert knowledge can unintentionally give rise to 'enclosures', tightly bound sites of vigorously defended professional expertise, resistant to the wishes of government (Rose and Miller, 1992, 190).

Moreover, such practices of governmentality are territorially demarcated. Space is an important element of governmentality because 'to govern it is necessary to render visible the space over which government is to be exercised. And this is not simply a matter of looking: space has to be re-presented, marked out' (Thrift, 2002, 205). This thereby locates the space of the state as one element in wider circuits of power and moves from a position that sees the state as simply an explanation of other events to one that regards the specific activities of the state as themselves something to be explained. The black box of the state must be opened up in order to explain how it can perform with a degree of functional coherence. As Jessop (1990, 229) puts it, such internal coherence can only be achieved through the successful realisation of specific 'state projects' which unite state agencies and officials behind a distinct line of action. Achieving such unity is thereby a contingent matter. Even if it is achieved, however, there is no guarantee that such projects will always and only have their intended effects, as the developmental history of the north east makes abundantly clear.

These concepts of regulation, governance and governmentality allow exploration of three sets of issues pertaining to that developmental history. The first concerns the relations between the 'regional problem' and notions of governmentality, linked to the transition (initially in the 1920s) from an analytic recognition of regional uneven development to the political identification of 'problem regions'. A key issue here is the ways in which 'problem regions' are made visible, constituted as objects of state policy via the construction of regional statistics, regional plans (with their focus on outputs) and regional strategies (with their focus on process and outcomes). Furthermore, there are important connections between the ways in which the 'regional problem' is defined and the perception of appropriate forms of regional policies to tackle it. This may involve seeking to help reinforce or to change forms of instituted behaviour and secure or alter the existing developmental trajectory.

The evolution in emphasis from plans (for example, Teesside County Borough Council, 1972) via strategic plans (Northern Regional Strategy Team, 1977) to strategies (ONE North East, 1999; 2001; 2003; 2007) is linked to a *political* shift from predominantly social-democratic politics to a neo-liberal politics. The UK state was at the forefront of making this transition, given particular impetus by the Thatcher governments of the 1980s and continued in the subsequent era of 'New Labour'. This has entailed a shift from a belief in the possibility, legitimacy and validity of socially progressive re-distributive planning via central state action to one that embraces the market as the main economic steering mechanism. This had definite implications for people in the north east as the state sought to cut back the extent of its direct engagement with economy and society there and, not entirely successfully, to encourage greater mobility in the labour market and encourage entrepreneurial behaviour. This switch also lends a certain political specificity to the experiences of the UK, as neo-liberalism penetrated widely into policy domains – competition, industrial and technology, employment and social – with spatially differentiating results, as well as into those of urban and regional policy. As such, the shift to neo-liberalism radically re-drew the boundaries between state, economy and civil society, at least in part because of fears of a fiscal crisis of the state, to create a UK-specific variant among the 'many national capitalisms' (Schmidt, 2002) of neo-liberal late modernity.

Part of this re-drawing of the boundaries has involved re-defining the geometry of state power, with a decentralisation of responsibility for regional development issues to the regional level within the state. Thus the region became socially constituted as an active subject in seeking to resolve the regional problem, the second issue that I want to consider here. Rather than regional policies designed and administered by the central state, there is now a more complex multi-level system of governance that conjoins EU, national, regional and sub-regional in a more complex geometry. However, these new arrangements devolve greater responsibilities to regional and sub-regional levels for dealing with issues of regional economic development and regeneration. This has been emphasised within the region by the creation of the ONE North East regional development agency, the four sub-regional partnerships to which it devolves most of its budget, and the Local Strategic Partnerships that were established across the region under the leadership of Local Authorities (Liddle and Townsend, 2002).

It is important to emphasise that these are not simply changes imposed externally upon the region. There were social forces within the region arguing in favour of such changes, with local politicians wanting greater decentralisation of power and resources to their authorities and an emergent small but vociferous lobby seeking a regional assembly and much greater regional autonomy. In principle, these three levels are intended to produce a seamless web of 'joined up' socio-economic development and regeneration policies in the region, with a heavy emphasis upon 'cluster' policies in economic development. Practice deviates somewhat from this principle, however – and there is scant recognition that successful 'cluster' policies could engender precisely the forms of lock-in that were previously seen as a diagnostic feature of the regional problem.

The emergent emphasis on regional and sub-regional strategies reflects a perception within neo-liberal policy circles and the UK state as to the need to balance two competing tensions. First, pressures arising from a perception as to the technical impossibility and normative undesirability of planning within the social relations of capitalism, and the uncertainties and unpredictabilities that these unavoidably create. Second, there were socio-political pressures for the state to be seen to be concerned with issues of democratic accountability and socio-spatial inequality. Responsibility for regional issues in north east England, however, has often been devolved to central government appointed QUANGOS (Quasi-Autonomous Non-Governmental Organisations such as Urban Development Corporations). This has generated new forms of 'democratic deficit' as these organisations are politically unaccountable within the region, with evident dangers in undermining the credibility of the case for devolving power as part of a new governmentality through which to address regional development problems (Beynon *et al.*, 1994).

In addition, decentralisation to the regional level has often involved greater reliance on institutions within civil society acting together ('in partnership') with regional, sub-regional and/or local state organisations. The notion of 'partnership' and collaborative working at and between these levels is important, although not all partners have equal power and influence in the partnership. In particular, many partnerships remain dominated or led by parts of the state. Even so, partnership signals a blurring of the boundaries between market, state and civil society as processes of governance partially replace those of government. Allied to this, there has been a discernible tendency towards 'the community' as both subject and object of intra-regional policies to tackle uneven development. This in turn has often been linked to an emphasis upon the 'third sector' or social economy as the route to tackling 'regional problems' and problems of intra-regional regeneration (Amin *et al.*, 2002).

The turn to the third sector signals recognition that state policy attempts to break unwanted forms of lock-in, for example by encouraging greater labour mobility and entrepreneurial activity via establishing new small enterprises in the mainstream economy, have largely been ineffectual. People wish to remain in their places but not to become entrepreneurs in the formal mainstream economy. The growing focus upon the social economy is recognition both of this and the fact that increasingly large swathes of the territory of regions such as north east England now fall outside the decisive circuits of capital. They have been eviscerated by capital flight and effectively abandoned by the state beyond a residual commitment to maintain a minimum level of welfare provision there. However, it is precisely the impoverished condition of such places that militates against the development of a vibrant 'alternative' social economy there, amplified by a more general state suspicion of potentially 'subversive' social economies such as LETS (Local Exchange Trading Systems). Thus the turn to the social economy represents an attempt to reconcile tensions between immanent accumulation and rationality crises on the one hand and legitimation crises on the other as both capital and the national state lose interest in the region as a space for the production of surplus-value. In its turn, however, it creates political tensions at local and regional levels as the developmental limits of the social economy become clear. For example, over much of north east England, the social economy is most notable by its absence, particularly in those areas in which it is needed most (Amin *et al.*, 2002), and where it does develop tends to reproduce the socio-economic inequalities of the mainstream within it (Bowring, 1999).

The third issue that I want to consider also flows directly from this growing marginalisation of the region in the concerns of capital and the national state. This is the emergence of Task Forces as a characteristic policy response of the new neo-liberal governmentality and, more particularly, of the particular politics of 'New Labour' to tackle place and/or industry specific problems of economic decline. There are marked similarities between such Task Forces and the 'project teams' that have come to characterise much of the contemporary economy (Grabher, 2002). Such Task Forces have exploded in number and have become endemic in north east England – though not only there. They have been established as ad hoc bodies intended to deal flexibly and rapidly with specific policy problems, typically associated with the (un)expected decline of a particular industry or sector (including coal mining, clothing, electronics, steel, textiles) and its consequences on the places in which it was formerly concentrated (Pike, 2002).[5] Others seek to arrest or reverse decline – for example the Teesside Chemical Initiative (Chapman, 2003) for reasons that are explicable in terms of sub-regional politics and the difficulties of imagining Teesside without chemical production, rather than a more realistic assessment of the global political economy of chemicals production. The membership of these bodies consists of a mix of private and public sector representatives, typically drawn from a cast of 'usual suspects'. Self-defined key players in the region find new niches in these partnerships from which to exercise power and preserve their own influence (Robinson and Shaw, 2000), often drawn together around notions of partnership and perception of a shared regional interest (as they first were in the 1930s). They can be characterised as non-statutory (that is, non-QUANGO) and multi-agency organisations, with selected and defined membership, with initially an indeterminate but always temporary lifespan. Typically, however, like the earlier QUANGOS they are opaque, unaccountable, closed off to wider political and public scrutiny, with the hand of central government often prominent and with limited links to and co-ordination with the actions of other public policy bodies. Fundamentally, they are designed to mop up and paper over the consequences of economic decline, a combination of sticking plaster and sponge. They symbolise the transition from a concern with planning to one with strategy, understood as developing ad hoc ways of coping with the consequences of unplanned, unexpected and emergent changes in economic circumstances in a region marked by long-term structural economic decline.

## Concluding comments

In this chapter, I have argued that concepts of path contingent and dependent development, instituted behaviour, especially in terms of cognitive and policy lock-in, and governmentality allow a deepened, more nuanced understanding of the changing position of regions such as north east England in/out of processes and circuits of capital accumulation. They thus facilitate a better understanding of processes of regional uneven development. Allied to structural political-economy understandings, they help reveal more subtle perspectives upon the practices of key social actors that recognise the power of structural constraints while revealing more about the determination of regional developmental trajectories within them.

Finally, by way of conclusion, I want to make some brief comments about the broader implications of the approach that I have explored to understanding regional change. While the empirical focus in this paper has been on a single region, the north east of England, this region exists, as it has done for centuries, as part of a global political economy. Other regions have experienced similar trajectories of growth, decline and occasionally renewal. The approach explored here could, therefore, be used as the basis both for analysis of other regions – both other declining 'old industrial regions' and contemporary 'hot spots' of growth – and for inter-regional comparative analysis. Focusing upon the determinants of trajectories of change and the specific institutional forms of different regions could help unravel the reasons as to why regions change in varying ways – some as 'winners', some as 'losers' – within the structural limits of a capitalist political economy. As such, it could help throw light on the key questions as to how and why regions experience different forms and trajectories of change, as to how the fortunes of different regions relate to one another and of how regional change both reflects and helps reproduce those systemic limits. The growing inter-connections between regions within a neo-liberal globalising economy in the twenty first century further reinforce the case for deepening understanding of the co-evolution of regional development trajectories.

## Notes

1 The re-invigorated debate as to how best to conceptualise 'the region' is summarised in Hudson, 2001a, chapter 9, and Hudson, 2003.
2 The steelworks was subsequently sold to SSI, based in Thailand, and remained vulnerable to closure (Hudson and Swanton, 2012). As this book was being completed, in September 2015 SSI announced the 'mothballing' of the plant for up to five years.
3 Both now closed.
4 This raises important and more general questions as to the rights as well as responsibilities of citizens, not least their right to lead decent civilized lives in places that

remain meaningful to them although abandoned by capital and the state as locations of production (see Hudson, 2001a, chapter 8).

5 Task Forces continue to be a policy response to closures. As I was completing work on this book, the latest one was created in response to the recently announced closure of the SSI steelworks on Teesside in September 2015.

# 6 Global production systems and European integration

## De-regionalising, re-regionalising and re-scaling production systems in Europe

### Introduction: globalisation, international investment and global production strategies

As Peter Dicken (2000, 276, emphasis in original) has put it, succinctly summarising a distinctive characteristic of his sophisticated approach to understanding geographies of economies, '*places produce* firms while *firms produce places*'. In this chapter I explore some of the ramifications of this perspective, in terms of inter-relationships between the globalisation of production systems, the political-economic re-definition of Europe, processes of de-regionalisation and re-regionalisation of production linked to changes in corporate (dis)investment strategies, and the changing character of places within Europe.

Whilst the volume of international investment has increased within the latest phase of globalisation – the latest and highest stage of capitalist development – it has displayed a distinctive macro-regional geography: the vast majority originates in North America, Western Europe and Japan while the former two form the main destinations. There is abundant empirical evidence about flows of international investment into and out of Europe, primarily by major multinational and transnational corporations but also by some small and medium-sized enterprises. These flows form constitutive moments in creating global production systems and changing geographies of production within Europe. Whilst European Union (EU)-based multinational corporations and transnational corporations seek investment opportunities in parts of Europe beyond their national territory and further afield outside Europe, major companies based in the USA and Japan in particular have invested within Europe. Whilst the volume of investment flows from Japan and other parts of south east Asia rose sharply in the 1980s and 1990s (Dicken *et al.*, 1997), the stock of foreign direct investment remains heavily dominated by USA-based companies, which have a long history of investment in Europe (Dicken, 1998). Moreover Europe continues to be a key destination for foreign direct investment by USA-based corporations (Deloitte Research, 2001). Furthermore, the balance between 'green field' investment in manufacturing and investment via merger and acquisition (which now accounts for 75 percent of international investment: Nitzan, 2001) has significantly shifted, often linked to unprecedented growth in the number of strategic alliances and other forms of co-operative linkages between major firms.[1]

This complex pattern of flows, mediated through corporate organisational structures, raises important theoretical, political and practical issues, which may be summarised as follows.

- How do the changing geographies of investment and production within Europe relate to processes of Europeanisation and globalisation of production systems and to processes of European political-economic integration and expansion, eastwards in particular?
- How do multinational corporation inward investment activities create new forms of cross-regional and cross-national integration within Europe and link parts of Europe with other parts of the world in global production systems that are both intra-corporate and inter-corporate?
- What forces underlie the (non-)coincidence of corporate and territorial development strategies within Europe, as articulated at EU, national and sub-national scales? How is this expressed in processes of re-regionalisation and de-regionalisation?
- How can territorially defined political subjects (the EU, national states, regions or cities) in Europe 'capture', if only temporarily, particular activities and parts of corporate global value-creation chains?
- Which places capture which activities? To what extent can public policies alter the characteristics of places to make them more attractive to particular sorts of inward investment?

## Re-regionalising and embedding production via new forms of multi-national and transnational investment?

Growing globalisation of the economy can be linked to the transition from multinational corporations to transnational corporations.[2] These changes in corporate form and strategy reflect an on-going search for more effective ways of creating new forms of uneven development and exploiting existing ones in pursuit of competitive advantage and profit.

As Dicken (1998, especially 201–41) has emphasised, transnational corporations and multinational corporations invest for diverse reasons in varied locations, thereby linking them in often complex ways within their intra-corporate but nonetheless global systems of production. These can be summarised under three headings, related to variations in corporate competitive strategy: accessing markets, often protected via tariff barriers, and taking advantage of economies of scale and differentiated consumer markets; lowering production costs via finding low cost locations and/or achieving economies of scale and scope; acquiring knowledge and other assets that allow radical change in techno-organisational production paradigms and in forms of competition, temporarily securing competitive advantages that translate into increasing market share for existing products or a monopoly position in markets for new products. This radically re-defines the forms, dimensions and scope of competition.

Reflecting these three qualitatively different forms of corporate strategy, transnational corporations create linkages and produce economic integration across national and supra-national boundaries in three analytically distinct ways (Dunning, 2000). The first two are asset exploiting.[3] First, horizontal integration, involving the same product (or locally customised versions thereof) being supplied by the same firm in different countries. Second, vertical integration, with different stages of the production process and value creation chain for a given commodity undertaken in different locations within an evolving international division of labour. Much inward investment in manufacturing in Europe involves these forms of integration, driven by asset-exploiting corporate competitive strategies.

While there has been some inward investment by manufacturing firms in activities such as European HQ offices and R&D in core regions, to date it has generally been limited in extent. Such activities typically remain deeply embedded in home countries, with this spatial concentration of R&D in the national base of the innovating firm memorably characterised as 'an important case of non-globalisation' (Pavitt and Patel, 1991). For example, there is a significant difference between the level of R&D investment by indigenous and foreign-owned companies (on average 5.0–7.0 per cent and 2.0–2.5 per cent, respectively). While there are variations within both groups, with several overseas companies investing heavily in R&D, 'these are the exceptions rather than the rule' (John Dodd of the UK Federation of Electronics Industries, quoted in Cane and Nicholson, 2001).

While these exceptions are important in relation to claims about new forms of more 'embedded' factories, most foreign direct investment in manufacturing, both in 'green field' factories and via acquisition of existing plants and companies, has been in routine production activities, either to guarantee access to European markets for key consumer goods (automobiles, 'white goods') and/or to find lower cost production locations, often exporting the resultant output beyond the EU's boundaries. New green field factories have typically been established in peripheral locations, characterised by high unemployment, abundant cheap and often highly skilled manual labour and generous state financial subsidies. In electronics in the UK, for example, 'Most foreign-owned companies are essentially offshore manufacturing sites' (Dodd, quoted in Cane and Nicholson, 2001). In many ways, such plants define the archetypical 'branch plant' economy, with low levels of local sourcing and an absence of advanced R&D. Such branch plants are located both in the peripheries of Europe and at the extremities of global chains of corporate command and control, vulnerable to closure because of decisions taken in distant locations. Moreover, continuing branch plant investment in Europe's peripheries bears a close resemblance to the specification of a 'global outpost', especially in regions within or just beyond but soon to be within the eastern boundaries of the EU (Hudson, 2002).

However, there are claims that radically new forms of branch plant investment began to be made in Europe from the 1980s, in response to the crisis of Taylorist mass production and corporate search for new models of more flexible high volume production (FHVP), combining the benefits of economies of scale and scope. As a consequence of the adoption of 'just-in-time' principles of production, this has often been associated with regional re-concentration of production in particular industries (archetypically automobiles) and 'embedding' in particular places. This is seen as denoting a greater permanence of investment and commitment to place – for example, via investment in R&D – than in the archetypical 'global outpost'. These processes of re-regionalisation and embedding come about because lead manufacturers develop component supply chains in the surrounding region, and secure provision of required 'hard' and 'soft' infrastructures – for example, via state investments in transport, telecommunications and IT networks and developing capacity for training required labour, often in collaboration with state organisations. However, 'just-in-time' is not necessarily equivalent to 'in-one-place'. As a result such new 'embedded' production complexes in Europe are also linked, often over great distances, with other factories both as sources of component inputs and markets for outputs within complex and distanciated globalised production systems.

Rather than regarding 'global outposts' and 'embedded branch plants' as dichotomous alternatives, however, it is useful to conceptualise them as located at opposite ends of a continuum, with particular plants tending more towards one pole or the other in a variety of hybrid forms. These conjoin company and territory in a variety of ways. The specific form depends upon the interplay of corporate strategy and the specific reasons for establishing (or acquiring) a particular plant in a particular time/space and the strategies, powers and competencies of relevant economic development organisations. Drawing on Kindleberger (1969) and his concept of the 'enclave economy', Phelps and MacKinnon (2000) conceptualise such production systems as industrial enclaves, exhibiting more connection to the surrounding region than 'global outposts' but less than the deep and far-reaching intra-regional connections, commitments and integration of 'embedded branch plants'. There is certainly evidence of continuing investment in 'global outposts' but there is also evidence of branch plant investment that approximates more closely to the specifications of 'embeddedness', in factories mandated to perform a wider range of functions than those 'traditionally' associated with 'branch plant' investment. For example Fiat's Melfi plant and the Nissan plant at Sunderland both have several of the attributes associated with 'embedded investment' – for example, intra-regional supply chains and close links with local economic development and training institutions.[4] Many multinational corporation plants in the IT sector in Ireland began as simple assembly operations but subsequently added R&D and product development functions (Brown, 2001). Furthermore, many foreign manufacturing plants incorporate both upstream (R&D) and downstream (sales and marketing) functions, as well as procuring inputs via intra-regional supply chains and linking with local institutions within the state and civil society.

In such instances, therefore, there *may* be evidence of the emergence of regional production complexes, with functional integration between co-located activities within and beyond the boundaries of the firm. Moreover, the growing recognition of the importance of incremental innovation and learning by doing within communities of practice suggests that branch plants within hybrid forms of 'enclave' may become repositories of practical know-how that provide localised competitive advantage (Morgan, 1997) and also a cognitive resource that can be deployed more widely within the firm. However, it is necessary carefully to distinguish between the presence of particular functions in a plant and the ways in which these integrate it into the surrounding regional economy and the (global) corporate production system. Co-location of functions does not *necessarily* equate to the presence of a regionally integrated production system. For example, there may be R&D or marketing activities but with these linked more closely to manufacturing activities in *other* locations. Such branch plant investment approximates more closely to the specifications of hybrid forms of 'enclave' rather than of deep 'embeddedness'. These contested claims about 'embedded' production complexes and the variety of forms of 'enclave' branch plant investment that have emerged raise questions about the ways in which global production systems are becoming 'fixed' in Europe as major corporations both use existing spatial differences and create new forms of spatial differentiation and link locations in complex ways as constitutive and integral elements within their global production strategies.

The first two forms of cross-border integration discussed above result from corporate strategies of asset exploiting weak competition within a given techno-organisational paradigm. The third type of integration results from corporate strategies of asset augmenting Schumpeterian strong competition that seek to re-define production paradigms and possibilities for creating and appropriating surplus-value. It involves seeking to capture 'local' knowledges and enhance R&D capabilities, often via acquiring or accessing assets created abroad to protect or enhance competitive advantage and core competencies. As such, growing emphasis upon asset-augmenting investment is linked to important changes in the form and 'territoriality' of transnational investment. In particular, it is linked in various ways with a tendency towards 're-regionalisation' of production in 'sticky places' (Markusen, 1996) and with corporate strategies that use merger and acquisition to find the locally constituted intellectual assets that such places create and exploit them within globalised production systems. These assets include 'local knowledge', tacit knowledge (firm-specific and place-specific) about production and new 'scientific' knowledge produced within the R&D laboratories of other companies and organisations about new, potentially revolutionary 'market disturbing' products and processes.

While acquisition is often a very cost-effective way of obtaining knowledge about products and processes, companies acquiring others in search of knowledge also acquire material and other assets. They must decide which of the activities of the newly acquired company are relevant to their own core competencies and, conversely, which activities are tangential and which product lines have surplus capacity and either close them down or divest them to others. Divestment, capacity reduction and 'exit' from 'non-core' activities are often key elements in post-acquisition rationalisations and have had marked effects on geographies of production in Europe.

There has also been a growing tendency to enter strategic alliances – on a multiple basis, with the same firm typically involved in several – amongst the major corporations, as they use these to acquire new knowledge, to learn new ways of producing via long-term strategic links with other major companies as well as with smaller and structurally less powerful firms. Such links are said to depend upon trust and 'trust' can undoubtedly offer considerable advantages in reducing time and effort, risk and uncertainty, and facilitating learning via enhancing the quality and quantity of information flows (Morgan, 2001). However, trust also carries costs – for example there are dangers of lock-in. There are definite limits to co-operative behaviour and trust because of the structural constraints that arise from the inherently antagonistic and competitive character of capitalist economic relations (Hudson, 2001a). Consequently, acquiring knowledge and learning in this way poses severe challenges for companies.

Globalised production systems are thus constituted via a complex dialectic of competition and co-operation, distanciation and localization/regionalization. As Dicken *et al.* (1994, 30) rightly emphasise, a key diagnostic feature of the 'newly emerging organisational form' of the 'complex global firm' is an 'integrated network configuration and ... capacity to develop flexible co-ordinating processes, both inside and outside the firm'. Understanding the ways in which places within Europe fit into changing geographies of globalising production systems requires such an analytic point of departure. Equally, the distinctions between asset exploiting and asset augmenting motivations for foreign direct investment are analytic. Actual firms operating in real historical time/space typically deploy them simultaneously, in varying combinations. Understanding changing geographies of economies within Europe requires recognition of this.

## Hollowing out industrial districts and related forms of regionalised production systems

The integration of Europe into global production systems is not, however, simply a consequence of the activities of big companies. Indeed, in other ways it is intimately linked to a transition in what were previously seen as very 'sticky' places in Europe, notably industrial districts such as those of the Third Italy. These have become less cohesive as the socio-economic glue of beliefs and material practices (rather than simply something 'in the air') that previously held them together strongly in place has, to varying degrees, dissolved.

From the early 1980s, the larger or leading firms in quintessential Italian clothing industrial districts such as Carpi and Prato initiated a far-reaching process of selective de-localisation of labour-intensive and unskilled stages of production. Conversely, they increasingly concentrated upon high quality products and those stages of production requiring skilled labour. More importantly, they focused upon design, marketing and brand development, as well as key HQ strategic functions, activities less sensitive to labour costs. Such de-localisation tendencies also reflected growing resistance by women, children and marginalised workers to 'super-exploitation', in strong contrast to the dominant image of these districts as characterised by egalitarian, progressive industrial relations (Hadjimichalis and Papamichos, 1990). Similar processes of 'hollowing out' production to surrounding localities with abundant cheap labour occurred elsewhere in southern Europe.[5] For example, in the 1980s there was a re-location of production to areas around the town of Kastoria in north west Greece, the one authentic industrial district in Greece, producing expensive clothing from imported fur (Hadjimichalis, 1998).

The 'hollowing out' of industrial districts can be a complex process, involving re-locating production beyond the national territory, as the example of Benetton illustrates. Benetton emerged as a major clothing company because of a complex combination of marketing, organisational and process innovations. This encompassed creating a new global product image, a refined just-in-time production system incorporating both out-sourcing and process innovation,[6] and a risk-minimising strategy of franchised outlets in over a hundred countries, while retaining key control, design and marketing functions in Treviso, northern Italy (Crewe and Lowe, 1996). Benetton was initially seen as an anomaly, a rare exception. But increasingly other districts unravelled in similar ways. The boundaries of clothing industrial districts became more permeable because of the emergence of powerful 'lead' firms or *gruppi*, a result of organic growth or, more often, of merger and acquisition activity among local firms, and the entry of externally owned larger firms that came to play dominant roles and shape local growth and development trajectories (Whitford, 2001). This created more complex structures of ownership and changed relationships between firms. Previously egalitarian horizontal relations have become much more hierarchical and asymmetric, radically re-shaping the anatomy of power relations between firms sharing the same location. In addition, lead firms established relationships with suppliers and sub-contractors beyond the boundaries of the district, and fractured the former territorially bounded coherence and integrity of the production system within the district. Consequently, there has been a growing tendency to re-cast these places as nodes in wider European or global corporate production systems.

In addition, however, such changes were also a consequence of developments beyond the boundaries of the districts. These changes enabled shifts in corporate behaviour, and indeed were necessary conditions for them. In particular, they were a result of the removal of previous constraints because of broader geo-political changes in Europe. The opening up of the formerly forbidden territories of central and eastern Europe to capitalist investment has been especially important in this regard. Two examples illustrate the point. Herning-Ikast in Jutland developed as a sophisticated industrial district, based on production of high value added woollen clothing (Maskell *et al.*, 1998). During the 1990s, however, production tasks, especially the most labour intensive ones, were sub-contracted to firms in Poland while the key decision making, marketing and design functions remained in Herning-Ikast. Around the same time, in the metal working industrial district around Brescia in northern Italy, basic steelmaking activities were increasingly sub-contracted to firms in Bulgaria and Rumania while keeping key design, marketing and decision making functions in and around Brescia. In both cases, there was a 'hollowing out' of the production structure of the industrial district in response to newly available locational opportunities, driven by increasingly fierce pressure on global product markets. In this way indigenous European small and medium-sized enterprises became enmeshed in evolving global production systems. In addition other small firms in many parts of Europe have become tied into global systems via the growth of sub-contracting and new forms of collaborative inter-firm relations. It is, however, important to emphasise that collaboration in this context does not mean equality of power between partners in such agreements. As a result, many small firms in Europe came to occupy vulnerable and precarious market niches within global production structures rather than within local or national markets, often subject to fierce price competition from locations outside Europe.[7]

However, there are also counter-tendencies that involve re-concentration of production in these same industries in other parts of Europe. While long-established industrial districts were being hollowed out and re-organised, new clothing clusters were emerging elsewhere. In central and eastern Europe, political change provided opportunities for a degree of re-regionalisation of clothing production as new clusters evolved, incorporating innovative forms of inter-firm relations, linked into local 'lead' production firms and in turn into export markets in Western Europe. Major European retailers have sought to supply from within Europe rather than lower cost non- European locations, linked to moves to smaller batch production and the need for rapid response to market changes (Crewe and Lowe, 1996). They are re-organising supply chains, often involving sourcing from locations in central and eastern Europe, in which labour is more expensive than in – say – India – but much less expensive than in Western Europe while transport times and communication problems are much less between Eastern and Western Europe than between Western Europe and distant parts of Asia (Dunford *et al.*, 2001). Similar processes were evident in parts of southern Europe, but focusing more upon specialised niche production. For example, in the rural areas of the Ave Valley in northern Portugal, clusters of clothing producers increasingly focused upon small batch production, manufacturing products for which the main modality of competition is quality rather than price (Thiel *et al.*, 2000).

Companies located in other forms of regionalised production systems within Europe are also increasingly seeking to 'hollow out' routine production activities in response to growing competitive pressures. One such region is Baden Württemberg in Germany. Although often classified as an industrial district (for example, see Scott, 1988), there are significant differences in industrial culture and structure that differentiate it sharply from the canonical industrial districts discussed above. In particular, in Baden Württemberg a hierarchically organised production system evolved around large 'lead' firms (some indigenous German, others inward investing multinational corporations) and very large factories (for example, the Singelfingen automobile factory of Daimler Benz employed over 40,000 people as recently as the early 1990s) at the centre of regionalised supply structures involving multiple sourcing within the region. These component supply companies were themselves often substantial. Some, such as Robert Bosch, are major multinational corporations. Even medium-sized component suppliers would typically have anything up to 2,000 employees in their factories. Increasingly, however, this regionalised production structure has become uncompetitive, rigid and inflexible. As a result Daimler-Benz, Audi, Robert Bosch, IBM, Hewlett Packard, SONY – all large multinational corporations based in Baden-Württemberg –

> have in fact begun engaging in [the] process of killing off the old regional division of labour that they were embedded in. This has involved a sharp winnowing of the number of suppliers that firms engage with not simply in general but also within the region itself.

Collaborative production in automobiles or electronics blurs the boundaries between firms but it also involves significantly fewer firm boundaries: 'multiple sourcing has been replaced with long-term contracting with smaller numbers of intimate firms. These firms can be local firms, *but they need not be*' (Herrigel, 2000, 296, emphasis in original). Consistent with this process of hollowing out and de-regionalisation, the large firms have shown a willingness to invite in foreign expert collaborative suppliers, such as the Canadian firm Magna, to establish green field operations in the region. Furthermore, expert collaborator firms can be accessed from their locations elsewhere in Germany and in Europe (including central and eastern Europe), without requiring relocation into Baden-Württemberg. Thus 're-regionalisation occurs but it does not have to occur within the old geographic boundaries of the traditional district' (Herrigel, 2000, 297).

In summary, there are increasing tendencies to 'hollow out' the production structures of regions that until recently were regarded as archetypical examples of regionalised production systems within Europe. Responding to growing competitive pressures and taking advantage of opportunities offered by technological and geo-political changes, established or emergent 'lead' firms in these regions are re-organising the socio-spatial structures of production systems, decentralising much of the materials transformation stages of production to other locations. As a result, the home regions of these lead firms are increasingly becoming systems integrators, sites of key decision making, design and marketing within wider, spatially dispersed production systems that link a variety of other firms and places. At the same time, the re-organisation of production may lead to a re-scaling of production, with the emergence of new clusters of firms in other locations, a process of re-regionalisation and possibly re-scaling of production as changes in corporate strategy create new scales of spatial organisation.

## Political-economic integration in Europe and the widening and deepening of the European Union

The creation of a common economic space over Europe forms one moment in a more general process of global macro-regionalisation, with the creation of free-trade areas in other parts of the world (such as NAFTA and MERCUSOR). Processes of political integration have produced a still evolving multi-scalar system of governance and regulation in Europe, especially the EU. The 're-organisation' of the state involves a triple process of de-nationalisation (hollowing out), de-statisation of the political system and the internationalisation of policy régimes (Jessop, 1997). De-statisation is important in changing the balance between the institutions of civil society and the state in governance but is not as relevant here as de-nationalisation and internationalisation of policy regimes. Furthermore there is growing complexity and, in some respects, new forms of uneven development in EU-level policy regimes. The deepening of the EU, notably via the Single European Market programme and the creation of the Euro single currency, has created important divisions between those national states that are members of Euro-land and those that are not, both within and outside the boundaries of the EU. These processes of re-organisation are changing the relations and balance of power between different levels of the state within the EU. At the same time, especially following the collapse of state socialism in central and eastern Europe and the subsequent initiation of processes of political and economic transformation there, the on-going process of European Union enlargement is adding to this complexity.[8]

While power, authority and competencies have to a degree been shifted 'up' from national to EU level, there have also been pressures to move decision making power and resources to sub-national levels of cities and regions, increasing the role of specifically regional and urban institutions in governance and regulation. However, there are also counter-tendencies that re-emphasise the significance of the national. Consequently, although the process of unbundling territoriality has gone further in the EU than elsewhere (Ruggie, 1993), national states in Europe are neither dying nor retiring – they have merely shifted functions (Mann, 1993). The claim of 'neo-medievalists' that the national state is largely rendered redundant in Europe is unfounded and reports of 'the exaggerated death of the nation-state' are premature (Anderson, 1995). Instead, national states are taking on different roles within complex multi-scalar structures of regulation and governance. There are complex links between this emerging multi-scalar political system and processes of economic internationalisation, both Europeanisation and globalisation. The latter are re-shaping the economic structure and geography of Europe while political subjects are seeking to influence international investment flows, both inward investment to and outward investment from the EU and its constituent national territories.

As an embryonic emergent 'super-state', the EU both encourages and seeks to resist processes of globalisation. The EU has long sought to encourage the formation of 'Euro-champions', European multinational corporations that can compete in global markets with those of the USA and Japan in particular. In part it has done so via pursuing strategic industrial policies that seek to shape market conditions confronting all firms in a sector, promoting inter-firm co-operation in order to ensure competitive success. For example, research and innovation initiatives such as ESPRIT aimed to encourage inter-firm collaboration in high tech industries over pre-competitive technological innovation. The EU has also encouraged the emergence of Euro-champions via its permissive and non-interventionist attitude towards acquisitions of EU companies by other EU companies and to intra-EU mergers.[9] Even so, it has had limited success in encouraging and facilitating successful cross-border mergers and acquisitions within Europe. In part, this is precisely because of the enduring significance of national differences in industrial cultures and attitudes towards such activity. Some cultures of capitalism encourage mergers and acquisitions (notably the Anglo-American model) while others are, or until recently have been, less receptive to such corporate behaviour, especially in cases in which this involves unwelcome 'hostile' acquisitions (the German and Swedish models, for example).

Moreover, while the European Union Commission encouraged the emergence of Euro-champions, many national governments have aimed to create 'national champions' to protect national interests in strategically significant industries, such as those in areas of emergent new technologies and defence (for example, the French and Italian governments).[10] However, the European Union Commission has actively sought to discourage or prevent mergers and acquisitions intended to create national champions (Guerrera, 2001).[11] This, as with the inability to agree regulations for cross-border mergers and acquisitions, is indicative of a continuing struggle between national states and the Commission over the architecture of multi-level governance within the EU territory and as to where regulatory authority and competence should reside in Europe. It is also a struggle over the preferred corporate anatomy of the EU. One, perhaps unintended, consequence of these varying political priorities and strategies towards mergers and acquisitions has been to enhance the role of inward investment from outside the EU in such activity. As a result, it has enhanced the significance of multinational corporations based outside the EU in shaping economic development trajectories within Europe. Consequently, while the Single European Market led to a surge in merger and acquisition activity within the EU in the 1980s and early 1990s, this mainly involved inward investment by multinational corporations based outside the EU. As a result, the EU has sought to influence the intra-EU geography of international inward investment via both its own industrial and regional policies and regulation of national industry and regional aids, including setting limits to national aids and limiting the extent of competitive bidding between countries and regions for major projects.

As noted above, national governments remain important actors in processes of economic governance and regulation, including the attraction of foreign direct investment from abroad. Virtually every European country has considered foreign direct investment to be sufficiently significant to warrant a set of specific policies and organisations focused on its attraction. Furthermore, there has been a growing sophistication in policy design and delivery at national level. However, national states in Europe vary in the extent to which they wish to embrace processes of international competition and global markets as economic steering mechanisms and seek to attract foreign direct investment. This can be related to the well-known persistence of national distinctiveness in forms of capitalism within Europe (Hudson and Williams, 1999). Broadly speaking, national states can be divided into three groups in terms of their attraction of foreign direct investment (Brown and Raines, 2000, 436–40). First, there are those with long-standing policies to maximise the attraction of foreign direct investment (the UK and Ireland). Second, there are those that have a continuing mis-trust of inward investment because of fears of losing national control of key economic sectors, or of indigenous firms losing out in competition with inward investors (Germany, Italy). Third, countries that were formerly hostile to foreign direct investment but which are becoming, or have become, much more favourably disposed towards it (France, and the countries of the Mediterranean and Scandinavia and, above all, after 1989, those of central and eastern Europe). However, while national variation and specificity remain, there is increasing convergence on a broadly neo-liberal Anglo-American model that encourages privatisation of sectors of the economy previously reserved for the state and public sector and creates space for international inward investment in this and other ways. This convergence is a consequence of the process of deepening economic integration in the EU and one that is increasingly driven by concerns with shareholder value rather than equity between the various social partners and stakeholders as a consequence of the effects of globalisation on financial markets.

At sub-national levels, cities and regions in Europe have engaged in an increasingly generalised place-marketing competition for foreign direct investment from other countries within and beyond the EU, especially the USA and Japan. Indeed, attraction of foreign direct investment has increasingly been devolved to local and regional levels as an integral part of the process of developing more sophisticated and sensitive national policies. Local and regional authorities within Europe have sought to construct their economic development strategies around varying types of foreign direct investment, depending upon their location and the characteristics of their areas. Choice of strategy often reflects the character and location of the place, linked to an evolving spatial division of labour within Europe that is increasingly differentiating qualitatively between places in terms of their location in circuits of value creation, appropriation and realisation (Hudson, 2001b). The key issue is what sorts of activities can be attracted to and – for a time – held down in what sorts of places? For example, within the United Kingdom it was feasible to seek to re-develop the London Docklands around international investment in high order financial and business services. In contrast, in peripheral places within Europe the focus of regeneration policies has been manufacturing branch plants (preferably embedded performance plants at the heart of new clusters rather than Taylorised global outposts, but if the latter are all that are on offer, welcoming them nonetheless), or the Taylorised 'back office' service activities of financial and business services. However, both the quantitative and qualitative employment creation effects of such investments in peripheral regions are very limited (Hudson, 1999; 2002), not least because the prevailing high levels of unemployment in these regions enable companies to be extremely selective in their recruitment policies.

The institutional character and performance of places, their 'soft' as well as their 'hard' infrastructures, has been increasing emphasised in both the academic and policy literatures about relations between foreign direct investment and regional economic performance. This has been linked with growing concerns to use inward investment to stimulate new 'clusters' and in this way re-regionalise production and revivify regional economies. Consequently, the form and content of local and regional development policies appropriate to first attract and capture, then – as the flows of foreign direct investment into the EU and applicant states in central and eastern Europe have declined – retain and nurture inward investment projects via 'after-care' policies has increasingly come under scrutiny. Indeed, the emphasis upon 'after-care' may lead to local and regional development organisations being 'captured' by inward investing multinational corporations, which can exert considerable influence over their actions and policies (Phelps *et al.*, 1998). In such cases the balance of corporate and territorial developmental interests tilts sharply in the direction of the former to the detriment of the latter.

## Conclusions

Geographies of economies within Europe have undoubtedly changed – and continue to change – in important ways, with simultaneous tendencies towards de-regionalisation and re-regionalisation of production, often at new spatial scales. These changes reflect the ways in which political actors seek to capture corporate investments and companies seek to use locations within Europe as part of their evolving strategies to develop more globalised production systems. This involves inward investment to and outward investment from Europe, as well as the creation of a variety of inter-firm linkages ranging from out-sourcing strategies to the creation of long-term strategic alliances. Increasingly these wider linkages are driven by the need to acquire knowledge and a variety of intangible assets and create complex ecologies of learning to enable companies to do so rather than merely to access lower cost production sites or to penetrate major markets. Consequently, there has been a switch in emphasis to asset augmentation in corporate strategies, although asset exploitation remains a major influence shaping many corporate geographies of production.

These changes in forms of material and knowledge production, and the resultant re-definition of intra-European geographies of production, are also connected in significant ways to the evolution of the EU. This is the case both in terms of its expansion to incorporate further parts of Europe (and arguably areas beyond Europe as conventionally understood) and in deepening processes of political-economic integration within this expanded space. As yet, deepening integration has not led to convergence in national economic structures or to increasing regional specialisation (Geroski and Gugler, 2001). However, these processes are still in their early stages and a corollary of their maturation could well be the creation of new forms of uneven development as places are increasingly qualitatively differentiated in terms of their position in wider European and global production systems. As a result, in some places there would be growing convergence between corporate and territorial development interests but in many others there would be growing divergence between these two sets of interests. Consequently, there may well be the simultaneous creation of virtuous circles of development for some places but vicious cycles of decline for others as the contours of the map of economic well-being in Europe become increasingly sharply delineated. The resultant widening of the map of inequality could have potential explosive implications for social cohesion within Europe. This in turn may create major political uncertainties as to the place that many parts of Europe can occupy within globalising production systems as the cycle of uneven development is reproduced in increasingly sharp form.[12] Understanding these processes of combined and uneven corporate and territorial development, as the emergence of global production systems runs up against the necessary territoriality of production, poses theoretical challenges for economic geographers.

## Notes

1 A considerable amount of inward foreign direct investment into the EU has been in service sector activities such as banks and financial services, with distinctive intra-EU geographies, different to those of investment in manufacturing (Dicken *et al.*, 1997: Hudson, 1999). However, in this chapter, because of constraints of space, I focus upon the globalisation of material production and manufacturing while recognising that the increasingly complex social division of labour and the growth of networks and of out-sourcing is rendering redundant the conventional statistical distinction between 'manufacturing' and 'services' (Hudson, 2001a). Indeed, much foreign direct investment 'service' investment within the EU has been by 'manufacturing' companies – for example in distribution functions.

2 Although there are very few genuinely transnational corporations, many exhibit some tendencies towards transnationalisation (Allen and Thompson, 1997). It may be more accurate to refer to a transition from multinational to transnational strategies within corporations of varying sizes.

3 The third type of strategy, asset augmenting, is discussed below.

4 However, following the strategic alliance between Nissan and Renault in 1999, there have been important changes that have loosened the degree of regional embedding of the Nissan plant – for example, purchasing decisions have been removed from plant level and centralised in Paris (Hudson, 2002).

5 While there are many concentrations – or clusters – of small firms specialising in specific products in southern Europe (Garofoli, 2002), most of these are not organised around the social relations of production that characterise industrial districts.

6 In 1972 Benetton introduced in-house dyeing at the final stage of production, crucially allowing piece (rather than batch) dyeing and so the dyeing of individual items to order.

7 Often the location of these firms in wider production structures has been decisively shaped by trade policies. For example, the Outward Processing Trade (OPT) regime established as part of the Multi-Fibre Arrangement (introduced in 1974 under the aegis of GATT) was critical in shaping sub-contracting relationships between small clothing producers in southern, central and eastern Europe and major clothing retailers in western Europe.

8 A corollary of this is an active debate as to where the boundaries of Europe are to be drawn, who is to be permitted to move across these boundaries, and who is to be defined as 'European' (Hudson, 2000b).

9 Since EU regulators began to scrutinise merger and acquisition proposals in 1990, only 16 have been blocked (Guerrera and Mallet, 2001).

10 One consequence of this is that the EU has been unable to establish agreed rules for cross-border mergers and acquisitions. Opposition of some national governments, especially Germany, has impeded moves towards the creation of European champions (Mann, 2001).

11 The Commission effectively seeks to force companies in national markets with highly concentrated sectors to acquire or merge elsewhere in Europe and create Euro-champions that conform to its normative vision of the corporate anatomy of the EU.

12 This was written a decade before the emergence of the deep crisis in Greece, and potentially other parts of southern Europe, in the aftermath of the global financial crisis in 2007/8.

# 7 Life on the edge

## Navigating the competitive tensions between the 'social' and the 'economic' in the social economy and in its relations to the mainstream

### Introduction: complex economies and concepts of economy beyond the mainstream

I begin with a seeming paradox: at a time of increasing emphasis on the certainties of the Reagan/Thatcher era as to the merits of a 'one size fits all' neo-liberal policy model and conception of the economy, there was in parallel a growing interest in the diversity of forms of capitalist economies, in different forms of capitalism, different ways of constituting capitalist social relations, different ways of combining capitalist and non-capitalist class relations, class and non-class relations and so on. Although in the last analysis these heterodox economies always remain decisively capitalist, there has been a growing acknowledgement of the plurality of competing forms in which capitalist economies can be conceived and constructed. There is a great variety of literatures that in various ways acknowledge this – institutional political economy, the 'varieties of capitalism' literatures, cultural political economy and so on (for example Chapter 2; Peck and Theodore, 2007).

The reasons for this growth of interest in diversity and variety of forms of capitalism are complicated but there is no doubt that, in part at least, they reflect a recognition that free-market capitalism, celebrating individualism, consumerism and excessive insatiable acquisitiveness, not only creates a yawning gap between the rich and poor but it also threatens ecological sustainability and human well-being, greatly increasing the risks to both economy and environment and indeed human life on the planet as we know it. The displacement of Keynesian demand management and welfarism and the rise of neo-liberalism involved a re-definition of relationships among economy, society and state. However, the growing interest in other ways of organising and regulating capitalist economies clearly indicated that this was only one of many possible models of capitalism.[1] Thus a corollary of this recognition of variety is renewed interest in the regulatory role of the state and in alternative ways of governing and organising capitalist economies – or even tentatively exploring the implications of non-capitalist alternatives – in seeking different ways of reconciling economic imperatives with concerns as to environmental and social justice. Nonetheless, while neo-liberal conceptions have to a degree been selectively modified in practice in response to these various critiques and alternative views, they remain dominant in economic policy and to pretend otherwise would be dangerously misleading but it would be equally misleading to deny the variety that does exist.

Capitalist economies and the accumulation process that is central to them are predicated upon the dominance of a narrow and very specific concept of value, with the exchange value of commodities taking precedence over their use values. In terms of day-to-day economic practices, what therefore matters is the price of commodities and 'fictitious' commodities such as labour-power. This immediately raises questions as to how to value those things that cannot be priced and whether the price attached to those things that can be priced properly reflects their ecological consequences and social value – an issue of central significance to those concerned with the social economy. It also raises questions about the relationship between 'the economic' and the 'social'.[2] Put another way, raising questions such as these recognises that a lot of 'economic' activity beyond the mainstream is informed and motivated by a diversity of values and ethical and moral concerns – but also that to a degree the reproduction of the mainstream depends on this being so and on the provision of certain things not being wholly commodified, not least labour that can be purchased as labour-power as and when needed by capital. In this sense the approach to the social economy advocated here, considering the developmental links between the mainstream and social economies, resonates with more general dynamic and relational approaches in contemporary economic geography (for example, see Yeung, 2005). This raises intriguing and important questions as to the extent to which, and ways in which, the existence of a 'social economy' may be actually functional for mainstream capital accumulation rather than posing a radical challenge to it.

## Creating a space for the social economy

It is important to recognise that the idea of the social economy is not new; it can be traced back to the nineteenth century. As poverty was then seen as natural and inevitable, the social economy was seen as a remedy for pauperism, understood as a state of moral turpitude. The social economy was driven by a set of moralising norms and philanthropic institutions for the 'undeserving' poor (Rose, 1998). In part this involved them engaging in self-help (Procacci, 1978). In a way that is echoed in much contemporary public policy discourse around the social economy that envisions this as tackling social exclusion via engaging with the socially excluded to provide goods and services for themselves and others like them, this economy was then seen as encapsulating a unity of labour and (moral) well-being for the poor. The re-discovery of the social economy within policy discourse as an object of regulation and governmental action (in a Foucauldian sense) can be seen as intimately connected with strategies to restructure the state and reduce the extent and re-define the content of its engagement with economy and society.

As well as this revised policy interest, however, the renewed interest in the social economy and varied forms of social economy organisations must also be situated in the theoretical context of recognition of complex and diverse capitalist economies. For one result of this revived interest in the diversity of capitalisms has been to create a space – theoretical, practical and political – for a (re)emergent interest in the social economy, broadly understood. The recognition of a variety of forms of capitalism has created differing opportunities for the development of a social economy and for varying forms of social economy organisations to emerge and evolve and so helped define the substantive meaning of the social economy in specific times and places (Amin *et al.*, 2002). Recognising the heterogeneity of the social economy, the diversity of organisational forms and of the specific concerns and values that motivate them, there is nonetheless one common shared distinguishing characteristic of *all* social economy organisations: that is, that they are not concerned with making a profit for distribution to individual capitalists and/or private shareholders of capital but with providing, directly or indirectly, socially useful goods and services, often explicitly in environmentally sustainable ways, that would not otherwise be provided through the mainstream channels of markets or state.[3] As such these organisations seek to create a space for humane, co-operative and sustainable forms of social and economic organisation that are 'alternative' to the markets of the mainstream economy and/or the mechanisms of the state as ways of producing and distributing goods and services.[4]

There is a wide range of forms of social economy organisations – from large near market social enterprises (that seek to produce a surplus for social uses) to co-operatives to social economy organisations that rely heavily on direct funding from the state or state contracts to small charitable organisations that rely wholly on voluntary labour (although volunteering is widespread to varying extents among almost all forms of social economy organisation and in that sense they can be thought of as forming part of a gift economy). These varying forms of social economy organisation have followed diverse and multiple developmental trajectories. Reflecting different concepts of value and processes of valuation to those of the capitalist mainstream, such not-for-profit ventures are established to supply services and goods to those abandoned by mainstream enterprises or by the welfare state. As such, they are seen to play a largely social role, helping to meet social needs, empower the marginalised or unemployed, form an Intermediate Labour Market bridge to help such people reintegrate into the formal economy, and sustain alternative lifestyles and systems of survival, of 'getting by' in difficult times and places. Many are content to continue in this mode.

Increasingly, however, there is an interest in some social economy organisations in exploring different ways of creating jobs and wealth generation and assuming a more explicitly economic role, seeking to become more market oriented, to become social *enterprises*, to trade their way to development and expansion. Such social enterprises have increasingly been seen as a legitimate form of economic entity by some social scientists, policy makers and practitioners. Numerous governments and other policy makers have begun to introduce legislative changes to recognise and support social enterprises, policy interventions to encourage their formation and growth, and discursive arguments placing the emphasis on individual responsibility, enterprise and economic achievements. Indeed, for some within the social economy, this risks compromising or concealing the raison d'être of social enterprises (and even more so the work of the broader spectrum of social economy organisations) in meeting otherwise unmet social needs.

In the rest of this chapter, I first further explore the motivations that lie behind the formation of social economy organisations and the multiple trajectories that these can then follow and the tensions to which this can give rise as the 'social' runs up against the 'economic'. This can, and often does, involve competition among these organisations in limited local markets and in search of state grant income. For those that seek to transcend these limits, the tensions between the 'economic' and the 'social' can become manifest and at times acute, especially as social economy organisations seek to become self-consciously social *enterprises*, with a growing focus upon their economic role and contribution and trading as the route to growth. This typically leads them into competition with firms in the mainstream capitalist economy, engendering tensions between the need to survive in competitive markets and the ethical and social motivations that informed their original formation. There is a varying tension between 'the social' and 'the economic' in all social economy organisations, but this is especially evident in those constituted as, or that seek to transform themselves into, near-market social enterprises. Exploring how in practice this tension is dealt with and managed, how the ethical and moral issues that this tension gives rise to are handled, is a major theme of the chapter. I then return to broader questions as to imaginaries about the social economy and its role, of how these conceive of the 'economic' and the 'social' and relations between them, of how the social economy is seen in the policy and academic literatures in terms of its socio-economic role, in light of the evidence as to how social economy organisations in practice handle the tensions between the 'economic' and the 'social'. Finally I offer some reflective comments as to the future for social economy organisations and the social economy and their contribution to social and economic life.

## Managing the tensions between 'the social' and 'the economic' in social economy organisations: some evidence from the UK

This chapter draws upon evidence collected in four large-scale collaborative research projects carried out between 1997 and 2007 into the practices and experiences of social economy organisations in the UK and the EU, using a variety of sources of primary and secondary evidence (for fuller accounts of the evidence base, see Amin *et al.*, 2002; Bennett *et al.*, 2000). These projects provide the basis for a considered and evidence-based account and assessment of the strengths, weaknesses and future potential of the social economy in these locations.

One way to approach the varying tensions between 'social' and 'economic' is in terms of the life course and trajectory of social economy organisations; something of an ideal-typical sequence but one that is useful in illustrating the shifting tensions between 'social' and 'economic', especially for those organisations that seek to become social enterprises. Given the differences that exist at the national scale in the ways in which the social economy is constituted (for example as a result of differing national regulatory regimes), it is important to recognise that the revival of interest in the social economy in the UK came in the context of an enthusiastic adoption of neo-liberal economic policies by national governments, Conservative and Labour alike. As such it has to be seen in terms of a selective restructuring of the state that cut across party political lines, tightening the boundaries of state involvement with economy and society. In other national states the social economy developed in markedly different contexts and ways.

## Origins: ethical and social concerns and 'doing social good'

While there is considerable emphasis in the literature (both academic and policy) on the activities of serial social entrepreneurs – and in specific circumstances they can be an important influence (for example, see Bennett *et al.*, 2000) – there is less in the way of empirical evidence to back up such generalised claims. In fact, the origins of social economy organisations more typically lie in the good intentions of a small number of altruistic individuals, motivated by ethical and/or social concerns, voluntarily giving their labour freely or working in poorly remunerated jobs, at much less than the wage rates that they could command in the formal mainstream economy. They are not primarily motivated by monetary concerns but work in this way because it provides a range of non-monetary satisfactions (Borzaga, 2008; Haugh, 2008). They do so in order to provide goods and services to disadvantaged people in disadvantaged places and to provide Intermediate Labour Market organisations to help the long-term unemployed back into the world of work and onwards into the mainstream labour market of the formal economy.

The origins of social economy organisations in ethical and social concerns with meeting otherwise unmet needs are grounded in a recognition that there are possibilities to do things and things that need to be done, socially, that aren't done precisely because they don't fall within the logic of the mainstream – in short, they aren't sufficiently profitable to attract the private sector, nor politically strategic enough to warrant direct state provision, especially in an era dominated by neo-liberal political-economic concerns. Social economy organisations typically seek to address issues to do with the environment, sustainability, recycling materials and reducing wastes, care for the elderly, training for the young and not-so-young, tackling social exclusion and so on. Often such initiatives are found in places that have been ravaged by the restructuring of capital and that remain unattractive to the mainstream economy, situated beyond the reach of major circuits of capital, but are by no means limited to them.

The reasons given for forming social economy organisations are typically a fusion of individual beliefs, values and motives and the specificities of place and institutional context. For instance, Five Lamps in Stockton-on-Tees, an area of north east England with serious problems of multiple deprivation, began because (Five Lamps, 2007):

> In the late 1980's a handful of people chose to do something about the rising problem of unemployment in this area. Many have followed in their footsteps as volunteers and workers, seeking to tackle the issues that are destroying the quality of life for whole communities. The vision of those pioneers means that the Five Lamps can celebrate two decades of 'making people matter'. Countless lives have been changed for the better. All because some people were willing to stand up and take action.

Another example of this theme of 'making people matter' and 'standing up and taking action' is provided by a social economy organisation in a deprived area of Salford, Manchester, which emerged in response to a perceived need for better health care to enhance the health and well-being of local residents and a desire to devolve power to local citizens. In the words of its director:

> We know ... that health care tends to be provided much more efficiently and effectively the wealthier and better social status that you have, so if you really want to deal with health inequalities you actually have to put more resources into areas of greatest deprivation, even in proportion to need ... What I am more bothered about is what difference do we make to people's lives ... and in order to do that we have to do it differently.

This ideal of 'standing up and taking action', 'doing it differently' and 'doing different things', informed by powerful ethical and moral imperatives and principled concerns to improve the lot of the disadvantaged, 'make a difference' and 'make people matter', lies at the heart of the foundation of a great many social economy organisations and constitutes one of their key distinctive defining characteristics.

## The next steps – more of the same

For many social economy organisations it is enough to continue in this mode of operation, maybe growing a little but with no ambition to transcend the limitations that working in this way unavoidably bring. Indeed these are not seen as limitations but rather as affirmation of the ethical and moral importance of providing goods and services that otherwise would not be provided to those that need them most. There are however a couple of points worth noting here. First, there are limited options in terms of the sorts of goods and services that can be provided in this way, typically in relation to meeting local needs in a small area, on the basis of largely voluntary labour with maybe a small number of paid staff. As a result there is a tendency towards serial repetition of social economy organisations, all informed by similar ethical and social concerns and seeking to survive if not prosper by providing the same sorts of goods and services and a sort of competition among them within the social economy. In South Wales, for example, there is a cluster of social economy projects in the valleys of the former coalfield, most of which have established some form of community enterprise and social economy organisations using national (both UK Government and the Welsh Assembly) and EU funds. The range of activities among them is quite narrow, consisting for the most part of semi-industrial potteries, carpentry workshops, furniture exchanges, catering, garden centres and landscaping services. All of these activities are conducted on a very small scale, reflecting their primary objective of providing jobs and services within the immediate neighbourhood. Whilst some of these social economy organisations are successful in meeting their own goals, their capacity for expansion or diversification is limited. They saturate the local market with similar products, and local labour markets can only absorb so many people being trained in the same skills which are often unrelated to the demands of the mainstream formal economy. The same limited range of activities serve the same set of local needs and chase the same limited local disposable income. The restriction on spending power further limits the possibilities of diversifying into 'new' products and services. Despite exhortations on the part of social economy umbrella organisations that locally focused social economy organisations should seek to break out of their immediate local areas, very little has been done in practice to overcome the inherent limitations of the activities pursued (West, 1999).

Acceptance of these limitations has a number of consequences, however. First, those social economy organisations offering poorer quality products and services, in a context of restricted demand for them and competition from others offering better quality goods and services, tend to fail or struggle to survive. Such weaker organisations typically have been born out of a response to a highly localised problem, without analysis of the potential for sustained demand for the goods and services they provide. In these circumstances their capacity to meet their social objectives is eroded by the economics of markets within the social economy and their demise as social economy organisations. Second, insofar as social economy organisations operate as Intermediate Labour Market organisations, there is a limited range of skills that they can impart and these too can be over-produced, swamping local labour markets with people chasing the same limited set of opportunities.

The uneven development of social economy organisations within the social economy can have perverse effects in further widening inequalities. Many places, especially areas of marked social exclusion and deprivation (as are clearly shown in England by data from successive Indices of Multiple Deprivation, for example), are often those bereft of the sorts of local capacities, resources and requisite skills that can facilitate the emergence of successful social economy organisations and sustain a vibrant social economy. As well as potentially important implications for theorising uneven development and its relationship to different forms of social relationships, this also has important policy and practical implications. Contrary to optimistic communitarian and policy perspectives that see the social economy as a way of tackling inequality and uneven development, insofar as a fledgling social economy emerges in such places, it comprises either highly precarious and short-lived social economy organisations that fail to meet local needs or social economy organisations reliant upon public sector leadership, peripatetic professionals and social entrepreneurs, or dedicated organisations such as religious or minority ethnic bodies. Rather than alleviate inequality and uneven development, the social economy may perpetuate it in new ways.

Insofar as such social economy organisations, especially those in multiply disadvantaged places, require funding to remain economically viable in order to meet their ethical and social objectives, this tends to come from the state – either directly in the form of grants or indirectly in the form of (sub-) contracts. Typically there is a heavy reliance upon public subsidy or public sector sub-contracts to provide markets. The majority of social economy organisations (even well-known 'success stories') rely heavily on grant income and/or service level contracts with public authorities. The alternative that the social economy offers with respect to the public sector, therefore, is less one of providing a different way of generating resources than a different way of using and distributing them. This creates a potentially dangerous relationship of dependence on the state and can, as a result, create tensions between meeting the 'economic' output/outcome targets required to qualify for funding and the 'social' and ethical concerns that drive social economy organisations. It can also create tensions as a result of the accounting and monitoring requirements of funders, diverting time from carrying out the socially useful work of providing needed goods and services to filling in forms to renew – or more generally seek new sources of – funding and complying with the differing accounting and monitoring requirements of multiple funders. Crucially, however, all cannot win in the competition for grants: there necessarily are 'losers' as well as 'winners' (and this is one reason why some social economy organisations seek to break free from the world of grant dependency).

In drawing attention to the close relations between many social economy organisations and the state as a source of funding, it is important not to obscure the point that relations with the mainstream private sector economy can, in some circumstances, be important in helping sustain social economy organisations economically, albeit precariously and unevenly. In places where the private sector economy is strong, such as in London and Bristol, social economy organisations have been able to derive considerable benefits. These include the secondment of staff from local firms, the acquisition of materials and financial donations, and the capacity of local labour markets to absorb trainees coming through Intermediate Labour Market organisations. In these circumstances social economy organisations can draw upon the mainstream economy for help and resources in meeting their social objectives: the 'economy' of the mainstream and the 'social' goals of social economy organisations can therefore, in *some* circumstances, be made to be, to a degree, compatible. In contrast, where the needs for alternative forms of provision through the social economy are often greatest, as in de-industrialised urban areas and former coalfield settlements and other former mono-industrial places, the private sector economy is much weaker. As a result, such links cannot develop precisely because there is insufficient density of private sector firms to provide the required aggregate level of support. In these circumstances, the 'economy' of the mainstream and the 'social' objectives of social economy organisations are dis-articulated and simply do not connect.

## Moving nearer the mainstream market: breaking the mould, creating hybrid forms and the transition to become a social *enterprise*?

For reasons alluded to above, some social economy organisations do seek to expand beyond the limitations of their local origins and the constraints of the social economy by pushing out their boundaries into the space of mainstream markets, seeking to expand the scope and scale of their activities via developing new lines of activity and trading in spatially more extensive markets. Successful ethically and socially driven social economy organisations that offer a quality product, perhaps with a unique selling point with potential beyond the local economy, and in markets of secondary interest to mainstream private sector firms or public welfare organisations can flourish. Typical niches in which social economy organisations can succeed include art materials for childcare organisations, recycled electrical goods and furniture for low income groups, low budget catering, shopping catalogues distributed by the homeless, and targeted services for ethnic minorities, the elderly or particular disadvantaged groups.

There are numerous examples of social economy organisations that have sought to transform themselves into social enterprises and to expand beyond their, typically local, roots and areas of operation. Moreover, they seek to expand by taking a share of mainstream markets, either by developing new lines of business or seeking to compete in their existing areas, entering direct competition with capitalist firms in those markets and impinging on the spaces of the mainstream. However, typically insofar as such social enterprises seek to grow, and become less reliant upon state funding and free labour and more reliant upon income from trading, two things happen: first, tensions are created between their social origins and objectives and their ethical and moral motivations and the imperatives of 'the economy'; second, competition between the dominant mainstream and the alternative to the mainstream is potentially increased. As a result, the latter increasingly looks like and behaves like the former.

Put another way, while ethical and social concerns are central to social enterprise organisations they are of necessity reconciled with a more pragmatic acknowledgement of other influences as they seek to grow, especially if they seek to become social enterprises. As Graham and Cornwell (2008, 29) have put it, such social enterprise organisations grow and develop 'through what we have called ethical negotiation, in which different principles, projects and participants are brought into balance'. However, '[f]or all the simplicity of their guidelines and maxims, it is clear that to be a community-led, evolving organisation is not a simple or straightforward process. There's no obvious or automatic way forward'. Often, then, this reconciliation is an experimental trial-and-error process of learning-by-doing, an open-ended process with no predefined end point. Sometimes it may reflect the internal dynamic of the social enterprise organisation but it may also reflect a response to external pressures and opportunities. For instance, SOFA (Shifting Old Furniture Around) in Bristol sought to increase capacity in order to position itself as a key local and regional player in the emerging Waste Electrical and Electronic Equipment market. This exemplifies the way in which such organisational development may be shaped by selectively targeted responses to opportunities 'as and when' they transpire. Nonetheless, such local responses can be intimately connected to wider social and ethical concerns expressed though state regulation – in this case the EU Waste Electrical and Electronic Equipment directives which came into force (in the UK) in January 2007. A second example is provided by a social enterprise in Bristol which provides a supported design and woodworking environment for clients with mental health needs, its founder viewing the organisation as marrying his experience in the woodworking industry with an external social objective:

> to fill the gap in day services employment ... what we really wanted to do was provide something that was going to be there for a long, long period of time, that people could come in and access – some of those people were less likely to access open employment [so] it was to provide a work environment for them forever, that's pretty much where we feel we are now.

This organisation detached itself from the local Primary Care Trust, contracting its services back to the National Health Service at 'market rate', in an attempt to secure a potentially more sustainable future. The wish to secure the provision of services for a 'long period of time' highlights two key dilemmas. First, that arising from a wish to respond to opportunities which promise a solution to immediate issues of economic survival balanced against wider moral, social and ethical concerns. Second, that arising from the nature of the social economy organisation as 'intermediary' positioned between civil society and the realm of formal mainstream labour market.

There are many other instances of well-established social economy organisations actively promoting an increased 'business orientation', buying into and deploying these new discourses in a way that is directly related to an ability to respond and adapt to a number of opportunities offered in the contemporary economy. A typical example comes from a social economy organisation that seeks to address community needs for transport in Bristol, which was able to take advantage of the opportunities offered by new funding schemes. Its manager explained how

> we were able, in partnership with Bristol City Council, to secure a government grant under the Urban Bus Challenge ... over the last two years [we've] ... started the community buses off, and we're hoping to keep them rolling out because the funding is coming through now, and it will probably run out about April/May next year.

This is simply one of a number of examples in which core activities have been modified and/or extended in response to opportunities as they arise. This process is tempered by the knowledge that opportunities and funding streams are invariably time-limited, and concomitantly additional openings must constantly be identified. However, this model of 'growth through opportunity' is not always guaranteed to be a smooth one. Nonetheless, there are pressures to develop new hybrid forms of organisation to retain a focus on ethical and social concerns while recognising the material realities of the political economy of capitalist social relationships. At many social economy organisations there is a perceptible struggle between ethical and pragmatic, social versus economic, concerns, with questions arising as to the extent to which the founding vision of the organisation can thrive when confronted with the economic realities of the markets within which the organisation has been positioned – or has chosen to position itself.

The need to create and sustain viable hybrid organisational forms as a social economy organisation moves more in the direction of becoming a social enterprise was highlighted by the director of an organisation in Bristol seeking to manage the tensions that this generated, who noted that:

> It's not just an ordinary business, my work would be much easier if we did stuff more cheaply, employed trained people, sourced the cheapest materials, ran more of a sweatshop. It'd be easier to get stuff made in China! You know – half the price, half the hassle, fantastic sellers, but that's not actually the point.

Precisely because these organisations are not just 'ordinary businesses', the extent to which any particular 'additional' element and modification to the way in which they work is *necessary* is often the key point of contention. Social economy organisations that seek to become social enterprises and as such become more exposed to the vicissitudes of mainstream economic markets are less clearly delineated from mainstream businesses in terms of their management style and business objectives (although they may of course be distinguished through other factors). Social economy organisations that are attempting to generate new outcomes – and attempting to either work within new markets, or provide a new way of working across different existing markets – may be more likely to achieve the transition to become economically sustainable social enterprises because they offer something which public sector organisations do not. Those organisations are also more likely to find a niche in the market, and may have the potential to expand further. Conversely, social economy organisations that are unable to find such a market or product niche or create a distinctive way of working must differentiate themselves from non-social economy organisations through a stress upon their non-profit, ethical or otherwise social character.

There are a number of examples of social economy organisations that have made the transition to successful social *enterprise*. Some of the larger and better established social enterprises in the UK have made the transition because they have been able to circumvent the limitations of the local by operating on much bigger and/or multiple scales. Such organisations are effectively detached from any identifiable area or community, sometimes operating up to and including the national level. Perhaps the clearest example of this is the Wise Group which is routinely cited as an exemplar of best practice in the 'local' social economy (see, for example, Social Exclusion Unit, 1998). When it first began in the early 1980s, Wise's services (provision of insulation, security devices and landscaping in areas of social housing combined with training) were delivered by community-based 'squads' scattered throughout Glasgow and responsible for particular local areas, neighbourhoods and/or communities. As the project grew, however, the Wise intermediate labour market in Glasgow became organised on a city-wide basis, with all operations based in its Charlotte Street offices. Following changes in the nature of employment services and Scottish devolution, Wise took on an increasingly regional and national role, looking to expand further as a provider of training and work experience throughout the UK, developing a number of subsidiaries and associated projects in other cities which, although more or less local depending on the nature of the local labour market, follow a model developed elsewhere. This is serial repetition of a rather different kind.

The ability to work beyond the local market has also contributed to the economic and political success of other successful social enterprises. The Furniture Resource Centre has been able to become financially independent in large part because of the wide social housing market that it has been able to tap into throughout Merseyside and, increasingly, the rest of England. Without access to a market on this scale, it would not have been able to grow or to diversify into other forms of social provision, recycling, training and manufacturing (Frances, 1988). Similarly, Coin Street Community Builders has been successful precisely because its location in central London has allowed it to transcend the limitations of local demand alone. As Coin Street Community Builders has developed local housing co-operatives, increasing amounts of private-sector housing have been developed on adjoining sites, attracted by the associated infrastructural and environmental improvements created by the project. By targeting its workspaces at the particular niche market of young creative designers, Coin Street Community Builders has been able to bring in a range of new industries and effect a considerable change in the nature of the local economy. More importantly, perhaps, the concentration of designers within one of the project's main building, the Oxo Tower, attracted further large numbers of designers, artists and their various customers and collectors to an area that they would previously have avoided. By encouraging the development of small cafeterias and bistros, as well as an internationally renowned restaurant, Coin Street Community Builders has been able to exploit the presence of large numbers of people working in local businesses and, increasingly, tourists and bon viveurs from throughout London and beyond.

In brief, local services have been created for local people but the resources assembled to enable this have not been exclusively those of local people. Rather, Coin Street Community Builders has been able fundamentally to alter the boundaries of the local economy by breaking down economic, social and political barriers that previously isolated this particular part of the inner city from the rest of London. This was greatly helped by the fact that Coin Street is situated within the wealthy and complex London economy. As a result, the process of 'reconnection' was very much easier than it would have been in more physically isolated communities. Prior to the development of the Coin Street site, the local economy was in sharp decline following the demise of the London Docks upon which many local businesses – primarily warehouses and processing plants – had depended. The local population was also falling, partly because of a lack of local employment and partly because social housing in the area was amongst the worst in London. By addressing these severe limitations of the local area, not least by connecting it to the wider political economy of London, conditions have been put in place that have allowed the creation of a successful social enterprise and the regeneration of the area.

In cases such as these, while working with the grain of the private sector mainstream and seeking to use it for their own purposes, social enterprises increasingly and unavoidably enter into competition with mainstream capitalist enterprises and have no choice but to seek to compete with them on the terrain of mainstream markets. As a result, tensions inevitably arise as they seek to balance these new competitive demands, with all that they imply for work within the social enterprise organisation and its modes of internal organisation and management as it becomes a social enterprise, with the original intention to do social good in the parts that mainstream markets and the state didn't reach. It is at this point, and in part a reflection of the emphasis given to 'professionalisation' in public policy towards the social economy, that many social enterprise organisations bring in new 'professional' managers who bring fresh perspectives to the issue of running the organisation explicitly as a social enterprise. These people are often refugees from the world of mainstream business or people who have had a successful career in business or in the public sector, retired early, and have time on their hands that they seek to use by engaging with the social economy (see Amin, 2008). However, 'professionalisation' also has implications for the balance of emphasis on the 'social' versus the 'economic'. While the goal of creating a bigger surplus for using in the pursuit of social purposes is fine and laudable, the organisational changes required to achieve this – for example in terms of modes of work organisation – often run counter to the original social objectives of the organisation.

Many aspirant social enterprises fail because of a lack of a clear sense of mission, an inability to reconcile their ethical and social objectives with market realities, and for that reason fail to align processes with aims. Typically, initiatives mixing business-driven aspirations and ethically informed goals that seek to address unmet social needs but lacking a clear-cut and conscious understanding of the differences between them, have had to sacrifice one or the other or have come unstuck and fallen between two stools because of contradictory organisational arrangements and competitive goals. For example, ethical ventures have been forced to lower wages or the quality of training because the product is commercially non-viable, or business-driven ventures have been forced by funding agencies to change direction because of poor social achievements. In contrast, the experience of initiatives with clear aims has been different. Those with clearly articulated social and ethical goals have consciously organised work, clients and products as a means of meeting needs or developing capabilities, which, in turn, has focused effort. Similarly, business-driven social enterprise ventures run by professionals, as for example has become the trend in Glasgow, are clear that equity must follow business success, perhaps – and not without controversy – even at the expense of social objectives.

Thus successful social enterprises are based upon a clear identification of real unmet social needs, with potential for expansion beyond the immediate neighbourhood and/or into related goods and services. However, in some instances, the local state has played an important role in underwriting demand as a contractor of the services provided. This highlights the point that for survival, beyond the important question of choosing the right product, there is a pressing need to secure a source of recurring demand and sustainable income streams. This presents a considerable challenge for nascent small social enterprises with fragile market expertise and thinly spread competencies.

## Reading the social economy: perspectives on the relationship between the 'social' and the 'economic' and on possibilities for the future

As the above section makes clear, there is a number of differing, even competing, perspectives as to the relationship between the social and the economic in social enterprise organisations in the UK, and as to the relative weight to be attached to these in practice. In this section I want to connect these different views as to the practical relationships between the 'social' and 'economic' with broader perspectives about the social economy and its place within contemporary capitalisms as seen from a variety of national, policy and theoretical perspectives, each with differing analytic and normative emphases. There are at least three such 'takes' on and interpretations of the social economy that I want to consider here, which can be mapped into the differential national and sub-national development of the social economy. In turn, there are perceptible relations with different national 'models' of capitalism (for example, see Albert, 1993; Lash and Urry, 1987) and the ways in which these embraced or resisted the propositions of neo-liberalism.

The first of these prioritises the ethical, moral and 'social' role of the social enterprise organisations, seeing them as a vital site of provision of goods and services, typically with a strong local focus, that otherwise would not be provided through the mainstream mechanisms of capitalist markets and states. As is clear from a weight of empirical evidence from the UK, virtually without exception social enterprise organisations are formed precisely with this intention and it remains their key priority, subordinating other issues to this. As a consequence, they choose to remain heavily dependent upon volunteer labour and the work of a few dedicated individuals who are prepared to accept much lower wages than they could earn in mainstream organisations. For some this is precisely because of their ethical and moral commitment to helping others less fortunate than themselves but for others it marks a recognition of limited opportunities – or indeed no opportunities – of finding employment in the mainstream economy. For them work in the social economy is typically mundane and 'extraordinarily ordinary' (Amin, 2008) and many are content to remain within the safe haven that it offers in an otherwise turbulent world. Furthermore, for those who founded these social enterprise organisations and continue to direct and manage them, any concern with issues such as growth via expanding markets remains off the agenda as this is seen as undermining their 'social' imperatives; if this means an uncertain future of reliance upon voluntary labour and precarious funding via contracts and/or grants from the state or grants from charitable trusts, so be it.

Such a view of social enterprise organisations and the social economy as driven by a concern to help meet the needs of those marginalised by or excluded from mainstream economy and society chimes neatly with a policy perspective that sees the social economy as a safety net and as a lower cost substitute for the provision of goods and especially services previously provided to citizens as of right via the state. This is clearly the perspective that has become dominant in UK policy discourse. From such a neo-liberal policy perspective the role of the social economy is to meet the needs or – still better – unlock the entrepreneurial capacities of those who are marginalised or indeed even damaged by the operations of markets and states, helping them to become future workers – or still better entrepreneurs – and citizens of the capitalist economy in whatever form it takes. The social economy is thus seen as an intermediate space through which those who have become economically and socially excluded as a result of the restructuring processes of capital and state can be reintegrated back into mainstream economy and society. From this perspective, the social economy is seen as an adjunct to the mainstream capitalist economy and a safety net for those that are marginalised by or surplus to its requirements (part of what Marxian political economists would refer to as the surplus population). Often this is expressed in terms of the social economy, understood as a local economy, becoming a panacea for problems of locally concentrated social exclusion. There is a very clear emphasis here that unequivocally accepts the dominance and primacy of the capitalist mainstream and its economic (il)logic and sees the social economy as a space in which those worst affected by its restructuring processes can be re-integrated into the mainstream – or if not that, then at least a space (or maybe more accurately a spacious cul-de-sac) in which they can be contained and challenges to the mainstream and its constituent social order can thereby be diffused.

There are, however, many who are actively involved in the social economy in the UK and elsewhere would vigorously contest and reject this first perspective. A second perspective therefore sees the social economy much more as an alternative to, rather than as an adjunct to, the mainstream capitalist economy, the motives that drive it and the values that underpin it. In contrast it sees the social economy as one that places addressing social need and enabling social participation before the imperatives of capital accumulation, corporate profits, shareholder value and individual gain rather than simply the space in which the individual and social costs of mainstream capitalism are absorbed and contained. For those who adhere to this view, the social economy represents an alternative to the values and economic logic of mainstream capitalism but one that also accepts the mainstream and, on occasion, seeks to compete with capitalist enterprises within the markets of the mainstream. Those social enterprise organisations that seek to make the transition to social enterprises and increase the scope and scale of their operations via competing with mainstream capitalist enterprises do so precisely because they see this as a way of generating greater resources and a social surplus that can then be used for collective and social purposes.

The social economy is thus conceived as a parallel sphere to the modalities of states and the mainstream economy, informed by different values and processes of valuation and organised differently, existing in parallel to and at times in competition with mainstream capitalist enterprises and states, but capable of both surviving and demonstrating the viability of a socially needs-based, humane and human-centred economy within contemporary capitalism (Pearce, 2008). Such a view of the social economy is common in France (Laville, 2008) and Italy (Borzaga, 2008), in the 'solidarity economy' of Quebec, where it is entangled in complex ways with issues of Quebec nationalism and identity, and in parts of South America. Crucially, however, in the last analysis it accepts the primacy of the mainstream and its conceptions of the economic, the social and the relations between them, but seeks to create a space for those whose ethical and moral values do not fit comfortably within the parameters defined by the mainstream. However, the interplay of the mainstream and the alternative to it raises issues of the regulation and structures of markets in complex and hybrid economies. How *can* markets be structured in such a way as to create a viable space for activities otherwise not attractive to capital? How can the environment in which social enterprises operate best be governed? What is the optimal balance between state and the institutions of civil society in governance arrangements? These are questions that in the final analysis can only be worked out in practice.

The third perspective to a degree overlaps with this second one but it is also distinct from it in one very important respect – that is, that it emphasises the disruptive qualities and radically transformational potential of the social economy to prise open the possibilities of a post-capitalist future. In intent if not pace of development, it is revolutionary. Rather than accept a de facto subordinate existence in a parallel social and economic world to the mainstream, it seeks potentially at least to challenge the dominance and hegemony of the mainstream and suggest alternative arrangements and definitions of the economic and social that could replace those of the mainstream. In principle it seeks to supplant the logic of capital rather than co-exist in parallel to it. From this perspective, and building upwards and outwards from radical locally based initiatives (while bearing in mind Williams' (1989) strictures and warnings as to the dangers of generalising 'militant particularisms' and translating them to places beyond their origins), the social economy offers, perhaps, the first green shoots of something beyond capitalist (dis)order, and not only in those places marginalised and ravaged by the devalorisation of capital or the restructuring of states but also in its very heartlands. For sure this is still grounded in a vision of constructing, regulating and shaping markets and bureaucracies but in ways that are sensitive to sustaining social needs, the needs of diverse individuals, communities and ecologies, and driven by values and ethical and moral concerns radically different from those of an economy driven by the imperatives of capital accumulation. From this perspective the social economy is seen as symbolising alternative definitions and meanings of economy and economic purpose, of recognising that the economy is always social and in that sense the debate about the relations between 'economic' and 'social' in the social economy needs to be radically re-cast as part of a more systemic process of socio-economic transformation (Amin *et al.*, 2002; Gibson-Graham, 1996).

## Conclusions: what about the future?

There is no doubt that in many parts of the world many social enterprise organisations perform a crucial function in providing goods, services and training opportunities for people in places that would otherwise be bereft of provision. They seek directly to improve the well-being of people, places and communities, to do so by working with the grain of the desires and wishes of local people, and move to a different collaborative and co-operative rhythm and tune to that of the mainstream economy. In that sense the 'social' continues to take precedence over the 'economic' and as a result there are sound ethical and moral reasons for supporting the social economy. Once seen as a residual and poor relation of the state and/or the market, a sphere of charity and social or moral repair, social enterprise organisations are now imagined as a mainstay of future social organisation in both the developed and developing world, seen as set to co-exist with or substitute for the welfare state, meet social needs in depleted and hard pressed communities, constitute a new economic circuit of jobs and enterprises in the socialised market composed of socially useful goods and services, empower the socially excluded by combining training and skills formation with capacity and confidence-building, and create a space for humane, co-operative, sustainable and 'alternative' forms of social and economic organisation. This is a pretty impressive agenda of diverse intended outcomes, although the extent to which they can be and are actually delivered in practice remains to be seen. What is clear is that the expectation – common in much policy thinking in the UK for example – that the social economy can be a major source of jobs, entrepreneurship, local regeneration and welfare provision in places marginalised by processes of capital accumulation and state restructuring is naïve and dangerous, with the manifest danger of generating disappointment as a result of unrealised expectations. More positively, social enterprise organisations – in some places, at varying spatial scales, and with appropriate support – can complement provision via state and mainstream market, perhaps even constitute a genuine 'Third System' of provision, and add to the range of goods and services and opportunities available to people in them. As such, in specific and typically but not necessarily simply local circumstances, they can achieve something genuinely different.

What can be said with much greater certainty is that it is difficult to envisage social enterprise organisations in aggregate having a radically transformative role such that a 'social economy' with its own distinctive values and concerns develops and displaces the (il)logic of capital accumulation from its position of systemic dominance within diverse capitalisms; rather they provide at best an alternative to the mainstream, at worst a safety net that serves to legitimise the inequalities inherent to the operation of mainstream capitalist markets and the process of capital accumulation. But whatever else social enterprise organisations and the social economy do or do not do, they do keep on the agenda the needs of those who the mainstream ignores and the possibilities of alterity and maybe radical alterity at that in terms of other ways of organising economy and society, and indeed of re-conceptualising what we mean by the economic, the social and the relations between them. Keeping open this window of potential practical and political as well as theoretical opportunity is vitally important – even if the short-term prognosis is less than rosy.

## Notes

1 It is worth noting that the recent post-2007 de facto nationalisation of major banks and insurance companies in the UK, USA and other major capitalist economies clearly shows that there are sharp economic limits to neo-liberal approaches as these threaten the viability of the accumulation process.

2 Although this is not to suggest that the economy can ever be anything other than thoroughly and unavoidably social or that the social is thoroughly and unavoidably economic. The issue is about the specific form of socio-economics and the priorities that inform it.
3 The social economy can be defined as follows (NICDA/CDS, 1999, 11):

> The 'Social Economy' constitutes a broad range of activities which have the potential to provide opportunities for local people and communities to engage in all stages of the process of local economic regeneration and job creation, from the identification of basic needs to the operationalisation of initiatives. The sector covers the economic potential and activities of the self-help and co-operative movements, that is, initiatives that aim to satisfy social and economic needs of local communities and their members. This sector includes co-operatives; self-help projects; credit unions; housing associations; partnerships; community enterprises and businesses. The Social Economy is the fastest growing sector in Europe and this context is fertile ground for the creation of many new enterprises locally.

4 It is also worth noting that while mainstream private sector organisations have developed Corporate Social Responsibility programmes, and that this to a degree seems to blur the boundary between mainstream and social economies, these organisations remain primarily motivated by the imperatives of accumulation and profitability and as such the qualitative divide between them and social economy organisations remains sharp. An analogous point can be made with regard to social economy organisations and major public sector organisations that develop Corporate Social Responsibility programmes.

# 8 Thinking through the relationships between legal and illegal activities and economies

## Spaces, flows and pathways

### Introduction

The starting point for this chapter is recognition of three things. First, that illegal activities form a significant component of capitalist economies. Second, that the legal and illegal are locked into a systematic symbiotic relationship which is contingently expressed in and constituted through their patterning in time and space and in the relationships between their flows, paths and spaces. Links between the legal and illegal are critical to the dynamic, trajectory and spatiality of accumulation globally. Legal and illegal practices can be seen as genetically entwined and encoded in the DNA and 'normal' operations of contemporary capitalism, integral to the workings of the capitalist economy rather than a marginal and unusual anomaly (Brown and Cloke, 2007; Murphy, 2011). While indeed arguably this has been the case within capitalism throughout its history (Bhattacharyya, 2005) recent regulatory and technological changes have facilitated a qualitative expansion in the significance of the illegal (Castells, 2010). As a result, illegal activities influence the configuration and broad sweep of accumulation and help shape the pattern of competitive advantage between companies engaged in activities that span the boundary of legal and illegal. Moreover, beyond the mainstream and legal circuits of capital illegal activities may also form a key element in the 'survival strategies' of those marginalised by or surplus to the requirements of the movers and shakers who direct and shape the major circuits of legal capital accumulation. Third, that while parts of the social sciences have been attentive to the illegal, others, not least economic geography, have not and have been largely blind to its significance, both empirically and theoretically. This is an absence that needs to be addressed.

The rest of the chapter is organised as follows. First, the absence of consideration of the illegal in the economic geography literature is discussed more fully and some consideration is given to the ways in which perspectives in economic geography could throw light on illegal activities while enabling a fuller and more nuanced approach to analyses of economic geographies. Then the definition and scope of illegality is considered, along with some consideration of important related concepts and perspectives within economic geography of relevance to understanding illegal activities and their geographies. Next, evidence as to the extent of the illegal economy is briefly considered and this is followed by a discussion of the practices and spaces of illegality in the processes of capitalist production. This is followed by some consideration of the governance of illegality, leading to a discussion of those spaces in which money from the illegal economy is sanitised and becomes money capital in the legal economy. The final section briefly summarises the main points of the chapter and this leads into some brief conclusions.

## A gap in the literature on economic geographies

There are extensive literatures in economic geography, political economy and economics, setting out the case for a variety of theoretical approaches, ranging from neo-classical economics to Marxian and other strands of heterodox political economy. In differing ways, some competitive, some complementary, these diverse approaches provide valuable knowledge about the socio-spatial forms of the economy, the ways it is governed and regulated, the production of commodities and value, how values are formed, and flows of value and the spaces through which commodities are produced and values flow. A corollary of this theoretical diversity is that economic geographers have become increasingly aware of the diversity of forms of social relationships within capitalist economies, expressed in the growth of interest in the social economy and 'diverse economies' more generally (Chapter 7; Leyshon *et al.*, 2003; Gibson-Graham, 1996).

While these theoretical approaches differ significantly, however, they do share one crucial common characteristic: that is, an almost total focus on the legal economy and the regulation of markets – for labour, for knowledge, for a vast range of commodities – and behaviour within it. Other than occasional reference to the informal economy[1] (for example, by Hadjimichalis and Vaiou, 1990a; 1990b) any consideration of illegal economies, and even more so of their relationship to the legal mainstream, is almost totally absent. As Pollard *et al.* (2009, 137) note, 'what is remarkable is that so much economic geography continues to presume that "the economy" can and should be theorised solely from the perspective of the formal spaces of western economies'.[2] For example, the indices in two landmark collections (Clark *et al.*, 2000; Shepherd and Barnes, 2000) contain no reference whatsoever to the illegal economy. This neglect continues. The introduction to a more recent collection of essays by leading economic geographers notes that '[a] major driving force of globalization is the economic geographies, legal and illegal, that compose and constitute the global economy' (Leyshon *et al.*, 2011, 7) but that is as far as consideration of the illegal goes in the rest of the book. There are a few exceptions in other economic geography literature (for example, Brown and Cloke, 2011; Hall, 2011; 2013) but in general this is very partial and fleeting in its coverage of the illegal (Chapter 2; Hudson, 2005). The overall impression is, at best, one of little more than a passing recognition by economic geographers that there is more to the economy than the legal mainstream.

Economic geography is not alone among the social sciences in having ignored the illegal economy (see Beckert and Wehinger, 2011, on economic sociology). It is also largely ignored in the economics literature (for rare exceptions, see Chaudhry and Zimmerman, 2010; Schelling, 1960). In contrast, however, in other social science disciplines such as anthropology, business studies, criminology, international relations and sociology there is greater recognition of the significance of the illegal and its relationships to the legal mainstream (Bhattacharyya, 2005; Dallago, 1990; Ditton, 1977: Hobbs, 1988; Nordstrom, 2007; Strange, 1998). In addition, there is quite a substantial literature in other social sciences such as sociology that considers 'informal' economies as well as outright illegal activities (Castells, 2010; Portes *et al.*, 1989).

Nonetheless, the absence of consideration of the illegal by economic geographers is surprising for several reasons. First, there are distinctive geographies of illegal economies. Second, illegal and legal are often closely linked. Third, economic geography has conceptual tools and theories (such as various strands of political economy and relational approaches) that could be brought to bear on the illegal to illuminate understanding of it, as I shall begin to illustrate in the following sections.

## Concepts and definitions: organisational forms, labour processes and value formation in the (il)legal economy

It is very difficult, not to say impossible, precisely to define the scope and delineate the boundaries of the illegal economy. It is also impossible to give a definition that is not specific to a given time/space context. There are definitional differences between national jurisdictions, between supranational and national definitions (Wohlfeil *et al.*, 2009), and between national and sub-national levels within a national territory (Erman, 2007). What is legal in some times and spaces is illegal in others and so there is a shifting boundary between them, with legal and illegal defined relationally and relatively, always contingent and provisional. The boundary between legal and illegal is thus socially defined, a matter of definition within the law (Bhattacharyya, 2005; Glenny, 2008).

These differing definitions and conceptions typically reflect power struggles between social actors, within and between state, civil society and economy and power struggles between national states, between central and regional governments, between and within social classes, between economic and environmental interest groups and so on. Of particular importance are the strategies of companies and fractions of capital to influence national states and supra-national regulatory bodies in labour market regulation (over issues such as working hours and conditions and wage rates) and in setting standards for products as part of the social process of creating and segmenting markets (Hudson, 2001a). The outcome of these struggles is the creation of different definitions of the legal and illegal, drawing the line between them in ways that favour some interests over others and forcing some firms and people to behave illegally if they are to seek to survive. Other forms of state involvement in the economy may unintentionally create spaces in which illegal activities can emerge and flourish. For example, the restructuring of the tobacco industry in China, focused around a small number of large-scale enterprises, resulted in 'a sizeable workforce of skilled labourers as well as production machinery [being] made available to the illicit tobacco business'. This was further reinforced by the 'formidable difficulties involved in obtaining a tobacco exclusive sale permit' (Shen *et al.*, 2009, 3).

Drawing the line between legal and illegal economic activities is further complicated because legal companies and legal regulators (typically state actors) engage in informal and illegal activities. The sharp line between legal and illegal becomes blurred. In extreme cases, the definition of the line is maintained by criminal organisations that practice extortion and demand protection fees from legal businesses as a condition of their being able to remain viable. In this way, the illegal sanctions the legal. More generally, illegal criminal organisations can operate as proxy agents of governance, extending a sort of order into spaces of illegality beyond the reach of the legitimate state (Glenny, 2008).[3] Moreover, drawing the line between illegal and legal activities can have unintended and, for some, undesirable consequences. For example, the banning of trade in e-wastes between 'developed' and 'developing' countries has had at least two unintended and undesirable consequences. First, it has disrupted the livelihood strategies of people and communities who were already poor, marginalised and dependent upon waste recycling, further increasing their economic insecurity. Second, it has enhanced the role of criminal networks involved in the illicit trade of e-waste (Williams *et al.*, 2008; Yu *et al.*, 2010).

There is an extensive literature dealing with the variety of organisational forms that capital can take in the formal legal economy (Hudson, 2001a, 96–216). Given the close links between legal and illegal activities as these are woven together into complex economies, the conceptual and theoretical tools of economic geography can also be focused on the illegal – for example, various strands of political economy and heterodox economics such as Marxian political economy and institutional and evolutionary economics and economic geography (Hudson, 2001a) as well as more recent perspectives such as those of relational economic geography (Bathelt and Glückler, 2003) and global production networks (Henderson *et al.*, 2002).[4]

There is a spectrum of illegal activities ranging from 'organised crime' on a large and increasingly global scale, with corresponding organisational forms, to smaller, flexible and often horizontally networked organisations, to small-scale localised and isolated illegal activities as part of individual and household 'survival strategies'. While the former may be organised through markets and closely tied to and functionally linked with legal circuits of capital, the latter may more often constitute part of a responsive 'survival strategy' in spaces that have been marginalised from or were never part of major circuits of capital. Exchange activities within them are typically organised through much more localised and personalised networks. As a result, there are many local organisations with a limited spatial reach (Castells, 2010; Glenny, 2008; Hobbs, 1998; Madsen, 2009) but also major illegal organisations that behave in some ways like mainstream transnational corporations with decentralised and devolved structures and 'profit centres' and links to other major illegal organisations (Saviano, 2008).

Moreover, the organisational forms of illegal activities and their focus and areas of operation can and do change over time. For example, in contrast to the rigid hierarchical structure of the Sicilian mafia, the Neapolitan Camorra emerged in the 1950s as a network of locally based clans, loosely and flexibly linked and based on petty crime undertaken as a survival strategy. By the 1990s it remained a network of local clans, but had evolved in two different though in part related directions. Some, based in the cities, developed into major economic actors, as a result of their growing involvement in the drugs trade in the 1980s and involvement in smuggling, extortion and illegal lotteries. Others, in the provinces of Naples and Caserta, evolved into a sophisticated political Camorra, closely interwoven with mainstream politics and dominating construction and other sub-contracts from the State (Allum and Allum, 2008).

In addition, echoing emerging organisational forms in the legal economy, illegal organisations have developed new structures of networked relationships. There is a constant re-grouping of clans and cartels, coming together for a time around particular deals and then dissolving as they come to an end, in a manner reminiscent of project working in the legal economy (Hagstrom and Hedlund, 1998; Grabher, 2002).[5] At the same time as these organisational forms evolved, all Camorra clans remained involved in extortion and drug trafficking, but also became involved in less risky but equally profitable activities such as making and selling counterfeit goods and in companies with global business networks and interests, such as food distribution. Some clans moved into environmental crime, notably the illegal management of recycled, often toxic, waste and the construction of buildings without permits and using unsafe materials (Saviano, 2008). Just as the mainstream legal economy has globalised in new ways, so too has the illegal economy, as Camorra clans have extended their links into Latin America and Europe. More generally, Castells (2010, 186; see also 212) argues that the 'combination of flexible networking between local turfs, rooted in tradition and identity, in a favourable institutional environment, and the global reach provided by strategic alliances, ... explains the organisational strength of global crime'. Put another way, the contemporary illegal economy is grounded in a subtle interplay between activities at different scales.

Quite a lot is known about labour processes, value formation and flows of value in the formal, legal economy. Much less is known about how work is organised and value is formed in the illegal economy, about flows of value within it and between the circuits of legal and illegal economies and the spaces in which these occur. As a first approximation, it seems reasonable to assume that both value construction and price formation in illegal markets draw on those processes in legal markets, and use the latter as a reference point. Indeed, the close interconnection between legal and illegal activities in many production networks suggests that processes of value creation within them are closely intertwined if not indistinguishable and are most appropriately considered as part of the same overall process. The connecting channels and shared spaces of exchange in which legal and illegal markets and other systems of exchange intersect are critical.

Three qualifications are worth making, however. First, commodities in the illegal economy command a price premium precisely because they are prohibited in a given institutional and regulatory jurisdiction. This is exemplified by the sequence of activities in the production and circulation of cocaine. As Allen (2005, 30) notes 'the most striking characteristic of the price structure of cocaine is the astonishing scale of value added during the production and distribution process' by virtue of the fact that cocaine is an illegal substance.[6] Second, actors in illegal markets have to deal with the issue of quality assessment and assurance in a rather different manner to those in legal markets. Personal relationships and network relationships, both involving trust, replace the formal mechanisms and quality standards of legal markets.[7] Third, relatively little is known about the effects of illegal activities on the accumulation process, both in terms of competition between capitals and competition between national states and other territorial jurisdictions (both supra- and sub-national) for capital investment, the overall pace and pattern of accumulation and the capacity of states to act because of loss of taxation and other revenues.

## Scale, magnitudes and empirical evidence about the illegal economy

As noted above, while it is impossible to give a precise definition of the magnitude of the illegal economy it is clearly of major significance. Moreover, I agree with Castells (2010, 173) that the difficulties of definition and measurement and in obtaining precise empirical data as to the extent of illegality should not stand in the way of seeking to understand its function and the relations between the legal and illegal. The illegal has clearly become an integral part of the contemporary phase of capitalist development. Put simply, it is too important – practically and theoretically – to ignore.[8]

Nonetheless, recognising the difficulties, there are credible 'order of magnitude' estimates of the size of the illegal economy. Illegal economic activities can be defined as '[t]hose productive activities that generate goods and services forbidden by law or that are unlawful when carried out by unauthorised producers' (OECD, 2002, 13). Authorities such as the International Monetary Fund and World Bank estimate that the illegal economy accounts for perhaps

20 per cent of global Gross Domestic Product and considerably more in particular territories and jurisdictions (for example, 40–50 per cent or more in (so-called) transitional economies and developing economies: Glenny, 2008). However, illegal activities are by no means confined to these parts of the world and are also present in a range of spaces in the core capitalist economies of the developed world – ranging from pivotal financial districts to peripheral marginalised spaces. In short, the illegal permeates the space-economy of contemporary capitalism.

The spaces in which the illegal can prosper have increased as socio-spatial inequality has widened because of the growing tendency to neo-liberalisation in economic policy, enabled by revolutionary advances in information and communication technologies and the greater freedom permitted by lightly regulated markets. The resultant expanded production of peripheral marginalised spaces, at best tangentially connected to the mainstream legal economy, provides ideal locations for illegality to flourish as people there seek to find ways to 'get by' and survive. Activities in such spaces often form the links between legal and illegal economies which combine in and through particular spaces, with illegal activities feeding into and sustaining legal circuits. Global geopolitical changes, notably the collapse of 'actually existing socialisms' in the USSR and central and eastern Europe and the emergence of capitalism alongside communism in China provided major opportunities for the expansion of illegal activities (Kan *et al.*, 2010). At the same time, growing inequality within the core states of advanced capitalism created spaces in which illegal activities could flourish, often precisely because of the lack of any legal alternative (Evans *et al.*, 2006).

Beyond accounts based on published official statistics, there are some very powerful investigative journalistic accounts of the illegal economy (García Márquez, 1998; Glenny, 2008; 2011; Saviano, 2008) and a wealth of empirical studies by non-governmental organisations and related organisations that give some consideration to illegal activities (several of which are drawn on here). While these may lack the rigour of social scientific investigations, they provide powerful indicative accounts of life in the illegal economy. So, in summary, while there is empirical evidence, it is partial and patchy though also suggestive of the scale and spatialities of the illegal economy.

## Spaces and practices of the illegal in the capitalist production process

In this section I will use concepts from political economy, specifically the Marxian conception of the circuit of productive industrial capital (Hudson, 2001a, 14–47), to help understand the relationship between the legal and illegal in the totality of the production process. There are two possible limit cases: either products and all the processes involved in their production are legal or they are illegal and so are all processes in production. Perhaps more common, however, are 'hybrid' cases in which legal products involve some illegal processes. A variety of illegal practices, typically unobserved and/or unremarked, may be involved in the production of legal commodities. Equally, illegal products may involve some legal processes. In their journey around a circuit of production commodities may therefore be subject to a variety of legal and illegal practices and pass through a variety of legally and illegally regulated spaces.

The circuit of production begins with capitalist enterprises laying out money capital to purchase inputs to the production process: labour-power; material inputs to production, both raw materials and components manufactured from them; and immaterial inputs in the form of intellectual property. Illegality may be involved in each of these. Labour is always produced as a fictive commodity and indeed has to be in order that commodified labour-power can come into existence (Elson, 1978). The price that capital has to pay to secure labour-power reflects the conditions under which labour is reproduced, and the distribution of the costs of that reproduction (as between family, community and state). While illegal labour can be provided by members of an indigenous population – for example via child labour or indentured labour – illegal migrants have a greater propensity to end up working illegally (Mingione, 1999). Illegal labour provided via migrant workers can have a doubly downward effect on costs. First, this is because the costs of its reproduction have already been displaced elsewhere in time and space. Second, and in addition, because illegal migrant labour by definition lacks citizenship and legal rights, and as a result is particularly vulnerable to further exploitation (Gatti, 2006). In some cases, workers who were initially legal migrants lose their jobs and so become illegal migrants as their work permits are no longer valid. Often, in these circumstances, they are unable to return to their country of origin because of indebtedness incurred in paying fees to agents in order to become migrants in the first place and so become vulnerable to recruitment as illegal labour with a very precarious existence. In others, especially involving agency contract workers, agencies deliberately arrange for people to become illegal immigrants in order that they can be employed on inferior conditions and lower wages (SOMO, 2009). Furthermore, such migrant workers, both legal and illegal, serve to displace indigenous workers and further help create labour reserves, further pushing down wages and thereby enhancing the rates of exploitation, profit and accumulation more generally.

The second element of input into production is raw materials or components manufactured from them, created via the transformation of elements of the natural world (raw materials, natural resources) into socially useful and valued commodities as a result of human labour. While much mining activity is legal, there are also numerous instances of mining activities depending on illegal labour – for example, children, indentured labour or workers working under conditions that otherwise violate labour laws (ACIDH, 2011; Earthworks and Oxfam America, 2004; Erman, 2007; Nordbrand and Bolme, 2007; Pöyhönen and Simola, 2007; Steinweg and de Haan, 2007). Minerals won in this way then enter complex patterns of international trade and the supply chains of major multinationals that use them as inputs to their production processes (Pöyhönen and Simola, 2007). The pathways through which such minerals make their way to legal manufacturing locations are typically opaque. The effect of such flows is to cut production costs for companies using these materials and components made from them, enabling them to undercut competitors, enhance market share and profitability.

The third element of input into the production process is knowledge and intellectual property. Much of this knowledge is legally acquired, embodied in workers or as fixed capital in the form of machinery and the means of production. Knowledge acquisition may, however, also involve the theft of intellectual property rights as a prelude to the production of counterfeit 'knock offs'[9] and illegal copies of branded goods. Illegal production of manufactured goods for mainstream legal markets is widespread: 'today nearly every consumer and industrial product is subject to counterfeiting' (OECD, 2007, cited in Chaudhry and Zimmerman, 2010, 26). Counterfeit goods account for about 7 per cent of global trade, with two thirds of these originating in spaces of production in China (Glenny, 2008; Phillips, 2005). Russia and some other south Asian and Latin American countries are also major sources of counterfeit production (Chaudhry and Zimmerman, 2010). Such goods may be produced by workers who are legitimate and legal (Phillips, 2005) but they may also be produced by illegal workers, resulting in 'good copies' (Saviano, 2008) being produced at very low labour cost.

The moment of production in which the various inputs to the production process are brought together under the control of managers of capital and in which surplus-value is produced is central to any form of capitalist production. In many parts of the world and sectors of the economy the organisation of production is critically dependent upon some combination of legal and illegal labour and legal and illegal working practices. Labour-power that is legally purchased on the labour market may be illegally employed – for example companies may withhold wages and force workers to work beyond the legal limit for overtime, violating both national legislation and international agreements such as the International Labour Organisation's Hours of Work Convention (ILO, 2002). Workers may also be forced to work in conditions that violate environmental, labour and health and safety legislation (Hudson, 2010) and indeed in buildings that are themselves illegally constructed and so dangerous and subject to fire risk or even collapse (for example, see Kazmin, 2013). Often workers have little choice but to work excessive and illegal overtime because their legal basic wage is below the level of a 'living wage' or because they are forced to work 'voluntary' unpaid overtime (Nordbrand and de Haan, 2009). Consequently, the boundaries between legal and illegal in production are frequently unclear.

Such illegal employment practices are often facilitated by the absence of trades unions (for example in 'no union no strike' Export Production Zones) or the presence of unions that are effectively under state control and/or the influence of employers. Such practices are widespread over much of south east

Asia and in central and eastern Europe, both in sectors such as consumer electronics and information technology that are commonly represented as 'high tech' and 'clean' production (Chan *et al.*, 2008: de Haan and Schipper, 2009; Ferus-Comelo and Pöyhönen, 2011; Mackay, 2004; Pöyhönen and Wan, 2011; SACOM, 2011; Wilde and de Haan, 2006)[10] as well as in those commonly seen as more traditional and labour-intensive in their production methods, such as brick making or clothing production (Coninck *et al.*, 2011; Oonk *et al.*, 2012; Upadhyaya, 2008). Commodities produced under these circumstances can then compete with and undercut those produced legitimately, reducing the market share and profits of those producers operating legally and conforming to the requirements of labour legislation. Commodities produced by illegal labour (whether directly or indirectly, knowingly or unknowingly) can undercut those produced by companies employing labour legally – with implications for uneven development among companies and spaces.[11] It is important to acknowledge that such working practices are also prevalent in activities such as mining, ship breaking and waste recycling, linked to the growing international trade in wastes, which are more commonly seen as 'dirty' and less desirable and so located in peripheral spaces in the global North as well as South (Buerk, 2006; Frandsen *et al.*, 2011; Nordbrand, 2009).

The illegal trading and sale of legitimate commodities and/or the trading of illegal commodities can be of great significance. Some commodities – for example, narcotics – are simply illegal. Others such as cigarettes and tobacco may be produced illegally as well as legally (Shen *et al.*, 2009). In addition, illegally produced goods may be packed and distributed by legal businesses, further blurring the boundary between legal and illegal. Conversely, commodities that are legally produced, such as cigarettes, consumer electronics or weapons, may avoid customs duties by smuggling, thereby underpinning the creation of 'grey markets' and conferring a competitive advantage to those that follow such a strategy, enhancing their profitability vis-à-vis those that do pay such duties. Illegal trade often flourishes precisely because it is focused on ports that lack the capacity to cope with the volume of goods passing through them (Glenny, 2008; Nordstrom, 2007). Commodities produced legally but then sold and traded illegally deny (territorially bounded) states taxation revenues that they would otherwise receive and could deploy in social and economic development projects (Nordbrand and Bolme, 2007).

In addition, in contravention of international regulations and treaties such as the Basel Convention, there is a burgeoning illegal trade in waste materials, such as flows of electronic wastes from developed to developing countries (Nordbrand, 2009),[12] increasingly linked to the growth of trade in counterfeit electronic parts (EE Times Asia, 2012). For example, as environmental regulation has been tightened in the European Union, and the costs of recycling there have risen, there have been unintended and unwanted consequences as pressures to export wastes illegally to spaces in which the costs of recycling are much less (typically by a factor of five or six) have grown. Commodities such as mobile phones, which have a rapid turnover and short product life, result in significant flows of illegal wastes. Moreover, they contain chemicals and metals such as arsenic and cadmium that are toxic and hazardous to human health but valuable once recycled (Wilde and de Haan, 2006). Consequently, they are exported to countries such as China, India, Pakistan, Indonesia and the Philippines, Ghana and Nigeria with abundant cheap informal and illegal labour (including child labour) in which such recycling activities can be carried out and toxic wastes dumped without regard to their detrimental effects on the environment and human health (Wilde and de Haan, 2006). The fact that people are prepared to undertake such activities is a reflection of their lack of alternative ways of getting by and generating some income.

Unless commodities can be sold, the surplus-value that they embody remains unrealised and as a result there is wide range of spaces and practices of sale for legally sanctioned commodities (for example, see Hudson, 2005, 145–66). In addition, however, there are also specific spaces in marginalised locations as well as iconic and well-known street markets in major global cities such as Beijing, London, Los Angeles and New York and Paris in which illegally produced commodities are sold (Chaudhry and Zimmerman, 2010, 42–3). Such markets – which state regulators regard with 'blind eyes' (see below) – enable producers to realise the surplus-value embodied in the commodities and consumers to acquire the symbolic value and prestige of premium brands at a fraction of the price of the genuine article, undercutting the latter in the market while to all intents and purposes appearing to be the genuine article.

Finally, it is important to stress that all economic activities have to take somewhere, emphasising the significance of identifying which sorts of activities, illegal and legal, occur in which sorts of spaces. Recently, there has been rapid growth of cyber-crime, and increasing consideration of its relationship to other aspects of both legal and illegal economies. In particular, the Internet has become a major market place for counterfeit goods via markets such as eBay, almost equivalent to China and Italy as a source of such goods (Chaudhry and Zimmerman, 2010, 137–52). As Jessop (2000) has emphasised more generally in relation to the cyber-economy, however, the Internet and electronic economy that it facilitates requires material grounding in specific spaces (as Glenny, 2011, demonstrates).

## How is the illegal governed?

There is a substantial and well-established body of state theory and theories of regulation, much of which is centred on the national state (Boyer, 1990; Jessop, 1990). This analyses the boundaries, scope and content of state involvement in the legal economy and in the definition and regulation of a variety of markets within it and so, by implication, de-limits the sphere of the illegal. As noted above, however, drawing the line between the legal and illegal varies between national states and their differing modes of regulation, and also as a result of definitions within incipient global regulatory bodies.

The governance literature focuses on relations between political actors and institutions (Held, 1989) and has little to say about the governing of economic practices in workplaces or between companies, let alone the interplay of the legal and illegal in the day-to-day dirty business of the quotidian economy. Ethnographies of workplaces (such as Beynon, 1973) explore such governance relationships, but by and large they remain detached from the mainstream governance literature.

While the worlds of illegal economies are by definition beyond the formal regulatory realm of the legal economy, illegal economies are nonetheless governed by distinctive sets of social relations and regulatory practices which are often tightly and precisely organised. While much illegal activity, especially more organised economic activity, is conducted within markets, it is also conducted through more personalised and localised networks of social relations. For example, this is typically the case when such activity is primarily part of a survival strategy to 'get by'. In the absence of legally enforceable contracts, trust assumes considerable importance in both markets and other systems of exchange (Gambetta, 2011, especially 39–53).[13] It is important to emphasise that illegal activities *are* regulated – typically, in the absence of the institutionalised trust provided by state regulation, via a combination of trust based in the social relations of family, clan or territory and, in extremis and occasionally brutally, via violence or death as a sanction should these mechanisms prove inadequate.[14]

Such activities are therefore generally highly regulated, although in different ways to those of mainstream legal regulation. As such, while they may be in conflict with the regulatory practices of the mainstream, they may also 'capture' elements of them, individually or institutionally – for example via the corruption of the police and/or politicians (Glenny, 2008; Saviano, 2008). More generally, this is symptomatic of 'blind eyes', of state officials and politicians deliberatively ignoring the illegal, or providing a cloak to hide it, becoming complicit in providing a 'protective umbrella' (Shen *et al.*, 2009) for it or even becoming active participants in it (Kazmin *et al.*, 2013; Upadhyaya, 2008).[15] In these varied spaces in which the sovereign state chooses to avert its eyes to illegality, the formal distinction between the legal and illegal becomes problematic, or even irrelevant.[16]

State officials and politicians may behave in these ways for a variety of reasons. First, they do so because of fear for their personal safety, or the temptations of bribery and personal material gain. Second, they do so because they see illegal activities as a justifiable route to local economic development (Kynge, 2006; 2009). As Shen *et al.* (2009, 13, emphasis in original) remark with reference to China that

> [s]ince cigarette counterfeiting, through the use of locally grown tobacco, is a source of revenue for the provincial government and provides employment for many individuals, *local* government seem reluctant to crack down on counterfeiting businesses, especially when the unauthorized production relates to international brands … or brands that are not produced in the particular province, and therefore does not cause a conflict of interests with local authorized manufacturers.

Moreover, as noted above, there are spaces in which theft of intellectual property rights to produce and then sell fake branded goods locally is seen as acceptable. Third, and relatedly, they do so because tolerating illegal activities is a necessary condition to enter into and retain a position, however marginal, in global circuits of capital and the supply chains of major transnationals. As Scott Nova of the Workers Rights' Consortium puts it, these are not industries 'driven by moral considerations but by the bottom line' (quoted in Brown *et al.*, 2013). Fourth, they may consider activities that are illegal to be morally justifiable and acceptable because there seems no alternative in spaces abandoned by, or never brought into, mainstream circuits of capital, a non-network of impoverished spaces that constitute the so-called 'Fourth World' (Castells, 2010). These include old former coal districts and de-industrialised industrial regions and cities in the 'North' of the global economy as well as spaces and people that never made it into or beyond the margins in the 'South' – such as small coca growers in Colombia (Allen, 2005). Illegal activities may be allowed as part of survival strategies in spaces detached from the mainstream, precisely because they and people living in them are excluded or have been expelled from the mainstream (Bhattacharyya, 2005; Glenny, 2008). In the absence of the legal mainstream, they offer an alternative mode of survival. Such spaces 'on the margins' are more likely to be those in which 'blind eyes' proliferate, raising theoretical questions as to the relationships between agency, institutions and structures. It is important to emphasise, however, that the illegal is often integral to activities in the core spaces of global capitalism, and also that legal activities (for example, banking and activities in offshore financial centres) may be seen as immoral although maybe necessary, as I show in the next section.

## Flows of money, spaces of sanitisation and disguise: the heightened significance of the illegal in globalising capitalism

In this section, the focus is the spaces and practices through which money generated through illegal activities becomes transformed into 'clean' and legitimate money, and especially money capital, in the legal mainstream economy. As Castells (2010, 183) points out, emphasising the symbiotic links between illegal activities and the overall accumulation process, '[t]he whole criminal system only makes sense if the profits generated can be used and reinvested in the legal economy'. Some money realised through illegal activities remains within circuits of illegal activity, in part financing activities that compete with those that are legally based. However, at least two thirds of the money earned in the illegal economy is immediately spent in the legal economy (Schneider and Enster, 2000). While the precise magnitude may be a matter for debate, the existence of the flow and the fact that it is significant is not. Some of it is used to support livelihoods and enables increased commodity consumption. A much greater proportion becomes money capital, however, invested in diverse legitimate activities and spaces in mainstream markets, enhancing the competitive position of those who own it, contributing systemically to the expanded reproduction of capital and to the sectoral and spatial distribution of growth. Furthermore, the flows of money from illegal activities that become invested in the legal mainstream raise the question of the spaces in which illegally acquired profits become 'clean' money.

This cleansing principally occurs in a particular type of space – offshore tax havens. These are legal jurisdictions, 'secrecy spaces' (Christensen and Hampton, 1999; Hampton, 1996) that provide an interface between legal and illegal economies. Offshore tax havens were originally established as spaces in which perfectly legal (though perhaps ethically and morally dubious) activities of tax avoidance were permissible. Created to facilitate the legal activities of transnational corporations, they subsequently have become the sites of a majority of many of the financial transactions of the global economy: over 50 per cent of international bank lending, approximately 33 per cent of foreign direct investment and 50 per cent of global trade is routed on paper via tax havens which only account for 3 per cent of world gross domestic product (Christensen, 2011, 178). The expansion of these tax havens has been enabled by developments in information and communication technologies and closely linked to the liberalisation of global capital markets and the growing dominance of neo-liberalisation (Sikka, 2003). As a result, however, 'legal institutions granted special status and privilege by society have been subverted to purposes for which they were never intended' (Christensen, 2011, 183) as this institutional structure became used by some (although by no means all: see below) criminals engaged in illegal activities to launder the money that they realised, obscuring it from the spatially limited gaze of state institutions (Picciotto, 2008).

Most offshore tax havens are closely linked to major OECD economies. About half are linked to the United Kingdom, either as Overseas Territories, Crown Dependencies or members of the Commonwealth (Christensen, 2011). Moreover, many offshore tax havens are not 'offshore' as the term is strictly a political statement about the relationship between the state and parts of its related territories (Palan, 1999). Indeed, such spaces have been created at the heart of the globalising economy in cities such as London and New York, with differential regulatory regimes that share one aspect in common: they differentiate regulatory standards as between domestic resident capital and non-resident international capital (Unger and Rawlings, 2008). As the recent

(2012) spate of press reports has emphasised, major banks such as Barclays, HSBC and Standard Charter may well have been routinely involved in money laundering through their bases in London, New York and so on. As Castells (2010, xx1, emphasis added) notes, '[w]orldwide, money laundering networks have taken advantage of a giant market of financial derivatives and loosely regulated institutions, *including institutions located in main financial centres*'. Advanced capitalist states (such as Switzerland, the UK and USA) frequently collude in preventing the development of effective international regulation to tackle illicit financial flows and police cross-border financial flows in and out of the offshore tax havens, precisely because they play a pivotal role in the global accumulation process and the 'new international order of disorder' that this generates. These powerful national states and the international institutions that they dominate, notably the World Bank and International Monetary Fund, and the interests represented and prioritised through them, have been instrumental in constructing the crisis generating invisible architecture of globalisation as well as its more publicly visible institutional forms. Far from this architecture being a *deus ex machina* imposed from above on hapless and helpless national states, powerful national states were and are integrally involved in its construction – although of course it was then imposed on hapless weaker and peripheral states at considerable cost to the majority of their populations.

As a result, offshore tax havens were central to the emergence of neo-liberal globalisation and the opaque practices that spawned innovative financial products such as complex derivatives that lay at the heart of the global financial crisis that exploded in 2008 (Kaletsky, 2010; Patterson, 2010). Because offshore tax havens are permissive spaces, they allow transactions and flows that elsewhere would be deemed illegal and so enable profits generated in the illegal economy to be sanitised and recycled into the circuits of the legal. Elaborate schemes are devised to 'weave dirty money' (Christensen, 2011, 183) into commercial transactions and disguise the proceeds of crime and tax evasion using complex multi-jurisdictional structures that exploit the asymmetries among regulatory spaces. Precisely because they involve activities on the fringes of or beyond the boundaries of formal legal regulation, such offshore financial activities require a high degree of trust to enable them to function successfully as socially constructed key nodes in global financial networks (Hudson A C, 1998).

The liberalisation of capital markets led to an eightfold expansion of cross-border financial flows between 1990 and 2006 (McKinsey Global Institute, 2008), of which around 20 per cent are illegal. A vast quantity of money – US$1.6 trillion annually – flows illegally into offshore accounts (Baker, 2006). Proceeds from bribery, drugs money laundering, human trafficking, counterfeit currencies and goods, smuggling, racketeering and illegal arms trading account for 35 per cent of such cross-border flows originating from developing and transitional economies. In contrast, 65 per cent originate from the proceeds of illegal commercial activity, incorporating mispricing, abusive transfer pricing, and fake and fraudulent transactions, indicative of the pervasive character of illegality in the mainstream ostensibly 'legal' economy and the blurred relationship between legal and illegal. However, national states and multilateral agencies have largely downplayed concerns about 'dirty money' and money laundering, except, revealingly and significantly, in relation to drugs and terrorism, which account for only a small proportion of illegal cross-border flows. This discursive selectivity reflects a tacit recognition of the intimate relationships between legal and illegal activities in the constitution of capitalist economies and of the pivotal role of offshore tax havens as the spaces in which the financial flows between them takes place. As Castells (2010, 172) puts it

> [a]t the heart of the system is money laundering by the hundreds of billions (maybe trillions) of dollars. Complex financial schemes and international trade networks link up the criminal economy to the formal economy, thus deeply penetrating financial markets and constituting a critical, volatile element in a fragile global economy.

This emphasises the way in which the contemporary capitalist economy encourages and facilitates the systematic and large-scale laundering of 'dirty money'. Such limited attention as is given to seeking to halt such flows is focused upon 'bribery of public officials and looting by despots and their cronies. ... the prevailing corruption discourse remains largely focused on pointing fingers at petty officials and ruling kleptomaniacs' (Christensen, 2011, 181–4).

In summary, since the criminal economy is a capitalist economy, the economic rationale for illegal activities depends upon the money that such activities realise becoming money capital invested in legitimate legal activities in the formal economy – and this crucially depends upon successful money laundering operations. At the same time, however, the economic sustainability of the mainstream depends upon continuous and substantial inflows of money from the illegal to the legal economy. The legal and illegal co-exist in a symbiotic relationship. As a result of the explosion of global financial flows offshore tax havens have become major players in global financial markets and have become closely entangled with servicing illegal economic activities, precisely because of the lack of transparency that surrounds transactions carried out in and through them, either because of banking secrecy laws or through *de facto* judicial arrangements and banking practices. As well as illegal tax evasion practices, secretive but legal instruments designed for legal tax avoidance are also used for a wide range of other criminal activities. Offshore tax havens encourage and enable large-scale corruption by providing an operational base used by legal and financial professionals, and their clients, to exploit legislative gaps and tax regulation. However, not all criminals can afford to use offshore tax havens. The high fees charged by 'specialist' accountants, corporate service provides, tax lawyers and multinational financiers limits their use to internationally organised crime syndicates and drug barons who can afford these costs of sanitisation. The bulk of money laundering operates via investments in securities and transfers of funds in global financial markets. Hidden behind a cloak of legal regulations, the legislative gaps are significant – while capital flows have become globally hypermobile, regulatory systems remain largely based on national territories, allowing 'dirty' money to be laundered through complex multi-jurisdictional ladders operating through the global banking system in which offshore tax havens are key locations. This may have systemic implications. Since criminal capital is involved in high risk activities in markets in which the speed, volatility and volume of electronic market transactions has increased greatly, it may well follow, and indeed amplify, speculative turbulence in financial markets. Thus, it may have become an important source of destabilisation of international financial and capital markets, not least in contributing to the global financial crisis that began in 2008. The systemic threats that this could pose to capitalist development are self-evident.

## Summary and conclusions

In summary, then, the key issues considered in this chapter have been the extent and form of the illegal economy, the systematic symbiotic relationships between legal and illegal activities, the spatialities of those links, and the relationships between the flows, paths and spaces of the illegal and legal in the processes of capitalist economic development. The key point to emphasise is that illegal practices are deeply embedded in this process. Economic geography – along with other strands of the social sciences – therefore needs to engage seriously with the illegal if it is to develop a deeper understanding of capitalist economies and their geographies. There is a variety of existing theories in economic geography – strands of political economy, evolutionary and institutional approaches, relational approaches and global production networks for example – that have the capacity to engage with the task of bringing consideration of the illegal more explicitly and fully into the scope of economic geography and which I have drawn on in this chapter. As I have demonstrated, a critical political economy perspective offers a more comprehensive account of the accumulation process and its geographies by engaging with the illegal. Global production networks would likewise benefit from considering the varying role of the illegal at different nodes and links in the network. Similarly, as I have begun to show, by engaging with the illegal and explicitly considering the regulatory structures and practices of illegal economies, institutional approaches could develop a more nuanced account of the institutional bases of contemporary capitalist economies while consideration of the illegal and its changing relationship to the legal could lead to more nuanced and powerful evolutionary approaches. In short, a systematic consideration of the illegal by a range of economic geographers pursuing different approaches to the discipline would add greatly to their theories while at the same time deepening understanding of the varying role of the illegal in constituting and shaping unevenly developed capitalist economies.

Grappling with the illegal has more than just a theoretical significance, however: it also has practical implications. Because capitalism is characterised by combined and uneven development, illegal activities are implicated in the expanded reproduction of socio-spatial differentiation at various scales. While lubricating and facilitating the activities of the legal mainstream economy, they can also make a significant positive contribution to urban and regional development, especially although not exclusively in spaces that are marginalised or excluded from mainstream economic processes and circuits of capital (Nordstrom, 2007). While illegal, they are considered as morally acceptable, an approved part of a moral economy. In some specific circumstances and spaces, then, illegal activities are accepted as legitimate and money acquired from illegal activities can have a positive developmental effect. Castells (2010, 209–10) points to the positive effects of the investment of revenues from the drug trade in parts of Colombia, a reflection of the fact that '[t]he attachment of the drug traffickers to their country, and to their region, goes beyond strategic calculation'. Ransoms from piracy in Somalia, some of which (estimated at around 33 per cent) finds its way from US$ to Somali shillings and the local economy and urban settlements (Garowe and Bosasso) in which the pirates are based, benefit casual labourers and pastoralists. This reflects a culture of sharing wealth that extends to that acquired illegally (Shortland, 2012). Examples such as these raise difficult moral and philosophical questions as to the relationships between the illegal and the morally defensible in poor and marginalised places. Others (Bhattacharyya, 2005), however, argue that the net developmental effect of illegality is negative because of the diversion of resources from the legal economy.

There are, in short, complex and integral relations between the flows and spaces of legal and illegal with contested developmental implications. Economic geographers need to get to grips with these issues if they are to deepen their understanding and theorisation of economic development within the parameters of capitalist social relations. While issues of reliable and valid evidence and of methodologies to create such evidence remain serious, economic geography has the conceptual and theoretical perspectives to grasp the nettle and take seriously the illegal in the constitution of economic geographies and to consider the implications of this in thinking about the practicalities of development.

## Notes

1 The informal economy refers to activities that are legal but carried out by people who are not authorised to do so and who fall outside the scope of legal regulation (ILO, 2002) and as such can be seen as part of the broader illegal economy. Over much of the world, especially but by no means only in the global South, informal employment is the dominant form: for example, between 75 per cent and 95 per cent of employment in national economies in south Asia is informal and unregulated (Upadhyaya, 2008). It has been mainly seen as an alternative mode of survival for those excluded from the formal legal mainstream economy rather than as necessarily and symbiotically linked to that mainstream.

2 While Pollard *et al.* were referring to the absence of consideration of the economies of the global South the point applies with equal force to the neglect of the illegal.
3 This suggests a challenge to state sovereignty and legitimacy, perhaps a different sort of legitimation crisis to that envisaged by Habermas (1976) and perhaps even the deeper corruption of democratic politics (Castells, 2010, 211). Issues of governance are discussed more fully below.
4 Given the complexity of contemporary capitalist economies no single theoretical perspective can encompass the illegal and its relations to the legal in the constitution of those economies. That said, some are more useful than others and emphasis here is on political economy and related approaches and those that focus on global networks and the spaces that they link.
5 This form of production organisation is found in many areas of illegal production. Shen *et al.* (2009, 10) describe how illegal cigarette production in China is a result of 'individual and small groups forming temporary collaborations in order for their shared objective, making profits, to be realised'.
6 While Allen refers to value added, this increase in price is more appropriately thought of as a rent reflecting the scarcity of cocaine and the risks associated with its illegal status.
7 Considerable emphasis has also been placed upon the role of network relationship of trust in the legal economy (Granovetter, 1985; Uzzi, 1996; 1997) but in the context of their complementary role to formal state regulation rather than as a replacement for it.
8 Providing a more thorough evidence base clearly is an issue for those who wish to study illegal economies. That is not, however, my concern here, beyond noting that there are obvious practical difficulties in researching in a rigorously social scientific manner illegal activities such as drug production and sale.
9 'Knock offs' may appear to be the same as branded products but do not abuse the intellectual property rights of any manufacturer, although they do affect sales and profitability of the branded commodities (Chaudhry and Zimmerman, 2010, 3).
10 While major Original Equipment Manufacturing multinationals that out-source production may have Corporate Social Responsibility policies that prescribe legal working practices, these commonly come into conflict with competitive pressures to cut costs. In response, managers deliberately falsify employment records to disguise illegal overtime and underpayment of wages (Sum and Ngai, 2005).
11 It has, however, been argued that illegal 'knock offs' can help 'protect' the value of the legitimate brands that they imitate, enabling the legitimate brand to maintain high prices and generate 'surplus profits' (Saviano, 2008).
12 Electronic materials are illegally exported for a variety of reasons. First, such exports occur because of the difficulties of distinguishing articles for re-use, perhaps after repair, from those that are wastes. Second, other forms of illegal trade take precedence in the concerns of state officials, reflecting a lack of political will. Finally, 'waste tourists' collect wastes that they then sell for profit in their home countries (Nordbrand, 2009). For whatever reason, illegal trade continues under the gaze of 'blind eyes'.
13 Gambetta (2011, 330–1) refers to the 'villain's paradox', whereby 'a criminal needs partners who are also criminals ... [who] are typically untrustworthy people to deal with when their self-interest is at stake. Criminals embody *homo economicus* at his rawest and they know it'.
14 Resorting to brute force and violence can attract unwelcome attention from the police, politicians and public as the history of the various mafia organisations in Italy demonstrates and for that reason is relatively uncommon: Glenny, 2008.
15 Commenting on the sequence of fires and building collapses in the Bangladeshi garment industry, Kazmin *et al.* (2013, 5; see also Brown *et al.*, 2013) note that

these raise serious questions as to the ability of the Bangladeshi government to regulate its main export-oriented industry because of the intimate ties between ownership of the industry and the country's political elite, as members of the government have significant financial interests in the industry. As a result, as Gareth Price Jones, OXFAM's country director in Bangladesh puts it, 'There is a very clear financial incentive for them to give the industry as much of a free pass as possible'. While extreme, this example is by no means unique.

16 It is worth noting one exceptional case – North Korea. The North Korean state practices 'criminal sovereignty', centred on 'penetrating organised crime' based upon its monopoly on the conduct of illegal activities. In particular, it is involved in the production and distribution of illegal drugs (heroin and metamphetamine), counterfeit cigarettes and counterfeit USA dollars. It actively colludes with organised crime networks and criminal syndicates (Chinese Triads, Japanese Yakuza and Russian Mafia) in the global distribution of these illegal commodities, laundering the receipts of such activities through offshore centres (see below) and using the money generated by these activities to finance other state activities and the lifestyles of key Party and state officials (Kan *et al.*, 2010).

# 9 Cultural political economy meets global production networks

## A productive meeting?

### Introduction

The starting point for this chapter is the conclusion reached by Neil Coe and Martin Hess (Coe and Hess, 2007, 22) in their discussion of global production networks that:

> there is a clear need to think about ways of integrating the material as well as the socio-cultural dimensions of global network development. In other words, what we are looking for is a relational network approach that neither under-socialises nor over-socialises current developments in the global economy (Hess and Yeung, 2006). This, we feel, moves us towards a 'cultural political economy' of Global Production Networks, that is capable of integrating both the system-world and life-world aspects of global networks and their related developmental outcomes while at the same time being aware of the pitfalls of conceptual 'imperialism', 'methodological nationalism' (Pries, 2005) and problematic binaries like global-local and culture-economy (Gregson *et al.*, 2001).

In this chapter, I want to take up this challenge and explore some of the implications of pursuing a cultural political economy approach to the analysis of global production networks, understanding production to encompass the whole gamut of activities comprising the circuit of production – that is, the production, exchange and consumption in various ways of what is produced, intentionally and unintentionally. Global production networks can be seen as constituted via a variety of flows (of capital in various forms such as commodities and money, knowledge and people) between a variety of nodes, sites and spaces (of production, exchange and consumption), with varying governance arrangements, both multi-scalar (supra-national, national, regional and urban) and non-scalar networked forms of governance. As these are *global* production networks these nodes and the flows linking them are, by definition, distributed around the globe, albeit unevenly. In pursuing the implications of exploring global production networks through the lens of cultural political economy or, more ambitiously, conjoining global production networks with cultural political economy, I wish to both acknowledge the innovative work of Jessop and Sum (2006) but also to begin to go beyond this and take up the challenge posed by Coe and Hess to integrate serious consideration of the material into cultural political economy. In their approach to cultural political economy Jessop and Sum consider political-economic and semiotic dimensions to great effect in a novel and sophisticated way (Hudson, 2007a). Furthermore, they integrate the treatment of time and space into their analysis, recognising the emergent properties of the complex economy, its development on an open-ended though still path dependent trajectory, and the spatiality of the economy in terms of its different sites and spaces and the connections between them. However, critically, they fail to engage seriously enough with the materiality of the economy (beyond the recognition that the production of use values necessarily involves people working on and with elements of the natural world and matter of various sorts and transforming them to create value) and so with the relations between the material, semiotic and political-economic. These links need to be systematically integrated into a more rounded cultural political economy.

I have argued elsewhere that a cultural political-economy perspective must involve understanding 'the economy' in terms of three registers, each constituted through a variety of circuits and (non-linear) flows linking a variety of sites and spaces (see Hudson 2001a and 2005 for some preliminary consideration of these issues). The first of these is political-economic, encompassing labour processes as well as processes of value creation, exchange and realisation, in addition to the consumption of commodities. The second is semiotic, relating to flows of knowledge and information and to the culturally endowed meanings that things come to acquire. The third is material, conceptualising the economy in terms of materials transformations – biological, chemical and physical – as well as flows of energy, matter and materials, drawing here on literatures in materials and natural sciences and reading these through the perspectives of political economy and semiotics drawn from the social sciences. Finally, it is important to emphasise the relations between these three registers and the flows and spaces through which they are co-constituted and the inter-relationships among them (see Chapter 2). For example, the issue of whether commodities cease to have use values and become 'wastes' or are re-valorised and take on new use values depends, inter alia, on issues of meaning and processes of re-valuation. The identification of the three registers of a cultural political economy approach implies the need to think of three sorts of circuits and the spaces and sites through which they flow and which they help constitute, as well as the relationships among and co-constitution of these flows in terms of the (re)production of global production networks. In addition, as well as the dangers identified by Coe and Hess, it is vital to avoid linear conceptions of flows and to acknowledge the complexity of the economy and of global production networks, the circuits and feedback loops that give rise to emergent properties.[1]

In the remainder of this chapter I will focus upon some aspects of the political-economic, semiotic and material registers of cultural political economy with the intention of deepening understanding of global production networks. The identification of these three registers implies the need to think through the relationships among and co-constitution of the various sorts of circuits, flows and transformations encompassed by them, as well as giving consideration to the spaces and sites through which they pass and which they help constitute. Of necessity this will be a partial and selective coverage but one that will, I hope, nonetheless, realise its intended effects and help deepen understanding of the concept of global production networks.

## Political economy and circuits of value

In the course of a single day, we – that is, those of us in the more developed parts of the global political economy – typically come into contact with a more or less sophisticated range of artefacts and material goods and objects that underpin our daily lives and, indeed, make them possible. Automobiles, frozen foodstuffs, mobile phones, shirts and shoes, the personal computer on which I'm writing this – the list is long, if not quite endless. Often, much of the time, we take their availability and presence for granted, even when we occasionally recall that many of them were produced on the other side of the world in China or parts of south east Asia. How do they come to be produced, acquire value and find their way to us? How can we begin to understand these processes of production, value creation and valuation?

As a starting point in seeking answers to these questions, it is critical to recognise the existence of different concepts of value and processes of valuation and the articulation and relations between different socio-economic systems (or social formations) grounded in different concepts of value. At a rather high level of abstraction and generalisation, all forms of economy and society may be conceptualised as reproduced via continuous flows of value as products circulate between people, times and places. These flows of value, moving through the sequence of production, exchange and consumption, are both constituted in and help constitute circuits of social reproduction. Value can be thought of as generated through relations and things which, via the material and social practices of the economy (production, exchange and consumption), come to be regarded as socially useful, helpful, uplifting or, more narrowly but generally, as fundamental to everyday life going on 'as normal'. These flows encompass the exchange of value embodied in products and may involve the exchange of money for work or the capacity to work, which could lead to an augmentation of future production and/or consumption. Social and material survival requires that circuits of social reproduction deliver such flows of value, in appropriate quantities, distributions and time/spaces. In turn, successfully maintaining such circuits necessarily involves often-subtle processes of regulation and complex intersections of material and social relationships and practices in the formation and definition of value.

The material and the social are intimately related via circuits of co-evolution and co-determination: 'the significance of any single moment of economic activity begins to make sense in material terms only in the context of circuits of material reproduction' (Lee, 2002, 336). Material relations, imbued with social meaning, involve the practice and co-ordination of circuits of production, exchange and consumption (and in a later section of the chapter I return to issues of materiality from a rather different perspective). Thus social relations, variable over time/space, define the meanings of material practices. These relationships and meanings may become hegemonic, voluntarily, often unquestioningly, accepted and confer a sense of social order via the recurrent practices of the economy. In other circumstances, maintaining social reproduction requires deployment of power within circuits of authority, control and direction to shape economic processes and circuits of material practices (and, viewed historically, hegemony has often been preceded by domination). The substantive content and meaning of conceptions of value are therefore spatio-temporally specific. What is seen as valuable in one socio-spatial context may not be so in another. The origins of these differences lie in different modes of socio-economic organisation and are expressed in different ways of conceptualising and theorising 'the economy'.

While recognising that contemporary capitalist economies are constituted via a variety of social relations and their associated concepts of value, however, it is equally important to acknowledge the dominance of capitalist concepts of value in the contemporary world, as this is what defines these economies *as* capitalist. Recognising that there are multiple circuits of capital (for example, a primary circuit constituted via co-existing circuits of commodity, money and industrial capital, as well as secondary and tertiary circuits: Chapter 2; Harvey, 1982; Hudson, 2005), I will take the (admittedly over-simplified) case of the circuit of industrial capital and the processes and regulatory mechanisms by which this improbable process of the circulation of capital is routinely reproduced to develop this point. Mainstream capitalist production is centred upon commodity production, the production of things with the intention of sale in markets, and value expansion via the production and realisation of surplus-value. Consider the production of that iconic commodity of mass produced modernity, the automobile – a result of workers assembling a huge variety of materials and components embodying a vast range of materials (various metals, glass, plastics, hydrocarbons, rubber, wood and so on), fixed in a particular order to create the finished product. More generally, and abstractly, capital brings together constant and variable capital – the necessary equipment, components and materials and labour – so that in the moment of production commodities are created that embody greater value than the value laid out to purchase the inputs to the production process. This is a consequence of the unique attributes of labour-power as a fictitious commodity, since people create surplus-value in excess of the value equivalent of the wages that they are paid for going to work (see Hudson, 2001a, 14–47). Consequently, capitalist production is simultaneously a labour process based upon the exploitation of labour (and so one that encompasses the life world at work of those engaged in production and waged work more generally), a process of valorisation and value expansion and a process of material transformation,[2] as a result of which commodities simultaneously possess the properties of use values and exchange values. This form of organising production is based on the class structural separation of, and dialectical relation between, capital and labour within the abstract conceptual space defined by the capitalist mode of production.

In actually existing capitalisms, or capitalist social formations, these social relations are extended and stretched over space and imposed upon people to define the character of social reproduction – although not without contestation and resistance – by commercial, industrial and financial institutions operating over multiple and mutually constitutive spatial scales from the very local to the global. Space in general and particular spaces are thus integral to the biography of commodities, which move between various sites of production, exchange and consumption as they flow around and beyond the circuits of capital, an insight that has been powerfully developed by the perspectives of global commodity chains, global value chains and, most recently, global production networks. In this sense, to conceptualise production in terms of global production networks is to do no more – and no less – than to recognise the practical realities of capitalist economies.

Commercial, industrial and financial institutions define highly focused and specific notions of value directed at profitability and accumulation and use them to constrain and direct capitalist circuits of social reproduction – that is, the expansion of capital and the socio-spatial extension (for example, in the contemporary period, to China and other emerging economies) and deepening (in existing centres of capitalism) of capitalist social relationships as these penetrate realms from which they were previously excluded such as the body, the family and the home (for example, see Bauman, 2005, 81–115). In this way, the social and material dimensions of social reproduction are mutually formative and inseparable and take a specific form within the parameters of capitalist social relationships. For example, in the formal capitalist economy value can be defined as market price (as in neo-classical and mainstream orthodox theories), or as socially necessary labour time (as in the orthodox Marxian labour theory of value or as in the value theory of labour: Elson, 1978).[3] Thus, in marked contrast to mainstream and neo-classical conceptions, Marxian analyses recognise in their conceptualisation of flows of value and circuits of capital in the specific context of the formal capitalist economy, that values and prices are not synonymous and that the relationships between them need to be considered. Not least this is because of the characteristics of money and monetary systems and the disciplining power of money on the practices and developmental trajectories of economies.

The routine performance of the social relationships of production, exchange and consumption and the day-to-day conduct and market transactions of a capitalist economy (such as declaring profits, paying wages or buying food and clothing) are conducted in terms of prices, not values. Economic agents freely enter into market relations mediated by monetary prices. Money thus serves as both a medium of exchange and a measure of value, though not one that equates to values defined in terms of socially necessary labour time (and the issue of how best to conceptualise relations between values and prices has become a matter of some, as yet unresolved and probably irresolvable, debate). What is clear is that monetary price is always a slippery, imperfect and unreliable representation of value. Discrepancies between supply and demand in markets result in commodities being exchanged at prices that diverge from their values. As production conditions diverge from social and technical averages, the amounts of labour time embodied in commodities deviate from the socially necessary amount that defines the value of a commodity. Commodities thus contain varying amounts of labour time but are sold at the same market price while money prices typically diverge from exchange values. As a result, there is a re-distributive flow of value between spaces, sectors and companies via the processes of competition. This re-distribution is critically important in relation to the systemic dynamism of capitalist economies, to processes of 'creative destruction' as firms seek competitive advantage via innovation and revolutionising the what, how and where of production, and so to their historical geographies of production and uneven development and the current configuration of global production networks.

Beyond the confines of the formal capitalist economy and theorisations of it but within the broader confines of capitalism and their theorisation, there are alternative conceptions of value in terms of labour time (as in Local Exchange Trading Systems, or LETS), or in terms of the intrinsic worth of things or affective dimensions such as friendship, love and respect – not all of which can be represented in terms of price. Indeed, there are things that people value that are, quite literally, priceless. It is impossible to put a price upon them because their value cannot be translated into a quantitative monetary metric. Such alternative conceptions of value influence economic practices within the spaces of mainstream economies of capitalism, while they also permeate the interstices that capital has abandoned or never found sufficiently attractive, or those areas from which, in a given time/space, it is prohibited by regulation or morality, custom and the force of tradition. It is also important to emphasise that these alternative conceptions of value often underpin the reproduction of the circuits of capital that constitute the formal economy (for example, through the reproduction of labour-power via domestic labour and the life world of the home as class and non-class relations become entwined in particular ways) while in turn for many people the successful reproduction of their daily lives depends upon their capacity to purchase and consume commodities (and so the entanglement of their life world in spaces of exchange and consumption). Similarly, circuits of capital are often augmented by processes of accumulation via dispossession (seeing this as an enduring feature of the process of accumulation rather than a transitory phase in the early history of capitalism: for example, see Wood, 2002), the appropriation of value from spaces of non-capitalist economic practices and values and their translation into circuits of capital.

The moment of exchange is a critical one as commodities move from the realm of exchange value to use value and the value (including the surplus-value) embodied in them is realised in monetary form and once again becomes money capital, and as such available to be thrown into the circulation process and advanced as capital for re-investment. The sale of commodities thus forms a decisive moment in the circuit of capital. Some commodities are sold to form inputs to other processes of production and the value embodied in them is transferred to new commodities. This 'productive consumption' is expressed in relations between firms and supply chains, often stretching around the world as a consequence of the production strategies of the transnational corporations and multinational corporations that construct and drive global production networks. For those commodities sold for final consumption, subsequent processes of consumption ensure that commodities move from the realm of exchange to that of use values. At the same time, they move from the life worlds and workplaces of those that produced them and become part of the material life worlds of those who consume them and are otherwise affected by their consumption. Often – increasingly – these life worlds are widely separated, to be found in distant parts of the world, as global production networks involve segmenting the global economy into discrete spaces of production, exchange and consumption for a given commodity. In addition, the subsequent post-sale life of things may, at the end of their useful lives to their initial purchasers or users, lead to their re-valorisation and use by others or to their categorisation as 'wasted' and no longer things with a use value (a point again taken up below in more detail).

In summary, the asymmetrical interdependencies between both people, as a result of their socio-spatial positionality, and concepts of value emphasise that capitalist economies involve complex and multiple flows of values, underlain by different conceptions of value. More generally, the fundamental point within a cultural political economy approach is that conceptions and circuitous flows of value vary with the form and type of economic organisations under consideration and the positionality of those constructing the category of value. This positionality, especially in terms of class relations, in turn is pivotal in determining which concepts of value become dominant, and the ways in which circuits of value become constructed. In similar fashion, relationships between capitalist and other non-capitalist forms of class relations and economy become constructed in ways that reflect differential power relations and this is of very direct relevance to the construction of global production networks.

Much recent literature in the 'new economic geography' and cognate disciplines has emphasised the role of relations of trust, non-market institutions and untraded interdependencies (Storper, 1995) forged in civil society as well as in the economy itself as both helping constitute and regulate the social relations of the contemporary economy, including those denoted by the concept of global production networks. The cultural and institutional 'turns' have placed heavy emphasis on such influences. There is no doubt that such influences can be significant in reproducing the social relations of the economy in particular times and places and in linking these places together as nodes in its constitutive circuits and global production networks. Equally, contra much of the recent new economic geography literature, I would argue that these influences are not new; indeed, they have been significant in the constitution of capitalist economies from the outset (for example, see Carney *et al.*, 1977). What *is* new is the claim as to the discovery of their contemporary significance as part of a new form of capitalist socio-spatial organisation by proponents of the new economic geography (cf. Hall, 1991).

Alongside this, however, and in contrast to much recent literature, I argue that it is necessary to pay attention to the continuing role of the national state in shaping these circuits and networks and the ways in which they are reproduced, as well as giving due recognition to other regulatory mechanisms and processes. The increased regulatory significance of both sub-national states and transnational policy régimes is undeniable. However, national states help constitute these other scales of regulation and co-exist in complex relationships with them so that the architecture of regulation is much more nuanced, subtle and multi-scalar. Nonetheless, both directly and indirectly national states continue to play an important role in shaping a range of commodity markets, such as those for products, labour and knowledge and so in shaping the spatiality of regulatory spaces. This is recognised in the varieties-of-capitalism literature and in the various strands of the regulationist approach (see Jessop and Sum, 2006), while at the same time acknowledging that the national cannot be a priori assumed to the main – or even less, the sole – scale of regulatory capacity. The point to emphasise is that while there has been growing regulatory influence at both sub-national and transnational scales, the (national) state continues to play a key role in ensuring that global production networks and the improbable processes of capital accumulation and the expanded reproduction of the circuit of capital are routinely made possible.

## Circuits of meaning, flows of knowledge: advertising, brands and the circulation of capital

The process of production within the circuit of industrial capital results in commodities that embody surplus-value – they embody more value than the commodities that were consumed in their production, precisely because of the unique attributes of the commodity labour-power and the fact that human labour creates more value than the value equivalent of the money received in the form of wages. However, until these commodities are sold, the value – to the capitalist – that they contain remains locked up, unavailable for further investment. For that value to be released in money form, so that it can again become money capital, the commodities must be sold. How and why should this happen?

To be sold, commodities must be seen to be useful to their purchasers – to have use value – and this in turn implies that they are seen as meaningful in the context of their life worlds. Such meanings may relate to strictly utilitarian aspects of commodities (for example, sheet steel purchased by automobile producers) or, increasingly in the case of final consumers, their affective dimensions and culturally coded symbolic meanings. The sale of commodities thus depends upon flows of information from their producers to potential purchasers, both other companies (buying commodities as inputs to the production of other commodities) and purchasers of commodities for 'final' consumption (although in practice many consumer goods are then re-sold on to others by their initial purchasers or recipients). In the context of global production networks, this implies that knowledge about commodities flows globally and commodities come to have shared meanings for people in different parts of the world. In this global context, advertising plays a critical role in the production and dissemination of knowledge about commodities, the creation of conceptual spaces of meaning and sale, seeking to construct intended meanings for them in the eyes of potential purchasers and consumers. Often, however, these intended meanings are contested and challenged, creating instead unintended meanings as a result of consumer resistance and subversion. Producers may respond to this by changing the projected image of the product through advertising or materially alter the commodity that they are trying to sell (Hudson, 2005, Chapter 4).

While now central to the contemporary global economy and the reproduction of global production networks, it is only quite recently that advertising has been more than a marginal influence on patterns of sales and production (Williams, 1980, 177–86). The formation of modern advertising was intimately bound up with the emergence of new forms of monopoly capitalism around the end of the nineteenth and beginning of the twentieth century as one element in corporate strategies to create, organise and where possible control markets, especially for mass produced consumer goods. Mass production necessitated mass consumption, and this in turn required a certain homogenisation of consumer tastes for final products. At its limit, this involved seeking to create 'world cultural convergence', to homogenise consumer tastes and engineer a 'convergence of lifestyle, culture and behaviours among consumer segments across the world' (Robins, 1989, 23). The reference to 'consumer segments' is crucial here, for globalisation does not imply the elimination of variations in consumer preferences and lifestyles but rather the socio-spatial segmenting of markets across the globe.

The development of modern advertising drew heavily on psychological theories about how to create subjects, enabling advertising and marketing to take on a 'more clearly psychological tinge' (Miller and Rose, 1997, cited in Thrift, 1999, 67). Increasingly, the emphasis in advertising has switched from providing 'factual' information to the symbolic connotations of commodities, since the crucial cultural premise of advertising is that the material object being sold is never in itself enough. Even those commodities providing for the most mundane necessities of daily life must be imbued with symbolic qualities and culturally endowed meanings via the 'magic system' (Williams, 1980) of advertising. In this way and by altering the context in which advertisements appear, things 'can be made to mean "just about anything" ' (McFall, 2002, 162) and the 'same' things can be endowed with different intended meanings for different individuals and groups of people, thereby offering mass produced visions of individualism. As such, representations of the consumer are a necessary component of the existence of markets. Consequently, contemporary capitalism could not function and global production networks could not exist as they do without advertising.

Consumers are susceptible to influence via advertising precisely because, as a result of their locations in specific socio-spatial-temporal structures, they have – and can *only* have – imperfect and partial knowledge of commodities and markets. This creates space for companies actively to seek to change or create consumer tastes and cultivate preferences for new products. Moreover, advertising practice 'constantly problematises the entire notion of "specific products" and constitutes a set of technologies for attempting both to de-stabilise markets and then to re-institutionalise them around new, strategically calculated product definitions'. In an environment in which markets and products are 'continuously and dynamically changing … advertising focuses on exploiting these environmental conditions, creating variations between product concepts as a means to reconfigure both consumer demand and competitive market structures' (Slater, 2002, 68–73). This powerfully emphasises the way in which advertising practices and products can be central to the re-definition of markets via re-creating the intended meanings of commodities as advertising signs and symbols are progressively de-coupled from specific commodities and so to the prosecution of destabilising 'market disturbing' strategies of strong Schumpeterian competition of the transnational corporations and multinational corporations that drive global production networks.

While there may well be limits to the de-coupling of brand logos and their meaning from specific commodities, as particular objects need to maintain a degree of stability of meaning in order that they can perform as commodities and so enable markets to be (re)produced (see also Chapter 2), the de-coupling of signs and symbols from any specific referent product has been further extended with the growing emphasis on the promotion of brands as opposed to advertising specific commodities. The increasing decoupling of signs and symbols from specific commodities has been a crucial move in the creation of global markets and global production networks. The increasing prevalence of 'enormously powerful and ubiquitous global brands or logos' with a 'fluid-like power' stems from the ways in which 'the most successful corporations over the last two decades have shifted from the actual manufacture of products to become brand producers, with enormous marketing, design, sponsorship, public relations and advertising expenditures' (Urry, 2001, 2). While retaining their pivotal headquarters, design and marketing functions in the core of the global economy, the production of material commodities and increasingly associated service functions has been shifted to new locations in the global economy (above all in the initial decades of the twenty-first century, China and India). As such, it signals a major change in the character of contemporary accumulation and the spatiality of global production networks, but it is important to stress that the creation of brands is a well-established development across a wide spectrum of commodities. Brands typically are tied to specific proprietary markers, such as hieroglyphs or logos (for example, the curly script and curvaceous bottle that encourage people all over the world to drink Coca-Cola) or a particular person (such as David Beckham, Richard Branson, Venus Williams or Tiger Woods), which both distinguish the brand and define particular brand families (Klein, 2000) and can be recognised all around the globe. Such logos are deliberately targeted and intended to force the viewer, wherever and whoever they may be, to take notice of them, 'to underscore the capacity of the brand to condense its message to its mark' (Franklin *et al.*, 2000, 69). This capacity is partly a result of extensive processes of market research and promotion and of the ways in which the phatic inscriptions of the brand create and maintain links among product items, lines and assortments.

Proprietary markers for brands thus operate as phatic images (Virilio, 1991), images that target attention, synthesise perception. As a result, 'the time of the brand is that of the instantaneity of recognition and thus discrimination: brands work through the immediacy of their recognisability' (Lury, 2000, 169). As a phatic image, the brand works to displace or de-contextualise bodily or biographical memory and re-contextualise it within its own body of expectations, understandings and associations, built up through market research, advertising, promotion, sponsorship and the use of themed retail space and manipulation of an object's environment or time/space context. As a result, brand owners frequently present branded objects in serially repetitive themed spaces of exchange and sale – parks, restaurants, pubs and shops – or contribute to the elaboration of themed lifestyles through the sponsoring of events or activities. The result is that 'these brands are free to soar, less as the dissemination of goods and services than as collective hallucinations' (Klein, 2000, 22). This creation of such distinct '(hallucinatory) spaces of brands' can extend across particular social strata scattered across the globe and exemplifies the dynamic dialectic between spaces and circuits of meanings as part of the process of (re)producing global production networks.

The significance of the brand as a phatic image is that it can, to an extent,

> recoup the effects of the subject or consumer's perception as the outcome of its own powers through an assertion of its ability to motivate the product's meaning and use. This is achieved through the ways the brand operates to link the subject and object in novel ways, making available for appropriation aspects of the experience of product use *as if they were the properties of the brand.*
>
> (Franklin *et al.*, 2000, 68–9, emphases in original)

More precisely, this is the intended way in which the potential purchaser should read the brand and be prepared to pay a premium for acquiring it. Purchasers who are able to thus pay for the brand name, the aesthetic meaning and cultural capital that this confers, rather than for the use value of the commodity per se. What matters is capacity to pay, irrespective of where in the world a person lives. These aesthetic and cultural meanings of brands and sub-brands then become ways of socio-spatially segmenting markets by ability to make the premium payments required to possess the desired brand. Successful global brands, such as Benetton, Bodyshop, Ford, Gap, Jurassic Park, Nike, McDonald's, Starbucks, Virgin have become powerful precisely because they have succeeded in the creation of 'family resemblances', a form of commodity kinship through which commodities become seen as sharing essential characteristics: 'the shared substance of their brand identities' (Franklin *et al.*, 2000, 69) thus becomes available to those who can and are prepared to pay for the cachet of the brand, irrespective of where they happen to live around the globe. Global commodity flows are then shaped by the distribution of specific groups of consumers, whose tastes and preferences have in turn been shaped by the advertising strategies of the global corporations that produce those commodities, whose identities have been constructed around the consumption of particular goods and brands (Lash and Urry, 1994, 140–1). In strong opposition to those who argue the case for 'consumer sovereignty', Williams (1980, 193) emphasises that 'in economic terms, the fantasy operates to project the production decisions of the major corporations as "your" choice, the "consumer"s selection of priorities, methods and style'. With the development and global diffusion of the mass media, especially TV, advertising linked to the emergence of dominant brands has become a greatly enhanced 'magic system' via more powerful and persuasive processes of sign production that penetrate into the day-to-day life worlds and living spaces of people across the globe.

Others argue that such a perspective over-emphasises the power that advertisers, allied to retailers, can exert over consumers (Jackson, 1993). Advertising is rarely the sole or even most important source of pre-purchase knowledge about the existence or qualities of particular commodities, 'seldom the single stimulator of wants and desires' (Pred, 1996, 13). According to Lash and Urry (1994, 277), consumers have become less susceptible to the illusions of mass consumption than was once the case. While true with respect to specific places and social groups, however, this is certainly not the case universally. They claim that people are increasingly reflexive about their society, its product and its images, 'albeit images which are themselves part of what one might term a semiotic society'. This raises critical questions as to *which* people have the capacity to become 'active consumers'. While this claim may have validity in some socio-spatial circumstances – for example, that fraction of the new middle class endowed with ample cultural capital and writing about itself? – there are evident dangers in over-generalisation here. There is, for example, little evidence of people becoming 'active consumers' over much of marginalised places of Europe and North America, let alone sub-Saharan Africa, as different people, their life worlds and spaces are included in or excluded from global production networks.

To better appreciate the significance of processes of advertising and branding requires a more nuanced and non-linear view of the production and circulation of meanings as a continuous process. The starting point is the creation, within given social conditions, of a series of texts by producers, which are then read and interpreted by different audiences according to their social conditions, positionality and lived cultures. Audiences undertake the cultural work of interpretation and their culturally constructed knowledges therefore play a key role in the decoding and interpreting of media messages and the ways in which adverts are understood. Such understandings, and the acceptance or contestation of messages, are likely to vary significantly between time/spaces and types of people. Moreover, this process of decoding is not simply a semiotic process; the uses to which people put things are a major factor in the determination of meaning. This work of interpretation can in turn give rise to recursive feedback loops from consumers to producers, and learning by producers from consumers. Recognition that advertisements are 'read' in ways that are culturally constructed and vary over time/space and with the class, gender, ethnicity, age and so on of the 'reader', allows companies to use advertising strategies as a way of segmenting markets by seeking to create meanings that are specific to these segments. In this sense, advertising is an inherently spatial practice, creating and differentiating circuits and spaces of meaning as integral elements of global production networks.

This recognition of the socio-spatial segmentation of markets renders redundant conceptions of globalisation that postulate the creation of a homogeneous global market. Indeed, they simply miss the point. One has only to consider the changes to the advertising strategies for Coca-Cola to appreciate this. After decades of a strategy based on the message of 'one sight, one sound, one sell', Coca-Cola has sought to devise an advertising strategy that seeks to respond to local specificities and 'to make Coca-Cola appeal to every type of consumer, of every culture and nation, on every occasion' (Mitchell, 1995, cited in Hudson, 2005). This exemplifies the way in which major multinationals are increasingly recognising the need to be aware of spatial differentiation in order to be successful globally and reproduce their global production networks. Increasingly they are devolving responsibility to local branches or agencies for creating adverts that are customised to local conditions – variations on a global theme, but tailor-made to fit local circumstances, increasingly multi-local rather than variations on a multinational theme. It is, however, important to recognise that these are very socio-spatially selective processes of inclusion in and exclusion from the spaces of global production networks.

Finally, while recognising that people can contest the intentions of advertisers, so that they 'do not *straightforwardly* draw upon meanings prescribed by retailers and advertisers' but contest and re-work commodity meanings (Leslie and Reimer, 1999, 433, emphasis added), there are dangers in going too far in celebrating consumer autonomy, reflexivity and resistance. While the process may not be straightforward, advertising undoubtedly can exert enormous influence in mediating and shaping the changing relationship between the sign values of commodities, their symbolic meanings, and their material content and form (Fine and Leopold, 1993, 28). Most fundamentally, companies continue to realise surplus-value via the successful sale of commodities, suggesting that their advertising and brand strategies have considerable efficacy in relation to reproducing capital on an expanded scale and in reproducing global production networks.

## Material circuits, flows of matter

As noted above, there is recognition of the materiality of the economy in Marx's own writing and in subsequent Marxian political economy but, in contrast to analyses of issues such as the labour process, value creation and the circulation of capital, this has remained relatively underdeveloped. While cultural and semiotic issues have been much more thoroughly integrated via the development of cultural political economy, allowing a more integrated treatment of issues of consumption, exchange and production, consideration of the economy in terms of materiality and flows of matter has remained largely conspicuous by its absence. It is an absence that needs addressing, not least as it may well have implications for our understanding of processes of value creation and the creation of meanings.

Irrespective of the specific social relationships of a given economy, economic activity involves the application of human labour, deploying a variety of artefacts and tools, to transform and transport elements of nature to become socially useful and valued products. In emphasising the articulation of people with inanimate objects and tools to produce the materials transformations that give rise to material goods, there are clear resonances with the 'performativity programme' (Callon, 2006). Every economic activity – production, exchange, consumption – therefore necessarily involves materials transformations, chemical and physical transformations of matter from one state to another but materials transformations that chronically exceed their intended effects, as unruly matter escapes the frame defined by a given transformative process. Consequently at every stage in the economy the transformation of materials has both intended and unintended – the latter often invisible or otherwise undetected as well as unwanted – effects. This leads to a conceptualisation of the economy as a complex socio-technical process with emergent effects, with important implications for a cultural political economy perspective. Any production process in turn always depends upon a particular material configuration of the means of production, an assortment of tools, artefacts, machines and so on (that is, an assemblage, or ensemble, of fixed capital within the social relations of capital), itself the product of previous materials transformations, that both enables new forms of transformation and is itself continuously transformed by this process.[4]

Recognising that the production of excess is a chronic feature of economies has important implications. Not least, we need to re-consider how we understand the category of 'waste' and the ways in which 'waste' is produced and this offers a productive route into consideration of the broader issue of the materiality of the economy and the material register of a cultural political economy approach. Conventionally 'waste' is seen as the end-of pipe/end-of-process unwanted and unvalued product of a linear process. In contrast, the concept of 'waste' that emerges here is one of 'waste' as endemic and unavoidable, an unintended consequence of every stage in the economy, every material transformation. From the point of view of capital such wastes represent value lost and so there are pressing imperatives both to minimise waste production and to find new uses for such materials as do become wastes and to re-valorise them, so that materials that, from the perspective of one set of economic processes have become wastes, literally wasted, once again become sources of value.

A corollary of viewing the economy in this way is that the environmental footprint (Jackson, 1995) of a global production network or indeed any socio-spatial form of organising economic activity and its practices, its socio-ecological and socio-spatial distribution, is always a mixture of intended and unintended effects and attempts to ameliorate the undesirable effects of both. Consider for example the production of steel: as well as the desired product, this gives rise to waste gases produced from the blast furnaces and basic oxygen steel shops; slag produced from blast furnaces; off-cuts of steel generated from the continuous casting machines and rolling mills; and so on. This in turn directs attention towards those practices that seek to reduce wastes by improving the efficiency of production processes, by recycling surplus at every stage in these processes (such as off-cuts of steel in steel mills), of finding ways of using wastes (such as using slag in construction), of finding new uses for products that have reached the end of their (original) socially useful life and so on. In this sense 'waste' is endemic but so too are strategies to seek to reduce it and re-valorise materials, in part for reasons of economic efficiency and competitiveness, in part because of ethical and moral concerns about waste in a society characterised by inequality and the ecological consequences of wastes. An important corollary of viewing wastes in these ways is that they and their effects become seen as endemic in the life worlds of virtually everyone, and not simply in the life worlds of production in which they are created. Indeed, the consequences of wastes on the health and well-being of people, especially marginalised people in marginalised spaces as these become the destination of wastes produced elsewhere and/or the location of heavily polluting activities (such as nuclear waste reprocessing) are an issue of major significance as spaces of waste are created as an integral part of global production networks. As *any* form of production, transport and consumption has a varied environmental footprint, the issue is not whether or not global production networks have such an ecological footprint but rather what sort of footprint they have and what the socio-ecological and socio-spatial distribution of this footprint is. Such issues have yet to be integrated within a global production network perspective, however.

The proposition that the economy can be productively conceived in terms of materials transformations can be explored further via drawing upon conceptualisations of the economy in terms of flows of energy and chemical and physical transformations of elements of nature that leave an unavoidable trace, with the laws of thermodynamics providing key insights in understanding these processes of materials transformation. Crucially, thermodynamics characterises *any* material transformation as conservative of materials and dissipative of energy. The conservation of materials is further discussed below but it is important at this point to note the critical systemic implications of the second law and the dissipation of energy in relation to entropy. As a result there is a constant tendency to disorder in the universe. Whilst order can be preserved locally, for example within a given socio-ecological system, this is on the basis of imported flows of energy – ultimately from the sun but in relation to the contemporary socio-ecological system, on the basis of carbon-based sources of energy such as coal, oil and natural gas. Consuming such sources of energy, however, results in emissions of greenhouse gases that in turn pose a threat to the continuing viability of the system (see Hudson, 2001a, chapter 9). The limits that these laws unavoidably impose upon any form of economic activity at all scales are critical and in the context of global production networks, linking diverse activities and locations around the globe, these limits may be particularly acute.

Each industrial process and economic activity *necessarily* involves the transformation of materials and energy from one form to another; this is an unavoidable truth. The laws of thermodynamics provide very specific rules and limits that govern these transformations; they cannot be altered or suspended by human intervention and in that sense set natural limits on social production and its relationships to nature (Georgescu-Roegen, 1971). Acknowledgement of such limits is, I would argue, a progressive move: 'in the face of realities which are genuinely invulnerable to human intentionality, adaptation by modifying or even abandoning our initial aspirations [to control nature] is to be recognised as a form of emancipation' (Benton, 1989, 58). The laws of thermodynamics state that energy is neither created nor destroyed during these transformations although it may change in physical form (for example, from kinetic energy to heat) and that the total mass of inputs to a transformation process is equal to the total mass of outputs. This identity also holds at the level of individual atomic elements during (non-nuclear) materials transformations. Inputs that do not emerge as desired products therefore necessarily appear as unwanted by-products or wastes. Crucially, however, in contrast to linear conceptions of the economy which see 'wastes' as the end product of linear processes, in the perspective of a critical cultural political economy 'wastes' are seen as created at each and every stage of a transformative process as this exceeds the capacity of the processes to contain them as intended, so creating an unwanted surplus. This in turn has implications for conceptualising the economy in terms of global production networks.

Furthermore, this focus upon the flow of materials and material transformations emphasises that the economy can be thought of as a (non-linear) sequence of configurations, each of which 'is more or less a transient event, a temporary (possibly long-lived but temporary) use of some set of atoms and energy'. Moreover, as Frosch (1997, 159) puts it, neatly summarising a well-established set of concerns,

> we can postulate a universe of material/energy paths through the production, life, and dissolution of any product or set of products. We can also consider each path to be a sequence of transformations from one material/energy embodiment to another. We can view the whole of material industry as a network of such paths and transformations, connected at each end (extraction of materials and disposal of products) to the environment external to the process and product and at places in the middle (disposal of incidental waste).

In referring to networks of paths and transformation, Frosch offers a perspective that seeks to emphasise the complexity of the economy and its grounding in continuous flows and transformations of matter. From this perspective, global production networks can be seen as a particular spatio-temporal 'fixing' of matter and material flows, held in place by socially specific regulatory practices.

This conception of economic practices as materials transformations in principle allows precise accounting of their environmental impacts. Consequently, it also provides the conceptual basis for industrial ecology and the methodologies of life-cycle analysis and industrial metabolism that seek to construct a set of accounts that centre on the notion of mass balance – that is, that the sum total of a particular chemical within a production process remains constant as it passes from production, to consumption, to disposal, with the social relations and institutions within which people behave providing the stabilising controls. However, while recognising the value of these methodologies as accounting frameworks and reminding us that there are chemical and physical limits to economic practices, my purpose in drawing upon them here is a different one; that is, to emphasise the ways in which matter changes state as it moves through the economy in flows that are socially shaped, with both intended and unintended effects. Once materials pass from one particular process, configuration and state, they simply re-enter the stream of the flow of matter until this flow is interrupted by their incorporation into another such socially constructed process and their configuration in new ways – for example, in a new Global Production Network. Moreover, the particular (bio)chemical and physical characteristics of particular configurations are crucial in shaping, if not quite determining, the possibilities for creating values. Consider, for example, the complex of materials flows and transformations within a major integrated chemicals complex and those within a clothing factory and the differing ways in which the characteristics of the varying materials and matter with which they work, their capacities and (chemical and physical) properties, influence the configurations into which they can be formed and held for varying periods of time and embody value, how they can be transformed into commodities for which markets can be created and the value embodied in them realised through sale. In terms of the relationships between processes of value creation and material flows and transformations, these specificities are therefore critical. Now of course capitalist production is an inherently speculative and risky activity, with all manner of possibilities of technical failure and breakdowns in the social relations of production within and between firms. As a result, there is no guarantee that commodity production will be successful and the circuit of capital completed – in that sense economies are always path contingent rather than path dependent (Chapters 2 and 5). But the point is that the very possibilities of specific sorts of commodity production – and particular forms of global production network – necessarily depend upon the sorts of materials configurations in which matter of particular sorts can be captured and held.

While it is the case that there is some attention paid to issues of materiality in the social sciences and this is valuable and informative, it is also the case that it is partial and limited. Material analysis in cultural anthropology and other parts of the social sciences is concerned with the meaning and representation of the material forms of artefacts, the ways they are represented and the meanings they come to have. This is fine as far as it goes but it remains focused upon issues of representation of the material form rather than addressing the dynamics of the flow of matter from one form to another. Cultural political economy to date likewise has little if anything to say on these issues and this forms a major limitation. In short, both cultural political economy and existing approaches to material analysis in the social sciences focus on the moments of 'interruption' of the flows and the fixing of matter into temporary configurations and forms via the social processes of the economy in particular places (for example as commodities or other forms of material product), albeit in different ways.[5] However, the laws of thermo-dynamics cannot be abolished or suspended by human intervention. Indeed, it is these that perhaps constitute the iron laws of the economy as a temporary 'interruption' of the continuous flow of matter. In this sense, focusing upon the materiality of the economy poses some interesting challenges and questions for those political economists for whom 'second nature' has been taken-for-granted, an unquestioned given.

Emphasising the material register of a more comprehensive cultural political economy therefore highlights the ways in which matter is conserved and energy dissipated during processes of transformation as they move through 'the economy', configuring matter in particular ways in the process of creating value. Conversely, the possibilities of value creation are in turn influenced by the chemical and physical properties of that matter. Focusing on the materiality of the economy highlights the point that wastes are endemic and as such represent value lost to capital – in turn offering possibilities of value creation if these waste materials can be configured in new ways to provide a new source of profit. In this way, we can obtain a deeper understanding of the relationships between processes of value creation and material transformation and the ways in which material possibilities and barriers influence the substance of commodity production.[6] By tracing the ecological impacts of varying combinations of technologies of production, exchange and consumption, and of different levels and compositions of output, the ecological implications of economic choices as to the composition of output and the socio-technical and socio-spatial configurations of various global production networks can be better understood. Equally the material effects of the devalorisation of capital and the creation of industrial wastelands, landscapes of abandoned factories, plant and machinery that then lie unused and decay, becoming transformed into new configurations of matter, can be better grasped and comprehended. This recognition of the significance of the material register therefore provides a perspective from which to review the ecological implications of the repertoire of possible social choices about how and what to produce, exchange and consume and where to do so. It allows fuller consideration of the determinants of where production occurs, for example in relation to companies' attempts to find 'spatial fixes' for pollutant and environmentally noxious and hazardous production and, linked to this, to the creation of 'regions of wastes', either regions that have always been on the margins of the global economy or those that were once central to it but no longer are, with such regions often in competition for the waged work that waste disposal offers. There are, therefore, considerable potential benefits in conceptualising economies in terms of materiality and materials transformation in thinking through different ways in which global production networks are currently organised and might in future be organised to ameliorate adverse ecological impacts as well as to deepening understanding of the links between processes of value creation and material transformation.

In summary, human societies and economies, however organised and whether or not conceptualised as global production networks, cannot escape the indeterminacies, uncertainties and limits set by the laws of thermodynamics. It is, however 'quite another thing to treat [these laws] as sufficient conditions for the understanding of human history' (Harvey, 1996, 140). These laws set limits within which there is scope for varying determinations. There is a degree of room for manoeuvre within these limits, allowing global production networks to be shaped in one way or another, subject to the limits of political economy and profitability. That said, these limits *are* non-trivial. Because the global ecological/economic system is complex and non-linear, its dynamic behaviour is potentially chaotic and its stability, its tendency to remain within its original domain, is indeterminate. Given this indeterminacy, there are good reasons to exercise the precautionary principle in considering relations between economy and environment. However, it remains an open question as to whether *any* form of economy, *any* set of social relations of production, any socio-spatial configuration of a global production network, can develop effective regulatory mechanisms to contain the consequences of human intervention into the cycles of natural processes over the long-term.

## Conclusions

Has the meeting between global production networks and cultural political economy been fruitful? I would argue that it has. I have argued for a conception of cultural political economy that encompasses a variety of circuits, flows and spaces within the three registers of the political-economic, semiotic and material. These co-constitutive circuits and flows intersect as people, things and knowledge flow into and out of spaces, both shaped by and shaping these spaces, linking them together into the intricacies of global production networks, constituted in and of time/space. Thus global production networks could become an extremely powerful way of representing 'the economy' in its essential complexity (that is with emergent effects, an entity that is not just complicated but complex), of representing the richness of the economy in terms of the links between the affective, cognitive and material, between circuits of value, meaning and matter, between the moments of production, exchange and consumption, and between political economies grounded in different concepts of value and processes of valuation. In particular global production networks highlight the particular spatialities of the global economy and the way in which different spaces and the everyday lives of those that live and work in them are entangled with or excluded from the processes of production, exchange and consumption through which global production networks are constituted. As a result, they bring together the 'system-world' and the 'life world', the imperatives of the accumulation process with the experienced realities of everyday life for people in varied sites of production, exchange and consumption.

However, consideration of the material and of the materiality of the economy, of the relationships between economy and nature, has yet to be fully brought into a cultural political economy perspective. It remains an open question as to the extent to which serious consideration of materiality forces a re-interpretation of issues of value and meaning within a cultural political economy perspective and the implications of this in turn for bringing together cultural political economy and global production network perspectives. Not least taking materiality seriously requires crossing disciplinary boundaries not simply within the social sciences but between the social and material and physical sciences, with all that this implies about different conceptions as to what constitutes valid knowledge and admissible evidence. As of now the global production network perspective gives minimal attention to the materiality of networks and to the material transformations that are, in practice, central to the constitution of global production networks. There is no doubt, however, that the material configurations in which matter can be temporarily stabilised and held has important implications for the way in which matter can be shaped to create value. Materialising global production network approaches therefore presents a significant challenge to its advocates and proponents – but also a significant opportunity to broaden the agenda of this exciting new way of thinking about economic geographies.

## Notes

1 It became clear in discussions with Nicky Gregson in the context of a major ESRC-funded project 'The Waste of the World' (www.thewasteoftheworld.org/) in which we are both involved that the metaphor of the circuit requires some further unpacking and elaboration, especially in the context of conceptualising the economy as a process with emergent properties. As a metaphor, 'circuit' speaks to two rather different aspects of connectivity and flow. First, it draws upon the notion of electrical circuits, with flows channelled between nodes via switching points, with the end point different to the origin, indicative of the complexity of the economy and its capacity to produce emergent effects – with such moments of emergence marked, perhaps, by the circuit blowing a fuse and subsequently being re-configured in a new way. Circuits and feedbacks loops may, then, under certain circumstances, give rise to emergent properties rather than simply reproducing existing properties and relations. In short, feedback does not necessarily imply a return to the same starting point or state; it may do, but it need not do even if this was the intention of those managing the process precisely because of the endless capacity of material to exceed or escape the frame established by the process of transformation itself. Second, it invokes the idea of circuits as recursive flows, with material of various sorts flowing through a variety of qualitative transformations and returning to its original qualitative starting form, as in the circuits of capital. However, this does not necessarily mean a return to the same starting point as these are flows in real time and may well involve a quantitative augmentation of value as well as physical transformation of material. It is important to note that some material transformations produce irreversible transformative effects so that return to the original qualitative state of matter is impossible. As this last point suggests the process of value creation and the creation of exchange and use values may well be decisively shaped by the possibilities – and limitations – of materials transformation.
2 Although as I shall argue this aspect of materials transformation has been neglected in much of political-economy and this is a neglect that requires rectification.
3 Note that the socially necessary is context dependent and specific and as such variable over time/space rather than this being an essentialised and invariant quantity.
4 There is a certain resemblance here to Sraffa's (1960) ideas as to the production of commodities by means of commodities but the point is that this applies to all forms of production, not just the commodity form.
5 Nicky Gregson has suggested that this may be an overly charitable interpretation of strands of cultural economy which simply take the process of 'fixing' for granted and focus upon the meaning of forms and things.
6 As noted above, for those who wish to pursue such an approach that focuses on material transformations per se, there are methodologies, notably those of industrial metabolism and life-cycle analysis, which allow a precise tracing of processes of the dissipation of energy and conservation of matter.

# 10 Critical political economy and materials transformation

> [T]he ever growing literature ... that deals explicitly with the subjects of *materiality* and *material culture* seems to have hardly anything to say about *materials*. I mean by materials the stuff that things are made of.
>
> (Ingold, 2007, 1, emphasis in the original)

> [A]n account of Fordism has yet to be written that takes seriously the properties of the new steels (hardness, ductility, physical and chemical stability, durability) in enabling the mass production of interchangeable parts and the cultural values associated with the mass consumption of standardized products.
>
> (Bakker and Bridge, 2006, 13)

## Introduction

The long history of various strands of critical political economy can be traced back to Marx's seminal analyses of capitalist development. As capitalism developed, these analyses became more sophisticated but nonetheless there are issues that require further exploration. I therefore have three aims in this chapter. First, I argue that critical political economy – as do the social sciences more generally – needs to engage more closely with the 'the stuff that things are made of', the properties of materials, their microstructures and transformations of these as such knowledge is crucial to understanding why materials acquire use values within the commodity production process. Put another way, critical political economy needs to open up the 'black box' of materials and their transformations in order to understand better why and how these can be manipulated in particular ways to create exchange value. Second, I offer an explanation in terms of competitive epistemologies, conceptions of theory and claims as to what constitutes valid knowledge as to why consideration of the micro-structures and properties of materials and their transformations has persisted as a lacuna in critical political economy. Filling it is a necessary pre-condition to consideration of the limits to and possibilities for progressive change in the socio-technical relations that shape the economy. Knowledge of what it is materially possible to produce is a necessary pre-condition for consideration of alternative conceptions that challenge the hegemony of capitalist material interests and imagine alternative ecologically sustainable and socially just visions of the economy. Third, I explore and exemplify the more general claims about the need to understand production as simultaneously a value-creation process and a materials transformation process, and that understanding the former requires grappling with the latter, via some illustrative examples drawn from the automobile and steel industries. While Bakker and Bridge correctly point to the neglect of materials transformations in analyses of Fordism, these issues have been addressed to some degree (for example see Best, 1990; Hounshell, 1984; Storper and Walker, 1989). To develop these analyses further, I focus upon relations between producers of steel and producers of automobiles and their component parts and the ways in which specific sorts of steels have been developed to meet the requirements of particular end uses in automobile production. In this way I will seek to develop existing analyses and respond both to Ingold's plea to engage more deeply with 'the stuff that things are made of' and how that 'stuff' is itself produced and Bakker and Bridge's challenge to explore the development of particular types of a material often treated as homogeneous and undifferentiated by social scientists for the production of perhaps the iconic commodity of twentieth century capitalism.

## Developments in and limits to critical political economy

In his analysis of the labour process in volume 1 of *Capital* Marx emphasised that production involved the application of human labour to materials taken from the natural world and their transformation into socially useful products. While Marx's focus was on capitalist production he was equally clear that, irrespective of the dominant social relations, any process of production was also one of materials transformation, with unavoidable material consequences and deleterious environmental effects.

However, having recognised that production always involves material transformation, Marx then focused upon production – and the economy more generally – as a socio-technical system driven by specific material interests, on the social relations and technologies of production and the way in which these were shaped in specific configurations to enable the continuing (expanded) reproduction of capital. Recognising the specificity of capitalist social relations had precise implications for the ways in which material transformations were shaped and de-limited and for which materials from nature became part of these social processes of value creation and commodity production. His focus – and that of those who followed him – was upon value creation and expansion, on the creation of surplus-value through the application of labour-power in production, the appropriation of surplus-value by capitalists and capitalist enterprises and its transformation into capital rather than on the properties of matter and material transformation per se.

The grounding of production in material transformations was thus acknowledged but then bracketed out. Its implications both for processes of value creation and the reproduction of the social and ecological conditions that enabled capitalist production to continue remained largely unremarked. This one-sided perspective remained dominant in subsequent developments in Marxian political economy: for example, in increasingly sophisticated analyses of the labour process (such as Braverman, 1974). The emphasis in analyses of capitalist economies upon circuits of capital and flows of value (for example, see Harvey, 1982; Palloix, 1977) further diluted the significance of the properties of matter for the possibilities of commodity production. Focusing on the commodity form emphasises the exchange of formally equivalent quantities of socially necessary abstract labour and neglects their material attributes and properties (Lütticken, 2008).

Furthermore, the development of modern capitalism and the practices of major capitalist enterprises increasingly emphasised the symbolic register of commodities and their socially ascribed meanings. Promoting the symbolic attributes of commodities through advertising, seeking to influence processes of consumer knowledge acquisition so that commodities are seen to be imbued with attributes that exceed their immediate functional and practical uses, and constructing the consumer via the deployment of psychological and social research were central to the rise of mass production/mass consumption in the 1920s and to subsequent capitalist development (for example, see Williams, 1960; 1980). Major companies, especially those producing for final consumer markets, became brand managers, creating extensive brand families incorporating diverse commodities under a particular brand label (Klein, 2000), thereby siphoning off monopoly rents. Systematic consideration of issues of meaning and semiosis is undoubtedly a major contribution to a more sophisticated critical political economy (or indeed the emergence of a cultural political economy). However, such approaches further divert attention from processes of materials transformation and the materiality of the processes and transactions of the economy.[1]

In general material matters, particularly concerns with 'the stuff that things are made of' and processes of materials transformation, remained the domain of the physical and engineering sciences, which developed extensive theories and laws about material properties and transformations. While physical scientists and engineers developed important knowledge about chemical and physical processes, the possibilities that these allowed to shape matter in particular forms and the ways in which these could be deployed in economic activities, they did so in ways and via methodological and theoretical positions that bracketed out the social context and relations in which the economy was performed. Meanwhile, although there was often a concern with R&D, and more recently with 'knowledge-based economies', social scientists overwhelmingly bracketed out from their analyses of economies any consideration of issues such as the effects of the physical and chemical properties of materials on the capacity to create commodities embodying value.

More recently, however, building on earlier work by a few pioneers (for example, see Ayres and Kneese, 1969; Benton, 1989; Georgescu-Roegen, 1971;

Kneese *et al.*, 1970), there has been the beginning of a revival of social scientific interest in issues of materials transformation and related material aspects of the economy. As Harvey (1996) notes, all processes of industrialisation are fundamentally socio-ecological projects. However, such concerns have largely remained at an aggregate level rather than engaging with the micro-scale properties of materials and processes of materials transformations and their implications for and relationships to commodity production.

Why then is it important for critical political economy better to understand the micro-scale properties of the materials and the materials transformations that lie at the heart of production? Knowledge of these properties and the ability to manipulate them, or transform them via combination with other materials, to give desired use value characteristics is central to industrial capitalism and capital accumulation. Value is created via such manipulations and transformations as materials with use values are produced and in turn provide a basis for exchange value and further value creation as they are transformed into new commodities. Equally such knowledge is a crucial pre-condition for serious consideration of a transition to either a different form of capitalist economy or, more radically, to non-capitalist relations of production. Such changes would incorporate modification to both the volume and composition of production and the material composition of products themselves, reflecting a much greater emphasis on socio-spatial and ecological equity and sustainability rather than simply economic growth and accumulation per se.

Furthermore thinking about the economy in the way outlined in this chapter, recognising the centrality of material flows and transformations, challenges and problematises established approaches that focus on firms and/or sectors. Emphasising flows of materials as well as of values among firms and across sectoral boundaries suggests that a more productive way of thinking about the economy is in terms of production systems of varying organisational composition, complexity and spatiality. Such an approach could begin with the final commodity and work back through the various firms, in different sectors, involved in its production and the complex array of material and social processes and flows that this entails, back to the initial extraction and appropriation of materials from nature. Equally it could begin with that initial extraction and appropriation and follow the flows in the opposite direction. Either way, it would emphasise the connectivity, complexity and uneven development of the capitalist economy, especially as these flows typically now involve global trade patterns.[2]

In this chapter, therefore, I want further to develop a concern with the properties of materials and materials transformations in critical political economic analyses, framed by a Marxian conception of the production process (understood in both its narrow and broad senses). I consider the properties of materials and materials transformation in greater depth because of their influence on use values and thus on their pivotal role in creating exchange value and the production of commodities and of the material worlds in which people live. Schematically three types of transformation can be recognised:[3]

molecular transformations that produce specific desired changes in the properties of the resultant materials and so directly affect their capacity to form use values and the uses that can subsequently made of them in production; forming and shaping of materials (into either final products or intermediate components); assembly into final products. These three types of transformation differ qualitatively in the character and scale of the changes that they encompass but are nonetheless related as changes of the first type can and typically do have implications for what is possible in terms of the other two forms of change and for relations between process and product innovation.

Schematically, these links may be sketched out as follows. Once a material has been produced with required use value characteristics, the competitive imperatives of capitalism result in continuous pressures to reduce the exchange value of that commodity via process innovations as producers of it seek to maintain or increase market share and profitability, reducing the socially necessary labour time involved in its production.[4] This may also lead to a search for alternative materials via new forms of molecular transformation. At the same time the invention of new materials can create opportunities for product innovation and the creation of new higher value products through forming and shaping new and existing materials into new commodities. Such product innovation requires bringing together requisite technical knowledge with 'softer' knowledge and skills in activities such as design and marketing. Product innovation may well also require process innovation but in this case driven by a different logic to that of cost-cutting and price competition. For a while these new commodities may confer monopoly advantages on their producers until they diffuse more widely and competition lowers their value and market price. This in turn can set in motion a fresh wave of product innovation, seeking to create value in further new commodities.

Much of the existing work in critical political economy (indeed more generally in social scientific work on the economy) focuses on the second and especially the third of these types of transformation. There is an extensive literature analysing the ways in which commodities are manufactured. Broadly speaking, this seeks to comprehend the various ways in which capitalist social relations are configured to ensure that the production of diverse components and their assembly into final products is successfully achieved such that the value embodied in the end product exceeds that of the inputs to the production process, creating the potential for capital to realise profits. Knowledge, know-how and know-who are crucial inputs to production processes. They include artisanal production, production through networks of small and medium-sized enterprises organised in industrial districts and a variety of methods of large-scale production such as Taylorist/Fordist mass production, lean production and just-in-time methods of flexible high volume production (for example, see Hudson 1994a; 2001a, 96–216). In this sense, this literature does indeed engage with issues of material transformation as diverse components and materials are assembled into often very complex commodities. Consider, for example, the way in which manufacturing automobiles involves combining and assembling diverse components of steel, aluminium, plastics, rubber and electronics.

Nevertheless, I want to argue that this represents simply the final stage in a series of material transformations that are integral to all processes of manufacture. For before these varied components can be assembled to give the desired final product, there are other fundamental transformations of materials that must be successfully undertaken. First, and critically, these involve molecular transformations so that materials from the natural world (typically referred to as having become natural resources) can be rendered into materials with use values in production. Knowledge of the chemical and physical properties of materials and the processes through which desired properties can be achieved is a necessary pre-condition for exploring and exploiting their possibilities in commodity production while, at the same time, their production as commodities requires that they can be produced sufficiently profitably.[5] Second, the forming, moulding and shaping of these transformed materials into commodities with exchange value, either products for final markets or components and parts that will in due course become part of products for final markets. The crucial point is that it is the interplay of the social relations of production, the imperatives that they bring, and the properties of materials and knowledge about them that shapes the anatomy of commodity production.

Knowledge of the properties of materials and of how to manipulate transformative processes to produce materials with desired properties has long been the domain of natural, physical and material scientists. Since this knowledge also allows profitable commodity production (and indeed is often created specifically for that purpose in the R&D laboratories of major capitalist enterprises or in university laboratories that they support) social scientists who wish to deepen understanding of capitalist economies must conceptualise them as conjoined processes of value creation and materials transformation and be cognisant of the latter processes.[6]

While social scientists have focused on the second and third types of transformation, the first has largely been left as the domain of physical/material scientists. My argument is that critical political economists (and indeed social scientists in general) analysing the economy need to engage with the first type of material transformations and its implications for subsequent types of transformation as there are clear relations between the chemical and physical properties of matter and the ways in which this can then be shaped, formed and used in the economy. Where there needed to be dialogue, there has been silence. The result has been an impoverished political economy. The character and properties of materials do not determine their use value or exchange value, or their capacity to underpin profitable commodity production, since these are always socially defined. However, knowledge about these properties is a necessary condition for deciding what is possible, technologically and economically, in terms of the logic of capital. As such, critical political economists who wish better to understand capitalist production with a view to progressively changing it ignore them at their peril. First of all, though, I begin by considering an epistemological dilemma in seeking to understand why critical political economy has generally remained blind to the central role of the first set of processes of material transformations in economic activities.

## An epistemological dilemma

Prima facie, it seems strange that critical political economists and social scientists interested in the economy have neglected the processes of transforming materials from one form to another, leaving this critical moment unexamined.[7] This is especially so of Marxian political economists, given the emphasis that Marx placed upon the labour process as also – and always – a process of material transformations. Why should this be so? One answer lies in the different conceptions of what constitutes valid knowledge and forms of theory in different disciplines and the purposes for which knowledge – or wisdom (Maxwell, 2007) – should be created.

There have been significant epistemological developments that have identified common ground in approaches shared by social and natural scientists since Horkheimer (1937) first drew a sharp distinction between 'traditional' and 'critical' forms of theory. Moreover, as Vogel (1996, 7) points out, 'little serious attention has been given to contemporary philosophy of science within the post-war tradition of critical theory, and this is a significant fault'.[8] Nonetheless, recognising this, I want to use Horkheimer's distinction as a point of departure and reference in seeking to account for the neglect by social scientists of physical processes. Whatever its limitations, it remains relevant to my purpose here. In the physical and natural sciences the dominant conception of theory has been and for many physical scientists remains that of 'traditional' theory, ideally deductive in structure, empirically verified and validated via inter-subjectively available knowledge and, crucially, by its predictive capacity and power. Moreover, prediction and explanation are seen as synonymous in a world regarded as governed by universally applicable and invariant laws. Such a form of theory developed in the natural sciences was intended to be socially progressive by emancipating people from the constraints of nature, rendering the natural world amenable to control and so change in those directions that people preferred (Lewis and Melville, 1977).[9]

There are still those who see a 'traditional' form of theory as relevant in the social sciences[10] but I take it as axiomatic that this is an inappropriate form of knowledge for understanding the social relations of the economy and the economy as a social process of value creation. In contrast, those working within the framework of critical political economy and critical social science more generally favour 'critical theory', with different criteria for assessing the value and validity of knowledge. This is because, irrespective of the intentions of the theorist, translating the 'traditional' form of theory from the natural into the social sciences leads to possibilities of social control and engineering, premised – even if only tacitly – on a view of society as unchanging in its underlying and formative social relationships and structures. The ability to predict the consequences of intervening in a process, whether social or natural, is a prerequisite for successfully manipulating it (Fay, 1975). Those who possess such (social) scientific knowledge thus have the possibility of exercising social control. In this way the progressive role of traditional theory in helping emancipate people from the constraints of nature can become a repressive role in maintaining structures of social domination and repression. This is clearly problematic for political economists and social scientists who wish to develop a notion of 'critical' theory that relates theory to practice, informed by an emancipatory intent. This requires producing forms of knowledge – theories – that reveal the hidden character of mechanisms and social relations of domination and repression as a necessary pre-condition for progressively intervening and changing them. Theory therefore becomes constitutive of, rather than simply descriptive of, the social world. Producing such change becomes the key criterion for validating theory.[11] A fortiori this is the case for those working from a Marxian or otherwise critical political economy perspective. The criteria for validating critical social theory are therefore radically different to those appropriate to 'traditional' theory developed in relation to the physical and natural worlds. As a result, there is a genuine epistemological dilemma for critical political economists and social scientists who recognise the need to engage seriously with the properties of matter and material transformations of elements of the natural world that are central to the production process and capital accumulation but can only do so via knowledge cast in the mould of 'traditional' theory.

What then to do? To reject a concern with the properties of materials and their processes of transformations because they are tied to a particular conception of 'traditional' theory would be unnecessarily restrictive and indeed counter-productive. Consequently, if we are serious about seeking a deeper understanding and integration of consideration of materials transformations and their relationship to commodity production within the realms of a critical political economy, there is no choice but to accept that different forms of knowledge are informed by different interests and purposes and to accept the dilemma that this poses.[12] Of course there is a need for eternal vigilance in pursuing such a path and to ensure that seeking to manage physical processes in socially progressive and ecologically sustainable ways via the approach of 'traditional' theory does not slide into the realms of social control. On the other hand, the danger of ignoring the implications of materials transformations as an unavoidable part of economic and social life is a greater risk, for two reasons. First, without an explicit recognition that social processes of value creation are always and necessarily processes of materials transformation, and that capital seeks to shape knowledge of these processes as well as the processes themselves to favour accumulation, then understanding of the accumulation process remains partial. The critical potential and transformational power of theory is thereby weakened. Second, therefore, ignoring the materiality of the economy, its transformational activities, their entanglement with processes of capital accumulation and their ecological impacts not only impoverishes theory but may well undermine the possibilities of moving to more equitable, humane and ecologically sustainable forms of economic relationships.

## Material matters, materials transformations and commodity production: the example of the automobile and steel industries

In this section, using the example of the automobile and steel industries and the links between them, I further explore the implications of examining the production process through the lens of materials transformations and the properties of matter. Contrary to popular misconception, steel is not a homogeneous commodity. Moreover, different components and parts of automobiles require steels with different properties appropriate to their specific uses in production. The central point is that the end uses of the steel, the forms into which it is transformed and the uses to which it will be put, are intimately connected to the properties of the metal. For example, engine parts require very different types of steel to body parts. Thus the automobile-steel nexus provides a good exemplar through which to explore the ways in which different types of steel are developed and customised to meet the requirements of particular components and parts and/or particular customers. Conversely, automobile companies seek to shape the R&D and production strategies of steel companies as they refine the development of their products in search of competitive advantage or to satisfy changing regulatory requirements.[13]

Contrary to popular perceptions of steel as a technologically backward 'smokestack' industry, 'steel making has now become a high tech industry … [with] major gains in productivity and product quality' (Llewellyn, 1995, 11). The costs of R&D have led to collaboration and strategic alliances between major producers (see Table 10.1)[14] and the demands of automobile producers have been an important motive for refining production processes and enhancing product quality. Production processes are highly automated, with sophisticated computerised process control systems (for example, see Arena *et al.*, 2006).[15] Furthermore because of continuous product and process innovation and the deployment of highly developed production technologies, it is possible to produce a great variety of cleaner, higher quality and higher value steels from the Basic Oxygen Steel (BoS) furnace.[16] At the same time, production of steel from scrap via the Electric Arc Furnace (EAF) route has increased, often forming the starting point for producing more complex steels. However, in both cases technological and process innovations in secondary steelmaking have been crucial in enabling the production of a wide range of steels customised to the requirements of specialised uses and users. Steel producers have sought competitive advantage via developing specific qualities of steel unique to them and protecting this via patents.

Advances in computer modelling and the incorporation of tacit knowledge into sophisticated expert systems allow the properties and qualities of steels

*Table 10.1* Production, R&D and partnerships of selected major steel companies, early 2000s

| *Company* | *Capacity (mt)* | *Automotive steel as % total production* | *R&D – average annual expenditure US$m and/or R&D staff* | *Global R&D partnerships* |
|---|---|---|---|---|
| Acelor | 46.0 | 68 | 175m, 1,500 staff | NS, TK |
| POSCO | 27.0 | 14 | 151m | NS |
| Nippon Steel | 25.2 | 67 | 74m | AG,PS |
| JFE Group | 23.9 | 37 | 307m | TK |
| Riva Group | 21.6 | N/A | N/A | N/A |
| Thyssen- Krupp | 17.0 | 16 | 176m, 3,500 staff | JFE, AC |
| US Steel | 14.4 | 55 | N/A | N/A |
| Bethlehem Steel | 11.3 | 20 | 200 staff | N/A |
| Baoshan Iron and Steel | 11.0 | N/A | 430 staff | NS |
| Corus | 8.8 | 16 | 199m | N/A |
| Dofasco | 4.4 | 35 | N/A | AG |

Notes: PS – Pohang Steel

Source: adopted from Warrian and Mulhern, 2005; with additional material from Acelor, 2005; Corus, n.d. (a); ThyssenKrupp, 2010.

to be predicted accurately as compositions and processing technologies are varied, increasing capacity to manipulate material transformations so as to give steels with a desired mix of properties and qualities. Knowledge of the effects of compositional changes, interactions between added alloys, heating/cooling sequences and other material transformations linked to particular forming processes, enable steels and parts made from those steels to be produced as saleable commodities with defined desired qualities. Conversely, seeking to understand these processes of commodity production presupposes scientific knowledge of the underpinning material transformations and properties of the resultant materials.

Drawing upon knowledge developed in the physical and materials sciences, therefore, steel can be produced with particular characteristics that are required for a given use. These characteristics depend upon the composition of the steel, the mix of alloys added to it and the type of production process and the way in which this is managed (for example, see Hawbolt *et al.*, 1983). In particular, different combinations of heating and cooling the metal can be deployed so that the steel has a particular crystalline microstructure and mechanical properties, such as hardness, malleability or ductility, which are appropriate for shaping it in particular ways into particular forms for particular uses (for example, sheet for automobile bodies or engineering steels for engine components).[17] The end uses of the steel, the forms into which it is transformed and the uses to which it will be put, are closely connected to the properties of the metal. Ensuring the appropriate properties often involves strategic collaboration between steel producers and users over R&D. Put another way, it is vitally important to have knowledge of materials, their properties and how these can be changed and manipulated, of how materials transformation processes can be managed so that steel can be produced with the characteristics – including an affordable price – required by customers and end users while yielding sufficient profit for the steel producer.

Automobiles constitute a major market for steel producers while steel is a major constituent of automobiles. For example, the automotive sector accounts for a majority of the production of Acelor, Nippon Steel and Bethelem Steel and is a significant market for other major steel producers (Table 10.1) while steel accounts for between 50 per cent and 70 per cent of the total vehicle weight (Llewellyn and Hudd, 2004, 115). Steel is far from being a homogenous commodity, however, and steel producers have sought to move up the value chain to produce more specialised higher value steels, drawing on knowledge of materials properties and transformation to create new products, ideally unique to them.[18] Manufacturing automobiles requires many types of steels, varying in their chemical composition, microstructure and mechanical and physical properties. Understanding which types of steel are required for particular uses, and having the capacity to produce such steels, depends upon detailed knowledge of the transformations that steel will undergo, depending upon its composition and the processes (heating, cooling, hot and cold rolling, stamping and so on) to which it is subjected. Knowledge of these properties and their various interactions allows the qualities of steels to be accurately modelled and predicted, using powerful computer simulation models, and matched to the required end uses in automobile construction.

Conversely, for over a century demand from the automobile industry has been a major driver of change in the steel industry. As Souther (1910, 437–8) noted: 'At the beginning [of the automobile industry] there was available ... Bessemer steel, open-hearth steel and cast or crucible steel. Variations within these classes were regarded as unimportant and heat treatment was an unknown term'. However, 'during the last few years ... the steel business has advanced and changed rapidly and ... the incentive is found in the manufacture of automobiles', an incentive that was to continue. In order to manufacture automobiles successfully and profitably as commodities, various steels must be available at appropriate prices, both high enough to enable steel producers to make sufficient profit while undercutting any potential substitute materials and low enough to enable automobile manufacturers to produce commodities that sell and realise the surplus-value embodied in them. Consequently different *types* of steel must be used for different parts and components, matching their characteristics with the required use.[19] Even so, a century or so ago, choice of steels for automobile production was fairly straightforward:

> With a given quality of automobile in view, the number of grades of steel necessary to construct it is few, namely, a good all-round forging steel, a steel of slightly better quality to be used for gears, a spring steel and a steel suited for the pressed-steel portions of it.
>
> (Souther, 1910, 459)

While initially automobile manufacturers had to learn about existing types of steel and their appropriateness to their activities, increasingly the emphasis switched to automobile manufacturers demanding new types of steel customised to their requirements. As Bensaude-Vincent and Stengers (1996, 190–1) put it: 'new industries – such as automobiles ... – called for specific materials with particular properties ... A new rationale for production was the result: given a function or performance to achieve, find the material that has the needed properties'. Consequently, major steel companies devote considerable expenditure to R&D (see Table 10.1) and there have been, and continue to be, close and symbiotic relations between major steel producers and automobile manufacturers over issues of process and product innovation and design. As a result, knowledge of different types of steels available to car manufacturers and of their suitability for different uses has expanded dramatically. Indeed, such links have deepened as more technically sophisticated types of steel have become necessary in response to regulatory requirements and market demands upon automobile manufacturers, expressed in a range of collaborative projects and strategic alliances and partnerships. As Schuberth *et al.* (2008, 637) note,

> [t]he automotive industry of today is characterised by faster cycles in materials invention, development and application, coupled with the ability to tailor materials to specific end-users requirements ... It is therefore essential for materials development to be closely integrated with the final product and process concurrent engineering practice.

As a result, there is increasing co-operation between steel producers (especially those for which the automobile sector, and indeed particular companies within it, constitute a major market), original equipment manufacturers and parts producers from the concept design and tooling/prototyping stages in early vendor involvement (EVI) programmes.[20] One consequence of this is that the boundaries between assemblers, component suppliers and steel producers have become more blurred as steel producers seek to move up the value chain by performing operations previously carried out by automobile companies.[21] At least one major steel producer, POSCO, is extending the concept of early vendor involvement to include component manufacture and sub-assemblies, especially those requiring highly advanced technologies and processes (Kwon and Biak, n.d.). The fundamental point, however, is that

> the key motivation behind innovation in the steel industry has been the revolution in vehicle manufacturing, as automotive steel represents the largest source of revenue for integrated mills ... [this has] increased the drive for innovation and process improvements in the value-added end of the automotive steel market.
>
> (Warrian and Mulhern, 2005, 162)

In the remainder of this chapter I will exemplify these points via reference to specific types of steel used in automobile production.

## Strip (sheet) steel and automobile production

The introduction of the continuous hot strip mill in 1923 was critical in enabling the growth of mass production in the automobile industry. Prior to this, steel was rolled in individual sheets, a slower and more expensive process. The automobile industry remains the largest consumer of strip steel, the predominant material for auto bodies (body-in-white[22] and other body components) and structural components. It has provided the greatest stimulus and challenge for R&D and the development of new improved grades of steel strip. Increasing demands from major automobile producers for higher quality steels – for example in terms of gauge control, flatness, surface texture, resistance to corrosion and strength/weight ratios – have been and continue to be a major driver of product and process innovation. During the 1970s and 1980s the character and qualities of steel strip demanded by automobile manufacturers changed significantly as they sought to reduce fuel consumption, enhance resistance to corrosion and improve passenger safety as these became important dimensions of competition and regulatory requirements became more stringent (Llewellyn and Hudd, 2004, 115–28). Typically this involved simultaneous consideration of varied aspects of material transformations due to the interrelationship between the microstructures of steel and the methods of working and forming it into components and parts. While steel can be hot rolled down to thicknesses of 2 mm, automobile producers demanded thinner and so lighter cold rolled steel. However, while cold rolling increases the strength of steel, it reduces ductility. Annealing enhances ductility and malleablility, restoring a high level of cold formability, making it easier to form complex shapes.[23] In response to pressures to enhance resistance to corrosion and provide more comprehensive warranties against structural and cosmetic deterioration, cold rolled strip for automobile bodies was increasingly zinc coated and in some cases also organically-coated (Fujita and Mizuno, 2007; Llewellyn, 1995, 58–60). At the same time, automobile manufacturers increasingly used different types of strip for different parts of the vehicle body, depending upon their exposure to corrosive elements and upon the mode of pressing the steel into the required shape[24] (Dasarathy and Goodwin, 1990; Takahashi, 2003).

Higher strength steels were also introduced, first in the USA, for structural members formed from steel strip, such as bumper reinforcements, side door beams and seat belt anchors, in response to regulatory pressures to improve in-vehicle safety. These components were manufactured principally from hot rolled, niobium-treated and precipitation-hardened micro-alloy steels. They had a favourable cost/weight ratio compared to conventional plain carbon steels and required only minor modification to manufacturing methods and facilities. Higher strength steel has higher yield strength and failure strength compared to mild steel and so improves the impact energy absorbing capacity and resistance to plastic deformation (Li *et al.*, 2003).

The oil crises of the 1970s greatly reinforced the impetus to increased use of higher strength but thinner and lighter steels, especially cold-reduced strip for inner and outer body panels, in order to reduce vehicle weight and fuel consumption.[25] This, however, posed problems in forming existing types of such steels into more complex or shape-sensitive components such as body panels. While strength increased, the formability of steel decreased and springback increased (as compared to plain carbon steels).[26] This stimulated further R&D and innovations in strip production as steel producers developed new grades of high performance advanced high strength steels (Kwon and Biak, n.d.; Llewellyn and Hudd, 2004, 56–85; Takita and Ohashi, 2001).[27] These steels have very high strength but are easily formed to produce complex automobile parts.[28] They have specific chemical compositions and microstructures, the latter produced via precisely manipulating sequences of heating and cooling, first slowly cooling, then rapidly cooling (quenching) the steel. This results in morphologies which provide the desired mechanical properties, qualities and strength characteristics for a given end use (Geck, 2010; Takahashi, 2003).[29] The critical element in the manufacturing process, therefore, is precise control of the processing conditions to optimise the microstructure of the steel and produce steels with very specific qualities for particular end uses.[30] On average replacing conventional steel designs with optimised advanced high strength steel designs in a typical five passenger compact vehicle results in a 25 per cent reduction in body structure weight, an 8 per cent reduction in vehicle weight, and a reduction of more than 5 per cent in fuel consumption and life-cycle emissions of greenhouse gases (Obenchain *et al.*, 2002; Opbroek, 2008). This allows compliance with tightening environmental regulation while enhancing the 'green' credentials of the vehicle and lowering running costs.[31]

At the same time as new advanced high strength steels have been developed, there have been significant related process innovations that optimise their use, contributing to further weight and cost reduction, linked to advances in computer simulation that enable optimisation of choice of steels and tools (Takita and Ohashi, 2001). For decades each body panel was formed from a single sheet of steel, cut to an appropriate blank size and shape prior to forming, with each part of a pressing made from the same grade of steel. As a result, certain parts of a pressing may have been stronger than strictly necessary or additional strengthening members may have been required to reinforce parts of a pressing that might otherwise have been too weak. In contrast, tailored blanking combines steels with different qualities and thicknesses into a single sheet by laser welding prior to pressing. Different parts of the component are designed to optimise shape, thickness and welding arrangements and produced with appropriate properties so as to maximise strength where needed and eliminate excess mass (Trem, 2004). The use of advanced forming technologies such as hot press forming and hydroforming has also increased (Kwon and Biak, n.d.; Obenchain *et al.*, 2002; Singh, 2003). Hot press forming, involving heating steel sheets to which boron has been added to above 900°C and then pressing with cold dyes, is used to produce bumpers, pillars and cross-members. Hydroforming involves forming parts via hydraulic pressure, increasing yield strength and the dimensional stability of steel components while enabling complex parts (such as pillar reinforcements and suspension members) to be formed via a single process. This obviates the need to combine the products of multiple stamping processes and enables advanced high strength steels to be used for a greater range of components and parts. However, the costs associated with fixed capital sunk into presswork technology and the resistance of engineers experienced in that technology have inhibited the speed with which automobile companies have adopted hydroforming in producing the body-in-white (Godwin, 1998).

As pressures to reduce the weight of vehicles continue, especially with the introduction of electrically powered automobiles with electric motors powered by heavy batteries, European automobile manufacturers and stainless steel producers collaborated in the Next Generation Vehicle (NGV) project. This involved exploring the use of stainless steels for various structural components of vehicle frames, such as door pillars.[32] In particular, nickel-containing grades of metastable, austenitic stainless steels were identified as particularly appropriate.[33] These austenitic steels have a high work hardening rate, becoming stronger as they are deformed and hydroformed or cold rolled into components. Moreover, in a collision they absorb more energy than carbon structural steels. They can therefore replace carbon steels while meeting regulatory crash-safety standards and providing greater protection to the vehicle occupants in a crash (Anon, 2008). Computer Aided Engineering programmes allow engineers to simulate crashes using dynamic material properties and ensure that vehicle designs maximise safety (Obenchain *et al.*, 2002).

Using austenitic stainless steels for structural components could reduce the weight of an average-sized European automobile by 90–110 kgs (Robert Gustafsson, manager of the Next Generation Vehicle project: cited in Gehm, 2009, 37). In addition, these steels can be welded to carbon steels, enabling different types of steel to be used as appropriate in the vehicle body (Schuberth *et al.*, 2008, 6). This is important, as austenitic stainless steels can be up to three times more expensive than carbon steels (Gehm, 2009). In the logic of commodity production it is important that they are only used in applications that optimise the benefits of their particular qualities and allow a cost effective trade-off of weight reduction against greater unit price.

Potentially more significant, however, is the further development as part of the Next Generation Vehicle project of software programmes that simulate all stages of production, taking metal through each step of forming and welding in the process of materials transformation. These programmes enable engineers to model the transformation process and see how substituting grades and fabrication processes can enhance the qualities of the finished part. According to Gustafsson,

> Without the software it wasn't really possible to simulate this [the transformation process] in a proper way, taking into consideration the deformation hardening and the way that happens. It's a big step forward, enabling car makers and other manufacturers to determine the best materials and applications without having to build and test parts that won't make the grade.
>
> (cited in Anon, 2008, 7)[34]

Consequently, these developments are important in minimising R&D costs as well as of subsequent production costs via optimising the use of materials.

## Engineering steels and automobile production

Very different types of high tensile strength (> 750 N/mm$^2$) steel are required for engine and transmission components that will be subjected to high levels of service stress. These engineering steels encompass a wide range of compositions, all of which until recently have generally been heat treated to produce the required tensile strength levels via generating lower temperature transformation microstructures, principally bainite and martensite. The critical property of engineering steels is their hardenability,[35] their capability to produce a particular level of strength in a specific section size (the ruling section) and harden in depth (rather than simply on a surface layer). Achieving hardenability depends upon the addition of appropriate alloying elements and the cooling rate on a specific composition or section size.

There have been important innovations in engineering steels, especially following the development of isothermal transformation (ITT) diagrams in the 1930s (Bain and Davenport, 1930, reprinted 1970). Until the late 1940s engineering steels for automobile engines and transmission parts were largely based on compositions containing substantial amounts of nickel and molybdenum (Ni-Mo) to give the required high levels of strength (from nickel) and toughness and wear (from molybdenum). During the 1950s, however, research revealed that many such steels were over-alloyed in relation to the hardenability requirements of the components and that the required levels of strength could be achieved with steels of leaner compositions – and so produced at lower cost, giving them a competitive advantage. In the 1960s, the emerging technology of fracture mechanics provided greater knowledge of the level of toughness required in engineering components and revealed that satisfactory performance could be provided by alternative steel compositions. Coupled with major advances in heat treatment technologies,[36] this led to the gradual replacement of Ni-Mo grades by cheaper steels involving additions of manganese, chromium and boron to enhance hardness and tensile strength.

By the 1970s the potential for alloy reduction had largely been exhausted but competitive pressures among automobile manufacturers translated into competitive pressures among steel producers as they fought for market share. As a result, there was increasing exploration of the scope for reducing manufacturing costs, especially those of heat treatment processes. The established method of producing components such as crankshafts or connecting rods involved specific sequences of heating and cooling.[37] In the mid-1970s German steel companies created a micro-alloy, medium-carbon steel[38] after air cooling following forging, eliminating the need for expensive heat treatments. Subsequently, other steel producers, especially in the rest of Western Europe and Japan, developed similar micro-alloy[39] forging steels, which gradually replaced quenched and tempered steels in the production of components such as crankshafts, connecting rods, steering knuckles, axle beams and tension rods (Korchynsky and Paules, 1989). Adoption of such micro-alloy steels generates substantial cost savings, for three reasons: they incorporate less expensive alloys than the alloy grades they replaced; they eliminate heat treatment costs; and they give improved machining characteristics. The ability to reduce costs became increasingly important to engineering steel producers in North American and Western Europe as the international division of labour in steel changed and newly industrialising countries, especially India and those in the Far East, developed the capacity to produce engineering steels. For example, by the latter part of the twentieth century, gearbox forgings from these places were 40 per cent cheaper (Corus Engineering Steels, 2001, 10).

Machinability is a particularly important attribute of engineering steels, since machining can account for up to 60 per cent of the cost of production of automobile components. It can be enhanced via adding small amounts of sulphur, calcium and tellurium (Llewellyn, 1995, 164–7). Machining involves a variety of operations (for example, turning, milling, grinding and drilling), several of which may be carried out in sequence on an automated lathe in the production of a single component, while each involves differing metal cutting actions and conditions of temperature, strain rate and chip formation. Indeed, for components that are mass produced at high machining rates, such as hose couplings and spark plug bodies, the mechanical property requirements of the steel are minimal and the pre-eminent requirement is a high and consistent level of machinability in low-carbon free-cutting steel.

For other components, however, machinability matters for different reasons. Automotive transmissions' components, such as gears and axles, must be produced to very demanding tolerances, minimising distortion in order to prevent misalignment, overloading and premature failure. Distortion represents a potentially significant problem in producing precision engineered gears and axles. Slight inaccuracies in shape lead to irregular tooth contact patterns and to problems ranging from a high level of noise in the gearbox or axle to premature fatigue failure because of overload. Given that dimensional change under fast-cooling conditions is inevitable, coping with it depends upon control and consistency of response and this requires predictable and appropriate properties in the steel used to form the component.

As a result, automobile manufacturers generally specify carburised steels with narrowly defined hardenability bands to minimise the variation in distortion such that changes can be accommodated in the pre-treatment geometry, while reducing temperature gradients during quenching to reduce the degree of irregular dimensional change. Carburised steels have a duplex microstructure combining a hard fatigue-resistant martensitic case with a lower strength but tough and ductile core.[40] Tempering at about 200°C then releases the internal stresses in the steel without causing any significant softening in either core or case, minimising distortion and allowing very accurate forming and machining of components (Llewellyn and Hudd, 2004, 210–27).

In summary, a considerable variety of types of steel can be made to meet the demands of automobile producers. In part this is a result of steel producers responding to competition on performance and costs from other materials (chiefly aluminium and plastics). In part it has been driven by competition among steel producers. The net result is that steel producers have found it imperative to improve production processes and devise new steel compositions and ways to produce and process them. There have been significant process and product innovations in steel production, which is now deeply grounded in scientific knowledge about materials, their properties and processes of materials transformation and in sophisticated computer-controlled production processes managed via expert systems that combine scientific knowledge created in research laboratories with knowledge that once was tacit but has now been captured in codified form. As a result, it is now possible predictably to manufacture an immense variety of types of steel, depending on the interplay of chemical composition, production processes, production costs and market forces, on the interrelations between processes of material transformation and those of value creation. Different combinations of alloying elements result in steels with different properties such as hardness, tensile strength and ductility. The properties of steels can be further manipulated via physical processing (such as rolling, pressing and forging) and sequences of heating and cooling. Consequently, the type of steel required for a particular end use – in this case automobile manufacture – can be precisely specified and the production process designed to result in steel with the required and desired properties. This ability to manipulate the properties of the metal is critical in establishing its use value, the use to which the steel will be put and the possibilities of using it as a component of constant capital in commodity production, although there is also an important relationship between the complexity of the transformation process, the cost of the product and demand for it.

## Conclusions

The starting point for this paper was that a critical political economy needs to take on board the challenge that originates in Marx's seminal contributions of conceptualising the economy as conjoined processes of value creation and material transformations, whatever the epistemological dilemmas this might pose. This is because, inter alia, the successful production of commodities requires knowledge of their constituent materials and their potential transformations and the ways in which these can be managed through the production process to allow the creation of surplus-value and profits.

Over a period of many years, chemists, metallurgists and physical scientists have built up, and continue to expand, a body of knowledge about the compositions and processes through which different kinds of steel can be produced. This enables them to predict the attributes and qualities of the resultant steels. Consequently, they can respond to the demands of – say – automobile producers for steels with particular characteristics. This is crucial since the ability to manufacture particular components of a vehicle to the required standard and accuracy depends upon the characteristics of the steel used for that component. The use value of the steel – and hence its potential exchange value – is a consequence of its microstructure and chemical and physical attributes. For example, to produce a smooth, efficient transmission system requires the use of appropriate types of engineering steel for each of its component parts. To produce light, corrosion-resistant and safe car bodies requires very different types of sheet steel. Understanding the basis of the use value and exchange value potentially contained in these steels – and so their potential for the creation of surplus-value – therefore presupposes knowledge of the material transformations involved in steel production. Clearly, the realms of value creation and materials transformation are inextricably conjoined as different steels are produced as commodities which in turn enter (in the form of constant capital or elements of fixed capital) as inputs into the creation of other commodities.

The example of the steel industry illustrates how a wide range of materials can be produced with a variety of desirable properties via combining alloying metals with iron and through careful (now typically computer) control of the production process, especially in terms of the composition of the metal and heating and cooling in particular ways. Manipulation and sophisticated management of the production process depends upon knowledge of the attributes and properties of materials and of the ways in which they can be combined and transformed to give types of steel with particular desired combinations of properties. Capitalist interests have increasingly shaped the processes of R&D through which knowledge about materials, their properties and their transformations have been developed and deployed to produce profits via producing steel and – inter alia – automobiles.

The chapter can then be seen as a response to the challenge laid down by Bakker and Bridge (2006, 13) to understand better how 'the properties of the new steels (hardness, ductility, physical and chemical stability) [enabled] the rise of production of interchangeable parts and the cultural values associated with the mass consumption of standardised products' that was central to the rise of Fordism and its high volume flexible production successors. Knowledge of material properties and transformations is certainly required for successful commodity production, but it is a necessary not sufficient condition. While there have been references to the economics of production, market competition and regulatory requirements and the influences that shape these, a more comprehensive critical political-economic analysis would need to bring together consideration of the properties of matter and material transformations with fuller consideration of the 'traditional' concerns of political economists and economic geographers, such as analysis of the labour process, production costs, intellectual property rights and patents, markets and profits and so on, and the ways in which these influences intersect with the characteristics of places to shape the spatiality of production. In this way a thorough recognition that production is always both a value creating process and a process of materials transformation could be restored to the centre of a critical political economy. As a necessary corollary, however, critical political economists need to engage with the forms of knowledge of 'traditional theory' used by physical scientists in their studies of materials and materials transformations in order to appreciate the material limits to and possibilities of transforming production.

Furthermore, while steels are very important materials in the economy, there are many others, with more complicated processes of transformation, such as carbon-based chemicals, that require analysis if the links between materials transformations and value creation are to be more fully explored within critical political economy, perhaps via detailed case studies of the production of particular commodities. Explicitly exploring the properties of materials and processes of material transformations alongside considerations of value creation, meanings and symbolic representation opens the possibility of filling a void in critical political economy and analyses of economies and their socio-spatial organisation.

I want to end, however, on a normative point that relates to the sort of economy that might be imagined as an alternative to contemporary forms of capitalism. What, to borrow and adapt a phrase from Vogel (1996, 168), could and should the communicatively and practically constituted economy be like? To begin to answer this question, not only do we need better understanding of the relationships between the properties of materials and the mix of commodities currently produced but also better understanding of the limits to and possibilities of what it is materially as well as socially possible to produce. Such knowledge is crucial to any consideration of different ways of organising the economy and of producing a different material world in which people could live (for example see Allwood *et al.*, 2011). Put another way serious consideration of what we ought to produce requires knowledge of the material possibilities for and limits to production.

## Notes

1 As Costis Hadjimichalis (personal communication) has pointed out, the postmodernism turn towards discourse analysis (in which everything was a linguistic construction) further diverted attention from any consideration of materiality.
2 Several approaches to studying global flows have emerged in recent years – commodity chain analysis, value chains, Global Production Networks, for example (see Coe *et al.*, 2004; Gereffi *et al.*, 2005; Gereffi and Korzeniewicz, 2004) but all neglect the materiality of these flows (see Chapter 9).
3 For a similar three-stage perspective (production; fabrication/manufacturing; use), see Michaelis and Jackson, 2000). The argument here is developed in relation to those commodities that involve such material transformations and that conventionally would be regarded as 'manufactures'.
4 Companies may adopt other strategies to combat falling market share and profitability – for example moving into other areas of manufacturing or services, as was the case with several steel companies in the 1980s (Hudson and Sadler, 1989).
5 Under certain circumstances, the state may step in (for example via nationalisation or public ownership) to ensure that materials that themselves cannot be produced profitably are actually produced and sold at prices that allow others to produce other commodities profitably. This was the case with steel in Italy and the UK, for example, for much of the latter half of the twentieth century (see Hudson and Sadler, 1989).
6 There are important differences between production processes based directly in nature and manufacturing processes. Biologically based processes that involve animals and plants as participants typically involve nurturing or enhancing natural processes of growth and development via manipulating the growth environment rather than materials transformation as an intentional strategy of production (for example, see Boyd *et al.*, 2001; Prudham, 2005). In addition, activities such as mining involve winning natural materials and perhaps some in-situ processing but not their molecular transformation. In both cases, there are critical issues relating to the appropriation of nature (Hudson, 2005, 45–54), especially acute when this involves modifying living organisms and associated deep ethical concerns. The transformation of natural materials into natural resources owned by specific capitalist interests, central to strategies of accumulation via dispossession (Harvey, 2003), can occur in diverse ways, ranging from military action and physical force linked to processes of (neo)colonialism to more subtle means, such as intellectual property rights legislation and the due processes of the rule of law (for example, see Prudham, 2007; Sneddon, 2007).
7 Social scientists – for example, some anthropologists, geographers and political economists – have of course shown interest in more general material aspects and forms of economy and society. As Ingold (2007), emphasises, however, they have had little to say about 'the stuff that things are made of'. Similarly, and going on from Ingold's observation, my point is that they have had little if anything to say about the preceding processes of material transformation that constitute a necessary condition for the creation of these forms (and indeed that follow the end of their lives as commodities) and shown little interest in knowledge and laws in the physical and natural sciences that explain and predict these transformations and allow them in principle to be managed and controlled.
8 Vogel (1996, 7) notes that Critical Theory has struggled to come to terms with such developments, which both elucidate and fundamentally complicate the epistemological and methodological accounts that it offers. For example Sayer's (1984) work on critical realism emphasises the unobservable causal structures that underlie both natural and social events. Since the realisation of their causal powers depends upon contingent effects, which may or may not be realised in a given set of circumstances,

the symmetry between explanation and prediction is shattered. From a different perspective, scholars working in the STS (science and technology studies) school and actor-network theorists (for example, see Latour, 2005) have emphasised the coupling of the social and the natural to produce hybrid actants and argued against drawing sharp distinctions between them. That said, there is equally a danger of reducing the material and the causal powers of materials to nothing more than a social construction.

9 The fact that it often had precisely the opposite effect because it led to unintended consequences is of great practical significance but is not the point at issue here.

10 It remains dominant in mainstream economics, for example.

11 However, the translation of theory into practice requires the undoubtedly problematic identification or constitution of subjects to effect such transformational change. This raises a different set of issues that are crucial but tangential to my main concerns here (for example see Castree, 1995).

12 Habermas (1968) sought to resolve this dilemma through his theory of 'knowledge-constitutive interests'; for a critique of his approach, see Vogel, 1996, especially chapters 5 and 6.

13 There are several other reasons for choosing automobiles and steel as exemplars: both are major global industries, the chemical and physical processes of materials transformation are *relatively* simple (as compared to, say, carbon-based petrochemicals) and both have attracted considerable attention from social scientists (for example, see Beynon, 1973; Burn, 1961; Carr and Taplin, 1962; Hudson and Sadler, 1989; Hudson and Schamp, 1995; Warren, 2001; Womack *et al.*, 1990).

14 Since the data in this table were compiled, there has been further major merger and acquisition activity in the global steel industry, notably the acquisition of Acelor by Mittal (2006) and of Corus by Tata (2007). Both were motivated by a desire to acquire more advanced technologies, know-how and higher value products. Automotive steels account for 25 per cent of AcelorMittal's annual R&D budget of US$250m (AcelorMittal, n.d.). There have also been significant mergers in China involving Baoshan and Shagang (see World Steel Association, 2011).

15 Occasionally, such control systems fail catastrophically (for example, see Health and Safety Executive, 2008). Converting tacit to codified knowledge within expert systems can enhance the risks of catastrophic failure if de-skilled operatives believe that monitoring systems are at fault rather than that the process is running out of control (Wiener, 1985). In this recognition of the limitations of human agency, there are similarities with approaches emphasising 'vital materialisms' and the agency or 'vitality' of matter (for example, see Bennett, 2010; Latour, 2005).

16 Steel cleanliness (that is, the reduction of non-metallic inclusions in the steel) and quality have been improved via innovations in secondary steelmaking, including vacuum degassing (1950s), argon shrouding of the molten metal stream (1960s) and vacuum steel making (1970s) (Llewellyn, 1995, 128–9).

17 Relationships between temperature, time and microstructures can be displayed as Isothermal Transformations (IT) diagrams, also referred to as TTT (Time, Temperature and Transformation) curves, or via Continuous Cooling Transformation (CCT) diagrams (Llewellyn and Hudd, 2004, 205–7).

18 For example, in 2007 ThyssenKrupp announced that its tailored stripe line 'is the first line in the world' capable of uninterrupted laser welds (ThyssenKrupp, 2007). Tailored blanks are discussed below.

19 As Souther (1910, 438–9) noted, while alloy steels began to be increasingly used in automobile manufacture:

> The alloy steel is no cure-all and must be used intelligently, if any compensation for increased cost is to be realised. Knowledge of steel is not sufficiently widespread. The history of the automobile is short and there has not been time enough to disseminate knowledge of so many special steels and special treatments.

20 For example, 34 steel producers, from 11 countries, collaborated in the ULSAS (Ultra-Light Steel Automotive Suspension) project, coordinated by the International Iron and Steel Institute (Corus Engineering Steels, 2001). The Auto/Steel Partnership (A/SP), formed in 1987, includes major North American automobile and sheet steel producers). The Next Generation Vehicle (NGV) project, 2005–9, brought together major European automobile and stainless steel producers (Anon, 2008; Gehm, 2009). In Japan the High Strength Steel Working Group was established in 1998 by the Iron and Steel Institute of Japan and the Society of Automotive Engineers of Japan (Takahashi, 2003). There are also collaborative links between the major automobile producers. For example EUCAR (The European Council for Automobile R&D) brings together 13 major producers to engage in pre-competitive R&D in areas where their combined efforts benefit all participants and feed into future competitive product innovations (EUCAR, 2010).

21 For example Corus has a dedicated Automotive Services Centre offering a wide range of first and second stage processing facilities for the volume production of car body panels and underbody components (Corus, n.d.(b)).

22 The body-in-white refers to the welded sheet metal components which form the vehicle's structure and to which the other components – engine, chassis, exterior and interior trim – will be added.

23 Reheating results in the grains within the structure recrystallising into many finer grains, enabling dislocations to move more easily. As a result the steel becomes softer.

24 There are four methods of press forming steel: that is, pressing the sheet steel between a punch and die, blanked to the appropriate size; deep drawing; stretching; stretch flanging; bending. The required properties of steel, for example ductility and formability, depend upon the press forming method(s) required for a given component (Takahashi, 2003). More recently hydroforming has become more common – see below.

25 Plastics or aluminium would have reduced weight further but at considerably increased cost (for example, see Kelkar *et al.*, 2001).

26 Springback refers to the tendency of a metal partially to return to its previous shape. It is positively correlated with the degree of work hardening or strengthening.

27 These included dual phase (DT), complex phase (CP), ferrite-bainite (FB), Transformation Induced Plasticity (TRIP), Twin Induced Plasticity (TWIP) and Martensitic steels. A 'phase' is a form of a material having an identifiable composition, characteristic microstructure and properties, and boundaries separating it from other phases (Gourgues *et al.*, 2000; Smith and Hashemi, 2006, 394–6; Toribio, 2004). Phase diagrams show the conditions in terms of temperature and composition that need to be satisfied to produce steels with particular crystal lattice microstructures and so particular properties suited for different uses, the use value of the steel being directly related to its composition and microstructure.

28 Dual-phase and TRIP steels have tensile strengths up to 600 and 800 $N/mm^2$ respectively. $N/mm^2$ is a measure of pressure, one Newton per square millimetre equating to 145.0377 pounds per square inch. Ultra-high strength steels have tensile strengths up to 1,200 $N/mm^2$.

29 Broadly speaking, end uses can be classified as: panels; structural members; reinforcements; and chassis. Steels are produced with the combination of attributes most appropriate to a given use (Takahashi, 2003).

30 Often the introduction of new advanced high strength steels has been synchronised with that of new automobile models (Takita and Ohashi, 2001).

31 The search for more cost-effective grades of steel via collaboration between automobile and steel producers in pursuit of competitive advantage via product

innovation is continuous and on-going. For example, following collaboration with several automobile manufacturers, Corus announced the creation of a new DP steel, 800 HyPerform, with a hot-dipped galvanised zinc coating, specifically targeted at the automobile sector. It is claimed to be the first to allow automobile manufacturers to use a single steel to produce highly crash resistant lightweight structural and reinforcement components while lowering their price (UK Government, 2010).

32 There are alternative materials such as aluminium alloys, against which stainless steels compete on both price and qualities.

33 Stainless steel, the most corrosion resistant type of steel (Ashby and Jones, 1992, 119), became increasingly used for vehicle exhausts from the 1970s, in addition to radiator grills and external and internal trims. Austenitic stainless steels contain a maximum of 0.15 per cent carbon, a minimum of 16 per cent chromium and sufficient manganese and/or nickel (at least 8 per cent) to retain an austenitic structure at all temperatures (Llewellyn and Hudd, 2004, 515–16, 330–2).

34 Individual steel companies make such software freely available to potential users (for example, see Corus, n.d. (b)). For a further example of developments in simulation via finite element modelling (FEM) of the fabrication and use of TRIP stainless steels see Schedin *et al.*, 2008. Finite element modelling involves computer simulation of a wide variety of different forming operations for 3-D shapes by computer-aided engineering (Llewellyn and Hudd, 2004, 35–6).

35 Although rather clumsy, this term is used in the technical literature on steel and so is used here.

36 Heat treatment allows manipulation of the properties of steel by controlling the rate of diffusion of carbon and the rate of cooling within the microstructure. Phase transformations in steel are heavily influenced by kinetics and result in varied crystalline microstructures and varying grain sizes, both of which are strongly influenced by the rate of cooling, and steels with varying mechanical properties appropriate to different end uses.

37 Cool to room temperature, reheat to about 850°C, and then quench in oil. Tempering at 550–650°C then yields a tensile strength in the range 800–1,100 $N/mm^2$.

38 A carbon content of between 0.30 per cent and 0.59 per cent balances ductility and strength.

39 The most commonly added alloy is vanadium, which effectively combines grain refinement and precipitation hardening, maximising the strengthening process: Korchynsky, 2001.

40 They have a surface layer with a carbon content of about 0.8 per cent and a lower carbon content core – around 0.2 per cent – a result of gaseous diffusion of carbon in the austenite state into the surface layers of low carbon steel.

# 11 Resilient regions in an uncertain world

## Wishful thinking or a practical reality?

### Introduction

Capitalism has proved to be a remarkably resilient form of social and economic organisation, able to both expand its influence extensively and intensify, absorbing and containing inherent systemic crisis tendencies and evolving on an open-ended, though certainly not unconstrained, developmental trajectory. At the same time, and seemingly paradoxically, in the course of this successful systemic evolution it has routinely created vulnerability and crises in regional economies precisely because processes of combined and uneven development lie at the heart of capitalist social relations. There have been various attempts to mitigate the effects of such crises and create more resilient regional economies via national state intervention. Typically these have been at best partially and temporarily successful, on occasion transmuting economic crisis tendencies into rationality and legitimation crises that question the role of the state. Consequently, the seeming paradox of systemic resilience depending in part upon undermining the resilience of many regional economies has continued as a chronic feature of capitalist development.

The recent (indeed still on-going) post-2007 economic crisis therefore is simply the latest – albeit very severe – in a series of crises of varying depth and temporality that have periodically afflicted the capitalist system, generating massive volatility in the global economy as crises in the banking and finance sectors translated into a generalised crisis of accumulation. As a result regions all around the world suffered precipitate economic decline – from previously seemingly shock-resistant sites of financial power such as the City of London to marginalised and peripheral regions everywhere. There is, however, one very important difference on this occasion: the coupling of a deep economic crisis with the perceived threat of an imminent global ecological crisis, above all because of climate change. Put another way, capitalism's blatant disregard for the grounding of economy and society in the natural world can no longer be ignored. This offers both new threats to, but perhaps also new opportunities for, those seeking to create new and more resilient forms of regional economy and society.

What might a resilient region look like in the face of such an unpropitious macro-environment? To begin to answer this question, the chapter first briefly reviews existing concepts of resilience. This forms the basis for seeking to specify the characteristics of resilient regions. First, in terms of their socio-economy, this begins with a critical review of the recently popular neo-liberal model, which is vulnerable to a variety of externally originating shocks and perturbations: for example, fluctuations in currencies, export markets and fuel costs. Addressing these vulnerabilities requires changes in regulatory and governance arrangements and a move to more diversified regional economic structures and greater regional economic closure. In seeking greater resilience there also needs to be a wider definition of the economy beyond the capitalist mainstream to include the 'third sector' and social economy/enterprises. Second, in terms of their ecological dimension, there is a need to close material loops, restructure processes to give an ecologically more efficient use of materials, shift to renewable energy sources, increase re-use and recycling and lower the $CO_2$ footprint of economic activities, acknowledging that the economy necessarily involves material flows, transformations and effects. These changes have clear implications for restructuring production, trade flows and consumption patterns. The final concluding section evaluates the limits to regional resilience in the face of global change.

## Resilience, adaptability and transformability

Resilience, along with adaptability and transformability, is one of three attributes of socio-ecological systems that shape their future trajectories (Walker *et al.*, 2006). The concept of resilience has a variety of disciplinary origins, including biology and ecology, business studies, engineering and materials science, and psychology (Gunderson, 2000; Holling, 1973; Hyslop, 2007). One consequence of these multiple origins is that the term has a variety of disciplinary specific definitions and meanings but in general it denotes the capacity of ecosystems, individuals, organisations or materials to cope with disruption and stress and retain or subsequently regain functional capacity and form. More recently, the concept of resilience became translated into the inter-disciplinary context of understanding relations between people and nature, resulting in the concept of a co-evolving social-ecological system (Berkes and Folke, 1998; Blaikie and Brookfield, 1987).[1] For socio-ecological systems, resilience requires consideration of three properties: the amount of change that a system can undergo while retaining its structure and functions; the degree to which it can re-organise; and the degree to which it can create and sustain the capacity to learn and adapt. Adaptability – the capacity of actors in the system to influence resilience – is critical in such systems.

The debate around resilience has also extended into a more general engagement with ideas from the social sciences (Adger, 2000; Arthur, 1989; Bonnano, 2004; Janssen *et al.*, 2006) and with related concepts of complexity, dynamics and disequilibria, transformability and thresholds, renewal, reorganisation and learning (Carpenter *et al.*, 2001; Walker *et al.*, 2006), although this has not been without debate (Kelman, 2008). Concepts such as adaptive capacity, self-organisation and learning are of particular importance for social scientific approaches to resilience. A resilient system is an adaptive system that adjusts and responds in ways that do not damage or jeopardise effective functioning, remaining on an existing developmental trajectory or making the transition to a new one. Creating resilience is therefore most appropriately thought of as a process of social learning, using human capacities and knowledge to reduce vulnerability and risk in the face of the unknown and unexpected. However, it may be that changes to ecological, economic or social relations and structures erode the adaptive capacity of a socio-ecological system so that it becomes locked into an undesirable state – in contrast, transformability refers to the capacity to learn and create a fundamentally new and different socio-ecological system, one that hopefully would possess the attributes of adaptability and resilience.[2]

More recently the concept of resilience has found its way into the policy literature where it is seen as a normative goal of environmental management and a key component of sustainable development. For example, systems can be managed to promote resilience and support adaptation and learning (Folke *et al.*, 2005). It is also beginning to be considered in relation to regional economic development policy (Hill *et al.*, 2008) and has also diffused into the disaster planning literature (Manyena, 2006).

Leaving aside the thorny but crucial question of power, and the distributional consequences of who has the power to determine what is acceptable, to whom, and via what political process, the extent to which change can be successfully managed and the effects of disasters effectively mitigated remains an open question and one that is critical in relation to issues of equity and social justice. A similar point can be made in the context of regional development and socio-spatial justice. This is particularly so given a recognition that regional economies evolve and move along open-ended developmental trajectories with an unknown end-point.[3] The extent to which regional economies can be rendered more resilient and less vulnerable to the damaging effects of externally controlled or originating processes within the contradictory social relations of capitalist development likewise remains an open question, one to which I return in the concluding section of the chapter.

It is also important to recognise that the analysis of resilience is still evolving, that there are absences and weaknesses in the social scientific conceptualisation of resilience (for example in terms of its recognition and treatment of power) and fundamental difficulties in translating concepts developed in the realms of one discipline into another, especially from the biological and physical to the social sciences. As such, it does not offer a ready-made 'off the shelf' solution to problems of defining the attributes that regions would need to develop to cope with the vulnerabilities inherent in an uncertain world. Nonetheless, it opens new perspectives in thinking about regional development. For example, regions and their socio-economies can be thought of as socio-ecological systems, which may or may not possess properties of socio-ecological resilience or the capacity to transform to a new and more resilient state.

What would a resilient regional economy imply and require? It would, inter alia, have a lighter environmental footprint, display a greater degree of internal closure, less dependence on decisions taken elsewhere, and less vulnerability to shocks emanating elsewhere (Hill *et al.*, 2008). Equally the meaning of resilience would depend upon the context of specific regional economies: for example, as between a region with a leading-edge and seemingly shock-proof economy and a vulnerable one confined to the periphery as a result of economic restructuring. In the former case the issue might be to maintain the existing regional economic structure and developmental trajectory but in the latter to effect a transformation to a new structure and trajectory. Before turning to consider these issues more fully, however, I first want to consider the effects of the most recent wave of neo-liberal policies in eroding resilience and creating more vulnerable regions.

## The rise of neo-liberal models of regional development: eroding resilience and creating vulnerable regions

While there may have been a time when the closed and self-contained region celebrated by Vidal de la Blache (1941) actually did exist, the rise of industrial capitalism ushered in a world of regional specialisation and inter-connection, with regions both partly constituted through and linked by flows of capital, commodities and people. Such regions nonetheless developed a degree of closure and coherence: consider, for example, the closely inter-connected production structures of the emergent regions of carboniferous capitalism in Western Europe and North America. In like manner, industrial districts, from their Marshallian variant in nineteenth century England to their late twentieth century neo-Marshallian successors in the 'Third Italy' were characterised by a substantial degree of intra-district closure and coherence in production structures, although their final markets were extra-regional. However, the passage of time and changes in the international division of labour led to the collapse of the original economic structure of what by then had become 'old industrial regions' and their transformation into 'global outposts' (Chapter 5). In similar fashion, the industrial districts of the Third Italy were 'hollowed out' as production was decentralised to cheaper locations elsewhere (Chapter 6).

This shift towards more 'open' regions as locations in global divisions of labour assumed greater significance with the rise of a neo-liberal political economy as the long post-war boom of the Fordist era ground to a halt and the global economy slid into crisis from the early 1970s, leading to a search in North America and Western Europe for a new regulatory framework to restore economic growth, linked to ideas of political devolution to regions which became seen as subjects responsible for their own economic well-being in global markets. As a result, patterns of regional inequality subsequently became more sharply etched and concepts of regions and regional development were re-worked as part of the narratives of a globalising economy, rooted in the regulatory policies and practices of neo-liberalism and the workfare state.[4] Two features of the political economy of neo-liberalism are particularly significant. First, a growing emphasis upon competitiveness and markets, a fortiori global markets, as the key mechanisms for disciplining and regulating economies and those who participate in them. Second, a further extension of the commodity form, re-defining the boundary between private and public sectors, introducing pseudo-market mechanisms into the residual public sector and extending the reach of the commodity form into areas of private life and civil society from which it was previously excluded by customary practice and tradition. The combined effect of these two tendencies has been to intensify competition between people and places for capital investment and jobs on a global scale.

The emphasis in development discourse, especially in the global 'North', has increasingly been placed upon 'competitiveness' and come to focus on the notion of (city) regions as the 'imagined unit of competition' (Lovering, 1999, 392), competitive actors and key nodes in global networks of production and consumption, and on their connections with other regions. For some, (city) regions have become *the* key territorial units (OECD, 2006; Scott, 1998; Storper, 1995). The discursive emphasis is placed firmly upon endogenous growth processes, regional institutions and regionally specific knowledges and learning as critical to competitiveness, often explicitly linked to the existence of regional clusters of related economic activities (Porter, 2003) – in short, on what has been termed the Territorial Innovations Models perspective on regional development (Moulaert and Sekia, 2003). However, while the rhetoric of development policy emphasised endogenous growth and entrepreneurship, inward investment by multinational corporations often remained the central element in such regional economies so that many of these regions remained 'global outposts'.

The key point is that while the emphasis is placed firmly upon deploying regional assets as the basis of regional economic success, this success is predicated upon the location of these regions in wider global circuits of capital: inputs flow in from other regions while outputs are sold outside the region. This is registered in the burgeoning literatures on global commodity chains, global value chains and global production networks (Chapter 9; Coe *et al.*, 2004; Gereffi *et al.*, 2005; Gereffi and Korzeniewicz, 2004). Building 'clusters' of activities within regions, fostering the intra-regional cohesiveness of economies, is seen as a way of enhancing global competitiveness. The 'success' of such regional economic structures therefore depends upon the ability to compete and sell in global markets in which they have little influence over issues such as price and quality standards and so they become more vulnerable as a result. Furthermore, there is scant regard for the environmental costs of the global mass movement of commodities that is central to such strategies.

This neo-liberal conception of regional development has also enhanced pressures to alter the built environments of and consumption patterns in regions in the global 'North' that aspire to become key nodes of economic activity. Just as production structures need to be modernised, so too do built environments and lifestyles. The shift to dual wage income households has been associated with the generalised consumption of consumer durables, substituting machines and power generated from fossil fuels for human labour. People consume fresh foodstuffs transported from the other side of the world as, for many, seasonality effectively disappears from diets and clothing and a range of consumer goods likewise are consumed thousands of miles from their site of production. Although such 'modernisation' tendencies have been visible for several decades in peripheral regions they have become intensified as the competition for investment and jobs has become increasingly global. Not least this is because such regions are seeking to compete to develop, attract and retain skilled, creative and entrepreneurial people (and their families) who are seen as crucial to constructing the desired (so-called) 'knowledge-based economy' (Chapter 4) but in the context of built environments constructed to accommodate the industrial workforce of an earlier era. Attracting and retaining such highly skilled labour requires the serial production of appropriate built environments that erode the specificities of places and typically leads to increased movement between sites of consumption, exchange and work.

For many regions in the global 'South', however, neo-liberal 'development' has been defined in much less sophisticated terms, with strong neo-colonial echoes of a colonial past.[5] For some, it has involved restructuring agricultural production systems from subsistence to cash-crop production, from production for domestic consumption to producing 'exotic' fruits, vegetables and flowers for sale in export markets and more latterly to producing crops as a source of bio-fuels. For others, the emphasis has been upon becoming regions of export-oriented manufacturing of consumer goods, via the attraction of foreign direct investment, typically tied into the supply chains of global brand owners based in the 'North'. In much of the global 'South' policies to develop key locations as nodes in global production networks have been associated with internal inter-regional and rural to urban migration on an unprecedented scale, most recently and visibly in China. This has led to massive urbanisation, with devastating consequences for the natural environment and human health (Walker and Buck, 2007). Such changes to structures of consumption and production have often been shaped by external pressures, such as those arising from the World Bank's structural adjustment programmes. One consequence of this has been to raise a range of ethical and moral concerns about the re-orientation of production to export markets, growing dependence on food imports, issues of health and safety at work and working conditions, the employment of child labour and so on, both among consumers and non-governmental organisations in the 'North' and among academic commentators (Hughes, 2006).

Parts of the global 'South' have also become increasingly vulnerable because of their growing incorporation into new global patterns of production of hazardous materials, location of polluting industries there and global trade in and markets for a variety of waste products. Such developments certainly were not simply a product of the neo-liberal turn (Hall, 2009) but, despite international regulatory and trade agreement via the Basel convention to limit such activities (see www.basel.int), they certainly became intensified as a result of it (Houveld, 2006; Yearley, 1995). A variety of wastes are routinely shipped from Europe and North America to regions of China, Indonesia and other parts of south east Asia for sorting and re-use while ships are driven onto beaches in Bangladesh and India to be taken apart and their constitutive material recycled (Buerk, 2006).

However, the global trade in wastes and the location of polluting activities is entangled in complex processes of uneven development that also affected some peripheral regions in the 'North', increasing their vulnerability as a result. Such regions have engaged in bidding wars with peripheral states within the 'South' seeking to become destinations for hazardous wastes in return for monetary payments and incomes, thereby increasing their vulnerability both economically, ecologically and in terms of risks to human health (Hudson, 2009). As Zonabend (1993) demonstrated in her analysis of the French nuclear industry on the La Hague peninsula, local communities in the 'North' have differential capacity – indeed willingness – to resist. In the 1990s Japanese nuclear waste was shipped to Sellafield in the UK for re-processing before being returned to Japan. At the same time, wastes from steel production in the UK were exported to Germany and Italy for remediation while derelict and heavily polluted USA and French navy 'ghost ships' were moved to Hartlepool in north east England for dismantling.[6]

In summary, the policy focus in peripheral 'losing' regions in both 'North' and 'South' shifted markedly and converged on an allegedly 'one best way'. Often with encouragement from influential consultants and think tanks, such regions sought to re-position themselves more favourably in global circuits of capital, commodity movements and flows of value as the route to socio-economic well-being and development. In this, they often sought explicitly to emulate the seemingly shock-proof 'winning' regions while ignoring the extent to which their bases of competitive success are grounded in the specifics of place and dependent upon the broader macro-political-economic climate and context. Regional development became de facto defined as successful re-positioning; to fail to achieve this meant remaining rooted at the bottom of the various chains or in the peripheries of networks. Successful regional development therefore required enhancing the attraction of the region so as to encourage a variety of flows (of commodities, money and people) into regions, promoting processes of transformation and value adding within those regions prior to the subsequent sale and movement of the resultant commodities out of them, creating flows between locations scattered around the world, driven by the (il)logic of capital accumulation with little or no regard for the ecological costs or, often, for the ethical consequences of so doing. However, as the recent global economic crisis has made only too clear, such a developmental model creates a vulnerable regional economy since its 'success' is predicated upon the ability to import raw materials and components at competitive prices and sell finished products profitably in export markets. When markets shrink and profits fall because of currency movements or a general collapse in the level of effective demand, the result is capacity closure and job losses in those regions – from south east China to north east England. In short, continuing with a mode of development that is predicated on encouraging global flows between regions widely dispersed around the world and is more generally blind to the materiality of the economy and its necessary grounding in 'First Nature' (Hudson, 2001a) creates a vulnerable rather than a resilient regional economy and is deeply and increasingly problematic.

## Moving towards more self-reliant and resilient regions?

Given the ecological impact of existing developmental models coupled with their failure to create resilient economies in many regions, might we not be forced to think seriously about returning to more place-based, localised and regionalised ways of living, predicated on a different and more materially aware conception of what constitutes development? Put another way, should we not engage seriously with a transformation to more resilient forms of regional economy and development?

In the remainder of this section of the chapter, I consider some issues that would need to be confronted in seeking to create more resilient regions, outline some indicative examples of how in practice regions can be made more resilient and examine some suggestions as to how such approaches could be developed further. This involves, inter alia, some regions seeking to increase their self-sufficiency, increasingly withdrawing and decoupling from national and international relations and structures and lowering their environmental footprint. This new approach is no longer based on stretching inter-regional networks to procure resources in more distant regions but seeks to develop a strategy of selective withdrawal and increased local autonomy via developing regional resources. These analyses and experiences of actually existing and planned regional development and the ways in which this goal has been pursued provide some hints as to future possibilities but also point to some limitations of existing and suggested approaches.

## A different regulatory regime and an enhanced capacity to learn and adapt

Growing vulnerability to the effects of decisions taken beyond the region was one of the defining aspects of the political economy of neo-liberalism. At the same time the neo-liberal approach involved greater devolution of responsibility for regional economic well-being to the regional level (MacLeod, 1999) – although typically without allocating resources commensurate with successfully carrying out this task in the face of global market forces. While granting greater power and resources to regions to devise economic development strategies that are appropriate to their condition and position in wider divisions of labour may be a necessary condition in moving towards greater resilience, it certainly is not a sufficient condition. There are limits to the capacity of regions to effect desired changes simply through action at the regional level. The switch to neo-liberal models of regional development reflected changes in national and, to a degree, supra-national, regulatory and governance regimes. It therefore follows that the capacity of regions to devise strategies for greater resilience will critically depend upon changes in national and, in some instances, supra-national modes of regulation and governing and on the articulation of regional, national and supra-national approaches. These policies would need to change in two important ways.

First, there would need to be changes to (dis)incentive and taxation structures to construct and regulate markets so as to encourage a shift to more ecologically sensitive processes, practices and behaviours (Hudson and Weaver, 1997). For example, there would need to be a shift to organisational forms and technologies of production and routine patterns of consumer behaviour that had a much lighter environmental footprint (not least via reducing the scale and scope of carbon-based mobility: see below). Second, greater priority would need to be given to issues such as the creation of socially useful (as opposed to simply profitable) work and socio-spatial equity, justice and well-being rather than economic growth per se and, as an important component of this, to seeking to optimise regional self-reliance and the degree of regional economic closure. This would undoubtedly require increased state involvement in the economy but it would not – and could not – simply involve a return to the 'command and control' Keynesianism that preceded neo-liberalism. Not least this is because of the scale of government borrowing and 'quantitative easing' (or more prosaically printing money) and direct involvement in the de facto nationalisation of many major banks undertaken as part of the attempt to kick-start the global economy. More fundamentally, however, a more radical approach to governing and regulation will be required to seek to cope with the unprecedented combination of deep economic and financial crises, the approach of 'peak oil' and the potentially catastrophic consequences of climate change (Green New Deal Group, 2008).

There has been considerable emphasis upon the creation of 'learning regions' as critical to regional competitive success in a neo-liberal world (Chapter 3; Morgan, 1995) and the capacity to learn and adapt will also be a key feature in the transition to resilient regions. However, the purpose of creating adaptive capacity and the capacity to learn would be rather different in the post-neo-liberal search for resilience. The emphasis would be upon moving to a proactive approach and upon learning how to anticipate and cope with a range of externally generated shocks and disturbances, learning how to create more self-contained regional economies, while securing a successful transition to ecologically sustainable and socially just forms of regional organisation of economy and society. This would entail recognising that there were benefits in looking beyond the boundaries of any given region to learn from others via networking and collaborating to share 'best practice' and learn about possible policy options.

## Greater intra-regional closure of the economy and greater regional self-reliance

There are clearly limits to the degree to which any regional economy can be closed off from the wider economy and a key issue would be to optimise the balance between intra-regional and extra-regional production and trade. In certain circumstances increasing intra-regional transactions is perfectly compatible with the mainstream logic of capital as it can cut both production and transport costs and enhance profits. This underlay the creation of major integrated chemicals and steel complexes, for example, as by-products from one process became inputs to another process rather than valueless wastes. The same logic underpins the development of eco-industrial development. The ecological benefits of this are discussed in the next section but the point to make here is that companies that practice eco-industrial development collaborate for mutual economic benefit, closing material loops via re-cycling, recovery or re-use of wastes and enhancing eco-efficiency via adjacent companies exchanging different kinds of by-product, based on bi-lateral commercial agreements, driven by concerns to minimise risks and wastes and maximise profits (Scharb, 2001; Stone, 2002). Eco-industrial development also offers possibilities to achieve greater efficiency through economies of systems integration in which networks and partnerships between businesses deliver common services, transportation and infrastructure needs. Knowledge exchange helps firms to discover new products and processes, so that they may become important spaces of innovation, knowledge creation and learning. Moreover, benefits spill over to local communities – for example via environmental improvements, increased employment and more co-operative industrial relations.

The emphasis on fostering networks and partnerships to optimise resource use and reduce costs has led to increasing recognition of the need to create wider regional networks to ensure economies of scale and sufficient supply of exchange materials (Scharb, 2001). Nonetheless, eco-industrial development clearly demonstrates the capacity to reduce the movement of materials in the process of manufacturing by regionalising at least part of supply chains. However, there are limits to eco-industrial development as at least some raw materials and components are typically imported into the region and finished products sold outside the region.

There are, however, also limits as to what can be produced for sale regionally because of the size of regional markets and consumption preferences within regions. Nonetheless there is considerable scope in many regions to enhance intra-regional transactions and the resilience of economies via public procurement policies. Consider, for example, the regionalisation of food supply chains over much of the European Union for schools, hospitals and other public sector activities (Hadjimichalis and Hudson, 2007). Such developments lead to greater consumption of fresh, locally produced foodstuffs, creating markets to sustain regional agriculture. This may also open up space for producers in the localised social economy, operating beyond the mainstream markets of capitalism (see below). It has also been argued that there is considerable scope to regionalise agricultural production by locating food production factories in densely populated regions (Weaver *et al.*, 2000), meeting regional demands from regional production and at the same time yielding major environmental benefits (which are discussed below).

There are, however, risks associated with increasing closure of regional economies, especially if this is linked to a concentration on a limited number of products. Greater resilience requires greater diversification, but of a radically different sort to the form of 'diversification' associated with the regional policies of the Fordist era. For while this brought a greater range of industries into regions previously dependent upon just one or a few industries, these were typically routine branch plants, involving de-skilled component production and/or assembly work. Diversification of industries led to homogenisation of labour processes based upon de-skilled work. In contrast, what is required is a diversification that involves a range of industries (manufacturing and services), firms of varied sizes and types (including social enterprises and 'Third Sector' organisations) and a range of functions, skills and occupations. Such a structure would be much better placed to cope with the unavoidable cycles of growth and decline that characterise capitalist development. How such a diversified structure could be achieved is, however, another question. What can be safely said is that it would require viewing the region not simply as a space in which to make profits but as a place to which key economic actors had a degree of attachment and commitment that was based on extra-economic motives, for example upon a regional identity and identification with the region (Hudson, 2001a).

Moreover, there are possibilities for some – but certainly not all – regions to create a resilient regional economy specialised in 'green' products (not least renewable energy) and the production of ecologically sensitive means of production for which there will be viable export markets. Firms in these regions that can achieve first-mover advantage in these emergent technologies and product markets will be able to pursue strategies of strong Schumpeterian competition and re-invest in R&D to maintain their competitive advantage. While there is no guarantee that this will not be eroded, the economic history of capitalism suggests that inherent to it are strong processes of cumulative advantage. Equally however this is no guarantee that profits made in a region would be re-invested there so that the risks to regional resilience that are endemic to capitalism would remain.

In addition, however, moving to more resilient regions will also require moving beyond the limits of the logic of capital and re-defining what counts as 'the economy', admitting the validity of differing concepts of value and processes of valuation and the outputs of goods and services that arise from them. As a result, much socially useful and environmentally enhancing activity that is currently consigned to the margins as the remit of the social economy, or 'Third Sector', would be accorded much greater recognition and significance (Amin, 2009; Amin *et al.*, 2002; Leyshon *et al.*, 2003). Often such activity is locally based, meeting local needs from locally produced products, or based upon recycling and re-use of existing goods and materials, so that in a variety of ways it has a much lighter environmental footprint. As well as creating socially useful work, often in regions plagued by high levels of worklessness, such social economy projects can also contribute to creating an ecologically more resilient economy.

## Acknowledging the materiality of the economy: restructuring consumption and production to lower the environmental footprint in resilient regions

While there is now a more widespread recognition that the economy involves flows and transformations of materials, with material effects on the natural environment, it was not until the late 1960s/early 1970s that a few economists and social scientists such as Ayres and Kneese (1969) and Georgescu-Roegen (1971) began seriously to engage with the economy understood in this way. Considering the economy through the lens of the laws of the physical sciences and concepts such as those of Life Cycle Analysis, industrial ecology, industrial metabolism and materials balance highlights the materiality of the economy and the economy as a series of continuous materials transformations. Regional economies can thus be thought of transient and temporary (possibly long-lived but always temporary and transient) assemblages of matter and energy, held in place by socially and spatially specific regulatory practices. The very possibilities of specific forms of production and economy – and hence of particular forms of regional economy and regional development – necessarily depend upon the sorts of materials configurations in which matter of particular sorts can be captured, formed and held.

However, these materials transformations chronically exceed their intended effects, as unruly matter escapes the frame defined by a given transformative process. Consequently at every stage in the economy the transformation of materials has both intended and unintended effects – the latter often invisible or otherwise undetected as well as unwanted and hence when visible typically referred to as 'pollutants' or 'wastes'. For a variety of reasons (economic, ecological and health) there are pressing imperatives to reduce such pollutants and wastes as well as the more general ecological footprint of economic activities.

As noted above, eco-industrial development offers the potential to regionalise production activities and reduce their ecological footprint, by minimising both wastes and the costs of moving materials between production processes and facilities. Eco-industrial development is grounded in a biological analogy that mimics the adaptive characteristics observed in nature, with clear similarities between eco-industrial development and the concept of socio-ecological systems. The most feasible locations for successful eco-industrial developments are big densely populated regions, which best meet three key conditions. First, firms within close proximity are sufficiently complementary to ensure an approximate balance between demand for and supply of by-products. Second, inter-firm relationships are based upon close individual connections or within an institutional framework that reduces transaction costs. Third, regulatory regimes encourage collaborative inter-firm relationships rather than the disposing of by-products as wastes. However, there are other environmental costs associated with major concentrations of population that need to be balanced against the benefits to be accrued from eco-industrial development in deciding, on a case-by-case basis, whether this offered a feasible way forward.

There are other ways of regionalising economic activities that can lower their ecological footprint. The regionalisation of food supply chains noted above can substantially reduce the ecological footprint of agriculture by reducing 'food miles' and $CO_2$ emissions as supply chains shorten and tonne-miles of food moved fall. Regionalisation of production and consumption does not automatically translate into a lower environmental footprint, however. For example, producing tomatoes in heated greenhouses in the UK may generate a greater carbon footprint than producing them out of doors in Spain and transporting them to the UK for sale, emphasising the need for a full Life Cycle Analysis.

It has also been claimed that agriculture could be made ecologically more efficient via food production 'factories' located in densely populated regions. Because production in controlled facilities would serve a known and defined population, feedback loops could be incorporated to allow customised production, with supply and demand dovetailed in terms of variety, quality, quantity and timing, lowering transport and storage costs.[7] Such a system could yield major eco-efficiency gains – for example in reducing energy and water use (Weaver *et al.*, 2000, 113–16). As with locating eco-industrial development in major populated regions, however, there would need to be a calculation of the environmental costs associated with such dense development offset against the environmental benefits of producing food in this way.

There is potential for further eco-efficiency gains but realising this would require more generalised changes in food production systems and major societal changes in diet, food preferences and tastes. This highlights the complexities of seeking to transform economic practices within a given region in pursuit of greater resilience. Novel foods could enable protein to be produced with substantially lower economic and ecological costs.

There are, however, major cultural, economic and social barriers to their adoption. As well as meeting nutritional needs, foods also provide sensual satisfaction through their aromas, flavours and textures and are used to confer and confirm social standing. Important relationships and family occasions are marked by eating important foods. As a result, 'the concerns of consumers over conventional foods in eating norms and habits constitute significant barriers to dietary change' (Weaver *et al.*, 2000, 121–2). So too do major capitalist concerns and agri-businesses with vested interests in reproducing existing food production and distribution systems on which their profits depend. Consequently, there are considerable pressures militating against innovative and potentially more eco-efficient food products and regionalised and resilient food production systems and it is an open question as to the extent to which these could be reduced via changes in national or supra-national regulatory systems.[8]

## Mobility, movement and land use patterns in resilient regions

Resilient regions will also require radical shifts in transport technologies and, over the longer-term, land use patterns. For many people there is an intimate link between automobility (Urry, 1999) and lifestyle as personal mobility is an important element of their quality of life. In turn, this reflects the long-established and well-known power of the 'road lobby' (Hamer, 1974) to promote its interests around the manufacture of cars and the construction of roads and related infrastructure. Thus land use patterns, transport demand and supply arrangements have co-evolved. The resultant environmental impacts could be reduced via some combination of demand management, more efficient methods of allocating people and goods to different modes of transport, changing modal splits and, in the longer-term, technological change to produce more energy-effective modes of movement and enable 'decarbonization of the economy', something that 'is clearly of paramount importance' (Wernick *et al.*, 1997, 138). Such changes would also have the beneficial effect of helping address inequalities in mobility that have resulted from prioritisation of the private car as a mode of transport over much of the world.

For many people, then, constructing more resilient regions within a decarbonising economy will require radically changing lifestyles as movement patterns are re-shaped, average distances travelled are reduced and people travel much more on foot, by bicycle or by various modes of public transport. Such changes will require major alterations to the spatial arrangement of built environments, the relative locations of spaces of work, exchange, leisure and residences and commensurate changes in people's activity patterns, activity spaces and dominant modes of travel. In brief, they will require a shift from built environments designed to maximise the movements required to go to work, shop and play to environments designed to minimise such movements between and within regions. Planning and designing built environments to minimise movement will drastically alter the relative locations of spaces of dwelling, work and so on and also the scales at which these activities occur.

There are already numerous examples around the world of planning projects that seek to construct built environments with a much lower environmental footprint, some of which claim also to address issues of socio-spatially uneven development. These include the Transition Towns movement (Brangwyn and Hopkins, 2009), which now embraces more than a hundred initiatives in different parts of the world, proposals to develop Mardar City as a carbon-neutral urban environment in Abu Dhabi and, drawing on proposals for the eco-neutral Dongtan eco-city in China, the proposed development of the Thames Gateway is intended to provide an important stimulus to the socio-economic regeneration of east London – although the flood risks associated with the planned development cast doubt upon its environmental sustainability and resilience (Lavery and Donovan, 2005).

There may well, however, also be resistance to such changes, even though innovations such as those information and communication technologies (notably the Internet) make them a feasible option. For example, telework has only led to a 0.7 per cent reduction in total commuting kilometres travelled in Finland (Helminen and Risitimäki, 2007). Only 2 per cent of Californian commuters wanted a 0–2 minute commute while almost 50 per cent preferred a commute of 30 minutes or more, suggesting resistance to the erosion of automobile-based lifestyles and the spatial separation of workplace and home (Button and Taylor, 2001, 30).

It would also be dangerous to under-estimate the inertia encapsulated in built environments precisely because they are constituted via major outlays of fixed capital, typically depreciated over decades. There are powerful economic imperatives to preserve existing socio-spatial structures, or at least slow the pace of change so that it does not endanger existing fixed capital investments and steer it so that it provides further scope for capital accumulation. It is an open question as to whether these economic imperatives are compatible with equally strong socio-ecological imperatives radically to alter patterns of human activity and mobility.

## Re-defining regional development? Moving towards resilient regions amidst the contradictions of capital

For some time now, there has been a strong emphasis in mainstream neo-liberal development discourse and policy on positioning regions more favourably in global production systems, up-grading their position in terms of links with other regions and locations. This in turn was seen as requiring major investment in transport and logistics infrastructure and in transforming built environments, not least in terms of attracting and retaining key highly skilled labour. So economic development and 'success' were seen as integrally linked to creating connections with and flows to other regions, maximising inter-regional flows, often on a global scale. Now there is an increasingly strong imperative to move towards more self-contained and sustainable models of regional development, to create more resilient regions by maximising intra-regional flows and connections (in part to help close materials loops) and by moving towards environmentally less damaging processes of production, exchange and consumption. Moreover, resilient regions can be thought of as those that seek to develop transformational strategies that anticipate and seek to prepare for the effects of adverse changes, developing the capacity to learn in order to do so and securing the necessary resources to put these proactive strategies into practice. There are numerous examples of 'local' solutions that address at least some of the issues, some parts of the problem. Nonetheless, all economic processes necessarily have an unavoidable ecological impact and it is also unrealistic to expect complete closure – or that all regions can be self-sufficient or indeed equally resilient, especially over issues such as energy supply. Consequently, this raises important questions as to the extent to which regional 'closure', autonomy if not autarky, and resilience are possible and the effects of such partial closure and resilience on the lifestyles and livelihoods of people who live and work in particular regions. Do moves to increase resilience in some regions simply defer environmental costs in time and/or displace them in space, thereby reducing the resilience of other regions while having no positive ameliorative impact systemically at global level? Does resilience simply become another dimension that regions deploy in the competition for mobile investment and so a key driver of new forms of combined and uneven development?

While the challenges posed in moving to more resilient and sustainable trajectories are severe in the global 'North', they are particularly acute for those marginalised regions in the 'South' that have embarked – often with little choice – on 'development' strategies based upon transforming local economies to find a niche in global production systems, whether in agriculture (a range of exotic fruits and vegetables, or cut flowers, or crops for bio-fuels) or as Free Production Zones for export-oriented manufacturing. While the ethical concerns and pressures from 'Northern' consumer groups and non-governmental organisations for 'fair trade' and better working conditions for factory workers (banning child labour, regulating terms, conditions and hours of work, improving health and safety and so on) are laudable and important, it is also important to bear in mind that they are predicated on these regions forming subordinate parts of global production systems. But what are the implications of these regions seeking to de-couple from such systems and switch to more autonomous and environmentally less damaging development trajectories, centred on maximising regionalised production and consumption, while acknowledging that there are limits to both what can be produced and sold in a given region? Would such a change enhance their resilience or deepen their vulnerability?

Indeed, more generally and crucially what are the practical possibilities for seeking to re-orientate regional development in these ways, given the imperatives of capital accumulation, the contradictory and uneven character of capitalist development and the difficulties of moving to non-capitalist models? Perhaps the biggest question of all is whether new forms of resilient and sustainable regional development – indeed development in general – can be made compatible with the social relations of capital and imperatives of capital accumulation? Eco-modernist optimists envisage ecological and economic imperatives as being compatible, provided that the appropriate institutional and regulatory arrangements are put in place. In short they imagine a managed 'green' capitalism that can ensure ecological sustainability. Others, me included, take a less sanguine view (Hudson, 2001a; 2005). The unintended consequences of seeking to move towards greater use of bio-fuels in creating an emerging crisis of food provision came as a sharp reminder of the contradictory character of a capitalist economy dogged by crisis tendencies. While there are encouraging local and regional examples, the possibilities of moving onto systemically non-capitalist development trajectories that would be more in tune with concepts of resilience and sustainability are hardly encouraging. The prognosis is, therefore, not a promising one, but the answer to these questions will have consequences that are not simply regional but global.

## Notes

1 This perspective is particularly associated with the Resilience Alliance (see www.resalliance.org).
2 The difference between adaptability and transformability is analogous to that between single and double loop learning (Levinthal, 1996).
3 This evolutionary concept of the economy and economic development sees resilience as the capacity to keep moving along a developmental trajectory (or to move to a more desirable one) rather than seeing resilience in terms of a return to a known fixed point of equilibrium.
4 At the time of writing (2009), the global economic crisis suggests that whatever the future may hold, the era of neo-liberal capitalism has had its day. Whatever the capitalist future may be, it will be a more and differently regulated one.
5 I draw a contrast, but also note some similarities, between changes in the global 'North' and 'South'. However, I recognise that this binary dichotomy is an over-simplification as the global movements of capital and people have led to elements of the 'South' locating in the 'North' and vice versa.
6 These issues of the production of, international trade in and re-use of wastes were investigated in a major research project funded by the UK Economic and Social Research Council. For further details see www.thewasteoftheworld.org/.
7 Such supply chain management is already virtually ubiquitous among major food retailers but driven by their concern to maximise corporate profits.
8 Densely populated regions also have potential to become more sustainable spaces of consumption in other ways, such as cleaning and washing clothing and other household textiles (Weaver *et al.*, 2000, 176).

# 12 The future of economic geography and economic geographies of the future

## Introduction

Let me begin by briefly précising the argument set out in Chapter 1. Economic geography has a rich history, with changing emphases over time, both empirically in terms of substantively what economic geographers have studied and of how they have done so, conceptually, theoretically and methodologically. Moreover, there have been connections between what and how. The engagement with location theories in the 1950s and 1960s was a pivotal moment in the transformation of economic geography – indeed human geography more generally – from a discipline concerned with description to one concerned with explanation of spatial form. It was not long, however, before location theories themselves became criticised because of their simplistic conception of social process, a reflection of their grounding in neo-classical economics, and their particular approach to explanation, emphasising deducing spatial form at the expense of understanding social process. This in turn led to the leading edge of economic geography being driven forward by Marxian political economy and analyses of the economy, its geographies and its uneven spatial development. Subsequently the Marxian approach, often with a critical realist tinge, became part of a new orthodoxy, emphasising that capitalist economies and their geographies were mutually constitutive – a socio-spatial turn. It too, in turn however became subject to critique for a variety of intellectual, sociological and political reasons. In the course of these changes, economic geographers engaged with scholars in other social science disciplines that were themselves coming to acknowledge the centrality of spatiality to economy and society and with disciplines in the natural sciences, especially those concerned with the environment and nature. As a result economic geography became a much more heterogeneous and contested field, developing links with emergent strands of economics that discovered the significance of space and spatial difference to the economy, sociological approaches to analyses of embeddedness drawing on the work of Polanyi and Granovetter, various strands of evolutionary and institutional economics, elements of the post-structuralism of Callon and Latour, as well as feminist approaches that emphasised the situated nature of all knowledges.

In short, some sought to elaborate more sophisticated political economy approaches, others to develop alternatives of various sorts to political economies.

I suggested in the opening chapter that we could identify five major shifts in the evolution of economic geography over the last five or six decades. Focusing more on the period since 1990, and on the socio-spatial rather than socio-natural dimensions of economic geography, Grabher (2009, 120) argues that '[i]n roughly two decades, our sub-discipline has readjusted its paradigmatic coordinates at least three times by going through cultural, institutional and relational turns'. As a result of this, he argues that there are four dimensions of socio-spatiality that run through approaches in contemporary economic geography – scales, networks, hierarchies and place making – which provide the analytic basis for comprehending the complex and multi-layered production of uneven spatial development within the contemporary economy (Brenner, 2011). Incorporating the effects of an evolutionary turn would help add a temporal dynamism to this framework. As well as this more sophisticated perspective on socio-spatiality, however, there has been an increasing recognition of the economy as constituted through socio-natural processes, registered in work thinking through the economy as processes of material transformation. These processes have both intended and, crucially, unintended consequences as bio-physical processes cannot necessarily be contained to have only the effects intended by people acting in the economy.

It seems certain that this heterogeneity will continue for the foreseeable future, as there are significant differences and in some cases deep epistemological and ontological incompatibilities among these approaches. This is not necessarily a bad thing insofar as it can be plausibly argued that it is unlikely that any single approach could be adequate to grasp the nuanced complexities of modern capitalist economies, to say nothing of their articulations with non-capitalist approaches to economic organisation (as emphasised by Gibson-Graham, 1996, for example). Views differ as to the merits of diversity of approach and perspective, however.

There are those who recognise that different perspectives are valuable and necessary and argue strongly that such variety could be the basis for a productive pluralism but nonetheless insist that this is in itself insufficient. In contrast, they argue that to be truly productive such pluralism requires more than the simple co-existence of diverse strands that mutually ignore one another and requires debates about boundaries defining the legitimate scope of different approaches and about relations of complementarity or incompatibility as a necessary condition for a more productive dialogue (Grabher, 2009). It also requires some agreement as to the criteria (empirical, conceptual and, given the contested character of capitalist economies, political) that could be used to decide what would constitute a more powerful explanation of the geographies of capitalist economies and that could be used to adjudicate among competing positions. In discussing the relationships between environmental and evolutionary economic geographies, Patchell and Hayter (2013) have helpfully suggested that varying conceptual approaches be thought of as 'passing conveniences', helpful staging posts on a journey to deeper understanding of economic geographies, as bases for constructive conversations that seek new ways forward rather than fixed positions to be defended at all costs. Such a perspective could be adopted more widely to good effect.

Others, however, suggest that, even with these caveats, there is also a downside to this multiplicity of views. For as Peck (2005) points out, instead of a cumulative evolution and continuous refinement of theoretical positions, the result has typically been short-lived theoretical and paradigmatic commitments and shifting methodological conventions and standards – often by the same individuals. In part, this can be thought of as simply part of the sociology of the discipline, as new generations of scholars seek to define and stake out their own territory. It is also, however, in part a result of fashion effects and social and political influences beyond as well as within the academy that are not necessarily conducive to deepening understanding of economies and their geographies and often result in people talking across one another rather than engaging in debate. I have considerable sympathy with Peck's view.

In part, it has been suggested that this confusion and babel of voices reflects that fact that theoretical positions are advanced without specifying how their validity may be tested. As such they become irrefutable. Sunley (2009, 17–18), for example, makes the point powerfully with respect to relational approaches which have entered a state of 'empirical immunity'. Because the terms and phrases are compatible with any empirical outcome, empirical research is solely confirmatory. Markusen's (1999) axiom of 'how do we know it when we see it?' is rendered redundant as any empirical results can be described as illustrations, outcomes and validation of network geometries and confirmation of the exercise of relational power. As a result, the end result is a push toward an economic geography that is immersed in managerial networks and uncritical descriptions of business elites and omniscient firms (see also Chapter 3). Furthermore, more generally, as Simandan (2011) emphasises, growing diversity in approaches has seen an increasing distancing from the concerns of political economy with systemic understanding of the economy, seemingly rejecting the possibility of integrating these various partial and competing knowledge claims within an overarching theoretical framework. While I have considerable sympathy with Simandan's anxieties and unease, I have sought to show that this is not necessarily the case.

## Persistent themes and future emphases: continuity amidst change

Nonetheless, amidst this welter of change and resultant uncertainty as to what the focus of economic geography should be and how it should be most appropriately thought and practised, there are a number of themes that have persisted across differing approaches and will continue to do so in the future. Conceptually, we can identify three inter-related themes or strands that have been important so far and will continue to be important in future in seeking to understand the changing geographies of economies and the significance of their constituent actors and institutions: value; meanings; materiality. These are discussed below.

First, though, a few words about empirical research. Economic geography has come a long way from the empiricism that once characterised it to a much more nuanced conception of careful and sophisticated theoretically informed empirical research. A future economic geography needs to pay continued attention to such empirical research to engage with the changing character of capitalist economies and their geographies of production, exchange and consumption. Sunley's (2009) comments about the dangers of 'empirical immunity' are particularly pertinent. Thus there is a clear need for sophisticated theoretically informed case studies of particular places, companies and industries, employing mixed methods approaches, including ethnographies to uncover meanings and understand behaviours as well as quantitative data on variables such as employment, wages, capital investment and profitability. In addition, however, an important part of future research agendas should be comparative empirical research that seeks to uncover the underlying mechanisms and processes that shape economic co-evolution across different spatial contexts (MacKinnon *et al.*, 2009, 145).

### *Value*

Value will continue to be of central concern to economic geography. In particular, there will be a continuing concern with understanding how value is produced, recognising that there is a variety of conceptions of value and that these too have a geography. Over the last two centuries or so capitalist conceptions of value have become increasingly dominant – and remain so – although they are by no means universal as people and places continue to resist their intrusion into their lives. Nonetheless, their growing presence and significance is reflected in the spread of capitalist forms of economic organisation and new forms of spatial divisions of labour, spatial forms of organising economies and geographies of economies. The continuing pressures for capital to extend its influence ever more deeply and widely are reflected in contemporary neo-imperial geographies of globalisation, the renewed significance of accumulation by dispossession and the emergence of 'the New Imperialism' (Harvey, 2003). The continuities with older geographies of Empire are crystal clear. It will be important therefore to continue to deepen understanding of how value is produced and distributed within capitalist relations of production, how capitalist economic geographies are made possible in terms of regulation and governance and the reproduction of the wider socio-political conditions on which capitalist markets depend, on how these are always economic geographies shaped in particular ways in space and time and shaping space. Economic geographers will – and will need to – continue to draw on the legacies of various strands of political economy and analyses of uneven development in future investigation of these issues.

While continuing to deepen understanding of the geographies of capitalist value production, circulation and realisation, it will be equally important to bear in mind that capitalist conceptions of value have been and continue to be contested. There are many economic spaces in which non-capitalist conceptions of value remain dominant, albeit these are typically limited and local. Understanding the boundaries and relationships between the spaces of capitalist and non-capitalist economies is important. Likewise, exploring the boundaries between legal and illegal economies within capitalism will remain a key issue, albeit one fraught with problems of empirical investigation. Recognising this variety both in forms of capitalism and in non-capitalist ways of organising economies links in important ways to normative and political questions related to understanding and responding progressively to the socio-spatial inequalities that are constitutive of capitalist social relations and the material inequalities that result from them.

### *Meanings*

The question of meanings is linked to that of different conceptions of value. A key question here is: what's the economy for? What are people seeking to produce through 'the economy'? What does it mean to them? Of course they seek to produce value in various ways, for this is intimately linked to the material basis of their lives and their ability materially to reproduce themselves, their families and communities. People cannot live by discourse alone. Material consumption (of food, shelter, clothing and so on) clearly matters and such consumption of use values pre-supposes production, whether through capitalist relations of production and exchange or in some other way. While the functional attributes of commodities remain of central importance for many, there is also evidence of the growing importance of particular brands, advertising and the aesthetic and symbolic attributes of commodities, for at least some people in some times and places, reflected in claims about the growth of a 'global' middle class. Consumption has further economic effects beyond the consumption of use values, however, in terms of the re-circulation of commodities, their potential recycling and re-consumption, and the production of wastes, depending upon the meanings that people attach to things that have reached the end of their useful life for them. This can lead to a more sophisticated recursive rather than linear view of the economy and a more nuanced view of the passage of things through it.

There is a further dimension to meanings of participation in the economy, however. Beyond the material necessity of production and consumption, what people do in the economy can give meaning to their lives in various ways, helping forge their identities through their activity as producers and/or as consumers. Investigating such issues entails encounters with new methodologies, new post-structuralist approaches that focused on how people construct (multiple) identities. To a degree, of course, identities have always been multiple and while they depend on where individuals are in terms of social class structures, this is not a rigidly deterministic relationship and the relationship of their (class structural) position in economic relations to characteristics such as ethnicity and gender is not predetermined.

For many people, then, participation in capitalist economic relations both provides a material basis for living via selling their capacity to work for a wage and helps define their identities and provide meaning for their lives. Given that people engage in wage labour as alienated labour and consume commodities that are the result of the alienated labour of others, these issues of identities can become complicated. For many others, however, excluded from or occupying marginal or subaltern positions in capitalist economies, 'getting by', subsisting, has and continues to be a very different process in terms of material provision and in terms of their identities as economic actors. For some, this entails engaging in different types of economies to those of the capitalist mainstream. For many it requires transgressing the boundaries of legality as they are enrolled into economies of illegality of various sorts as part of strategies for 'getting by'.

### *Materiality*

All economic activities have an unavoidable material dimension, involving socio-ecological interactions of various sorts. This is as true of 'service' activities as it is of those of material production. They all involve material transformations of one sort or another in activities of production, circulation, exchange and consumption, whether in commodity or other forms. This impact of economic activities on 'nature' at various spatial scales is unavoidable, and its significance is increasing. Material transformations have unintended as well as intended effects, however. As a result, it is also important to recognise that there is an epistemological challenge involved in bringing together environment and economy. Collective engagements with nature's effectivity – the difference that nature makes to economic processes and conversely the difference that economic processes make to nature – raise the question of how we understand the materiality of nature. There is a tension here that centres on an epistemological distinction between a (critical realist) position that regards nature as a material force and a (post-structural) position that sees nature as a cultural artefact; that is, as an effect of ways of thinking that are typically classified as 'science'. The objective of the former is to explain how the structures and internal processes of the natural world function; while that of the latter is to identify the practices through which nature and/or its various structures and processes are able to acquire their social status as material properties (Bridge, 2011, 228).

Environmental impact in part depends upon choice of economic developmental model, the dominant form of capitalist development: for example, globally in the recent past credit-fuelled globalisation has intensified a set of environmental risks and externalities, especially those of resource depletion and carbon emissions. So far at least, both national states and global institutions have proved unable or unwilling to deal with these costs. Whether this is a sustainable position remains a moot point. What, then, would a transition to ecologically sustainable production entail? Is such a transition possible, politically? Is there a viable technological 'fix' that can avoid the need for hard political choices? These are key questions for the future – is an environmentally sustainable capitalism possible? Or if not that, then what alternative futures for economy, environment and society are possible?

There will be no simple answers to these questions. Not least, this is because the problem for any analysis of economy, grounded as it necessarily must be in material and social circumstances, and for any radical alternative, is how to grapple with the challenge of reconciling the inherent social, cultural and environmental aspects of economic activity with the 'brute material imperative' of producing at least as much value as is needed to sustain all those materially dependent upon it (Leyshon *et al.*, 2011, 18). Central to this reconciliation are the complex relationships between material value and the values – both moral and ethical – that guide and shape economic activity. In short, economic geographers need explicitly to confront the question: what sort of economy, and what of economic geography, for whom?

## So where are we now, and where next?

In many ways I would argue that, like it or not, there will continue to be strong continuities with the past. While not without problems, this heritage can be seen to provide a strong basis for a vibrant discipline of economic geography, with strong links to other parts of the social and, to a degree, physical sciences. Furthermore, a practical implication of broadening conceptions of the economy and the scope of economic geography is to create conceptual space for new approaches to spatial economic policies, including those that challenge the imperatives of capital and the mainstream economy. However, while there undoubtedly are many examples of imaginative alternative social economy and social enterprise projects, these very rarely, if ever, can escape specific time/space context in which they arose and become the basis of broader alternative approach to the economy. Realistically, at least for the foreseeable future, economies will remain dominated by capitalist social relations but there are varieties of capitalism, some of which are more socially just and environmentally sensitive than others, and radical alternatives to capitalisms can continue to thrive in the spaces between and within these differing versions of capitalism. This variety provides both political possibilities and theoretical challenges in understanding the relationships between these differing political-economic spaces.

In terms of theory, then, it seems highly likely that economic geography will continue to be characterised by a diversity of approaches and that tensions, for example between formal deductive and inductive contextual approaches, between quantitative and qualitative methodologies, will continue to exist. My own preference – as will by now be clear – is for a geographical political economy grounded in a Marxian approach because this alone offers the systemic perspective necessary to grasp the complexities of uneven development but drawing upon other perspectives to give a more nuanced view of processes of capitalist development and how they operate. Others will no doubt have other views. For some, epistemological variety and lack of a canon represent an intellectual strength rather than a weakness. There are those who argue that the lack of a canon in economic geography can be seen as advantageous in trying to come to terms with contemporary economic and environmental dilemmas which strike at the heart of the sustainability of human life. Conversely, to others this variety can be seen as evidence of a discipline subject to fashion effects, blown in the direction of the latest fad to emerge elsewhere in the social sciences or responding to winds of changes in the political climate. But irrespective of such conceptual and theoretical variety, and whether this is seen as a good or bad thing, what seems certain is that in future issues of long-term sustainability of existing economic arrangements and their constituent economic geographies will become of growing significance. No doubt new issues, themes and approaches will emerge in future that aren't foreseeable now. But, provided that economic geographers do not lose sight of the need for systemic perspectives, the rich variety of intellectual position within economic geography will leave it well-placed to contribute to their understanding and to informing – hopefully progressive – responses to them.

# References


Acelor, 2005, *Newsletter ACELOR Auto*, No. 10, Paris.

AcelorMittal, n.d., 'Worldwide research and development centres', available at www.acelormittal.com/automotive/about/automotive/rd [accessed 21 February 2011].

ACIDH (Action Against Impunity for Human Rights), 2011, *Unheard Voices: Mining Activities in the Katanga Province and the Impact on Local Communities*, ACIDH and SOMO – Centre for Research on Multinational Corporations, Amsterdam, 49 pp.

Adger W, 2000, 'Social and ecological resilience: are they related?', *Progress in Human Geography* 24, 347–64.

Aghion P and Howitt P, 1998, *Endogenous Growth Theory*, MIT Press, London.

Aglietta M, 1979, *A Theory of Capitalist Regulation*, New Left Books, London.

Albert M, 1993, *Capitalism against Capitalism*, Whurr, London.

Allen C M, 2005, *An Industrial Geography of Cocaine*, Routledge, New York.

Allen J, 2002, 'Symbolic economies: the "culturalization" of economic knowledge', in du Gay P and Pryke M (Eds.), *Cultural Economy*, Sage, London, 39–58.

Allen J and Thompson G, 1997, 'Think global, then think again – economic globalization in context', *Area*, 29, 3, 213–27.

Allen J, Massey D and Cochrane, A., 1998, *Re-thinking the Region*, Routledge, London.

Allum F and Allum P, 2008, 'Revisiting Naples: clientelism and organised crime', *Journal of Modern Italian Studies*, 13, 340–65.

Allwood J M, Ashby M F, Gutowski T G and Worell E, 2011, 'Materials efficiency: a white paper', *Resources, Conservation and Recycling*, 55, 362–38.

Amin A, 1998, 'An institutionalist perspective on regional economic development', Paper presented to the Royal Geographical Society Economic Geography Research Group Seminar, Institutions and Governance, 3 July, UCL, London.

Amin A, 2008, 'Extraordinarily ordinary: working in the social economy', mimeo, University of Durham, 19 pp.

Amin A (Ed.), 2009, *The Social Economy: International Perspectives*, Zed Press, London.

Amin A and Cohendet P, 1997, 'Learning and adaptation in decentralised business networks', Paper presented to the Final EMOT Conference, 11–13 September.

Amin A and Cohendet P, 2003, *Architecture of Knowledge*, Oxford University Press, Oxford.

Amin A and Hausner J, 1997 (Eds.), *Beyond Market and Hierarchy: Interactive Governance and Social Complexity*, Edward Elgar, Aldershot.

Amin A and Thomas A., 1996, 'The negotiated economy: state and civic institutions in Denmark', *Economy and Society*, 25, 2, 255–81.
Amin A and Thrift N, 1994, 'Living in the global', in Amin A and Thrift N (Eds.), *Globalization, Institutions and Regional Development in Europe*, Oxford University Press, Oxford, 1–22.
Amin A and Thrift N, 2004, 'Cultural economy: the genealogy of an idea', in Amin A and Thrift N (Eds.), *Cultural Economy: A Reader*, Sage, London.
Amin A, Cameron A and Hudson R, 2002, *Placing the Social Economy*, Routledge, London.
Amin S, 1977, *Unequal Development*, Harvester, Lewes.
Anderson J, 1995, 'The exaggerated death of the nation state', in Anderson J, Brook C and Cochrane A (Eds.), *A Global World?*, Oxford University Press, Oxford, 65–114.
Anderson P, 1984, *In the Tracks of Historical Materialism*, Verso, London.
Anon, 2008, 'Stainless steel car frames: the next generation', *Nickel*, 24, 1, 6–7.
Appadurai A (Ed.), 1986, *The Social Life of Things*, Cambridge University Press, Cambridge.
Arena R, Lazaric N and Lorenz E, 2006, 'Trust, codification and epistemic communities: implementing an expert system in the French steel industry', *DIME Communities of Practice Working Paper No. 12*, available at www.dime-eu.org/node?page=4 [accessed 29 April 2011].
Arrow K, 1962, 'The economic implications of learning by doing', *Review of Economic Studies*, 29, 155–73.
Arthur D Little, 2001, *Realising the Potential of the North East's Research Base*, ADL Ltd, Harrogate.
Arthur W B, 1989, 'Competing technologies, increasing returns, and "lock-in" by historical events', *Economic Journal*, 99, 106–31.
Ashby M F and Jones D H R, 1992, *Engineering Materials 2*, Pergamon, Oxford.
Asheim B and Coenen J, 2005, 'Knowledge bases and regional innovation systems: comparing Nordic clusters', *Research Policy*, 34, 1173–90.
Athreye S, 1998, 'On markets in knowledge', *ESRC Centre for Business Research Working Paper 83*, University of Cambridge.
Ayres R U and Kneese A V, 1969, 'Production, consumption and externalities', *American Economic Review*, 59, 282–97.
Bain E C and Davenport E S, 1970, 'Transformation of austenite at constant subcritical temperatures', *Metallurgical and Materials Transactions B*, 1, 12, 3503–30.
Baker, R, 2006, *Capitalism's Achilles Heel*, Wiley, New Jersey.
Bakker K and Bridge G, 2006, 'Material worlds? Resource geographies and the "matter of nature"', *Progress in Human Geography*, 30, 5–27.
Barnes T, 1996, *Logics of Dislocation*, Guilford, New York.
Barnes T and Sheppard E, 2010, ' "Nothing includes everything": towards engaged pluralism in anglophone economic geography', *Progress in Human Geography*, 34, 193–214.
Bathelt J, 2006, 'Geographies of production: growth regimes in spatial perspective 3 – towards a relational view of economic action and policy', *Progress in Human Geography*, 30, 223–36.
Bathelt J and Glückler J, 2003, 'Toward a relational economic geography', *Journal of Economic Geography*, 3, 117–44.
Bauman Z, 1992, *Intimations of Postmodernity*, Routledge, London.
Bauman Z, 2005, *Liquid Life*, Polity, Cambridge.

Beckert J and Wehinger F, 2011, 'In the shadow: illegal markets and sociology', *Discussion Paper 11/9*, Max Planck Institute for the Study of Societies, Cologne, 24 pp.

Bellet M, Colletis G and Lung Y (Eds.), 1993, 'Économie de proximités', *Revue d'Écononomie Regionale et Urbaine*, 3, 357–602.

Bennett J, 2010, *Vibrant Matter: A Political Ecology of Things*, Duke University Press, Durham, NC.

Bennett K, Beynon H and Hudson R, 2000, *Coalfields Regeneration: Dealing with the Consequences of Industrial Decline*, Policy Press, Bristol.

Bensaude-Vincent B and Stengers I, 1996, *A History of Chemistry*, Harvard University Press, Cambridge, MA.

Benton T, 1989, 'Marxism and natural limits: an ecological critique and reconstruction', *New Left Review*, 178, 51–86.

Berkes F and Folke C (Eds.) 1998, *Linking Social and Ecological Systems: Management Practices and Social Mechanisms for Building Resilience*, Cambridge University Press, Cambridge.

Best M, 1990, *The New Competition: Institutions of Industrial Restructuring*, Polity, Cambridge.

Beynon H, 1973, *Working for Ford*, Penguin, Harmondsworth.

Beynon H, 1995, 'The changing experience of work in Britain in the 1990s', Paper presented to the Conference on Education and Training for the Future Labour Markets of Europe, University of Durham, 21–24 September.

Beynon H and Austrin T, 1979, *Global Outpost: The Working Class Experience of Big Business in the North East of England, 1964–79*, Department of Sociology, University of Durham.

Beynon H and Austrin T, 1994, *Masters and Servants*, Rivers Oram, London.

Beynon H, Hudson R and Sadler D, 1991, *A Tale of Two Industries: The Decline of Coal and Steel in North East England*, Open University Press, Milton Keynes.

Beynon H, Hudson R and Sadler D, 1994, *A Place Called Teesside: A Locality in a Global Economy*, Edinburgh University Press, Edinburgh.

Beynon H, Cox A and Hudson R, 2000, *Digging Up Trouble: The Environment, Protest and Opencast Coal Mining*, Rivers Oram, London.

Bhattacharyya G, 2005, *Traffick: The Illicit Movement of People and Things*, Pluto Press, London.

Blaikie P and Brookfield H, 1987, *Land Degradation and Society*, Longman, London.

Blyton P and Turnbull P (Eds.), 1992, *Re-assessing Human Resource Management*, Sage, London.

Bonnano G, 2004, 'Loss, trauma and human resilience: have we underestimated the human capacity to thrive after extremely adverse events?', *American Psychologist*, 59, 20–8.

Borzaga C, 2008, 'Working for social enterprise: does it make any difference?', Paper presented to the International Workshop on Ethnographies of the Social Economy, Durham, 14–15 March.

Boschma R and Frenken K, 2009, 'Notes on institutions in evolutionary economic geography', *Economic Geography*, 85, 151–8.

Boschma R and Frenken K, 2011, 'The emerging empirics of evolutionary economic geography', *Journal of Economic Geography*, 11, 295–307.

Boulding K, 1985, *The World as a Total System*, Sage, London.

Bourdieu P, 1977, *Outline of a Theory of Practice*, Cambridge University Press, Cambridge.

Bourdieu P, 1981, 'Men and machines', in Knorr-Cetina K and Cicourcel L (Eds.), *Advances in Social Theory and Methodology*, Routledge and Kegan Paul, Boston, 304–18.
Bowring F, 1999, 'LETS: an eco-socialist alternative', *New Left Review*, 232, 91–111.
Bowring F, 2003, 'Manufacturing scarcity: food biotechnology and the life-sciences industry', *Capital and Class*, 79, 107–44.
Boyd W, Prudham W S and Schurman R A, 2001, 'Industrial dynamics and the problem of nature', *Society and Natural Resources*, 14, 555–70.
Boyer R, 1990, *The Regulation School: A Critical Introduction*, Columbia University Press, New York.
Boyer R and Drache D (Eds.), 1995, *States Against Markets*, Routledge, London.
Braczyk H-J, Cooke P and Heidenreich M (Eds.), 1998, *Regional Innovation Systems*, UCL Press, London.
Brangwyn B and Hopkins R, 2009, 'Transition initiatives primer – becoming a transition town, city, district, village, community or even island. Version 26', available at http://transitionstowns.org/TransitionNetwork/TransitionNetwork#Primer [accessed 8 June 2009].
Braun B, 2006, 'Environmental issues: global natures in the space of assemblages', *Progress in Human Geography*, 30, 644–54.
Braverman H, 1974, *Labor and Monopoly Capital*, Monthly Review Press, New York.
Brenner N, 2011, 'Critical sociospatial theory and the geographies of uneven spatial development', in Leyshon A, Lee R, McDowell L and Sunley P (Eds.), *The SAGE Handbook of Economic Geography*, Sage, London, 135–48.
Brenner N, Jessop B, Jones M and MacLeod G, 2003, *State/Space: A Reader*, Blackwell, Oxford.
Brenner R and Glick M, 1991, 'The regulation approach: theory and history', *New Left Review*, 188, 45–120.
Bridge G, 2011, 'The economy of nature: from political ecology to the social construction of nature', in Leyshon A, Lee R, McDowell L and Sunley P (Eds.), *The SAGE Handbook of Economic Geography*, Sage, London, 217–30.
Brown E and Cloke J, 2007, 'Shadow Europe: alternative European financial geographies', *Growth and Change*, 38, 304–27.
Brown E and Cloke J, 2011, 'Critical perspectives on corruption: an overview', *Critical Perspectives on International Business*, 7, 116–24.
Brown J, Duncombe A and Short E, 2013, 'High street urged to put safety ahead of profits', *Independent*, 26 April, 8–9.
Brown J M, 2001, 'Why Irish eyes are still smiling over IT sector', *Financial Times*, 7 May.
Brown R and Raines P, 2000, 'The changing nature of foreign investment policy in Europe', in Dunning J H (Ed.), *Regions, Globalization and the Knowledge-Based Economy*, Oxford University Press, Oxford, 435–58.
Buerk R, 2006, *Breaking Ships: How Supertankers and Cargo Ships Are Dismantled on the Beaches of Bangladesh*, Penguin, London.
Burn D, 1961, *The Economic History of Steel Making, 1867–1939: A Study in Competition*, Cambridge University Press, Cambridge.
Button K and Taylor S, 2001, 'Towards an economics of the internet and e-commerce', in Leinbach T R and Brunn S D (Eds.), *Worlds of E-Commerce*, Wiley, Chichester, 27–44.

Callon M, 2006, 'Why Virtualism paves the way to political impotence: a reply to Daniel Miller's critique of *The Laws of the Market*', *Economic Sociology European Electronic Newsletter*, 6, 3–20.
Camagni R, 1991, 'Local "milieu", uncertainty and innovation networks: towards a new dynamic theory of economic space', in Camagni R (Ed.), *Innovation Networks: Spatial Perspectives*, Belhaven, London, 121–42.
Cane A and Nicholson M, 2001, 'Thousands of job losses feared at Motorola', *Financial Times*, 19 April.
Carney J and Hudson R, 1978, 'Capital, politics and ideology: the north east of England, 1870–1946', *Antipode*, 10, 64–78.
Carney, J Hudson R and Lewis J, 1977, 'Coal combines and inter-regional uneven development in the UK', in Batey P W and Massey D (Eds.), *Alternative Frameworks for Analysis, London Papers in Regional Science, No 7*, Pion, 52–67.
Carpenter S, Walker B, Anderies J M and Abel N, 2001, 'From metaphor to measurement: resilience of what to what?', *Ecosystems*, 4, 765–81.
Carr J C and Taplin W, 1962, *History of the British Steel Industry*, Harvard University Press, Cambridge.
Castells M, 1996, *The Rise of the Network Society*, Blackwell, Oxford.
Castells M, 2010, *End of Millennium*, Blackwell, Oxford (2nd edition).
Castree N, 1995, 'The nature of produced nature: materiality and knowledge construction in Marxism', *Antipode*, 27, 12–48.
Chan J, de Haan E, Nordbrand S and Torstensson A, 2008, *Silence to Deliver: Mobile Phone Manufacturing in China and the Philippines*, SOMO and Swedwatch, Amsterdam.
Chapman K, 2003, 'From "growth centre" to "cluster": restructuring, regional development and the Teesside chemical industry', Paper presented to the International Workshop, The Restructuring of Old Industrial Areas in Europe and Asia, University of Bonn, 11–12 July.
Chapman K, 2005, 'From "growth centre" to "cluster": restructuring, regional development and the Teesside chemical industry', *Environment and Planning A*, 37, 597–615.
Chaudhry P and Zimmerman A, 2010, *The Economics of Counterfeit Trade: Governments, Consumers, Pirates and Intellectual Property Rights*, Springer, Berlin.
Christensen J, 2011, 'The looting continues: tax havens and corruption', *Critical Perspectives on International Business*, 7, 177–96.
Christensen J and Hampton M, 1999, 'A legislature for hire: the capture of the state in Jersey's Offshore Finance Centre', in Hampton M and Abbott J (Eds.), *Offshore Finance Centres and Tax Havens: The Rise of Global Capital*, Macmillan, Basingstoke, 166–91.
Clark G, 1992, 'Real regulation: the administrative state', *Environment and Planning A*, 24, 615–27.
Clark G L, Feldman M P and Gertler M S (Eds.), 2000, *The Oxford Handbook of Economic Geography*, Oxford University Press, Oxford.
Coe N and Hess M, 2007, 'Global production networks: challenges and debates', Paper prepared for the GPERG workshop, University of Manchester, 25–26 January.
Coe N, Kelly and Yeung H, 2007, *Economic Geography: A Contemporary Introduction*, Blackwell, Oxford.

Coe NM, Hess M, Yeung H W-C, Dicken P and Henderson J, 2004, 'Globalizing regional development: a global production networks perspective', *Transactions of the Institute of British Geographers, New Series*, 29, 468–84.

Coninck N, Theuws M and Overeem P, 2011, *Captured by Cotton: Exploited Dalit Girls Produce Garments in India for US and European Markets*, SOMO and ICN, Amsterdam and Utrecht.

Cooke P and Morgan K, 1998, *The Associational Economy*, Oxford University Press, Oxford.

Corbridge S, Martin R and Thrift N (Eds.), 1994, *Money, Space and Power*, Blackwell, Oxford.

Corus, n.d.(a), 'Corus in automotive: Working in partnership – making a difference', available at www.corusautomotive.com [accessed 20 February 2011].

Corus, n.d.(b), 'Making strip steels work harder in automotive components', available at www.corusautomotive.com [accessed 20 February 2011].

Corus Engineering Steels, 2001, 'Automotive supply chains and the engineering steel supplier', *Corus Engineering Steels Technical Paper Prod/A5*, Rotherham, 13 pp.

Crewe L and Lowe M, 1996, 'United colours? Globalization and localization tendencies in fashion retailing', in Wrigley N and Lowe M (Eds.), *Retailing, Consumption and Capital: Towards the New Retail Geography*, Longman, London, 271–83.

Dallago B, 1990, *The Irregular Economy: The Underground Economy and the 'Black' Labour Market*, Dartmouth Publishing Company, Dartmouth.

Dalton H, 1953, *Call Back Yesterday: Memoirs, 1887–1931*, C F Müller, Karlsruhe.

Damette F, 1980, 'The regional framework of monopoly exploitation', in Carney J, Hudson R and Lewis J (Eds.), *Regions in Crisis: New Perspectives in European Regional Theory*, Croom Helm, Beckenham, 76–92.

Dasarathy C and Goodwin T J, 1990, 'Recent developments in automotive steels', *Metals and Materials*, 6, 21–8.

David P A, 1985, 'Clio and the economics of QWERTY', *American Economic Review*, 75, 332–7.

Davis M, 2015, 'Marx's lost theory', *New Left Review*, 93, 45–68.

De Haan E and Schipper I, 2009, *Configuring Labour Rights: Labour Conditions in the Production of Computer Parts in the Philippines*, SOMO and Swedwatch, Amsterdam, 52 pp.

Dean M, 1999, *Governmentality*, Sage, London.

Deloitte Research, 2001, *Global Manufacturing Trends of US Manufacturers: Building the Global Network*, Deloitte Consulting and Deloitte & Touche, New York.

Dicken P, 1998, *Global Shift*, Paul Chapman, London (3rd edition).

Dicken P, 2000, 'Places and flows: situating international investment', in Clark G, Feldman M and Gertler M (Eds.), *The Oxford Handbook of Economic Geography*, Oxford University Press, Oxford.

Dicken P and Yeung H, 1999, 'Investing in the future', in Olds K, Dicken P, Kelly P, Kong L and Yeung H W-C (Eds.), *Globalization and the Asia Pacific: Contested Territories*, Routledge, London.

Dicken P, Forsgren M and Malmberg A, 1994, 'The local embeddedness of transnational corporations', in Amin A and Thrift N (Eds.), *Globalization, Institutions and Regional Development in Europe*, Oxford University Press, Oxford.

Dicken P, Tickell A and Yeung H, 1997, 'Putting Japanese investment in Europe in its place', *Area*, 29, 3, 202–12.

Ditton J, 1977, *Part-time Crime: Ethnography of Fiddling and Pilferage*, Macmillan, London.

Dosi G, Freeman C, Nelson R, Silverberg G and Soerte L (Eds.), 1988, *Technical Change and Economic Theory*, Pinter, London.

DTI, 2000, *Excellence and Opportunity: A Science and Innovation Policy for the 21st Century* (Cm 4814), HMSO, London.

DTI and DfEE, 2001, *Opportunity for All in a World of Change* (Cm 5052), HMSO, London.

Du Gay P and Pryke M, 2002, 'Cultural economy: an introduction', in Du Gay P and Pryke M (Eds.), *Cultural Economy*, Sage, London, 1–20.

Dugger W M, 1989, 'Radical institutionalism: basic concepts', in Dugger W M (Ed.), *Radical Institutionalism: Contemporary Voices*, Greenwood Press, Westport, CT, 1–20.

Dugger W M, 2000, 'Deception and inequality: the enabling myth concept', in Pullin R (Ed.), *Capitalism, Socialism and Radical Political Economy*, Edward Elgar, Cheltenham, 66–80.

Duke C, Hassink R, Powell J and Puukka J, 2006, *Supporting the Contribution of Higher Education Institutions to Regional Development. Peer Review Report: North East of England*, OECD, Directorate of Education, Programme on Institutional Management of Higher Education, Paris.

Dunford M, Hudson R and Smith A, 2001, 'Restructuring the European clothing sector', Sussex European Institute, mimeo.

Dunning J H, 2000, *Regions, Globalization and the Knowledge-Based Economy*, Oxford University Press, Oxford.

Earthworks and Oxfam America, 2004, *Dirty Metals: Mining, Communities and the Environment*, Earthworks and Oxfam America, 32 pp.

EE Times Asia, 2012, 'Conference finds fake electronics parts problem growing', available at www.eetasia.com/ART_8800667596_480200.HTML [accessed 23 May 2012].

Elson D, 1978, 'The value theory of labour', in Elson D (Ed.), *Value: The Representation of Labour*, CSE Books, London.

Erman E, 2007, *Rethinking Legal and Illegal Economy; A Case Study of Tin Mining in Gangka Island*, 34 pp, available at http://globetrotter.berkeley.edu/GreenGovernance/papers/Erman2007.pdf [accessed 14 January 2012].

Essletzbichler J, 2009, 'Evolutionary economic geography, institutions and political economy', *Economic Geography*, 85, 159–65.

Etzkowitz H and Leydesdorff L, 2000, 'The dynamics of innovation: from national systems and "mode 2" to a triple helix of university-industry-government relations', *Research Policy*, 29, 109–23.

EUCAR (European Council for Automobile R&D), 2010, *Collaborative R&D for Automobile Innovation, 2010–2911*, EUCAR, Brussels, 61 pp.

Evans M, Syrett S and Williams C, 2006, *Informal Economic Activities and Deprived Neighbourhoods*, Department of Communities and Local Government, London, 113 pp.

Fay B, 1975, *Social Theory and Political Practice*, George Allen and Unwin, London.

Featherstone M, 1991, *Consumer Culture and Postmodernism*, Sage, London.

Ferus-Comelo A and Pöyhönen P, 2011, *Phony Equality: Labour Standards of Mobile Phone Manufacturers in India*, Finnwatch, Cividep and SOMO – Centre for Research on Multinational Corporations, Amsterdam, 50 pp.

Fine B and Leopold E, 1993, *The World of Consumption*, Routledge, London.
Five Lamps, 2007, *Annual Review 2006–7*, Stockton-on-Tees.
Florida R, 1995, 'The industrial transformation of the Great Lakes Region', in Cooke P (Ed.), *The Rise of the Rustbelt*, University of London Press, London, 162–76.
Folke C, Hahn T, Olsson P and Norberg J, 2005, 'Adaptive governance of social-ecological systems', *Annual Review of Environment and Resources*, 20, 441–73.
Foray D, 1993, 'Feasibility of a single regime of intellectual property rights', in Humbert M (Ed.), *The Impact of Globalisation on Europe's Firms and Regions*, Pinter, London, 85–95.
Frances N 1988, *Turning Houses into Homes*, Fabian Society, London.
Frandsen D M, Rasmussen J and Swart M U, 2011, 'What a waste: how your computer causes health problems in Ghana', *Dan Watch*, 31 pp.
Franklin S, Lury C and Stacey J, 2000, *Global Nature, Global Culture*, Sage, London.
Frosch R A, 1997, 'Towards the end of waste: reflections on a new ecology of industry', in Ausubel J H and Langford H D (Eds.), *Technological Trajectories and the Human Environment*, National Academy Press, Washington DC, 157–67.
Fujita S and Mizuno D, 2007, 'Corrosion and corrosion test methods for zinc coated steel sheets on automobiles', *Corrosion Science*, 49, 211–19.
Gambetta D, 2011, *Codes of the Underworld: How Criminals Communicate*, Princeton University Press, Oxford.
García Márquez G, 1998, *News of a Kidnapping*, Penguin, Harmondsworth.
Garofoli G, 2002, 'Local development in Europe: theoretical models and international comparisons', *European Urban and Regional Studies*, 9, 3, 225–40.
Garrahan P and Stewart P, 1992, *The Nissan Enigma: Flexibility at Work in a Local Economy*, Mansell, London.
Gatti F, 2006, 'I was a slave in Puglia', *L'Espresso*, 1 September, 7 pp, available at http://espresso.repubblica.it/dettaglio/i-was-a-slave-in-puglia/137395 [accessed 22 February 2012].
Geck P, 2010, 'Advanced high-strength steels add strength and ductility to vehicle design', available at http://machinedesign.com.article/advanced-high-stength-steels-add [accessed 27 September 2010].
Gehm R, 2009, 'A stainless future', *aei*, June, 36–8.
Georgescu Roegen N, 1971, *The Entropy Law and the Economic Process*, Harvard University Press, Cambridge, MA.
Gereffi G and Korzeniewicz M (Eds.), 1994, *Commodity Chains and Global Capitalism*, Greenwood Press, Westport, CT.
Gereffi G and Korzeniewicz M, 2004, *Commodity Chains and Global Capitalism*, Praeger, Westport, CT.
Gereffi G, Humphrey J and Sturgeon T, 2005, 'The governance of global value chains', *Review of International Political Economy*, 12, 78–104.
Geroski P and Gugler K P, 2001, 'Corporate growth convergence in Europe', *Discussion Paper 2838*, Centre for Economic Performance, London.
Gertler M, 1997, 'The invention of regional culture', in Lee R and Wills J (Eds.), *Geographies of Economies*, Arnold, London, 47–58.
Gibbs D, 2006, 'Prospects for an environmental economic geography: linking ecological modernization and regulationist approaches', *Economic Geography*, 82, 193–215.
Gibson-Graham J K, 1996, *The End of Capitalism (As We Know it)*, Oxford, Blackwell.
Gibson-Graham J K, Cameron J and Healy S, 2013, *Take Back the Economy: An Ethical Guide for Transforming Our Communities*, University of Minnesota Press, Minneapolis.

Giddens A, 1990, *The Consequences of Modernity*, Polity, Cambridge.
Giddens A, 1991, *Modernity and Self-Identity: Self and Society in the Late Modern Age*, Polity, Cambridge.
Glaeser E L, 2000, 'The new economics of urban and regional growth', in Clark G L, Feldman M P and Gertler M (Eds.), *The Oxford Handbook of Economic Geography*, Oxford University Press, Oxford, 83–98.
Glenny M, 2008, *McMafia: A Journey through the Global Criminal Underworld*, House of Anasi Press, Toronto.
Glenny M, 2011, *Dark Market: Cyberthieves, Cybercops and You*, The Bodley Head, London.
Godwin J, 1998, 'Hydroforming starts to make an impression', *Materials World*, 5, 483–4.
Gough J, 2003, 'Review of *Producing Places*', *Economic Geography*, 79, 96–9.
Gourgues A-F, Flower H M and Lindley, T C, 2000, 'Electron backscattering diffraction study of acicular ferrite, bainite, and martensite steel microstructures', *Materials Science and Technology*, 16, 26–40.
Grabher G, 1993, 'The weakness of strong ties: the lock-in of regional development in the Ruhr area', in Grabher G (Ed.), *The Embedded Firm: On the Socio-Economics of Industrial Networks*, Routledge, London, 255–77.
Grabher G, 2002, 'The project ecology of advertising: tasks, talents and teams', *Regional Studies*, 36, 245–62.
Grabher G, 2009, 'Yet another turn? The evolutionary project in economic geography', *Economic Geography*, 85, 119–27.
Graham J and Cornwell J, 2008, 'Building community economies: two community enterprises in the Pioneer Valley of Massachusetts, USA', Paper presented to the International Workshop on Ethnographies of the Social Economy, Durham, 14–15 March.
Gramsci A, 1971, *Selections from the Prison Notebooks*, Lawrence and Wishart, London.
Granovetter M, 1985, 'Economic action and social structure: the problem of embeddedness', *American Journal of Sociology*, 91, 481–510.
Green New Deal Group, 2008, *A Green New Deal: Joined-up Policies to Solve the Triple Crunch of the Credit Crisis, Climate Change and High Oil Prices*, New Economics Foundation, London, 44 pp.
Gregson N, 1995, 'And now it's all consumption?', *Progress in Human Geography*, 19, 135–41.
Gregson N and Crewe L, 1997a, 'Excluded spaces of regulation: car boot sales as an enterprise culture out of control', *Environment and Planning A*, 29, 1717–37.
Gregson N and Crewe L, 1997b, 'Performance and possession: rethinking the act of purchase in the space of the car boot sale', *Journal of Material Culture*, 2, 241–63.
Gregson N, Simonsen K and Vaiou D, 2001, 'Whose economy for whose culture? Moving beyond oppositional talk in European debates about economy and culture', *Antipode*, 33, 616–47.
Gregson N, Crang M, Ahamed F, Akter N and Ferdous R, 2010, 'Following things of rubbish value: end-of-life ships, "chocky chocky" furniture, and the Bangladeshi middle class consumer', *Geoforum*, 846–54.
Gregson N, Crang M, Ahamed F, Hudson R, Akter N, Ferdous R and Mahmud F, 2012, 'Bhatiary, Bangladesh as a secondary processing complex', *Economic Geography*, 88, 37–58.

Grundy Warr C, 1989, 'Engineering linkages within the coal chain', unpublished PhD thesis, University of Durham.

Guerrera F, 2001, 'Brussels' face set against "national champions" ', *Financial Times*, 3 October.

Guerrera F and Mallet V, 2001, 'Brussels blocks Schneider deal with Legrand', *Financial Times*, 11 October.

Gunderson L H, 2000, 'Ecological resilience in theory and practice', *Annual Review of Ecology and Systematics*, 31, 425–39.

Habermas J, 1968, *Knowledge and Human Interests*, Beacon Press, Boston.

Habermas J, 1976, *Legitimation Crisis*, Heinemann, London.

Hadjimichalis C, 1998, 'Small and medium enterprises in Greece', University of Thessaloniki, mimeo, 21 pp.

Hadjimichalis C, 2014, 'Crisis and land dispossession in Greece as part of the global "land fever" ', *City*, 18, 4–5, 502–8.

Hadjimichalis C and Hudson R, 2006, 'Networks, regional development and democratic control', *International Journal of Urban and Regional Research*, 30, 858–72.

Hadjimichalis C and Hudson R, 2007, 'Re-thinking local and regional development: implications for radical political practice in Europe', *European Urban and Regional Studies*, 14, 99–113.

Hadjimichalis C and Hudson R, 2014, 'Contemporary crisis across Europe and the crisis of regional development theories', *Regional Studies*, 48, 208–18.

Hadjimichalis C and Papamichos N, 1990, ' "Local" development in southern Europe: towards a new mythology', *Antipode*, 22, 181–210.

Hadjimichalis C and Vaiou D, 1990a, 'Whose flexibility? The politics of informalization in Southern Europe', *Capital and Class*, 42, 79–106.

Hadjimichalis C and Vaiou D, 1990b, 'Flexible labour markets and regional development in Northern Greece', *International Journal of Urban and Regional Research*, 14, 1–24.

Hagstrom P and Hedlund G, 1998, 'A three-dimensional of changing internal structure in the firm', in Chandler A, Hagstrom P and Solvell U (Eds.), *The Dynamic Firm: The Role of Technology Strategy, Organisation and Regions*, Oxford University Press, Oxford, 166–91.

Hall D, 2009, 'Pollution export as state and corporate strategy: Japan in the 1970s', *Review of Radical Political Economy*, 16, 260–83.

Hall S, 1991, 'The local and the global: globalization and ethnicity', in King A D (Ed.), *Culture, Globalization and the World System*, Macmillan, London, 19–30.

Hall T, 2011, 'Economic geography and organised crime: a critical review', *Geoforum*, 6, 841–6.

Hall T, 2013, 'Geographies of the illicit: the case of organised crime', *Progress in Human Geography*, 37, 366–85.

Hamer M, 1974, *Wheels Within Wheels*, Friends of the Earth, London.

Hampton M, 1996, *The Offshore Interface: Tax Havens in the Global Economy*, Macmillan, Basingstoke.

Hardy J, 2002, 'An institutionalist analysis of foreign investment in Poland: Wroclaw's second great transformation', Unpublished PhD thesis, University of Durham.

Harvey D, 1982, *The Limits to Capital*, Oxford, Blackwell.

Harvey D, 1996, *Justice, Nature and the Geography of Difference*, Blackwell, Oxford.

Harvey D, 1998, 'The body as an accumulation strategy', *Society and Space*, 16, 401–22.

Harvey D, 2002, 'Reflecting on *The Limits to Capital*', Paper presented to the Annual Conference of the Association of American Geographers, Los Angeles, 19–23 March.

Harvey D, 2003, *The New Imperialism*, Oxford University Press, Oxford.

Harvey D, 2014, *Seventeen Contradictions and the End of Capitalism*, Profile Books, London.

Harvey G, 1917, *Capitalism in the Northern Coalfield*, City Library, Newcastle on Tyne.

Harvey M, Quilley S and Beynon H, 2002, *Exploring the Tomato: Transformations in Nature, Economy and Society*, Edward Elgar, Cheltenham.

Haugh H, 2008, 'Working in the social economy: an exploration of rewards and motivations', Paper presented to the International Workshop on Ethnographies of the Social Economy, Durham, 14–15 March.

Hawbolt E B, Chau B and Brimacombe J K, 1983, 'Kinetics of austenite-pearlite transformation in eutectoid carbon steel', *Metallurgical and Materials Transactions A*, 14, 1803–15.

Health and Safety Executive, 2008, *The Explosion of No. 5 Blast Furnace, Corus UK Ltd, Port Talbot, 8 November 2001*, HSE, available at www.hse.gove.uk [accessed 23 September 2009].

Held D, 1989, *Political Theory and the Modern State: Essays on Power, State and Democracy*, Stanford University Press, Stanford, CA.

Helminen V and Risitimäki M, 2007, 'Relationships between commuting distances, frequency and telework in Finland', *Journal of Transport Geography*, 15, 331–42.

Henderson J, Dicken P, Hess M, Coe N and Yeung H W-C, 2002, 'Global production networks and the analysis of economic development', *Review of International Political Economy*, 9, 436–64.

Herod A, 2001, *Labor Geographies: Workers and the Landscapes of Capitalism*, Guilford, New York.

Herrigel G, 2000, 'Large firms and industrial districts in Europe: de-regionalization, re-regionalization and the transformation of manufacturing flexibility', in Dunning J H (Ed.), *Regions, Globalization and the Knowledge-Based Economy*, Oxford University Press, Oxford, 286–302.

Hess M and Yeung H W-C, 2006, 'Guest editorial: whither global production networks in economic geography: past, present and future', *Environment and Planning A*, 38, 1193–1204.

Hill E W, Wial H and Wolman H, 2008, 'Exploring regional economic resilience', *Working Paper 2008–04*, Institute of Urban and Regional Development, University of California, Berkeley, CA.

Hobbs D, 1988, *Doing the Business: Entrepreneurship, the Working Class and Detectives in the East End of London*, Oxford University Press, Oxford.

Hobbs D, 1998, 'The case against: there is not a global crime problem', *International Journal of Risk, Security and Crime Prevention*, 3, 139–46.

Hodgson G, 1988, *Economics and Institutions: A Manifesto for Modern Institutional Economics*, Polity Press, London.

Hodgson G, 1993, *Economics and Evolution: Bringing Life Back into Economics*, Polity Press, Cambridge.

Holling C S, 1973, 'Resilience and stability of ecological systems', *Annual Review of Ecology and Systematics*, 4, 1–23.

Hollingsworth J Rogers, 2000, 'Doing institutional analysis', *Review of International Political Economy*, 7, 595–640.

Hollingsworth J Rogers and Boyer R (Eds.), 1997, *Contemporary Capitalism: The Embeddedness of Institutions*, Cambridge University Press, Cambridge.

Holloway L, 2007, 'Subjecting cows to robots: farming technologies and the making of animal subjects', *Society and Space*, 25, 1041–60.

Horkheimer M, 1937, *Critical and Traditional Theory*, re-printed in Delanty G and Strydon P (Eds.), 1983, *Philosophies of Social Science: The Classic and Contemporary Readings*, Open University Press, Milton Keynes.

Hounshell D, 1984, *From the American System to Mass Production, 1800–1932*, John Hopkins Press, Baltimore.

Houveld K, 2006, 'Toxic fumes unleash panic in the Paris of Africa', *Sunday Times*, 16 September, 26.

Hudson A C, 1998, 'Placing trust, trusting places: on the social construction of offshore financial centres', *Political Geography*, 17, 915–37.

Hudson R, 1980, 'Women and work in Washington New Town', *Occasional Paper No. 18 (New Series)*, Department of Geography, University of Durham.

Hudson R, 1982, 'Accumulation, spatial policies and the production of regional labour reserves: a study of Washington New Town', *Environment and Planning A*, 14, 665–80.

Hudson R, 1986, 'Nationalised industry policies and regional policies: the role of the state in the deindustrialisation and reindustrialisation of regions', *Society and Space*, 4, 7–28.

Hudson R, 1989a, 'Labour market changes and new forms of work in old industrial regions: maybe flexibility for some but not flexible accumulation', *Society and Space*, 7, 5–30.

Hudson R, 1989b, *Wrecking a Region: State Policies, Party Politics and Regional Change in North East England*, Pion, London.

Hudson R, 1990, 'Re-thinking regions: some preliminary considerations on regions and social change', in Johnston R J, Hoekveld G and Hauer J (Eds.), *Regional Geography: Current Developments and Future Prospects*, Routledge, London, 67–84.

Hudson R, 1994a, 'New production concepts, new production geographies? Reflections on changes in the automobile industry', *Transactions of the Institute of British Geographers*, NS, 19, 331–45.

Hudson R, 1994b, 'Institutional change, cultural transformation and economic regeneration: myths and realities from Europe's old industrial regions', in Amin A and Thrift N (Eds.), *Globalization, Institutions and Regional Development in Europe*, Oxford University Press, Oxford, 331–45.

Hudson R, 1995, 'The role of foreign investment', in Evans L, Johnson P and Thomas B (Eds.), *Northern Region Economy: Progress and Prospects*, Cassell, London, 79–95.

Hudson R, 1997a, 'Regional futures: industrial restructuring, new production concepts and spatial development strategies in Europe', *Regional Studies*, 31, 5, 467–78.

Hudson R, 1997b, 'The end of mass production and of the mass collective worker? Experimenting with production, employment and their geographies', in Lee R and Wills J (Eds.), *Geographies of Economies*, Arnold, London, 302–10.

Hudson R, 1998, 'Restructuring region and state: the case of north east England', *Tijdschrift voor Economische en Sociale Geografie*, 89, 15–30.

Hudson R, 1999, 'The new economy of the New Europe: eradicating divisions or creating new forms of combined and uneven development?', in Hudson R and Williams A (Eds.), *Divided Europe: Society and Territory*, Sage, London, 29–62.

Hudson R, 2000a, *Production, Places and Environment*, Prentice Hall, London.

Hudson R, 2000b, 'One Europe or many? Reflections on becoming European', *Transactions of the Institute of British Geographers*, NS, 25, 409–26.
Hudson R, 2001a, *Producing Places*, Guilford Press, New York.
Hudson R, 2001b, 'Regional development, flows of value and governance processes in an enlarged Europe', *Working Paper 6–01*, Regional Economic Performance, Governance and Cohesion in an Enlarged Europe, available at www.geog.susssex.ac.uk/research/changing-Europe/wprkpaper.html [accessed 7 January 2002].
Hudson R, 2002, 'Changing industrial production systems and regional development in the New Europe', *Transactions of the Institute of British Geographers*, NS, 27, 262–81.
Hudson R, 2003, 'Geographers and the regional problem', in Johnston R and Williams M (Eds.), *A Century of British Geography*, Oxford University Press, Oxford, 583–602.
Hudson R, 2005, *Economic Geographies*, Sage, London.
Hudson R, 2006a, 'On what's right and keeping left: or why geography still needs Marxian political economy', *Antipode*, 38, 374–95.
Hudson R, 2006b, 'Firms as political actors in processes of capital accumulation and regional development', in Taylor M and Oinas P (Eds.), *Conceptualising the Firm: Capabilities, Cultures and Coalitions*, Oxford University Press, Oxford, 169–88.
Hudson R, 2006c, 'Regional devolution and regional economic success: myths and illusions about power', *Geografiska Annaler B*, 88, 159–71.
Hudson R, 2007a, 'Beyond the regulation approach: putting capitalist economies in their place: a review', *Economic Geography*, 83, 325–6.
Hudson R, 2007b, 'Regions and regional uneven development forever? Some reflective comments upon theory and practice', *Regional Studies*, 41, 1149–60.
Hudson R, 2009, 'The costs of globalisation: producing new forms of risk to health and well-being', *Journal of Risk Management*, 11, 13–29.
Hudson R, 2010, 'Multiplicant els riscs per a la salut I el benestar: els costos inadmissibles de la globalització/Multiplying risks to health and wellbeing: the unacknowledged costs of globalisation', *Treballs de la Societat Catalana de Geografia*, 70, 101–27.
Hudson R, 2015, 'Does illegality enable or undermine the sustainability of the globalising economy', in Redclift M and Springett D (Eds.), *Handbook of Sustainable Development*, Routledge, London, 41–54.
Hudson R and Sadler D, 1989, *The International Steel Industry*, Routledge, London.
Hudson R and Schamp E W (Eds.), 1995, *Towards a New Map of Automobile Manufacturing in Europe: New Production Concepts and Spatial Restructuring*, Springer, Berlin.
Hudson R and Swanton D, 2012, 'Global shifts in contemporary times: the changing trajectories of steel towns in China, Germany and the United Kingdom', *European Urban and Regional Studies*, 19, 6–19.
Hudson R and Weaver P, 1997, 'In search of employment creation via environmental valorisation: exploring a possible Eco-Keynesian future for Europe', *Environment and Planning*, 29, 1647–61.
Hudson R and Williams A, 1995, *Divided Britain*, Wiley, Chichester (2nd edition).
Hudson R and Williams A, 1999, 'Re-shaping Europe: the challenge of new divisions within a homogenised political-economic space', in Hudson R and Williams A (Eds.), *Divided Europe: Society and Territory*, Sage, London, 1–28.

Hughes A, 2006, 'Learning to trade ethically: knowledgeable capitalism, retailers and contested commodity chains', *Geoforum*, 37, 1007–19.
Hyslop M, 2007, *Critical Information Infrastructures: Resilience and Protection*, Springer, New York.
ILO, 2002, *Decent Work and the Informal Economy*, ILO, Geneva.
Ingold T, 2007, 'Materials against materiality', *Archaeological Dialogues*, 14, 1–16.
Jackson P, 1993, 'Towards a cultural politics of consumption', in Bird J, Curtis B, Putnam T, Robinson G and Tickner L (Eds.), *Mapping the Futures: Local Cultures, Global Changes*, Routledge, London, 207–28.
Jackson P, 2002, 'Commercial cultures: transcending the cultural and the economic', *Progress in Human Geography*, 26, 3–18.
Jackson T, 1995, *Material Concerns*, Routledge, London.
Janssen M, Schoon M and Börner K, 2006, 'Scholarly networks on resilience, vulnerability and adaptation within human dimensions of global environmental change', *Global Environmental Change*, 16, 240–52.
Jensen M, Johnson B, Lorenz E and Lundvall B-A, 2007, 'Forms of knowledge and modes of innovation', *Research Policy*, 36, 680–93.
Jessop B, 1990, *State Theory: Putting Capitalist States in Their Place*, Cambridge University Press, Cambridge.
Jessop B, 1997, 'Capitalism and its future: remarks on regulation, government and governance', *Review of International Political Economy* 4, 561–81.
Jessop B, 2000, 'The state and the contradictions of the knowledge-driven economy', available at www.comp.lancs.ac.uk/sociology/soc044rj.html [accessed 23 October 2001].
Jessop B, 2001, 'Institutional (re)turns and the strategic-relational approach', *Environment and Planning A*, 33, 1213–35.
Jessop B and Sum N-L, 2006, *Beyond the Regulation Approach: Putting Capitalist Economies in Their Place*, Edward Elgar, Cheltenham.
Johnson B, 1992, 'Institutional learning', in Lundvall B-A (Ed.), *National Systems of Innovation: Towards a Theory of Innovation and Interactive Learning*, Pinter, London, 23–44.
Johnson M and Reed H, 2008, *Entrepreneurship and Innovation in the North*, Institute for Public Policy Research North, Newcastle, 38 pp.
Jones M, 2008, 'Recovering a sense of political economy', *Political Geography*, 27, 377–99.
Kaletsky A, 2010, *Capitalism 4.0: The Birth of a New Economy*, Bloomsbury, London.
Kan P R, Bechtol B E and Collins R M, 2010, *Criminal Sovereignty: Understanding North Korea's Illicit International Activities*, Strategic Studies Institute, available at www.StrategicStudiesInstitute.army.mil/ [accessed 11 April 2012].
Kazmin A, 2013, 'Factory collapse adds to pressure on Dhaka', *Financial Times*, 25 April, 5.
Kazmin A, Jopson B and Lucas L, 2013, 'Factory's collapse highlights failure to enforce basic rules', *Financial Times*, 26 April, 5.
Kelkar A, Roth R and Clark J, 2001, 'Automobile bodies: can aluminium be an economical alternative to steel?', *JOM*, 53, 28–32.
Kelman I, 2008, 'Critique of some vulnerability and resilience papers, Version 2, 17 November 2008', available at www.isalndvulnerability.org/docs/vulnrescritique.pdf [accessed 17 November 2008].

Kindleberger C, 1969, *American Business Abroad*, Yale University Press, New Haven, CT.

Kitson M and Michie J, 1998, 'Markets, competition and innovation', *ESRC Centre for Business Research Working Paper 86*, University of Cambridge.

Klein N, 2000, *No Logo*, Harper Collins, London.

Klepper S, 2010, 'The origin and growth of industry clusters: the making of Silicon Valley and Detroit', *Journal of Urban Economics*, 67, 15–32.

Kneese A V, Ayres R U and d'Arge R C, 1970, *Economics and the Environment: A Materials Balance Approach*, Resources for the Future, Washington DC.

Korchynsky M, 2001, 'A new role for micro-alloyed steels: adding economic value', Paper presented at Infacon 9, Quebec City, 6 June, 7 pp.

Korchynsky M and Paules J R, 1989, 'Micro-alloyed forging steels: a state of the art review', *SAE Technical Paper 890801*, Detroit.

Krugman P, 2000, 'Where in the world is the "New Economic Geography" ', in Clark G L, Feldman MP and Gertler M (Eds.), *The Oxford Handbook of Economic Geography*, Oxford University Press, Oxford, 49–60.

Kwon O and Biak S K, n.d., 'Manufacture and application of advanced high strength steel sheets for auto parts manufacture', POSCO, Pohang, 5 pp.

Kynge J, 2006, 'Shock and ore – China tightens its steely grip', available at www.rewerx.com/shock_and ore.htm [accessed 28 January 2011].

Kynge J, 2009, *China Shakes the World: The Rise of a Hungry Nation*, Phoenix, London.

Lane C and Wood G (Eds.), 2011, *Capitalist Diversity and Diversity within Capitalism*, Routledge, 189–208.

Lash S and Friedman J (Eds.), 1992, *Modernity and Identity*, Blackwell, Oxford.

Lash S and Urry J, 1987, *The End of Organised Capitalism*, Polity, Cambridge.

Lash S and Urry J, 1994, *Economies of Signs and Space*, Sage, London.

Latour B, 1987, *Science in Action: How to Follow Scientists and Engineers Through Society*, Open University Press, Milton Keynes.

Latour B, 2005, *Reassembling the Social: An Introduction to Actor-Network Theory*, Oxford University Press, Oxford.

Lavery S and Donovan B, 2005, 'Flood risk management in the Thames Estuary looking ahead a 100 years', *Philosophical Transactions of the Royal Society A*, 363, 1455–74.

Laville P, 2008, 'Local initiatives in Europe: social and solidarity economy facing public policies', Paper presented to the International Workshop on Ethnographies of the Social Economy, Durham, 14–15 March.

Law J, 2002, 'Economics and interference', in Du Gay P and Pryke M (Eds.), *Cultural Economy*, Sage, London, 21–38.

Lee D, Hampton, M and Jeyacheya J, 2015, 'The political economy of precarious work in the tourism industry in small island developing states', *Review of International Political Economy*, 22, 194–223.

Lee R, 2002, ' "Nice maps, shame about the theory"? Thinking geographically about the economic', *Progress in Human Geography*, 26, 3, 333–54.

Leinbach T R and Brunn S D (Eds.), 2001, *Worlds of E-Commerce*, Wiley, Chichester.

Leslie D and Reimer S, 1999, 'Spatializing commodity chains', *Progress in Human Geography* 23, 401–20.

Levinthal D, 1996, 'Learning and Schumpeterian dynamics', in Dosi G and Malerba F (Eds.), *Organisation and Strategy in the Evolution of the Enterprise*, London, MacMillan, 27–41.

Lewis J and Melville B, 1977, 'The politics of epistemology in regional science', in Batey P W J (Ed.), *Theory and Method in Urban and Regional Analysis*, Pion, London, 82–101.

Leyshon A, Lee R and Williams C C (Eds.), 2003, *Alternative Economic Spaces*, Sage, London.

Leyshon A, Lee R, Sunley P and McDowell L, 2011, 'Introduction', in Leyshon A, Lee R, McDowell L and Sunley P (Eds.), *The SAGE Handbook of Economic Geography*, Sage, London, 1–20.

Li Y, Lin Z, Jiang A and Chen G, 2003, 'Use of high strength steel sheet for lightweight and crashworthy car body', *Materials and Design*, 24, 177–82.

Liddle J and Townsend A, 2002, 'Reflections on the development of local Strategic Partnerships: key emerging issues', Paper presented to the annual conference of the British Academy of Management, 9–11 September, London.

Lipietz A, 1977, *Le Capital et Son Espace*, Maspero, Paris.

Lipietz A, 1987, *Mirages and Miracles*, Verso, London.

Llewellyn D T, 1995, *Steels: Metallurgy and Applications*, Butterworth-Heinemann, Oxford (2nd edition).

Llewellyn D T and Hudd R C, 2004, *Steels: Metallurgy and Applications*, Butterworth-Heinemann, Oxford (3rd edition).

Lovering J, 1999, 'Theory led by policy: the inadequacies of the "new regionalism" (illustrated from the case of Wales)', *International Journal of Urban and Regional Studies*, 23, 379–95.

Lundvall B-A (Ed.), 1992, *National Systems of Innovation: Towards a Theory of Innovation and Interactive Learning*, Pinter, London.

Lundvall B-A, 1995, 'The learning economy – challenges to economic theory and policy', revised version of a paper presented to the EAEPE Conference. Copenhagen, 27–29 October 1994.

Lundvall B-A and Johnson B, 1994, 'The learning economy', *Journal of Industry Studies*, 1, 2, 23–42.

Lundvall B-A and Maskell P, 2000, 'Nation states and economic development', in Clark G L, Feldman M and Gertler M (Eds.), *The Oxford Handbook of Economic Geography*, Oxford, Oxford University Press, 353–72.

Lury C, 2000, 'The united colors of diversity', in Franklin S, Lury C and Stacey J (Eds.), *Global Nature, Global Culture*, Sage, London, 146–87.

Lütticken S, 2008, 'Attending to abstract things', *New Left Review*, 54, 101–22.

McCord N, 1979, *North East England*, Batsford, London.

McDowell L, 1997, 'A tale of two cities? Embedded organizations and embedded workers in the City of London', in Lee R and Wills J (Eds.), *Geographies of Economies*, Edward Arnold, London, 118–29.

McDowell L, 2004, 'Work, workfare, work/life balance and an ethic of care', *Progress in Human Geography*, 28, 145–63.

McFall L, 2002, 'Advertising, persuasion and the culture/economy dualism', in Du Gay P and Pryke M (Eds.), *Cultural Economy*, Sage, London, 148–65.

Mackay S, 2004, 'Zones of regulation: restructuring labor control in privatized export zones', *Politics and Society*, 32, 171–202.

MacKinnon D, 2000, 'Managerialism, governmentality and the state: a neo-Foucauldian approach to local economic governance', *Political Geography*, 19, 293–314.

MacKinnon D, Cumbers A, Pike A, Birch K and McMaster R, 2009, 'Evolution in economic geography: institutions, political economy and adaptation', *Economic Geography*, 85, 129–50.

McKinsey Global Institute, 2008, *Mapping Global Capital Markets: Fourth Annual Report*, McKinsey Global Institute, San Francisco.

MacLeod G, 1997, 'Globalizing Parisian thought waves: recent advances in the study of social regulation, politics, discourse and space', *Progress in Human Geography*, 21, 530–53.

MacLeod G, 1999, 'Place, politics and scale dependence', *European Urban and Regional Studies*, 6, 231–53.

McRobbie A, 1997, 'Bridging the gap: feminism, fashion and consumption', *Feminist Review*, 55, 73–89.

Madsen F, 2009, *Transnational Organized Crime*, Routledge, New York.

Mandel E, 1975, *Late Capitalism*, New Left Books, London.

Mandel E, 1978, *The Second Slump*, New Left Books, London.

Mann M, 1993, 'Nation-states in Europe and other continents: diversifying, developing, not dying', *Proceedings of the American Academy of Arts and Sciences*, 122, 3, 155–40.

Mann M, 2001, 'Brussels tries again for agreement on cross-border takeover rules', *Financial Times*, 5 September.

Manyena S B, 2006, 'The concept of resilience revisited', *Disasters*, 30, 433–50.

Markusen A, 1996, 'Sticky places in slippery space; a typology of industrial districts', *Economic Geography*, 72, 293–313.

Markusen A, 1999, 'Fuzzy concepts, scanty evidence, policy distance: the case for rigor and policy relevance in critical regional studies', *Regional Studies*, 33, 869–84.

Martin R, 2015, 'Rebalancing the spatial economy: the challenge for regional theory', *Territory, Politics, Governance*, 3, 235–72.

Martin R and Sunley P, 2006, 'Path dependence and regional economic evolution', *Journal of Economic Geography*, 6, 395–437.

Maskell P, 1998, 'Low-tech competitive advantage and the role of proximity', *European Urban and Regional Studies*, 5, 2, 99–118.

Maskell P and Malmberg A, 1995, 'Localised learning and industrial competitiveness', *BRIE Working Paper No. 80*, Berkeley Roundtable on the International Economy, University of California, Berkeley.

Maskell P, Eskelinien H, Hannibalsson I, Malmberg A and Vatne E, 1998, *Competitiveness, Localised Learning and Regional Development*, Routledge, London.

Massey D, 1995, *Spatial Divisions of Labour: Social Structures and the Geography of Production*, Macmillan, London (2nd edition).

Massey D, 2014, ' "Stories so far": a conversation with Doreen Massey', in Featherstone D and Painter J (Eds.), *Spatial Politics: Essays from Doreen Massey*, Wiley-Blackwell, Chichester, 253–66.

Massey D and Meegan R, 1982, *The Anatomy of Job Loss*, Methuen, Andover.

Maxwell N, 2007, *From Knowledge to Wisdom*, Pentire Press, London (2nd edition).

Metcalfe J S, 1996, *Technology Strategy in an Evolutionary World*, The Honeywell/Sweatt Lecture, Centre for Development of Technological Leadership, University of Minnesota.

Metcalfe J S, 1998, 'Evolutionary concepts in relation to evolutionary economics', *Working Paper No. 4*, Centre for Research on Innovation and Competition, University of Manchester.

Michaelis P and Jackson T, 2000, 'Material and energy flow through the UK iron and steel sector, Part 1, 1954–1994', *Resources, Conservation and Recycling*, 29, 131–56.

Miles N and Daniels R, 2007, *The State of the Innovation Economy in the UK – 2007*, O2C Arc, Milton Keynes.
Miller D, 1987, *Material Culture and Mass Consumption*, Blackwell, Oxford.
Miller D, 2002, 'The unintended political economy', in Du Gay P and Pryke M (Eds.), *Cultural Economy*, Sage, London, 166–84.
Miller D and Rose N, 1997, 'Mobilising the consumer: assembling the subject of consumption', *Theory, Culture and Society*, 14, 1–36.
Miller P, Pons J N and Naude P, 1996, 'Global teams', *Financial Times*, 14 June.
Mingione E, 1999, 'Introduction: immigration and the informal economy in European cities', *International Journal of Urban and Regional Research*, 23, 209–11.
Minton A, 2002, *Building Balanced Communities: The US and UK Compared*, Royal Institute of Chartered Surveyors, London.
Mitchell A, 1995, 'Un-American activities', *London Evening Standard*, 13 September.
Morgan K, 1995, 'The learning region: institutions, innovation and regional renewal', *Papers in Planning Research No. 157*, Department of City and Regional Planning, University of Wales, Cardiff.
Morgan K, 1997, 'The learning region: institutions, innovation and regional renewal', *Regional Studies*, 31, 5, 491–503.
Morgan K, 2001, 'The exaggerated death of geography: localise learning, innovation and uneven development', Paper presented to The Future of Innovation Studies Conference, The Eindhoven Centre for Innovation Studies, Eindhoven University of Technology, 20–23 September.
Moulaert F and Sekia F, 2003, 'Territorial innovation models: a critical survey', *Regional Studies*, 37, 289–310.
Murphy J, 2011, 'Capitalism and transparency', *Critical Perspectives on International Business*, 7, 125–41.
Nelson R R and Winter S G, 1982, *An Evolutionary Theory of Economic Change*, Harvard University Press, Cambridge, MA.
NICDA/CDS, 1999, *Building a Social Economy for the New Millennium*, NICDA Social Economy Agency and Co-operative Development Society, Belfast.
Nitzan J, 2001, 'Regimes of differential accumulation: mergers, stagflation and the logic of globalisation', *Review of International Political Economy*, 8, 2, 226–74.
Nonaka I and Takeuchi H, 1995, *The Knowledge-Creating Company*, Oxford University Press, New York.
Nordbrand S, 2009, *Out of Control: E-waste Trade Flows from the EU to Developing Countries*, Swedwatch, Amsterdam, 46 pp.
Nordbrand S and Bolme P, 2007, *Powering the Mobile World: Cobalt Production for Batteries in the DR Congo and Zambia*, Swedwatch, Amsterdam, 83 pp.
Nordbrand S and de Haan, E, 2009, *Mobile Phone Production in China: A Follow up Report on Two Suppliers in Guangdong*, SOMO and Swedwatch, Amsterdam, 27 pp.
Nordstrom C, 2007, *Global Outlaws: Crime, Money, and Power in the Contemporary World*, University of California Press, Berkeley.
North G, 1975, *Teesside's Economic Heritage*, Cleveland County Council, Middlesbrough.
Northern Regional Strategy Team, 1977, *Strategic Plan for the Northern Region, Volumes 1–5*, HMSO, London.
Northern Way, 2005, Moving Forward: The Northern Way Business Plan, 2005–8, available at www.thenorthernway.co.uk [accessed 6 December 2005].

Obenchain W A, van Schalk M and Peterson P, 2002, 'Green engineering case study: reducing automobile emissions and saving energy', *ULSAB – Advanced Vehicle Concepts*, American Iron and Steel Industry, Washington DC, 16 pp.

Odgaard M and Hudson R, 1998, 'The misplacement of learning in economic geography', Universities of Durham and Roskilde, mimeo, 20 pp.

OECD, 2002, *Measuring the Non-Observed Economy: A Handbook*, OECD, Paris.

OECD, 2006, *Territorial Review: Newcastle in the North East*, OECD, Paris.

OECD, 2007, *The Economic Impact of Counterfeiting and Piracy, Part 1*, 146 pp, available at www.oecd.org/dataoecd/36/36/39543408.pdf-3 [accessed 27 February 2008].

Offe C, 1975, 'The theory of the capitalist state and the problem of policy formation', in Lindberg L N, Alford R, Crouch C and Offe C (Eds.), *Stress and Contradiction in Modern Capitalism*, DC Heath, Lexington, MA, 125–44.

Okamura C and Kawahito H, 1990, *Karoshi*, Mado-Sha, Tokyo.

ONE North East, 1999, *Regional Economic Strategy: Unlocking Our Potential*, ONE North East, Newcastle on Tyne.

ONE North East, 2000, *Regional Economic Strategy: Fulfilling Our Potential*, ONE North East, Newcastle on Tyne.

ONE North East, 2001, *Strategy for Success*, ONE North East, Newcastle on Tyne.

ONE North East, 2003, *Regional Economic Strategy: Realising Our Potential*, ONE North East, Newcastle on Tyne.

ONE North East, 2007, *Leading the Way: Regional Economic Strategy Action Plan 2006–2011*, ONE North East, Newcastle on Tyne.

Oonk G, Overem P, Peepercamp M and Theuws M, 2012, *Maid in India: Young Dalit Women Continue to Suffer Exploitative Conditions in India's Garment Industry*, SOMO and ICN, Amsterdam, 71 pp.

Opbroek E G, 2008, 'Reinventing automotive steel for environmentally friendly vehicles', *AUTO FOCUS ASIA*, available at www.autofocusasia.com/automotive_materials/reinventing_steel.htm [accessed 27 September 2010].

Palan R, 1999, 'Offshore and the structural enablement of sovereignty', in Hampton M and Abbott J (Eds.), *Offshore Finance Centres and Tax Havens: The Rise of Global Capital*, Macmillan, Basingstoke, 18–42.

Palloix C, 1977, 'The self-expansion of capital on a world scale', *Review of Radical Political Economics*, 9, 1–28.

Patchell J and Hayter R, 2013, 'Environmental and evolutionary economic geography: time for EEG?', *Geografiska Annaler: Series B*, 95, 2, 1–20.

Patterson S, 2010, *The Quants: How a Small Band of Maths Wizards Took Over Wall Street and Nearly Destroyed it*, Random House, London.

Pavitt K and Patel P, 1991, 'Large firms in the production of the world's technology: an important case of non-globalisation', *Journal of International Business Studies*, 22, 1–21.

Pearce J, 2008, 'Social economy: engaging in a third system?', Paper presented to the International Workshop on Ethnographies of the Social Economy, Durham, 14–15 March.

Peck J, 2005, 'Economic sociologies in space', *Economic Geography*, 81, 129–75.

Peck J and Theodore N, 2007, 'Variegated capitalism', *Progress in Human Geography*, 31, 731–72.

Phelps N and MacKinnon D, 2000, 'Industrial enclaves or embedded firms? Overseas manufacturing operations in Wales', *Contemporary Wales*, 13, 46–67.

Phelps N, Lovering J and Morgan K, 1998, 'Tying the firm to the region or tying the region to the firm?', *European Urban and Regional Studies*, 5, 119–37.

Phillips T, 2005, *Knockoff: The Deadly Trade in Counterfeit Goods*, Kogan Page, London.
Picciotto S, 2008, 'Constitutionalizing multilevel governance?' *International Journal of Constitutional Law*, 6, 457–79.
Pike A, 2002, 'Task forces and the organisation of economic development: the case of the North East region of England', *Environment and Planning C*, 20, 717–39.
Pike A, 2005, 'Building a geographical political economy of closure: the case of R&DCo in North East England', *Antipode*, 37, 93–115.
Pike A, 2013, 'Economic geographies of brands and branding', *Economic Geography*, 89, 317–39.
Pine B J, 1993, *Mass Customization: The New Frontier in Business Competition*, Harvard University Press, Harvard.
Polanyi K, 1944, *The Great Transformation*, Rinehart, New York.
Pollard J, McEwan C, Laurie N and Stenning A, 2009, 'Economic geography under postcolonial scrutiny', *Transactions of the Institute of British Geography*, 32, 313–30.
Pollert A, 1988, 'Dismantling flexibility', *Capital and Class*, 34, 42–75.
Porter M, 2003, 'The economic performance of regions', *Regional Studies*, 37, 549–78.
Portes R, Castells M and Benton L A (Eds.), 1989, *The Informal Economy: Studies in Advanced and Less Developed Countries*, John Hopkins University Press, London.
Pöyhönen P, 2008, 'Illegal ground: Assa Abloy's business in occupied Palestinian territory', Swedwatch, available at www.swedwatch.org [accessed 10 January 2012].
Pöyhönen P and Simola E, 2007, *Connecting Components, Dividing Communities: Tin Production for Consumer Electronics in the DR Congo and Indonesia*, FinnWatch and SOMO, Amsterdam, 59 pp.
Pöyhönen P and Wan D, 2011, *Game Console and Music Player Production in China*, FinnWatch, SACOM and SOMO, 39 pp, available at www.makeITfair.org [accessed 11 January 2012].
Pred A, 1996, 'Interfusions: consumption, identity and the practices and power relations of everyday life', *Environment and Planning A*, 28, 11–24.
Pries L, 2005, 'Configurations of geographic and societal spaces: a sociological proposal between "methodological nationalism" and "the space of flows" ', *Global Networks*, 5, 167–90.
Procacci G, 1978, 'Social economy and the government of poverty', *Ideology and Consciousness*, 4, 55–72.
Prudham S, 2003, 'Taming trees: capital, science and nature in Pacific slope tree improvement', *Annals of the Association of American Geographers*, 93, 636–56.
Prudham S, 2005, *Knock on Wood: Nature as Commodity in Douglas-Fir Country*, Abingdon, Routledge.
Prudham S, 2007, 'The fiction of autonomous invention: accumulation by dispossession, commodification and life patents in Canada', *Antipode*, 39, 406–29.
Putnam R, 1993, *Making Democracy Work*, Princeton University Press, New Jersey.
Ray L and Sayer A, 1999, 'Introduction', in Ray L and Sayer A (Eds.), *Culture and Economy After the Cultural Turn*, Sage, London.
Robins K, 1989, 'Global times', *Marxism Today*, December, 20–7.
Robinson F and Shaw K, 2000, *Who Runs the North ... Now? A Review and Assessment of Governance in North East England*, Department of Sociology and Social Policy, University of Durham, 160 pp.
Robinson F and Storey D, 1981, 'Employment change in manufacturing industry in Cleveland, 1965–76', *Regional Studies*, 15, 161–72.

Rose N, 1998, 'The crisis of "the social": beyond the social question', in Hänninen S (Ed.), *Displacement of Social Policies*, Jyväskylä, SoPhi.

Rose N and Miller P, 1992, 'Political power beyond the state: problematics of government', *British Journal of Sociology*, 42, 202–23.

Rosenberg N, 1982, *Inside the Black box: Technology and Economics*, Cambridge University Press, Cambridge.

Routledge P, 2011, 'Capitalism and social justice', in Leyshon A, Lee R, McDowell and Sunley P (Eds.), *The SAGE Handbook of Economic Geography*, Sage, London, 175–88.

Ruggie J G, 1993, 'Territoriality and beyond: problematizing modernity in international relations', *International Organization*, 27, 1, 139–74.

SACOM, 2011, 'iSlave behind the iPhone: Foxconn workers in Central China', SACOM, 14 pp.

Sadler D 1997, 'The role of supply chain management in the "Europeanisation" of the automobile production system', in Lee R and Wills J (Eds.), *Geographies of Economies*, Arnold, London, 311–20.

Sassen S 1991, *The Global City: New York, London, Tokyo*, Princeton University Press, New Jersey.

Sassen S, 2003, 'Globalization or denationalisation?', *Review of International Political Economy*, 10, 1–22.

Saviano R, 2008, *Gomorrah: Italy's Other Mafia*, Pan, London.

Sayer A, 1984, *Method in Social Science*, Hutchinson, London.

Scharb M, 2001, 'Eco-industrial development: a strategy for building sustainable communities', *Review of Economic Development Interaction and Practice 8*, Cornell University and US Economic Development Administration, 43 pp.

Schedin E, Jansson M, Groth H L, Santacreu P-O and Ratte E, 2008, 'Design of a stainless B-pillar – concept evaluation using finite element simulation', International Deep Drawing Research Group 2008 International Conference, 16–18 June, Olofström, Sweden, 8 pp.

Schelling C T, 1960, *The Strategy of Conflict*, Harvard University Press, Cambridge, MA.

Schmidt V A, 2002, *The Future of European Capitalisms*, Oxford University Press, Oxford.

Schneider F and Enster D H, 2000, 'Shadow economies: size, causes and consequences', *Journal of Economic Literature*, 37, 77–8.

Schuberth S, Schedin E and Frolich Hand Ratte E, 2008, 'Next generation vehicle – engineering guidelines for stainless steel in automotive applications', Proceedings of the 6th Stainless Steel Science and Market Conference, Helsinki, 10–13 June, 637–44.

Scott A J, 1988, *New Industrial Spaces*, Pion, London.

Scott A J, 1998, *Regions and the World Economy*, Oxford University Press, Oxford.

Seers D, Schaffer B and Kiljunen M L (Eds.), 1979, *Underdeveloped Europe: Studies in Core-Periphery Relations*, Harvester, Brighton.

Sheller M and Urry J, 2000, 'The city and the car', *International Journal of Urban and Regional Research*, 24, 737–57.

Shen A, Antonopoulos A and Von Lampe K, 2009, ' "The dragon breathes smoke": cigarette counterfeiting in the People's Republic of China', *British Journal of Criminology*, doi: 10.1093/bjc/azp069, 20 pp, available at http://bjc.oxfordjournals.org [accessed 11 April 2012].

Sheppard E and Barnes T (Eds.), 2000, *A Companion to Economic Geography*, Blackwell, Oxford.
Shortland A, 2012, 'Treasure mapped: using satellite imagery to track the developmental effects of Somali piracy', Paper presented to a Chatham House seminar, January, 28 pp.
Sikka P, 2003, 'The role of offshore financial centres in globalization', *Accounting Forum*, 27, 365–99.
Simandan D, 2011, 'Is engaged pluralism the best way ahead for economic geography?', *Progress in Human Geography*, 35, 568–52.
Simmie J (Ed.), 1997, *Innovation, Networks and Learning Regions*, Jessica Kingsley, London.
Singh H, 2003, *Fundamentals of Hydroforming*, Society of Manufacturing Engineers, Dearborn, Michigan, 219 pp.
Slater D, 2002, 'Capturing markets from the economists', in Du Gay P and Pryke M (Eds.), *Cultural Economy*, Sage, London, 59–77.
Smith A, Rainnie A, Dunford M, Hardy J, Hudson R and Sadler D, 2002, 'Networks of value, commodities and regions: reworking divisions of labour in macro-regional economies', *Progress in Human Geography*, 26, 41–64.
Smith N, 1984, *Uneven Development: Nature, Capital and the Production of Space*, Blackwell, Oxford.
Smith W F and Hashemi J, 2006, *Foundations of Material Science and Engineering*, McGraw Hill, New York (4th edition).
Sneddon C, 2007, 'Nature's materiality and the circuitous paths of accumulation: dispossession of freshwater fisheries in Cambodia', *Antipode*, 39, 167–93.
Social Exclusion Unit, 1998, *Bringing Britain Together: A National Strategy for Neighbourhood Renewal* (Cm. 4045), The Stationery Office, London.
SOMO, 2009, 'On the move: the electronics industry in central and eastern Europe', 6 pp, available at www.makeITfair.org [accessed 10 January 2012].
Souther H, 1910, 'The selection and treatment of alloy steels for automobiles', *Journal of the Franklin Institute*, 170, 437–60.
Sraffa P, 1960, *The Production of Commodities by Means of Commodities*, Cambridge University Press, Cambridge.
Steinweg T and de Haan E, 2007, *Capacitating Electronics: The Corrosive Effects of Platinum and Palladium Mining on Labour Rights and Communities*, SOMO – Centre for Research on Multinational Corporations, Amsterdam, 70 pp.
Stone C, 2002, 'Environmental consequences of heavy-industry restructuring and economic regeneration through industrial ecology', *Transactions of the Institute of Mining and Metallurgy*, 111, A187–91.
Storey D, 1982, *Entrepreneurship and the New Firm*, Croom Helm, Beckenham.
Storper M, 1995, 'The resurgence of regional economies, ten years later: the region as a nexus of untraded interdependencies', *European Urban and Regional Studies*, 2, 191–222.
Storper M, 1997, *The Regional World: Territorial Development in a Global Economy*, Blackwell, Oxford.
Storper M and Walker D, 1989, *The Capitalist Imperative Territory, Technology and Industrial Growth*, Blackwell, Oxford.
Strange S, 1988, *States and Markets*, Pinter, London.
Strange S, 1998, *Mad Money*, Manchester University Press, Manchester.
Streek W, 2014, 'How will capitalism end?', *New Left Review*, 87, 35–64.

Sum N-L and Ngai P, 2005, 'Globalization and paradoxes of ethical transnational production: code of conduct in a Chinese workplace', *Competition and Change*, 9, 181–200.

Sunley P, 2009, 'Relational economic geography: a partial understanding or a new paradigm?', *Economic Geography*, 84, 1–26.

Swyngedouw E, 1999, 'Modernity and hybridity: nature, regeneracionismo and the production of the Spanish waterscape, 1890–1939', *Annals of the Association of American Geographers*, 89, 443–65.

Takahashi M, 2003, 'Development of high strength steels for automobiles', *Nippon Steel Technical Report*, 88, 2–7.

Takita M and Ohashi H, 2001, 'Application of high-strength steel sheets for automobiles in Japan', *Review de Metallurgies*, October, 899–909.

Teesside County Borough Council, 1972, *Teesside Structure Plan: Report of Survey*, Teesside County Borough Council, Middlesbrough.

Thiel J, Pires I and Dudleston A, 2000, 'Globalisation and the Portuguese textiles and clothing filière in the post-GATT climate', in Giunta A, Lagendijk A and Pike A (Eds.), *Restructuring Industry and Territory: The Experience of Europe's Regions*, Stationary Office, London, 109–26.

Thrift N, 1999, 'The globalisation of the system of business knowledge', in Olds K, Dicken P, Kelly P, Kong L and Yeung H W-C (Eds.), *Globalization and the Asia Pacific*, Routledge, London, 57–71.

Thrift N, 2000, 'Performing cultures in the new economy', *Annals of the Association of American Geographers*, 90, 674–92.

Thrift N, 2002, 'Performing cultures in the new economy', in du Gay P and Pryke M (Eds.), *Cultural Economy*, Sage, London, 201–34.

Thrift N, 2005, *Knowing Capitalism*, Sage, London.

ThyssenKrupp, 2007, 'ThyssenKrupp tailored strips open up new possibilities', available at www.newmaterials.com/Customisation/News/General/German/Thyssen Krupp/ [accessed 21 February 2011].

ThyssenKrupp, 2010, *Annual Report 2009/2010*, available at www.thyssenkrupp.com/fr/09_10/en/innovation.html [accessed 21 February 2011].

Toribio J, 2004, 'Relationship between microstructure and strength in eutectoid steels', *Materials Science and Engineering A*, 387–9, 227–30.

Trem R, 2004, 'The future of automaking: tailor welded blanks', *Welding*, 1 February, available at http://printthis.clickability.com/pt/cpt?action-pt&title_The+Future+of+Automaking [accessed 28 September 2010].

Tsing A, 2005, *Friction: An Ethnography of Global Connection*, Princeton University Press, Princeton.

Tully J, Hudson R and Tanner B, 2006, *Creating a Regional Knowledge Economy in North East England: Factors Affecting Knowledge Exchange*, Final Report to the Cambridge MIT Institute and ONE North East.

UK Government, 2010, 'Future cars to be built with "super steels" made in UK', available at www.ukti.gov.uk/uktihom/localisation/print/113244.html [accessed 7 September 2010].

Unger B and Rawlings G, 2008, 'Competing for criminal money', *Global Business and Economics Review*, 10, 331–52.

Upadhyaya K P, 2008, *Poverty, Discrimination and Slavery: The Reality of Bonded Labour in India, Nepal and Pakistan*, Anti-Slavery International, London.

Urry J, 1999, 'Automobility: car culture and weightless travel: a discussion paper', available at www.comp.lancs.ac.uk/sociology/soc008ju.html [accessed 14 August 2002].

Urry J, 2000a, *Sociology beyond Societies: Mobilities for the Twenty First Century*, Routledge, London.

Urry J, 2000b, 'Time, complexity and the global', available at www.comp.lancs.ac.uk/sociology/soc030ju.html [accessed 14 August 2002].

Urry J, 2001, 'Globalising the tourist gaze', available at www.comp.lancs.ac.uk/sociology/soc079ju.html [accessed 14 August 2002].

Uzzi B, 1996, 'The sources and consequences of embeddedness for the economic performance of organisations: the network effect', *American Sociological Review*, 42, 35–67.

Uzzi B, 1997, 'Social structure and competition in inter-firm networks: the paradox of embeddedness', *Administrative Science Quarterly*, 61, 674–98.

Vidal de la Blache P, 1941, *La personalité géographique de la France*, Hachette, The University Press, Paris.

Virilio P, 1991, *The Lost Dimension*, Semiotext(e), New York.

Vogel S, 1996, *Against Nature: The Concept of Nature in Critical Theory*, State University of New York Press, New York.

Walker B H, Anderies J M, Kinzig A P and Ryan P (Eds.), 2006, *Exploring Resilience in Social-Ecological Systems: Comparative Studies and Theory Development*, Collingwood Press, CSIRO Publishing, Victoria, Australia.

Walker R and Buck D, 2007, 'The Chinese road', *New Left Review*, 46, 39–68.

Warren K, 2001, *Big Steel: The First Century of the United States Steel Corporation, 1901–2001*, University of Pittsburgh Press, Pittsburgh.

Warrian P and Mulhern C, 2005, 'Knowledge and innovation in the interface between the steel and automotive industries: the case of Dofasco', *Regional Studies*, 39, 161–70.

Weaver P M, Jansen L, van Grootveld G, van Spiegel E and Vergragt P, 2000, *Sustainable Technology Development*, Greenleaf, Sheffield.

Wiener E L, 1985, 'Beyond the sterile cockpit', *Human Factors*, 27, 75–90.

Weiss L, 1997, 'Globalisation and the myth of the powerless state', *New Left Review*, 225, 3–27.

Wernick I D, Herman R, Govinch B and Ausubel J H, 1997, 'Materialization and dematerialization: measures and trends', in Ausubel J H and Langford H (Eds.), *Technological Trajectories and the Human Environment*, Washington DC, National Academy Press, 135–56.

West A 1999, 'Regeneration, community and the social economy', in Haughton G (Ed.), *Community Economic Development*, The Stationery Office/Regional Studies Association, London, 23–29.

Whitford J, 2001, 'The decline of a model? Challenge and response in the Italian industrial districts', *Economy and Society*, 30, 1, 38–65.

Whitley R, 1999, *Divergent Capitalisms: The Social Structuring and Change of Business Systems*, Oxford University Press, Oxford.

Wilde J and de Haan E, 2006, *The High Cost of Calling: Critical Issues in the Mobile Phone Industry*, SOMO – Centre for Research on Multinational Corporations, Amsterdam, 117 pp.

Wilkenson E, 1939, *The Town That Was Murdered*, Left Book Club, London.

Williams E, Kahhat R, Allenby B, Kavazanjian E, Kim J and Xu M, 2008, 'Environmental, social and economic implications of global reuse and recycling of personal computers', *Environmental Science and Technology*, 42, 6446–54.

Williams R, 1960, 'Advertising: the magic system', *New Left Review*, 4.

Williams R, 1980, *Problems in Materialism and Culture*, Verso, London.

Williams R, 1989, *Resources of Hope*, Verso, London.
Williamson O, 1975, *Markets and Hierarchies*, Free Press, New York.
Wohlfeil J, Herlaouil S, Baars G, Nordbrand S and Nilsson P-U, 2009, *Legal and Illegal Blurred: Update on Tin Production for Electronics in Indonesia*, Finnwatch/MakeITfair, 31 pp, available at www.makeITfair.org [accessed 10 January 2012].
Womack J P, Jones D T and Roos D, 1990, *The Machine That Changed The World*, Macmillan, New York.
Wood E M, 2002, *The Origin of Capitalism: A Longer View*, Verso, London.
Wood G and James P (Eds.), 2006, *Institutions, Production and Working Life*, Oxford University Press, Oxford.
World Steel Association, 2011, *World/s Top 30 Steel Companies 2010–2011*, available at www.steelads.com/info/largeststeel/TOP30-Worlds-Largest-Steel-Companies.html [accessed 7 February 2011].
Yearley S, 1995, 'Dirty connections: transnational pollution', in Anderson J, Brook C and Cochrane A (Eds.), *A Global World?*, Oxford University Press, Oxford, 209–48.
Yeung H, 2005, 'Rethinking relational economic geography', *Transactions of the Institute of British Geographers*, 30, 37–51.
Yeung H W-C and Coe N, 2015, 'Toward a dynamic theory of global production networks', *Economic Geography*, 91, 29–58.
Yu J, Williams E, Ju M and Yang Y, 2010, 'Forecasting global generation of obsolete personal computers', *Environmental Science and Technology*, 44, 3233–7.
Zimmerman E, 1951, *World Resources and Industries*, Harper and Row, New York.
Zonabend F, 1993, *The Nuclear Peninsula*, Cambridge University Press, Cambridge.

# Index

For Product Safety Concerns and Information please contact our EU representative GPSR@taylorandfrancis.com
Taylor & Francis Verlag GmbH, Kaufingerstraße 24, 80331 München, Germany

www.ingramcontent.com/pod-product-compliance
Ingram Content Group UK Ltd.
Pitfield, Milton Keynes, MK11 3LW, UK
UKHW021010180425
457613UK00020B/882

* 9 7 8 0 3 6 7 8 7 0 7 1 3 *